DATE DUE

DEMCO 38-296

CONTEMPORARY MUSICIANS

ISSN 1044-2197

R

CONTEMPORARY MUSICIANS

PROFILES OF THE PEOPLE IN MUSIC

**JULIA M. RUBINER,
Editor**

VOLUME 8
Includes Cumulated Indexes

Gale Research Inc. • DETROIT • WASHINGTON, D.C. • LONDON

0930851

STAFF

Julia M. Rubiner, *Editor*

Suzanne M. Bourgoin, Nicolet V. Elert, L. Mpho Mabunda, *Associate Editors*

Marilyn Allen, *Editorial Associate*

Robin Armstrong, David Bianco, Barbara Carlisle Bigelow, Susan Windisch Brown, Marjorie Burgess, Tim Connor, Stewart Francke, Simon Glickman, Nina Goldstein, Joan Goldsworthy, Joyce Harrison, Barry Henssler, Anne Janette Johnson, Janice Jorgensen, Paula Kepos, Michael L. LaBlanc, Ondine E. Le Blanc, Jeanne M. Lesinski, James M. Manheim, Greg Mazurkiewicz, Louise Mooney, John Morrow, Rob Nagel, Nancy Pear, Nancy Rampson, Heather Rhodes, Isaac Rosen, Megan Rubiner, B. Kimberly Taylor, Jeffrey Taylor, Tim Taylor, Jordan Wankoff, Elizabeth Wenning, Christian Whitaker, Denise Wiloch, *Contributing Editors*

Peter M. Gareffa, *Senior Editor, Contemporary Biographies*

Jeanne Gough, *Permissions Manager*
Margaret A. Chamberlain, *Permissions Supervisor (Pictures)*
Pamela A. Hayes, *Permissions Associate*
Amy Lynn Emrich, Karla L. Kulkis, Nancy M. Rattenbury, Keith Reed, *Permissions Assistants*

Mary Beth Trimper, *Production Director*
Shanna Philpott Heilveil, *Production Assistant*
Cynthia Baldwin, *Art Director*
C.J. Jonik, Yolanda Y. Latham, *Keyliners*

Special thanks to the Biography Division Research staff

Cover Illustration by John Kleber

Contents

Introduction   ix

Photo Credits   xi

Cumulative Subject Index   289

Cumulative Musicians Index   301

Introduction

Fills the Information Gap on Today's Musicians

Contemporary Musicians profiles the colorful personalities in the music industry who create or influence the music we hear today. Prior to *Contemporary Musicians,* no quality reference series provided comprehensive information on such a wide range of artists despite keen and ongoing public interest. To find biographical and critical coverage, an information seeker had little choice but to wade through the offerings of the popular press, scan television "infotainment" programs, and search for the occasional published biography or expose. *Contemporary Musicians* is designed to serve that information seeker, providing in one ongoing source in-depth coverage of the important figures on the modern music scene in a format that is both informative and entertaining. Students, researchers, and casual browsers alike can use *Contemporary Musicians* to fill their needs for personal information about the artists, find a selected discography of the musician's recordings, and read an insightful essay offering biographical and critical information.

Provides Broad Coverage

Single-volume biographical sources on musicians are limited in scope, focusing on a handful of performers from a specific musical genre or era. In contrast, *Contemporary Musicians* offers researchers and music devotees a comprehensive, informative, and entertaining alternative. *Contemporary Musicians* is published twice yearly, with each volume providing information on 80 to 100 musical artists from all the genres that form the broad spectrum of contemporary music—pop, rock, jazz, blues, country, new wave, New Age, folk, rhythm and blues, gospel, bluegrass, rap, and reggae, to name a few, as well as selected classical artists who have achieved "crossover" success with the general public. *Contemporary Musicians* will occasionally include profiles of influential nonperforming members of the music industry, including producers, promoters, and record company executives.

Includes Popular Features

In *Contemporary Musicians* you'll find popular features that users value:

- **Easy-to-locate data sections**—Vital personal statistics, chronological career summaries, listings of major awards, and mailing addresses, when available, are prominently displayed in a clearly marked box on the second page of each entry.

- **Biographical/critical essays**—Colorful and informative essays trace each personality's personal and professional life, offer representative examples of critical response to each artist's work, and provide entertaining personal sidelights.

- **Selected discographies**—Each entry provides a comprehensive listing of the artist's major recorded works.

- **Photographs**—Most entries include portraits of the artists.

- **Sources for additional information**—This invaluable feature directs the user to selected books, magazines, and newspapers where more information on listees can be obtained.

Helpful Indexes Make It Easy to Find the Information You Need

Contemporary Musicians features a Musicians Index, listing names of individual performers and musical groups, and a Subject Index that provides the user with a breakdown by primary musical instruments played and by musical genre.

We Welcome Your Suggestions

The editors welcome your comments and suggestions for enhancing and improving *Contemporary Musicians*. If you would like to suggest musicians or composers to be covered in the future, please submit these names to the editors. Mail comments or suggestions to:

The Editor
Contemporary Musicians
Gale Research Inc.
835 Penobscot Bldg.
Detroit MI 48226-4094
Phone : (800) 347-4253
Fax: (313) 961-6241

Photo Credits

CONTEMPORARY MUSICIANS

John Adams

Composer

The musical style known as "minimalism" has been ridiculed by some critics as "going nowhere music" or "needle-stuck-in-the-groove music." Composers Philip Glass and Steve Reich have been criticized for writing what some consider repetitive and monotonous works devoid of either intellectual rigor or expression. John Adams, who could be considered a successor to Glass and Reich, has put minimalist music on a fresh path—one that has won both admirers and detractors.

Adams grew up in New England. His music study was encouraged by his parents, both of whom were amateur musicians. As a youth, he studied clarinet with Felix Viscuglia, a member of the Boston Symphony Orchestra. At home, all types of music were considered equally important. "In the house where I grew up, we had Mozart and we had Benny Goodman on the record player, and I was not raised to think there was a difference between them," Adams told Nancy Malitz in the *New York Times.*

While at Harvard College, where he enrolled in 1965, Adams studied composition with Leon Kirchner, Roger Sessions, and Earl Kim, conducted the Bach Society Orchestra, and was substitute clarinetist for the Boston Symphony Orchestra and the Boston Opera Company. He also played clarinet for the American premiere of Austrian-born composer Arnold Schoenberg's opera *Moses und Aro* and in 1969 was the soloist at the world premiere of American composer Walter Piston's Clarinet Concerto at New York City's famed Carnegie Hall. Adams was the first undergraduate in the history of Harvard University to be allowed to submit a musical composition in lieu of a prose work as his honor's thesis—a remarkable event particularly in light of the roster of distinguished composers who had earned degrees there.

Moved to California

Adams received his B.A. magna cum laude from Harvard and completed his M.A. there in 1971. Then, tired of the East Coast academic music scene—which he considered outmoded and hostile—he moved to San Francisco, where he came under the influence of composers John Cage, Morton Feldman, Christian Wolff, and Robert Ashley, who, with the exception of Ashley, were not based in California but whose experimental, open techniques of composition appealed to Adams. Adams's works of the mid-1970s, including *Grounding* and *Onyx,* were composed largely for electronic media. Also in the mid-seventies, what has become known as "minimalism"—music based on repeated and shifting rhythmic, melodic, and harmonic patterns—

was coming into its own, with Californians Terry Riley and La Monte Young leading the way, followed by the younger, East Coast composers Steve Reich and Philip Glass. Adams, roughly ten years junior to Reich and Glass, developed his own broader, and more expressive, style of minimalism; earlier minimalists generally composed music for small groups, but Adams, beginning with 1980's *Harmonium*—a piece for huge chorus and orchestra set to texts by early 17th-century English poet John Donne and 19th-century American poet Emily Dickinson—wrote, and continues to write, primarily for large performing forces.

Adams's growing prominence was apparent in 1982, when *Time* contributor Michael Walsh wrote: "The fastest-rising minimalist composer—and potentially the most influential of all—is John Adams. . . . The least 'minimal' of the three [Glass, Reich, and Adams], Adams has forged a big, strong, personal style, expressed in complex forms that employ a more extensive use of dissonance than other minimalists. . . . His highly accessible music makes a bridge between the avant-garde and traditional concert-hall fare."

Debate Over *Grand Pianola Music*

Though he was rapidly becoming one of the most popular composers of his time, some thought that Adams went too far with *Grand Pianola Music,* composed in 1981 and 1982, and that by incorporating all kinds of music, serious and humorous, he had created a piece that bordered on the ridiculous. Others disagreed; Gregory Sandow defended the piece in the *Village Voice,* asserting, "In *Grand Pianola Music,* [Adams] revels in sounds we've heard before—and that's his greatest victory. There's nothing wrong with recycling familiar music. Composers of the past did it a lot; they were writing in the style of their times. . . . A classical composer who wants to write music that sounds like anything the classical audience has heard before is all but forced to use styles of the past, which can only be responsibly done if something in your tone suggests you know you're doing it. Adams succeeds with triumphant exuberance—and so *Grand Pianola Music* has been damned as vulgar by people uneasy about the age they live in."

Two of Adams's later works, both operas, likewise fell under considerable scrutiny. 1987's *Nixon in China* is a dramatization of President Richard M. Nixon's historic visit to Beijing in 1972. Although its creators—Adams, director Peter Sellars, and librettist Alice Goodman—considered it a satire, *Nixon in China* met with objection from some reviewers, partly because they believed the characters' mythic portrayal was unsuitable given their less-than-pristine reputations.

Terrorist Event Inspired Opera

More controversial, in 1991, was *The Death of Klinghoffer,* an operatic retelling of the 1985 hijacking by Palestinians of the Italian cruise ship Achille Lauro and subsequent assassination of a disabled Jewish passenger, Leon Klinghoffer. Some critics and operagoers were offended by what they considered a pro-Palestinian bias; others believed that the event dramatized was inappropriate for operatic treatment. Adams summed up the controversy in the *New York Times Magazine*: "It is so clear that we haven't taken sides, but that won't prevent people from leaping to judgment. I am sure that there will be people who think that having Palestinians sing music which is not ugly or aggressive, but which is expressive and sometimes personal and beautiful, is to glorify hideous facts. And I am sure there are some who feel that to portray this event at all is just further Zionist propaganda."

Despite disagreement among critics and the public about his work, Adams's star continues to rise; in November of 1991 his piece *El Dorado* was premiered by the San Francisco Symphony. Of his career, Adams was quoted as saying in *Time,* "[Before,] I thought that if I wrote something that was attractive there must be something wrong with it. Now I feel there are a lot of people out there actually waiting for my next piece."

Continued acclaim has proven the composer's words prophetic.

Selected compositions

Chamber music

American Standard (for unspecified ensemble), 1973.
Grounding, 1975.
Onyx, 1976.
Phrygian Gates (for piano), 1977.
Shaker Loops (for string septet), 1978.

Orchestral music

Common Tones in Simple Time (for orchestra), 1979.
Harmonium (for large chorus and orchestra), 1980.
Grand Pianola Music (for small orchestra, two sopranos, and two pianos), 1981-82.
Harmonielehre (for large orchestra), 1984-85.
El Dorado (for orchestra), 1991.

Other

Matter of Heart (film score), 1982.
Nixon in China (opera), 1987.
The Death of Klinghoffer (opera), 1991.

Selected discography

Shaker Loops, Philips.
Harmonium, ECM.
Grand Pianola Music, EMI/Angel.
Harmonielehre, Elektra/Nonesuch.
Nixon in China, Elektra/Nonesuch.
The Death of Klinghoffer, Elektra/Nonesuch, 1992.

Sources

Books

Baker's Biographical Dictionary of Musicians, 7th edition, edited by Nicholas Slonimsky, Schirmer, 1984.
Marshall, Ingram D., *The New Grove Dictionary of American Music,* edited by H. Wiley Hitchcock and Stanley Sadie, Macmillan, 1986.

Periodicals

Esquire, December 1984.
New York Times Magazine, August 25, 1991.
Time, September 20, 1982.
Village Voice, January 29, 1985.

Additional information for this profile was obtained from liner notes by Allan Kozinn to *Grand Pianola Music,* EMI/Angel.

—*Joyce Harrison*

Debbie Allen

The word "multi-talented" could have been coined just to refer to Debbie Allen. As a song-and-dance entertainer, she thrilled Broadway audiences with her work in revivals of *West Side Story* and *Sweet Charity.* On television, she not only choreographed and helped direct the award-winning series *Fame,* she starred in it as well. Her long string of film credits for both the large and small screen includes *Ragtime; Jo Jo Dancer, Your Life Is Calling;* and *Women of San Quentin.* Beginning in the late 1980s she earned credentials as producer and director of the hit situation comedy *A Different World.*

"I'm very fickle—whatever I'm doing at the moment is the thing I like best," Allen confessed in *McCall's.* She added: "I'm a passionate woman, and I'm moved to work because it makes me feel so good. If I didn't love my work, I wouldn't have the energy to do all the things I've done. But my work is a discipline, a way of life."

Those who know Allen describe her as a consummate professional who is serious, focused, and determined. Both behind the camera and in front of it, she resembles the character she played in the television series *Fame*—a dance teacher who constantly prodded her students to work harder and longer, to strive for perfection. Performing, she asserted in *Essence,* is "beat up and mixed up in a lot of sweat and blood and tears. Anyone who talks about the glamour of this profession should experience a show like *Fame* to know that the glamour is only icing on the cake."

Credits Family for Achievements

Allen attributes her success to her unorthodox childhood with her mother, Vivian Ayers. The youngest daughter in a family of four children, she showed an interest in the performing arts, especially dance, at a very early age. "When I was five my mother saw that I could be a great dancer," Allen declared in *Essence.* "So she helped make it happen for me. If she had let it slide, I might be in a real different place right now." Allen was born and raised in Houston, Texas, and though her parents divorced when she was four, she remained on cordial terms with both of them. In *Ebony,* the performer described her dentist father as a "wonderful, fantastic man."

Allen also received encouragement from her older sister, Phylicia Rashad. "Everything I've done, Phylicia's helped me do," Allen acknowledged in *McCall's.* "We were very close growing up, and I guess we've gotten even closer as we get older." Although the sisters

For the Record. . .

Born Deborah Allen, January 16, 1950, in Houston, TX; daughter of Andrew Allen (a dentist) and Vivian Ayers (an artist); married Win Wilford (a record executive; divorced); married Norman Nixon (a former professional basketball player and real estate broker), 1984; children: (second marriage) Vivian, Norm, Jr. *Education:* Howard University, B.A. (cum laude).

Actress, dancer, and singer appearing in plays, including *Purlie,* 1972, *Raisin,* 1973, *Ain't Misbehavin',* 1978, *West Side Story,* 1980, *Louis,* 1981, and *Sweet Charity,* 1986; in motion pictures, including *The Fish That Saved Pittsburgh,* 1979, *Fame,* 1980, *Ragtime,* 1981, and *Jo Jo Dancer, Your Life Is Calling,* 1986; in television films, series, and specials, including *Roots: The Next Generations,* 1979, *Fame,* NBC, 1982-87, *The Kids From Fame,* 1983, *Motown Returns to the Apollo,* 1985, and *Celebrating a Jazz Master: Thelonious Sphere Monk,* 1987. Choreographer for *Fame,* 1982-87. Producer and director of television series, including *A Different World,* 1988—, and episodes of *Family Ties, Quantum Leap,* and *The Fresh Prince of Bel Air;* director of *Stompin' at the Savoy,* CBS, 1992.

Awards: Drama Desk Award for outstanding featured actress in a musical, 1980, for *West Side Story;* Tony Award nomination, 1986, for *Sweet Charity;* Emmy Award nomination for best actress in a dramatic series, for *Fame;* two Emmy Awards for choreography for *Fame;* received a star on Hollywood Walk of Fame, 1991.

Addresses: c/o NBC Inc., 3000 W. Alameda Ave., Burbank, CA 91523.

followed very different routes, both wound up in show business. Phylicia remains best known for her portrayal of Mrs. Claire Huxtable on the long-running television series *The Cosby Show.*

Both Debbie and Phylicia were encouraged to excel in the arts by their mother, who ran a museum, wrote poetry, and exposed all of her children to different cultures and points of view. "Even when we were little kids Mother would call us together for conversations about all kinds of things—history, the arts, the value of meditating and fasting," Allen remembered in *Ebony.* "She always wanted us to reach a higher consciousness. She wanted all of her children to be excellent in everything."

Overcame Rejection

The road to excellence was not always fair, however. At the age of eight, Allen was refused entry into the Houston Foundation for Ballet. She studied privately for six years before a Russian teacher at the foundation insisted she be admitted—on scholarship. After high school, Allen auditioned for the dance program at the North Carolina School of Arts but was rejected and told she did not have "the body of a dancer." Crushed, she returned to Houston and did not dance for an entire year.

Allen decided instead to enroll at Howard University and study classics. She slowly drifted back into dancing and singing, though, and her confidence in her performing abilities was gradually restored due to the praise she received from such important choreographers as Donald McKayle and Twyla Tharp. Allen pointed out in *Ebony* that her experience at Howard helped to convince her that she had been the victim of prejudice in both Houston and North Carolina. She concluded that, in retrospect, she was glad to have experienced "all that racism, because it helps me deal with it today and I can pass along my experiences to younger people."

Allen graduated from Howard with top honors and moved to New York City. For some time, she and her sister Phylicia helped one another as they sought work on the stage. Debbie began to make some progress, earning small but noticeable roles in *Purlie* in 1972 and *Raisin* in 1973. By 1978 she had landed a bigger role in the popular musical *Ain't Misbehavin'.* The role that finally put her over the top was that of the fiery Anita in a 1980 revival of *West Side Story.* Her rendition of "(I Like To Be in) America" absolutely "stole the show," according to a *People* magazine reviewer, and she was nominated for a Tony Award for the performance.

Fame Brought Stardom

A brief, two-line appearance in the movie *Fame* brought Allen to a career crossroads. The film portrayed the struggles of students at New York City's School for the Performing Arts. When the film was adapted for a television series, Allen was tapped to star as a teacher and to choreograph many of the show's high-energy dance numbers. The television version of *Fame* found a following and ran for six years, from 1982 to 1987. Allen won two Emmy Awards for her choreography on the series, and she was nominated for an Emmy as best actress in a drama as well. As Lydia Grant on *Fame,* Allen gave the show its most memorable lines: "You want fame, honey? Well, fame costs. And right here is where you start paying. In sweat."

In 1986 Allen returned to Broadway for a well-received revival of *Sweet Charity*. Allen's name was billed above the title of the show in the advertising, and she brought great verve to the role of Charity Hope Valentine, a luckless dance-hall girl. Her musical numbers in that play included "If My Friends Could See Me Now," "Where Am I Going?" and "I'm a Brass Band." *Newsweek* reviewer Jack Kroll praised Allen's performance, noting that she "does everything that a star can do: a fine actress, a rousing singer, a knockout dancer, a true comedienne, she explodes with . . . sheer joy."

Allen's vocal talents have always been somewhat eclipsed by her acting and dancing, but she did release a pop album, *Special Look,* in 1979. Allen confessed in *Essence* that her experience with that recording convinced her that she had not cleared every hurdle in her path. "Getting out there, getting [the record] played is tough," she said. "I didn't realize what a difficult, even racist, struggle it would be to get visibility in the music business."

The lackluster performance of her album has been the only setback for the hardworking Allen. She gained further prestige as the producer-director of the television situation comedy *A Different World,* and she has also directed episodes of *Family Ties, Quantum Leap,* and *The Fresh Prince of Bel Air.* Allen disclosed in *Ebony* that she is particularly comfortable with the subject matter on *A Different World.* "I'm a graduate of a Black college so I have *lived* what [fictional] Hillman is all about. . . . College life is about young adults coming of age; about their intellectual, political and sexual maturity." Describing the school she helped create on

A Different World, she added: "This is a college where you go to the cafeteria and they have fried apples and grits for breakfast."

In 1991 Allen received the 1,940th star on the Hollywood Walk of Fame. The award recognized her contributions to musical comedy, drama, and directing since her debut in her early twenties. Allen, who is the mother of two children by her second husband, Norm Nixon, promises that she has scores of other projects she wants to develop for stage and screen. In *Jet* magazine she ventured, "I guess you could say I've been planting a lot of seeds for a while, and after tending the garden, everything is really starting to grow."

Selected discography

(With others) *Sweet Charity,* EMI America, 1986.
Special Look, MCA, 1989.

Sources

Ebony, March 1983; March 1991.
Essence, March 1984; June 1990.
Glamour, March 1983.
Jet, May 15, 1986; July 31, 1989; October 28, 1991.
McCall's, July 1987.
Newsweek, May 12, 1986.
New York Times, January 7, 1982.
People, March 10, 1980; April 19, 1982.
USA Weekend, November 21-23, 1986.

—Anne Janette Johnson

Marian Anderson

Classical, spiritual, and opera singer

Acclaimed as much for her gentle demeanor as for her rich voice, Marian Anderson effectively bridged entrenched racial gaps with her powerful renditions of classical, spiritual, and operatic songs. At age 89, as always, Anderson's characteristic grace, nobility, and modesty were evident; honored as the subject of a 60-minute 1991 PBS documentary, she was described as "a queen, a national treasure, an inspiration, a great lady and an icon," according to the *New York Times.* Yet the singer portrayed herself in typically humble fashion, saying, "I hadn't set out to change the world in any way. Whatever I am, it is a culmination of the goodwill of people who, regardless of anything else, saw me as I am, and not as somebody else."

Anderson's nearly 40-year career as a classical singer was, in fact, marked by racial prejudice and discrimination. Although she won an important singing contest in 1925, she was for years unable to advance her career in America; it was in Europe that Anderson first became a star. She captured the attention of millions of Americans, however, when in 1939 she was refused the use of Constitution Hall by the Daughters of the American Revolution (D.A.R.). Her operatic debut was delayed until 1955, when she became the first African-American to sing with New York City's Metropolitan Opera.

Supported Family

Anderson was born in Philadelphia on February 17, 1902. Her father sold coal and ice, and her mother, who had been a schoolteacher before marrying, took in laundry and did housework to make ends meet. Anderson's father died when she was 12; five years later, her mother contracted a serious case of influenza, leaving young Marian to take over support of the family.

Anderson's earliest vocal training came at Philadelphia's Union Baptist Church, where she began singing spirituals and hymns in the junior choir at age six. Her early experience there helped develop her astonishing range, which embraced three octaves at its peak. Singing "The Lord Is My Shepherd," Anderson made her debut performance at the age of eight and received 50 cents for her recital. She studied with local voice teachers in Philadelphia, but by the time she was 18 she had outgrown them. Almost single-handedly supporting her family, she could not afford expensive vocal coaches. Knowing this, the parishioners of Union Baptist Church collected a "Marian Anderson Fund" to pay for instruction by Giuseppe Boghetti, a famous voice teacher who worked in Philadelphia and New York City. In 1925, following a recital at New York's Town Hall, Boghetti was sufficiently encouraged by his pupil's performance to enter her in a vocal contest. Competing

For the Record. . .

Born February 17, 1902, in Philadelphia, PA; daughter of a coal and ice vendor and a former schoolteacher; married Orpheus Fisher (an architectural engineer), July 24, 1943. *Education:* Studied with vocal teachers Giuseppe Boghetti, Frank LaForge, and Michael Raucheisen.

Classical, spiritual, and opera singer. Debuted professionally, with Union Baptist Church junior choir, Philadelphia, 1910; won vocal contest and performed with the New York Philharmonic, c. 1925; studied in Europe, 1929-30, 1931; performed throughout Europe; signed contract for U.S. performances, 1935; performed at the White House and at presidential inaugurations; performed at the Lincoln Memorial, Washington D.C., 1939; established Marian Anderson scholarship awards; made operatic debut at Metropolitan Opera, New York City, 1955; served as U.S. delegate to the United Nations; gave farewell concert performance at Carnegie Hall, New York City, 1965. Author of *My Lord, What a Morning* (autobiography), Viking, 1956.

Selected awards: Rosenwald scholarship, 1931; decorated by King Gustaf of Sweden, c. 1933; Prix de Chant, Paris, 1935; Spingarn Medal, NAACP, 1939; Bok Award (Philadelphia), 1941; Presidential Medal of Freedom, 1963; Presidential Medal of Arts, 1988.

Addresses: *Home*—Portland, OR. *Management*—ICM Artists, Ltd., 40 West 57th St., New York, NY 10019.

against three hundred singers, Anderson took first prize in the contest and won the opportunity to sing at Lewisohn Stadium with the New York Philharmonic Orchestra. It was a victory she long considered a keystone of her career. Singing "O Mio Fernando" from Donizetti's opera *La Favorite,* she gave a smashing performance that was widely acclaimed.

Studied in Europe

In spite of her triumph, though, Anderson's career did not advance as expected. Studying and under contract with Frank LaForge, her concerts were given primarily under the auspices of black organizations for black audiences. Despite the racial prejudice she encountered daily, she refused to abandon the high musical road upon which she had set out. In the summer of 1929 she sailed to England and studied there with various teachers. But she returned to the United States the next year, the trip to Europe having had little impact on her career.

Then, after a 1931 concert in Chicago, Anderson was approached by a representative from the Julius Rosenwald Fund, a foundation set up to advance higher education for blacks. At the time, Anderson desperately wanted to study in Germany. With the aid of a Rosenwald scholarship, she returned to Europe that year and stayed with a German family in Berlin. She studied with Michael Raucheisen, a German vocal coach, to learn the language and lieder.

Success came more quickly to Anderson in Europe than in America. She gave concerts in Norway, Sweden, and Finland, then returned briefly to America. In 1933 she went back to Europe for a 20-concert Scandinavian tour financed by the Rosenwald Fund. Anderson sang before King Gustav in Stockholm, Sweden, where she was decorated by him. She also sang before King Christian in Copenhagen, Denmark. In Finland she received a rare invitation from the great composer Jean Sibelius, who later dedicated his song "Solitude" to her. In 12 months, she gave 108 concerts.

"A Voice Heard but Once in a Century"

Following her Scandinavian tour, Anderson gave concerts in Paris and London and toured Italy, Austria, Spain, Poland, Latvia, and Russia. She was particularly well received in Russia, where the famous theater director Constantin Stanislavsky requested that she study Bizet's opera *Carmen* under his direction. In Salzburg, Austria, she gave a spectacular performance at the Mozarteum with revered conductor Arturo Toscanini in attendance. On hearing her sing, Toscanini reportedly told Anderson that she had "a voice heard but once in a century."

By the end of her tour on the Continent, Anderson was a widely heralded sensation throughout the capitals of Europe. In Paris, American impresario Sol Hurok signed her to 15 concerts in the United States. She was also awarded the Prix de Chant in Paris, where she was known as "The Black Venus." Hurok managed Anderson's career from 1935 on, once telling a reporter that she was the only artist he'd ever handled who never became temperamental with him.

At Last, Triumph at Home

Anderson's first recital on returning to the United States was given at New York's Town Hall on December 30, 1935. She had fractured a bone in her left foot on the ocean liner before she landed; at the concert, the cast on her foot was hidden by her gown. Despite this encumbrance, the performance, which included songs by Handel, Schubert, Verdi, and Sibelius, as well as a group of spirituals, was glorious. After the recital, critics welcomed her as a "new high priestess of song." The *New York Times* called Anderson "one of the great singers of our time."

Within the next few years Anderson became so popular that she was invited to sing at the White House for U.S. president Franklin Delano Roosevelt, where she had her only attack of stage fright. She was invited back to perform for King George and Queen Elizabeth of England during their state visit. She embarked on several cross-country tours and was soon being requested for engagements two years in advance. Every appearance was an automatic sellout, and one year Anderson covered 26,000 miles in the longest tour in concert history, giving 70 concerts in five months. When touring the deep South, her theater contract specified equal, though separate, orchestra seating for blacks.

Snubbed by D.A.R.

In 1939, an incident involving the Daughters of the American Revolution, members of which are directly descended from soldiers or patriots of the Revolutionary period, brought Anderson's name to the attention of millions of Americans, many of whom would never have been acquainted with her otherwise. The D.A.R. denied her use of their Constitution Hall in Washington, D.C., for an April 9 concert. A huge outcry ensued, and first lady Eleanor Roosevelt subsequently resigned from the organization. With permission from the federal government, Anderson instead gave a free Easter Sunday outdoor concert at the Lincoln Memorial. A live crowd of 75,000 and a radio audience numbering into the millions heard the performance, which began with the patriotic song "My Country 'Tis of Thee."

Later that year, Mrs. Roosevelt presented Anderson with the Spingarn Medal. The prestigious award, named for NAACP president Joel E. Spingarn, is awarded by the NAACP to the black American who "made the highest achievement during the preceding year or years in any honorable field of human endeavor," as defined in the *New York Times;* she used the $10,000 award accompanying the medal to set up the Marian Anderson awards—cash scholarships given each year to ten aspiring young singers regardless of race or creed.

In 1942 the D.A.R. again refused to let Anderson use Constitution Hall, this time reportedly over her demands that the audience for her war benefit concert not be segregated on the basis of color. The issue was finally resolved in 1943, when Anderson sang at Consti-

tution Hall for a China Relief Fund benefit. The following year, the singer gave a performance at Carnegie Hall that included the spiritual "My Lord, What a Morning," which Anderson would later adopt as the title of her autobiography. An enthusiastic *New York Times* reviewer proclaimed of the appearance: "It became apparent that something very unusual was taking place, one of the rarest of things—a really great song recital." Of the spirituals, the reviewer observed, "[They] displayed a pathos and a profundity of feeling that made them possibly the most moving music of the evening."

In 1948 Anderson underwent a dangerous operation for the removal from her esophagus of a cyst that threatened to damage her voice. For two months she was not permitted to use her voice and was unsure if

---

"I hadn't set out to change the world. Whatever I am, it is the goodwill of people who saw me as I am, and not as somebody else."

---

she would ever be able to sing again. When she was finally allowed to rehearse, her voice returned free of impairment. Following her recovery, Anderson made her first post-World War II tour of Europe, including stops in Scandinavia, Paris, London, Antwerp, Zurich, and Geneva.

Long Delayed Operatic Debut

Although Anderson had once expressed a desire to sing opera, she later revealed in a press release, "When some of the things I did in concert gratified me, it did not become a necessity." And so, it was not until January 7, 1955, at the age of 52, that Anderson made her operatic debut in the role of Ulrica in Verdi's opera *Un ballo in maschera* ("The Masquerade Ball"). It was the first time an African-American had sung with the company of New York's Metropolitan Opera (Met) since it opened in 1883; her presence in the company opened the doors for many black opera singers. When Anderson was offered the chance to sing Verdi's opera at the Met, she made a point of carefully examining the score with conductor Dimitri Mitropoulos to determine whether it was within her vocal range. Commenting in the *New York Times* on winning her first opera role, Anderson exclaimed, "Ever since [I] was in high school in Philadelphia, [I] wanted to sing opera—at the Metropolitan, if that could be. Now [I am] speechless."

Over the years, Anderson continued to add to her accomplishments. She sang at the presidential inaugurations of Dwight D. Eisenhower and John F. Kennedy, served as a U.S. delegate to the United Nations, and toured the Far East in a 40,000-mile trek sponsored by the U.S. State Department and filmed by CBS-TV. On Easter Sunday of 1965, Anderson gave a farewell concert at Carnegie Hall. The audience of 2,900 included actor Montgomery Clift, who remarked in the *New York Times* of Anderson's gift, "This marvelous thing comes across and it's so rare, so beautiful." The program was typical for Anderson, consisting of songs by Handel, Haydn, Schubert, Samuel Barber, and a selection of spirituals. She gave four encores, including "Ave Maria" and "Let My People Go."

On the occasion of her farewell concert, *New York Times* music critic Harold C. Schoenberg wrote: "It was Miss Anderson who stood as a symbol for the emergence of the Negro; and while she herself never militantly participated in the civil-rights movement, she was revered as one who, by the force of her personality, talent and probity, was able to become a world figure despite her humble birth and minority status. In a way, she was part of the American dream. And her success story was an inspiration to younger Negro musicians." Describing the range and quality of her voice, Schoenberg noted, "Those who remember her at her height . . . can never forget that big, resonant voice, with those low notes almost visceral in nature, and with that easy, unforced ascent to the top register. A natural voice, a hauntingly colorful one, it was one of the vocal phenomena of its time."

Selected discography

(Gustav Mahler) *Kinder-Tontenlieder* (title means "Songs on the Death of Infants"), Victor, 1951.

Marian Anderson Sings Beloved Songs of Schubert, Victor, 1951.

(Giuseppe Verdi) *Un ballo in maschera* (title means "The Masquerade Ball"), Victor, 1955.

Marian Anderson (songs by Schubert, Schumann, Brahms, Straus, and Haydn), Victor, 1964.

Jus' Keep on Singin' (spirituals), Victor, 1965.

Spirituals, Victor, 1976.

Marian Anderson: Bach, Brahms, Schubert (recorded 1924-55), Victor, 1989.

Marian Anderson, Pearl, 1990.

Sources

Books

Anderson, Marian, *My Lord, What a Morning* (autobiography), Viking, 1956.

Hitchcock, H. Wiley, and Stanley Sadie, *The New Grove Dictionary of American Music,* Macmillan, 1986.

Sims, Janet L., *Marian Anderson: An Annotated Bibliography and Discography,* Greenwood, 1981.

Tedards, Anne, *Marian Anderson,* Chelsea House, 1988.

Vehanen, Kosti, *Marian Anderson: A Portrait,* McGraw-Hill, 1941.

Periodicals

Christian Century, February 21, 1940.

Detroit Free Press, May 8, 1991.

National Review, September 29, 1989.

New York Times, July 3, 1939; March 18, 1941; November 13, 1944; October 8, 1954; April 19, 1965; May 8, 1991.

New York Times Magazine, December 30, 1945.

Stage, December 1938.

Time, December 30, 1946.

Additional information for this profile was obtained from a press release, c. 1949, housed in the E. Azalia Hackley Collection of the Detroit Public Library.

—*David Bianco*

Desi
Arnaz

Bandleader, actor, television producer

Desi Arnaz will forever be identified with nightclub entertainer Ricky Ricardo, the character he played on the classic television series *I Love Lucy*. The role mimicked at least two aspects of his real life: he was married to his costar, Lucille Ball, and before becoming involved in television he made his living as the hard-working leader of a rumba band. His achievements as a musician, actor, producer, and director were all a far cry from the career planned for him while he was growing up in Cuba. The son of a powerful politician and a woman said to be one of the great beauties of Latin America, he spent his youth enjoying his family's vast wealth. He was to study law at the University of Notre Dame in Indiana, then return home to a ready-made practice.

Those plans crumbled on August 12, 1933, when the first Batista revolution, in which Fulgencio Batista y Zaldivar organized a military coup and eventually became president, swept Cuba. Arnaz's father was jailed, and his money and property were confiscated. Sixteen-year-old Desi and his mother fled to Miami, Florida, where they spent the next six months negotiating the release of Desi, Sr. Young Desi, who barely spoke English, struggled through classes at St. Patrick's High School in Miami during the day, then worked to help pay the rent at the dingy boardinghouse that was now home. His first job was cleaning birdcages; he later graduated to working in a railyard, bookkeeping, and driving taxis and trucks.

The expensive education his family had envisioned for Arnaz was now out of the question, so he began considering other ways to advance himself. In 1937 he auditioned as a singer for Miami Beach's high-class Roney Plaza Hotel. He borrowed a suit for the occasion and convinced his former classmates from St. Patrick's to crowd the audience at his trial performance. Thanks to their enthusiastic cheering, he was hired to front the Siboney Septet for $50 a week. Bandleader Xavier Cugat saw Arnaz perform at the Roney and asked the young singer to tour with him. The pay was only $35 a week, but the experience and exposure were invaluable. After a year with Cugat, Arnaz confidently struck out on his own and was soon bringing in $750 per week as the headliner at the La Conga Cafe. Before long, he and his newly formed orchestra were playing dates at the best clubs in the United States, including New York City's Copacabana.

Married Lucille Ball

During a Copacabana engagement, Arnaz was spotted by George Abbot, who gave the Cuban a leading role in his musical *Too Many Girls.* RKO Studios bought

For the Record. . .

Born Desiderio Alberto Arnaz y de Acha III, March 2, 1917, in Santiago, Cuba; immigrated to United States, 1933; died of lung cancer, December 2, 1986, in Del Mar, CA; son of Desiderio Alberto (a politician) and Lolita (de Acha) Arnaz; married Lucille Ball (an actress), November 30, 1940 (divorced, 1960); married Edith Mack Hirsch, March 2, 1963; children: (first marriage) Lucie Arnaz Luckinbill, Desi, Jr. *Education:* Attended Colegic de Dolores and St. Patrick's High School, Miami, FL.

House singer at the Roney Plaza Hotel, Miami, FL, 1937; vocalist with Xavier Cugat's orchestra, 1938; leader of the Desi Arnaz Orchestra, 1939-51; musical director of Bob Hope's radio program, 1947-48; host of radio game show/ Latin American musical showcase *Your Tropical Trip,* 1951; costar and executive producer of television comedies *I Love Lucy* and *The Lucy-Desi Comedy Hour,* 1951-60; president of Desilu Productions, 1951-63. Author of *A Book,* William Morrow, 1976.

1946 and 1947, when Arnaz replaced Stan Kenton as the musical director of Bob Hope's radio show, but in 1948 he headed out on the road again.

America's Favorite Couple

Ball saw a way to save her marriage when CBS approached her in 1949 with the idea of turning her very successful radio program, *My Favorite Husband,* into a television show. She agreed, on the condition that Arnaz would be cast opposite her, thereby giving him a job that would not require constant touring. CBS rejected the idea, believing that the notion of an all-American woman married to a Cuban orchestra leader would be unacceptable to audiences. To prove them wrong, Arnaz and Ball put together an ambitious vaudeville revue featuring a series of comic routines about a woman trying to crash her bandleader husband's show. Vaudeville was nearly dead at the time, but the Lucy-Desi act drew rave reviews and large audiences. Once convinced, CBS agreed to let Arnaz costar in Ball's television show, *I Love Lucy.*

the film rights to the hit show and invited Arnaz to Hollywood to recreate his character. The female lead was filled by an RKO contract actress, Lucille Ball, who became romantically involved with Arnaz soon after they met. Everyone from studio executives to gossip columnists considered the relationship a bad idea, but the pair continued seeing each other even after filming stopped and their careers took them to different parts of the country. On November 14, 1940, Ball went to New York City on a personal appearance tour. Arnaz was there, playing the Roxy Theatre. After the band's last show, Ball and Arnaz eloped, taking their vows before a justice of the peace at the Byram River Beagle Club in Greenwich, Connecticut.

The marriage was troubled from the start, largely due to the conflicting schedules of the two performers. Ball's contract with RKO kept her tied to Hollywood and necessitated early morning makeup calls. Arnaz traveled constantly with his band, and even when he had a local engagement, he usually arrived home just as his wife was leaving. Although he had parts in several films—*Cuban Pete* and *Holiday in Havana* were written especially for him and featured music he composed— his movie career never developed enough to take him away from the nightclub circuit. The couple once estimated that in the first eleven years of their marriage, they spent just three years' time together and paid more than $29,000 in telephone and telegraph charges to each other. Their lives stabilized somewhat during

Behind the Scenes

The program was an immediate success and is now regarded as a classic of television comedy. Arnaz was the perfect foil for Ball's antics, and his musical numbers, set in the fictional Tropicana nightclub, lent variety and interest to the program. Behind the camera, Arnaz immersed himself in work as the head of Desilu Productions, the couple's production team, and proved to be a shrewd television executive. He produced many other popular series, including *December Bride, Our Miss Brooks, The Untouchables,* and *The Danny Thomas Show,* and he created the three-camera technique still used for filming situation comedies.

Despite all efforts to save it, the Arnaz marriage ended in divorce in 1960, and the Lucy-Desi comedy partnership terminated as well. Arnaz went into semiretirement a few years later, spending most of his time on his horse farm in Del Mar, California. He did occasional television work, producing several pilots and the comedy series *The Mothers-in-Law.* In 1982 he played a straight dramatic role in Francis Coppola's film *The Escape Artist.* Poor health plagued him throughout the 1970s aand 1980s, however, and in 1986 he died of lung cancer at his home in Del Mar.

Sources

Books

Andrews, Bart, *The "I Love Lucy" Book,* Doubleday, 1985.
Arnaz, Desi, *A Book,* William Morrow, 1976.

Periodicals

Look, June 3, 1952.
Newsweek, February 18, 1952.
New York Times, December 3, 1986.
People, February 18, 1991.
Time, June 6, 1952, December 15, 1986.

—Joan Goldsworthy

The Beastie Boys

Rap trio

"**W**e're probably a parent's worst nightmare," Mike Diamond, member of the rap trio the Beastie Boys, disclosed in *People*. Diamond and his songster cohorts Adam Yauch and Adam Horovitz are the controversial core of a group whose first LP, *Licensed to Ill,* sold more copies than any debut album in Columbia Records history. Called the Bowery Boys and Three Stooges of rock-rap, the Beastie Boys are clowns of a raunchier variety of stage imagery and antics than their comic forebears. During their concerts of the mid- to late 1980s, for example, grand finales climaxed with the hydraulic rise of a 20-foot pink penis from a black box rostrum while "King Ad-Rock" Horovitz, "Mike D" Diamond, and "MCA" Yauch urged audiences to "Fight for Your Right (to Party)." The group has been credited with making rap accessible to a broader audience, mouthing obscenities in the syntactically proper phrasing of the Jewish, bourgeois New Yorkers they are. With their debut and subsequent albums, the Beastie Boys intend to offend.

The offspring of professionals, Adam Yauch is the son

of a school administrator and an architect, and Mike Diamond is the son of an interior decorator and an art dealer. Adam Horovitz's father is playwright Israel Horovitz, who wrote *The Indian Wants the Bronx.* After his mother died in 1986, Horovitz dedicated *Licensed to Ill* to her.

The members of the Beastie Boys were not high school or college classmates. Yauch dropped out of public school to attend Elizabeth Seeger. He divulged to David Handelman in *Rolling Stone* that Seeger was "a little hippie school with sixty kids in it where I smoked pot all day." Although he pursued a higher education, Yauch remained at Bard College only two years. Diamond attended Brooklyn Height's posh St. Ann's followed by one semester at Vassar College. Gathering credits working in a recording studio in New York City as a part of a school program, Horovitz spent a total of two hours enrolled at Manhattan Community College. The group discovered each other during their early teen years club-hopping in a warehouse district that included the Rock Lounge, Tier 3, and the Mudd Club.

Rooted in Hardcore Tradition

Originally punk rockers in early adolescence, Diamond and Yauch performed together in the hardcore band the Young and the Useless in 1979. The duo played guitar and bass, respectively, after they created their own punk band. They dubbed themselves the Beastie Boys, Diamond revealed to Handelman, since hardcore music groups propagated "stupid names, and it was the stupidest name we could come up with." When they enlisted Horovitz to join the group in 1983, the band remained punk but experimented with rap that same year. Their crank call to the toll-free number of Carvel Ice Cream, during which the Boys harangued female employees, was the impetus behind the rap song that achieved cult status, "Cookie Puss."

With their venture into the rap genre officially underway, the Beasties enlisted Rick Rubin, whom they knew from an earlier hardcore band, to serve as DJ for onstage performances. Rubin had founded Def Jam Records as a college student at New York University; he eventually became the group's producer, taking "Rock Hard," a sample of the Boys' work, to Russell Simmons of Rush Productions. Recognizing the potential of the group to "be able to cross a lot of boundaries that a lot of other rap groups couldn't," as Rubin explained to Anthony DeCurtis in *Rolling Stone,* Simmons signed the trio.

Undaunted by Boos

In 1985 the Beasties contributed the single "She's on It" to the film *Krush Groove.* Less successful that same year as the opening act for pop icon Madonna, the group was booed off stage during their six-week stint of her Virgin Tour. Undaunted, the Beasties shouted obscenities back at the crowds. "We were going for the boos," Yauch explained in *People.* "We didn't want any bland reaction. If they aren't going to walk out happy, they'll walk out mad, but they *won't* walk out wondering who played." The following year, the Beasties opened the Raising Hell Tour for Run-D.M.C., prior to the success of their debut album *Licensed to Ill.*

"You probably knew kids like the Beastie Boys in high school: wiseasses who wore beat-up clothes, smoked dope, cut classes and partied till dawn in grungy rock clubs—too antsy to be studious but too upper-middle-class and smart to be real delinquents," wrote Handelman, summing up his impression of the group upon the release of *Licensed to Ill* in 1986. Although Jim Miller in *Time* called the album "loud, disgusting, without redeeming social merit" and "a perverse kind of slapstick comedy," he credited the group for the authenticity of its most famous single. "Still, when the Beastie Boys gleefully shout, 'You gotta fight for your right to PAAARTY,' you can almost taste the beer and smell the barf."

Creators of the fastest-selling debut album in the annals of Columbia's history, the Beasties did not endear themselves to the older generation with their crotch-grabbing and use of expletives at the Grammy Awards. "If you don't see the joke in three white, relatively privileged art brats' affecting the manners and morals of street hoods," penned Anthony DeCurtis in *Rolling Stone*, "you missed the point—not to mention the fun."

Earned Critical Respect

After the Beastie Boys severed their relationship with Rick Rubin and Def Jam Records over a heated royalty dispute, they released their second album, *Paul's Boutique*, on Capitol Records. The LP, featuring a sampling of a radio advertisement from the Brooklyn store after which it is named, only went gold, but made the Beasties musically credible. Critics who surmised that *Licensed to III* was a one-shot product of Rick Rubin's artistry, began to take serious notice of the white rappers. "Although the album doesn't boast an anthem on the order of 'Fight for Your Right,' *Paul's Boutique* certainly marks a musical advance for the trio," wrote Fred Goodman in *Rolling Stone*. "At the risk of sounding ridiculous, let us assert right off the bat that *Paul's Boutique* is as important a record in 1989 as Dylan's *Blonde on Blonde* was in 1966," wrote David Hiltbrand in *People*. "Everyone who thought the Beasties were just rude, crude, moronically loutish delinquents, the Three Stooges of rap, think again."

With their legal battles with Def Jam behind them, the Beastie Boys began work on a new album in 1990, this time in their own studio, which Bob Mack described in *Spin* as "a kid's bedroom, with freaky color photos of the band . . . and two Tijuana black velvet portraits of [singer] Michael Jackson." Their efforts there yielded the well-received 1992 release *Check Your Head*, an admitted departure for the trio, who, as they had in their punk rock days, returned to playing their own instruments. "We kinda got back into it from the stuff we were sampling on our other records," Yauch told Gary Graff of the *Detroit Free Press*. "A lot of the records we were listening to [in order] to find loops and samples had really amazing playing on it. We had a lot of funk records that had these really great instrumentals. You listen to that playing, and . . . it got us into playing again."

Though Alan Light commented in *Rolling Stone* that "it remains to be seen . . . whether people are ready for rappers playing their own instruments for the first time," it took only a week for *Check Your Head* to break into the Top Ten. Some reviewers found the album—an eclectic blend of styles ranging from funk to punk— "murky and messy," in the words of a *People* contributor. *Spin's* Steven Blush, however, declared that "what makes *Check Your Head* so vital and timely is the groove quotient. No longer silly, yet steadfastly sardonic, the Beasties take their rap-rock hybrid audience on an aural joyride."

Despite the skepticism of many critics after the hugely successful *Licensed to III* was followed by the poor sales of *Paul's Boutique*, the Beastie Boys, as they demonstrated with the release of *Check Your Head*, continue to earn notice in the music industry for their rambunctious forays into a variety of genres. "If there's a secret to the Beastie Boys' survival," Light remarked, "it is [their] willingness to wear their influences on their raggedy sleeves. They have never claimed to be anything they're not or to play anything but music they like listening to."

Selected discography

Licensed to III (includes "Fight for Your Right"), Def Jam, 1986.
Paul's Boutique, Capitol, 1989.
Check Your Head (includes "Jimmy James," "Pass the Mic," "The Biz vs. the Nuge," "So What'cha Want," and "Groove Holmes"), Capitol, 1992.

Also recorded single "She's on It," 1985, and EP *Polly Wog Stew*.

Sources

Billboard, February 20, 1988; August 5, 1989.
Creem, May 1992.
Detroit Free Press, May 15, 1992.
Entertainment Weekly, May 1, 1992.
Interview, April 1988; April 1992.
Newsweek, February 2, 1987; June 29, 1987.
People, February 9, 1987; August 28, 1989; June 1, 1992.
Playboy, September 1989.
Pulse!, April 1992.
Rolling Stone, February 12, 1987; April 23, 1987; June 15, 1989; August 10, 1989; November 15, 1990; May 28, 1992; June 25, 1992; July 9, 1992.
Spin, May 1992.
Teen, July 1987.
Time, May 18, 1992.

—Marjorie Burgess

Harry Belafonte

Singer, actor, activist

It is said that the worlds of music and morality do not collide, but rather balance harmoniously in the life and work of entertainer Harry Belafonte. In the 1950s Belafonte introduced the colorful, bouncy melodies of calypso music to the United States, and American listeners began swaying to the jaunty Caribbean beat and singing "Day-O" along with the masterful crooner. Since that time Belafonte has used his visibility as an entertainer to cast a political spotlight on humanitarian causes ranging from world hunger to civil rights to the plight of children in the Third World. Belafonte's accomplishments, and the awards bestowed on him in the spheres of entertainment and activism, show a man equally committed to musical excellence and political virtuousness.

Known as the "consummate entertainer," Belafonte was born in Harlem, New York, in 1927. His parents were West Indian, and he moved with his mother to her native Jamaica when he was a child. In the five years he spent on the island he not only absorbed the music that was such a vital part of the culture but also observed the effects of colonialism, the political oppression that native Jamaicans had to endure under British rule. "That environment gave me much of my sense of the world at large and what I wanted to do with it," Belafonte was quoted as saying in the *Paul Masson Summer Series.* "It helped me carve out a tremendous link to other nations that reflect a similar temperament or character."

Once back in Harlem, another culturally and artistically rich environment, Belafonte became street smart, learning the hard lessons of survival in the big city. When the United States entered World War II, he ended his high school education and enlisted in the U.S. Navy. After an honorable discharge he returned to New York City, where he bounced between odd jobs. His first foray into the world of entertainment came in the late 1940s when he was given two tickets to a production of the American Negro Theater. He was hooked after one performance. "I was absolutely mesmerized by that experience," he told the *Ottawa Citizen* in 1990. "It was really a spiritual, mystical feeling I had that night. I went backstage to see if there was anything I could do." His first leading role with the company was in Irish playwright Sean O'Casey's *Juno and the Paycock.* Impressed by the power and message of O'Casey's words, and by the promise of theater in general, Belafonte enrolled in the Dramatic Workshop of the New School for Social Research, studying under famous German director Erwin Piscator, whose other students included Rod Steiger and Bea Arthur.

For the Record. . .

Born Harold George Belafonte, Jr., March 1, 1927, in New York, NY; son of Harold George and Melvine (Love) Belafonte; married, 1948; wife's name Marguerite (divorced); married Julie Robinson (a dancer), March 8, 1957; children: Adrienne, Shari, David, Gina. Education: Attended Dramatic Workshop of the New School for Social Research, studying under Erwin Piscator.

Singer, actor, producer, political activist. Joined the American Negro Theater, late 1940s, appearing in *Juno and the Paycock;* performed at such clubs as the Royal Roost Nightclub and the Village Vanguard, New York City, late 1940s and early 1950s; appeared on Broadway in *John Murray Anderson's Almanac,* 1953; appeared in television adaptation of *Carmen Jones,* 1955; released *Calypso,* 1956; appeared in films, including *Island in the Sun,* 1957, *Uptown Saturday Night,* 1974, *First Look,* 1984, and *The Player,* 1992; produced television program *A Time for Laughter,* 1967; helped organize *We Are the World* recording session, 1985. Named cultural adviser to the Peace Corps by President John F. Kennedy; named member of the board of directors, Southern Christian Leadership Conference; chair of Martin Luther King, Jr., Memorial Fund; appointed a UNICEF Goodwill Ambassador, 1987. *Military service:* U.S. Navy, 1943-45.

Selected awards: Tony Award for best supporting actor, 1953, for *John Murray Anderson's Almanac;* Emmy Award, 1960, for *Tonight With Harry Belafonte;* Grammy Award, 1985, for *We Are the World.*

Addresses: *Office*—Belafonte Enterprises Inc., 830 8th Ave., New York, NY 10019.

Voice Captivated First Audience

Belafonte was concerned about the scarcity of work for black actors but got a break when, as a class project, he sang an original composition called "Recognition." His audience was spellbound. Among the listeners was the owner of the Royal Roost Nightclub, a well-known Broadway jazz center. Belafonte was offered a two-week stint that, due to such positive reception, blossomed into a twenty-week engagement. At the Roost and later at other clubs, such as the Village Vanguard in New York City's Greenwich Village, Belafonte charmed audiences with his husky-yet-sweet-voiced adaptations of popular and West Indian folk songs.

Armed with a recording contract with Capital Records

and the praise of critics, this bright new talent started making his mark. He first appeared on Broadway in *John Murray Anderson's Almanac,* for which he won a Tony Award. In 1955, in a television adaptation of the film *Carmen Jones,* Belafonte played the lead role and endeared himself to a national audience. Throughout the next few decades he continued to act in films such as *Island in the Sun* and *Uptown Saturday Night,* and produced television programs such as *A Time for Laughter,* in which he introduced U.S. audiences to then nationally unknown humorists Richard Pryor and Redd Foxx.

Career Soared With *Calypso*

It was in 1956, with the release of his album *Calypso,* that Belafonte sealed his status as a superstar and consummated America's love affair with Caribbean music. His most famous recordings, "Banana Boat Song" (popularly known as "Day-O") and "Matilda," recalled the melodies, rhythm, and spirit of Jamaica and other West Indian cultures. Throughout the sixties, seventies, and eighties, Belafonte reached into the lore and music of other cultures, most notably those of South America and Africa. He also continued with his celebrated interpretations of American folk ballads and spirituals, but he is always most closely associated with the zest and spunk of calypso.

Belafonte's *Calypso* was the first album to sell more than one million copies, a benchmark that led to the establishment of the Grammy Awards. The album was only one of many illustrious firsts in Belafonte's life. He was the first black man to win an Emmy Award as well as the first black television producer. He was also the first entertainer to be named cultural adviser to the Peace Corps by President John F. Kennedy.

Belafonte's success on vinyl and tape has always translated well in his live concerts, where he uses sing-alongs, dialogue with audience members, and a contagious energy and excitement to get the crowds responding jubilantly. Dave Hoekstra wrote in the Chicago *Sun-Times* in 1990 that Belafonte "sings from discovery and fulfillment. . . . So when you listen to the Belafonte songbook on a perfect summer night, you know the dignity, poise and spiritual exploration will still be heard long after the voice has passed. That is Harry Belafonte's lasting contribution to American popular music."

Dedicated to Humanitarian Causes

As important as his accomplishments in music are

Belafonte's political activities on behalf of humanitarian causes around the world. And more often than not he has been able to successfully merge these two passions. In 1985 Belafonte helped organize the recording session for the philanthropic and inspirational *We Are the World,* which won a Grammy Award, and he has been involved in many projects aimed at helping those suffering from poverty, homelessness, and famine around the world. As a result of his efforts to fight segregation in the United States, Belafonte was named to the board of directors of the Southern Christian Leadership Conference, a leading civil rights organization, and he has been chair of the memorial fund bearing the name of his friend, the late Dr. Martin Luther King, Jr. In 1987 he was appointed a UNICEF Goodwill Ambassador, and he has been dubbed the "Children's Patron Saint" by *Ebony* magazine.

Belafonte's interest in Africa—particularly in those suffering under apartheid's white minority rule in South Africa—and his admiration for African National Congress leader Nelson Mandela, inspired his critically acclaimed 1988 album *Paradise in Gazankulu.* Banned on South African radio, the album was praised for beautifully capturing in music the painful and haunting stories of life in a land infamous for its oppressiveness. In 1990 Howard Reich, appraising Belafonte's role as both entertainer and activist, wrote in the *Chicago Tribune:* "Like very few entertainers, he knows how to lure an audience to his point of view—or his political cause—without preaching. Belafonte's message is one of hope and optimism, even in the face of the global tragedies he decries."

Selected discography

Mark Twain, RCA, 1954.
Calypso (includes "Banana Boat Song"), RCA, 1956.
Belafonte (includes "Matilda"), RCA, 1956.
An Evening With Belafonte, RCA, 1957.
Harry Belafonte Songs of the Caribbean, RCA, 1957.
Belafonte Sings the Blues, RCA, 1958.
Love Is a Gentle Thing, RCA, 1959.
(With Lena Horne) *Porgy and Bess,* RCA, 1959.
Belafonte at Carnegie Hall, RCA, 1959.
My Lord What a Mornin', RCA, 1960.
Swing Dat Hammer, RCA, 1960.

Belafonte Returns to Carnegie Hall, RCA, 1960.
Jump Up Calypso, RCA, 1961.
To Wish You a Merry Christmas, RCA, 1962.
Midnight Special, RCA, 1962.
The Many Moods of Belafonte, RCA, 1962.
Streets I Have Walked, RCA, 1963.
Belafonte at the Greek Theater, RCA, 1964.
Ballads, Blues, and Boasters, RCA, 1964.
(With Miriam Makeba) *An Evening With Belafonte/Makeba,* RCA, 1965.
(With Nana Mouskouri) *An Evening With Belafonte/Mouskouri,* RCA, 1966.
In My Quiet Room, RCA, 1966.
Calypso in Brass, RCA, 1967.
Belafonte on Campus, RCA, 1967.
Belafonte Sings of Love, RCA, 1968.
Homeward Bound, RCA, 1970.
Belafonte by Request, RCA, 1970.
Belafonte Warm Touch, RCA, 1971.
This Is Belafonte, RCA, 1971.
Don't Stop the Carnival, RCA, 1972.
Play Me, RCA, 1973.
Turn the World Around, Columbia Records, 1977.
Loving You Is Where I Belong, Columbia Records, 1981 (Europe).
Paradise in Gazankulu, EMI, 1988.
Harry Belafonte: All Time Greatest Hits, RCA, 1988, volumes 2 and 3, 1989.
Belafonte '89, EMI, 1989 (Europe).
Belafonte '89 (abridged version), EMI, 1990 (United States).
Pure Gold, RCA.

Sources

Chicago Tribune, July 26, 1990.
Ebony, September 1988.
Fun & Gaming, March 1, 1990.
Ottawa Citizen, January 13, 1990.
Paul Masson Summer Series, June 1989.
Sun-Times (Chicago), July 27, 1990.

Additional information obtained from a 1991 Belafonte Enterprises Inc. biography.

—*Isaac Rosen*

Pat Benatar

Singer, songwriter

Pat Benatar burst onto the rock scene in 1979 with the scathing single "Heartbreaker." Her shag haircut, dark eye makeup, spike heels, and skin-tight pants combined with an angry, opera-trained voice to make her a unique rock commodity. In fact, Benatar's looks and voice were imitated by female rockers for years as she dominated the charts with hard-driving hit after hit. With her 1984 album, *Tropico,* however, Benatar began to slow down and produce a more mature sound. In 1991 she departed even further from her rock beginnings, immersing herself in the blues on the album *True Love.*

Benatar originally longed to be an opera singer, but she instead married and moved from New York City to Virginia with her husband. The young couple soon split, and Benatar returned to New York with a new agenda: to make it as a rock singer. Lean times followed, literally, as Benatar often found herself eating rice and beans. She sang oldies and standards at a club called Catch a Rising Star until 1978, when she was discovered there by Chrysalis Records executives.

In just a year's time, Benatar had released her first album, *In the Heat of the Night.* The record jolted the music industry; Benatar presented herself as a tough, rebellious woman scorned with the single "Heartbreaker," which warned listeners "Don't you mess around with me!" Fans relished her strong, sexy image and powerhouse songs. But the singer found herself at a loss to accommodate her sudden fame, commenting in the *Detroit News,* "I'm scared to watch the charts. I still don't understand what's going on. There have been packed houses everywhere we've gone, but every night when I step off that bus, I'm afraid there's going to be no one in the hall."

Consolidated Stature as Rock High Priestess

Success continued to follow Benatar. 1980's *Crimes of Passion* zoomed to *Billboard's* Top Twenty within three weeks of its release. "Hit Me With Your Best Shot," a rocking tribute to female independence, earned a particularly enthusiastic response from fans. One of the biggest singles from the album tackled a difficult social issue, which was atypical of the average rock song of the period. "Hell is for Children" looked into the problem of child abuse. "It started with a curiosity," Benatar told the *Detroit Free Press.* "I didn't know much about it, and I began to look into it. It was a big surprise to me. . . . I wanted it to be a great rock 'n' roll song—but it was never meant to be a commercial success."

Benatar ascended to *Billboard's* Number One spot with the release of her 1981 album, *Precious Time.* Though

For the Record. . .

Born January 10, 1953, in Brooklyn, NY; daughter of Andy (a sheet-metal worker) and Mildred (a cosmetologist) Andrzejewski; married Dennis Benatar (a video editor), c. 1972 (divorced, 1979); married Neil Geraldo (a musician, songwriter, and producer), February, 1982; children: (second marriage) Haley. *Education:* Trained briefly as an opera singer; studied health education.

Worked as a bank teller, and lounge singer in bars and Holiday Inns, Richmond, VA, 1972-74; worked as a singing waitress; "discovered" at a New York City club and signed by Chrysalis Records, 1978; recording and performing artist, 1979—.

Awards: Grammy Awards for best female rock vocal performance, 1981-84; Grammy Award nomination for best female rock vocal performance, 1986, for "Invincible."

Addresses: *Home*—Tarzana, CA. *Agent*—Premier Talent Agency, 3 East 54th St., New York, NY 10022.

sold-out shows were common on the tour supporting the record, critical response was mixed; a few reviewers commented that Benatar seemed to stick to a standard formula rather than venture into new ground. But the real story of *Precious Time* took place behind the scenes. Due to the stress of working constantly together over the previous two years, personnel problems erupted in Benatar's backup group. "Everybody was fighting," the singer remembered in the *Los Angeles Times.* "It was the everybody-kill-each-other stage of the band. It was a horrible, depressing experience. We couldn't get along anymore. Personal problems overshadowed everything." As Benatar strove for more artistic freedom, conflict with her producer compounded the tension.

Personal Conflict

Perhaps at the center of the difficulties surrounding *Precious Time* was Benatar's relationship with guitarist-writer-producer Neil Geraldo, which was falling apart under the strain. The two barely communicated during the taping sessions, and the situation deteriorated while Benatar and Geraldo toured with the rest of the band. "It was an all-time low for everything," she explained in the *Los Angeles Times.* "Everybody was so disgusted. We were oversaturated with everything—music and each other. . . . We didn't know if the band was going to stay together." Benatar decided to take a

year off after the tour to gain perspective on her life and career.

The smoke began to clear during her hiatus. She and Geraldo decided that they were better together than apart; they married in Hawaii in February of 1982. When a rested Benatar went back into the studio to record *Get Nervous,* she was much better equipped to weather record company problems and band stresses. *Get Nervous* showed Benatar in top form and was considered her best album by several critics. Using the tumultuous preceding years as inspiration, Benatar showed considerable depth and range in her compositions.

Tropico, Benatar's next release, was a decided departure from her established hard-edged, confrontational tone. Songs about romance and motherhood were featured. Benatar was pregnant while she developed much of the release, and her band had matured and changed. They no longer went into each recording session just to bang out hard rock; they were now taking more time to formulate their artistic vision and plan its execution. Sales of *Tropico* did not match those of Benatar's previous efforts, but the singer remained steadfast about her career's direction. "Instead of making records that are expected of me," Benatar told the *Detroit News,* "I'm making the records I want to make."

With the 1986 release of *Seven the Hard Way,* Benatar's band sought to combine their new-found sophistication with some of their older, more aggressive energy. As Benatar said in the *Detroit News* of the album's intent, "If anyone doubted that we would ever kick ass after I became a mother, think again." The single "Sex as a Weapon" became a hit. It was Benatar's way of trouncing the media for forcing sex into people's lives—something she had experienced first-hand during her days of being touted as a sex symbol.

Singin' the Blues

In 1991 Benatar released *True Love,* a collection of blues compositions. A complete departure from her previous work, *People* contributor Craig Tomashoff said of the record, "This come-back-to-basics disc is what [Benatar] should have been doing all along," though some critics were not as spirited about the effort. Backed by the popular outfit Roomful of Blues, Benatar's skillful voice rendered each song—both old and new—her own. Despite *True Love*'s only marginal connection to rock and roll, a single, the B. B. King-penned "Payin' the Cost to Be the Boss," received some airplay on mainstream and classic-rock radio stations.

With her singularly powerful voice and potently

unconstrained image, Benatar has made a significant mark on rock and roll—one that has since paved the way for many women entering this male-dominated field. And in shunning the limelight to pursue her not-always-commercial artistic vision, Benatar has further provided an independent alternative for would-be singer-songwriters. Where she once felt the need to please her record company first and foremost, Benatar asserted in *Spin* that concerning song choices for future albums, "From now on they will all be *my* favorites."

Selected discography

In the Heat of the Night (includes "Heartbreaker"), Chrysalis, 1979.
Crimes of Passion (includes "Hit Me With Your Best Shot" and "Hell Is for Children"), Chrysalis, 1980.
Precious Time, Chrysalis, 1981.
Get Nervous, Chrysalis, 1982.
Live From Earth, Chrysalis, 1983.
Tropico, Chrysalis, 1984.
Seven the Hard Way (includes "Sex as a Weapon"), Chrysalis, 1986.
Wide Awake in Dreamland, Chrysalis, 1988.
Best Shots, Chrysalis, 1989.
True Love, Chrysalis, 1991.

Sources

Christian Science Monitor, September 21, 1984; December 4, 1984.
Detroit Free Press, November 2, 1979; September 17, 1981; November 26, 1982; February 14, 1986.
Detroit News, November 5, 1979; November 26, 1982; February 14, 1986.
Guitar Player, December 1980.
Los Angeles Times, March 13, 1983.
Mother Jones, June 1982.
Ms., December 1982.
People, May 12, 1980; December 29, 1980; September 28, 1981; January 17, 1983; January 6, 1986; February 3, 1986; May 6, 1991.
Rolling Stone, May 1, 1980; December 16, 1980; November 13, 1980; December 25, 1980; May 1, 1981; June 25, 1981; October 29, 1981; December 24, 1981; November 25, 1982; December 9, 1982; November 24, 1983; January 31, 1985; January 16, 1986; June 27, 1991.
Spin, September 1985.
Stereo Review, April 1991; September 1991.
Variety, January 4, 1989.

—*Nancy Rampson*

Irving Berlin

Composer, pianist

Although he was born in Russia, Irving Berlin created songs that epitomize American music. As Michael Walsh said in *Time,* "Berlin's songs are as much part of American culture as any folk song. They seem to have been with us always, defining the spirit of a nation in an artless melody, or an unexpected harmonic twist." During his lifetime, Berlin published more than one thousand songs, some failures and many successes; some have been forgotten, and some, such as "White Christmas" and "God Bless America," will be remembered always. Berlin could not read music, but he is one of the twentieth century's most beloved composers.

Berlin's life began in poverty. He was born Israel Baline on May 11, 1888, the youngest of the six children of Lena and Moses Baline. Fleeing Russian persecution of Jews, his family arrived in the United States in 1893 and settled into an immigrant tenement neighborhood in New York City. The older members of the family took jobs where they could find them, but money was still too scarce. Shortly after his father's death in 1901, young Israel left school and home to earn his living.

Between the ages of 14 and 17, Israel Baline made money as a busker, or a street singer. He would roam from brothel to bar, singing for the coins the generous would toss. In 1905 he secured a full-time job as a singing waiter at Mike Salter's Pelham Cafe in New York City's Chinatown. When the bartender at a rival bar scored a big success by writing a new song to sing in his bar, young Baline set out to do the same. In 1907 he published his first song, "Marie From Sunny Italy." The artist who drew the cover for the printed music of the song misprinted his name as I. Berlin; thinking the name sounded more American than Israel Baline, the composer renamed himself Irving Berlin.

In the last decades of the nineteenth century, New York City became the business center of music publishing. Firms would hire songwriters and lyricists to mass-produce songs according to a musical and textual formula that pleased the public. These songwriters worked on the premises, often at pianos in large rooms where others like themselves also sat at pianos. They would then play their tunes for arrangers who would add the accompaniment to the published version. The companies hired "pluggers" to sell the new songs by singing them everywhere sheet music was sold or the public gathered; they plugged their songs in dime stores, departments stores, bars, and on the streets, and busin᠁ ᠁ ᠁

Birth of Tin Pan Alley

During the early years of the twentieth century, many publishing firms established their offices by the theater district, on West 28th Street between Fifth Avenue and Broadway. In 1909 journalist and songwriter Monroe Rosenfeld wrote a series of articles on the music publishing industry. Walking through that district, he was amazed by the clamor the industry produced and later in print likened the cacophony of the pianists, pluggers, and composers to the clatter of pots and pans and dubbed the area Tin Pan Alley.

Between the ages of 19 and 21, Berlin worked odd jobs in the Tin Pan Alley and Broadway areas. He plugged songs, sang in vaudeville, and sometimes played bit parts in shows. After business hours he would find pianos to play on and taught himself to plunk out songs.

In 1909 he got his first Tin Pan Alley job, as lyricist for the publishing firm of Waterson & Snyder. These early years of plugging and writing served as his initiation and education in the songwriting industry, and he learned well the art of pleasing the public. In 1911 he published "Alexander's Ragtime Band," which immediately thrust him into songwriting fame; his song was such a hit that he was instantly dubbed the "King of Tin Pan Alley."

Played in Only One Key

He developed at this time the work habits he would retain all of his life. After dinner Berlin would sit down at the piano and write songs until dawn. Since he had no formal musical training, he could only play the piano in one key. To be able to take full advantage of all the harmonies the piano had to offer, he used a special transposing keyboard. He just had to push a lever and the piano would start playing in another key while he still played the same notes on the keyboard. Berlin could not read music. He consequently would work out all of the details of the song in his head, and then sing and play it for his musical transcriber who would then write it down, playing it back to Berlin until it was right. This method of working was not uncommon for songwriters of his generation, and others used both the transposing keyboard and a musical secretary.

It is said that Berlin succeeded in part because he followed a strict work ethic. The composer had "Nine Rules for Writing Popular Songs," which appeared in an interview in *American Magazine* in 1920; he explained one of them thusly: "The song writer must look upon his work as a business, that is, to make a success of it, he must work and *work,* and then WORK." Between 1912 and 1916 Berlin wrote more than 180 songs, including many that would appear later in films; "Snooky Ookums" and "I Love a Piano," for example, were included in the 1948 film *Easter Parade.* Even Berlin's off hours were filled with his business: he spent his free time in the Broadway and vaudeville theaters. In 1914 he wrote his first complete Broadway musical, *Watch Your Step.* This was quickly followed by *Stop! Look! Listen!* in 1915 and *The Century Girl* in 1916.

Attained U.S. Citizenship

When World War I broke out, Berlin decided it was time to become an American in fact as well as in spirit. After several years of paperwork and delays, he took his oath on February 6, 1918, and became a citizen of the United States. Several months later he was drafted into the army. The hardest adjustment at Camp Upton in

Yaphank, Long Island, for this notorious night owl was to rise to reveille every day. He turned this experience into a song, "Oh! How I Hate to Get Up in the Morning," which became one of the most popular tunes of the day. Berlin subsequently was asked to write a musical show to raise money for the army. Yip! Yip! Yaphank! played on Broadway for a month, raising $83,000 before the cast—300 army soldiers—was sent to France.

After the war, life for Berlin returned to normal, and he continued to turn out song hits. In the 1920s he fell in love with heiress Ellin Mackay, who was Catholic. She reciprocated his feelings, but her father disliked Berlin for his undistinguished origins and theater ties and sent his daughter to Europe to forget him. During their months of separation Berlin wrote several of his most lovely ballads, "What'll I Do," "All Alone," and "Remember." Mr. Mackay's ruse did not work; the heiress returned from her year abroad in 1925, and the following year she and Berlin eloped.

1929 was a year of both success and setback for Berlin. Along with the rest of the country, he lost a fortune in the stock market crash. But that year, sound came to moving pictures, and Berlin began to write film scores. His first two films, Puttin' on the Ritz (1929) and Cocoanuts (1929), were adaptations of Broadway shows. His next film, Top Hat (1935)—featuring Fred Astaire and Ginger Rogers—was written expressly for Hollywood. Some of his most famous and memorable songs were in this film, including "Top Hat, White Tie, and Tails" and "Cheek to Cheek." More films followed, such as Follow the Fleet (1936), On the Avenue (1937), Carefree (1938), Alexander's Ragtime Band (1938), and Holiday Inn (1942), which contains the song that has sold more recordings than any other, "White Christmas."

World War II

When the Second World War broke out in Europe, Berlin needed to make a musical statement. "I'd like to write a great peace song, but it's hard to do, because you have trouble dramatizing peace," he said in an interview with the New York Journal American. "Yet music is so important. It changes thinking, it influences everybody, whether they know it or not." He found a song that he had written for his World War I show but had not included in it. He updated it a bit and found a radio singer who wanted a peace song for Armistice Day. When Kate Smith sang Berlin's "God Bless America" on November 11, 1938, the country gained a new— if unofficial—national anthem. Feeling uncomfortable about capitalizing on such sentiments, Berlin donated

the copyright and royalties to the Girl Scouts of America and the Boy Scouts of America.

When the United States entered World War II, Berlin took it as a personal call to action. He offered his services to the army, and created This Is the Army. The stage show toured the United States and then played for the troops in Europe; it was made into a movie in 1942 and earned ten million dollars for the Army Emergency Relief fund. Even more important to the country and composer than the money was the moral support it drew for the war effort. Writer Laurence Bergreen said in As Thousands Cheer: The Life of Irving Berlin, "Through his songs, Berlin managed to inject human touches that made life in the armed services comprehensible to civilian audiences."

Once the war was over Berlin returned to working for himself. He continued to turn out the hits. Annie Get Your Gun (1946) contained more hit songs than any other musical on Broadway and was his most successful show ever. Movie moguls in Hollywood also demanded his songs. The almost universal popularity of

---

"Irving Berlin has no place in American Music. He is American Music."
—Jerome Kern

---

his music insured their appeal for years. Songs that Berlin wrote in his early career were given new life in the movies. White Christmas (1954) not only included the title song, which was written for an earlier movie, but also used "Mandy" and "Oh! How I Hate to Get Up in the Morning," both of which were written in 1918 for Yip! Yip! Yaphank!

In the 1950s Berlin's creativity began to slow down. While his old hits played well, he wrote fewer new songs, and they were less successful. Financially secure, he did not need to work, for his royalties exceeded the income of any other songwriter ever. In 1954 he earned $101,000 in royalties, and in 1956 he earned $102,000. Finally, after his last Broadway show, Mr. President (1962), flopped, he retired.

Last Years Spent Privately

Resigning from songwriting, Berlin also withdrew from public life. He spent the last decades of his life privately in his New York City town house, or in retreat at his estate in the Catskill Mountains. He made no public appearances. In 1972, when the cast of *This Is the Army* held a reunion party, he did not attend. But the public did not forget him. His 100th birthday in 1988 spawned many public tributes, including a televised celebration at Carnegie Hall, complete with old and new stars and even Girl Scouts and Boy Scouts marching on stage singing "God Bless America." The National Museum of American History in Washington, D.C., had a six-month exhibit of Berlin memorabilia, including his transposing piano. He also received many private tributes as well. For almost 20 years, a small group of people met on Christmas Eve outside his home in New York City and sang to him their favorite carol, "White Christmas."

Berlin died on September 22, 1989. The number and length of the subsequent printed obituaries and articles attests to the respect the world holds for him. To many, he symbolizes the sentiments of an era and the music of a nation. Fellow songwriter Jerome Kern was quoted as saying in Alexander Woollcott's biography of Berlin: "Irving Berlin has no place in American Music. He *is* American Music."

Selected discography

Annie Get Your Gun (selections), RCA Victor, 1966, reissued, 1988.
Call Me Madam (selections), MCA, 1973.
The Vintage Berlin, New World Records, 1977.
Say It All with Music, Monmouth Evergree, 1978.
The Girl on the Magazine Cover, RCA Victor, 1979, reissued, 1988.
Blue Skies, Nonesuch, 1985.
Rosemary Clooney Sings the Music of Irving Berlin, King Record Co., 1985.

Bennett/Berlin, Columbia Records, 1987.
Remember: Michael Feinstein Sings Irving Berlin, Elektra, 1987.
Songs of Irving Berlin, CRI, 1988.
Irving Berlin: A Hundred Years (recorded 1930-58), Columbia, 1988.
The Irving Berlin 100th Anniversary Collection, MCA, 1988.
The Irving Berlin Songbook: A Centennial Celebration, RCA, 1988.
Holiday Inn and Blue Skies (soundtrack), Vintage Jazz Classics, 1990.
Mr. President, Sony Broadway, 1992.

Sources

Books

Bergreen, Laurence, *As Thousands Cheer: The Life of Irving Berlin,* Viking, 1990.
Freedland, Michael, *Irving Berlin,* W. H. Allen, 1974.
Whitcomb, Ian, *Irving Berlin and Ragtime America,* Century, 1987.
Woollcott, Alexander, *The Story of Irving Berlin,* Putnam, 1925.

Periodicals

American History Illustrated, May 1988.
American Magazine, December 1920.
Commentary, October 1990.
Esquire, January 1990.
New York Journal American, September 4, 1938.
Newsweek, October 2, 1989.
Opera News, December 9, 1989.
People, October 9, 1989.
Stereo Review, February 1988.
Time, May 16, 1988; October 2, 1989.
U.S. News and World Report, May 9, 1988.

—Robin Armstrong

Carla Bley

Composer, arranger, bandleader, pianist

Carla Bley has been a vital force in the jazz world for more than 30 years. As a musician and composer, her flair for the outrageous and her engaging sense of humor, combined with a profound dedication to her art and audience, have continually placed her on music's cutting edge. As an entrepreneur in the recording and publishing businesses, her creativity and financial savvy have nurtured the careers of many new artists who, because of their reluctance to conform to set standards of commerciality, found difficulty securing financial support from traditional channels. That she accomplished her success with no formal training—and in a male-dominated field—is proof of her talent and perseverance.

Bley was born Carla Borg in Oakland, California, in 1938. Her mother died when Carla was eight years old, and Bley was raised in a strict religious atmosphere by her father, a choir director and piano teacher. Bley's earliest musical experiences revolved around the church; as she recalled *Contemporary Keyboard,* "I spent the first 15 years of my life playing music only for Jesus." But even in this environment her witty and irreverent approach to music began to take shape. According to an interview in *Jazz,* she composed "twelve variations on 'Onward Christian Soldiers,' one a march, one a waltz, a polka version, ending up with a dirge and a 'Hallelujah Chorus.'"

Bley quit school at age 15, worked briefly at a music store, and then moved to New York City, where she found a job as a cigarette girl at the famed Birdland jazz club. In those surroundings she first began seriously listening to jazz, and the influences of the musicians she heard at the time—pianist Thelonius Monk, trumpet player Dizzy Gillespie, saxophonist John Coltrane and many others—can be detected in her compositions and solo improvisations. It was also at Birdland that Bley met her first husband, Canadian pianist Paul Bley. They were married in 1959 and moved back to the West Coast, where they kept company with some of the most important avant-garde jazz musicians of the 1960s, notably saxophonist Ornette Coleman, bassist Charlie Haden, and trumpeter Don Cherry. During this period Bley began composing, mainly through her husband's prodding. "He'd come in and say, 'Well, I got a record date tomorrow and I need six hot ones,'" she divulged in *Contemporary Keyboard.* "I'd sit down and write six of them. I just functioned like that. Instead of cooking the dinner, that would be my job."

Free-lanced as Composer and Arranger

Bley first came to the attention of the general public in the late 1960s. In 1967 vibraharpist Gary Burton recorded her cycle of pieces, *A Genuine Tong Funeral.* Two years later Bley provided both arrangements and original compositions for Charlie Haden's *Liberation Music Orchestra,* an album celebrating the spirit of the Spanish Civil War. Bley finished a five-year project, *Escalator Over The Hill,* a kind of surreal opera that she subtitled "a chronotransduction" in 1970. The piece, one of her most ambitious works, was subsequently issued by the Jazz Composer's Orchestra Association (JCOA), which Bley cofounded to produce her own work as well as that of other jazz composers.

During the 1970s and 1980s Bley toured extensively with her ten-piece band, a group founded specifically to perform her own music, and she recorded several albums for her own label, Watt. In the early 1990s, while continuing her work as composer and bandleader, Bley also focused on her talents as an improvisor at the piano, both as soloist with her band and in a duet setting with bassist Steve Swallow, with whom she toured extensively in 1988.

Developed Unique Style

Bley's method of composing and arranging is considered among the most eclectic of all jazz artists. Her work has displayed an instantly recognizable style that combines musical elements of swing, bebop, marches, rock and roll, waltzes, and even German cabaret music. Yet in spite of her unconventional style, she has always remained something of a conservative in her melodies and harmonic structures; as Gary Burton told a *Down Beat* correspondent, "I know a Carla Bley tune the minute I hear it. It's direct. It is not complicated. It is not layer upon layer of subtle interaction. It's very strong melody, very strong harmony, simply constructed. Carla wants her music to hit you square between the eyes."

Although Bley's keyboard improvisations are strongly influenced by such jazz pianists as Thelonius Monk and Bill Evans, in many ways her solo work is as striking and individual as her compositional style. Because she received no formal training, she has developed an idiosyncratic method of fingering that produces a unique tone and manner of phrasing. Her improvisations are notable for their economy; she relishes a sense of space while improvising, and the listener has the sense that every single note is meaningful. In fact, Bley once asserted to *Down Beat* writer Don Palmer, "When I do a solo and when it's good, there's a word for every note I play. I speak the solos while I play."

Although Bley has occasionally made concessions to commercial trends in music—her 1985 album *Night Glo* would easily fit on the playlists of most adult contemporary radio stations—she has for the most part remained true to her unique musical ideals. Her 1991 release *The Very Big Carla Bley Band,* for example, features a 15-minute work titled "United States," in which big band jazz, blues, salsa, polka music, snatches of John Philip Sousa marches, and even "The Star Spangled Banner," are combined to provide an amazingly cohesive portrait of the 50 states.

A Force Behind the Scenes

Carla Bley's musical accomplishments alone warrant her acceptance as a crucial figure in modern jazz. Yet her success offstage, as a leader in the intensely competitive music industry, has been equally remarkable and has profoundly affected the careers of many innovative artists. In 1965, along with Austrian musician—and future second husband—Michael Mantler, Bley helped found the Jazz Composer's Orchestra, an ensemble dedicated to the performance of new works by aspiring jazz composers. "The Jazz Composer's

Orchestra was everybody's band, the community's band. All the composers who wanted to write for a large orchestra got to write for one," Bley informed Linda Dahl, author of *Stormy Weather: The Music and Lives of a Century of Jazzwomen.*

Bley and Mantler subsequently founded the Jazz Composer's Orchestra Association—a nonprofit organization that produces, records, and distributes jazz considered too experimental by the major recording companies for the mainstream market—and New Music Distribution Service, a branch of JCOA serving as an umbrella organization that supports more than two hundred independent record companies. The work of these organizations has been financed largely by copyright royalties from Bley's compositions.

For Bley, these business ventures remain an enormous source of pride. She has been able to lend a hand to fellow struggling artists and also maintain her artistic integrity. As she told *Jazz's* Sy Johnson, "I feel proud and sort of like a shining example, mainly because I'm independent. I don't belong to a stable. I'm not a pet of the recording industry. I put out my own records. We book our own band. I have my own publishing company. I have my own recording studio. Everything I do is totally controlled by me." It is this fierce self-reliance that has made Carla Bley an innovative and influential figure in American music.

Selected compositions

"3/4" (for piano and orchestra), 1975.
Mortelle randonnee (film score), 1985.

Selected discography

A Genuine Tong Funeral, RCA, 1967.

The Jazz Composer's Orchestra, JCOA, 1968.
Charley Haden, *Liberation Music Orchestra,* Impulse, 1969.
Escalator Over the Hill, JCOA, 1971.
Tropic Appetites, Watt, 1973.
13-3/4, Watt, 1975.
Dinner Music, Watt, 1976.
The Carla Bley Band—European Tour 1977, Watt, 1977.
Music Mecanique, Watt, 1979.
Fictitious Sports, Columbia, 1980.
Social Studies, Watt, 1980.
Carla Bley Live!, Watt, 1981.
The Ballad of the Fallen, ECM, 1983.
Heavy Heart, Watt, 1984.
I Hate to Sing, Watt, 1985.
Night Glo, Watt, 1985.
Duets, Watt, 1988.
Fleur Carnivore, Watt, 1989.
The Very Big Carla Bley Band, Watt, 1991.

Sources

Books

Dahl, Linda, *Stormy Weather: The Music and Lives of a Century of Jazzwomen,* Pantheon, 1984.
Placksin, Sally, *American Women in Jazz, 1900 to the Present: Their Words, Lives, and Music,* Seaview Books, 1982.

Periodicals

Contemporary Keyboard, February 1979.
Down Beat, March 30, 1972; June 1, 1978; August 1984; April 1991.
Jazz, Spring 1978.
New York Times, February 10, 1985.

—*Jeffrey Taylor*

Paul Brady

Singer, songwriter, instrumentalist

Paul Brady comes from a small town in Northern Ireland near the border with the Republic of Ireland. Like many Catholics in Northern Ireland, Brady learned to play and sing Irish traditional music at an early age; his earliest recordings, in fact, were made up of strictly traditional songs. He quickly established himself as one of the great guitarists in the genre and made recordings with some of the best Irish musicians of the day. Brady also performed vocals on a few songs from some of these early, mostly instrumental folk music recordings, showing himself to be one of the finest exponents of traditional Irish song.

Brady performed with several Irish folk groups throughout the late 1960s and 1970s. He founded the Johnstons and remained with them until 1972. After a brief stay in the United States from 1972 to 1973, the musician returned to Ireland to join the prominent Irish folk group Planxty. Brady had a tough act to follow, for he replaced the popular singer/songwriter/guitarist Christy Moore, who had left to pursue a quieter lifestyle. Though he never recorded with Planxty, listeners—including *Melody Maker*'s Colin Irwin—felt that when he joined the band they were at their peak. Planxty considered making a farewell album, but decided against commercializing the band's demise. After Planxty disbanded, Brady did record some of the group's material with Planxty's former members, such as Andy Irvine, a fellow instrumentalist and singer.

Switched From Folk to Rock

By the early 1980s Brady felt that he had done all he could do with traditional music. His *Welcome Here Kind Stranger* won *Melody Maker*'s award for best folk album of 1978, and Brady made it clear that this was his last album in that genre. By this time Brady had already begun writing his own songs and wanted to try to break into the pop market. Based on songs recorded in early 1980, Warner/Elektra/Atlantic Corp. offered him a deal to record singles that resulted in "Crazy Dreams"/ "Busted Loose," which went to Number One in Ireland in late 1980.

Brady told a *Melody Maker* correspondent in 1981, "Making the break with traditional music to rock music involved a complete change in the way I thought about various things. Rock music is so open compared to traditional music. In rock music, there are no rules except the ones you make yourself." Brady commented in the same interview, "I felt I'd exhausted all the possibilities of interpreting traditional music. The bottom of the well had been reached, there was nowhere else to go. There's only so much you can do with traditional music, after you've reached a certain point you begin to realize you're just screwing around with it."

Born Paul Joseph Brady, May 19, 1947, in Strabane County, Tyrone, Northern Ireland. *Education:* Attended University College, Dublin.

Singer, songwriter, producer, and instrumentalist. Irish folk musician; member of the Johnstons, late 1960s-1972; joined Planxty, 1974; recorded with numerous Irish traditional musicians, including fiddlers Kevin Burke and Tommy Peoples and flutist Matt Molloy. Shifted to rock music, opening for Dire Straits and Eric Clapton, recording original songs, and writing for various recording artists, including Bonnie Raitt.

Selected awards: *Welcome Here Kind Stranger* voted best folk album of the year by *Melody Maker,* 1978; single "Crazy Dreams"/"Busted Loose" reached Number One in Ireland in 1980.

Addresses: *Agent*—Monterey Peninsula Artists, P.O. Box 7308, Carmel, CA 93921. *Record company*—Mercury/Polygram, 901 18th Avenue South, Nashville, TN 37212.

Because of his switch to rock, some of Brady's folk fans thought that the musician was "selling out," or falling prey to commercialism. Brady himself acknowledged the problems that accompanied his move from folk to rock. "It was ludicrous, really," he admitted in *Rolling Stone.* "A lot of people thought I was crazy, that I could go on forever as a folk act making a good living. I went form the top of one ladder to the bottom of another, and I didn't know anybody in rock. It was a very scary time."

Honed Songwriting Skills

Brady's new style was not considered folk-rock fusion, but bore the signs of many of the musician's influences—including jazz, folk, and rhythm and blues—which other Irish rock musicians like Van Morrison, also from Northern Ireland, have drawn on in various ways. Brady has pointed to Wilson Pickett, Otis Redding, and Ray Charles as his favorite singers when he was growing up.

Unlike the work of some other Irish musicians, Brady's music is not usually recognizably Irish and not usually political, despite his border hometown in Northern Ireland, an area often embroiled in religious and civil strife. "I don't feel the need or the desire to clothe my music in the obvious signals of Irishness," he explained

to *Rolling Stone* in 1991. And when he does make use of Irish sounds—for example, a tin whistle on his *Trick or Treat* album—he tends to use them in nontraditional ways.

A political song or two does find its way into Brady's work, however. "The Island" on 1986's *Back to the Centre,* for example, is about the problems between the Catholic minority and Protestant majority on his home island of Ireland. "Nobody who lives in Northern Ireland can escape what's happening there," Brady stated in *Rolling Stone* in 1986. My audience is both Protestant and Catholic, and frankly I'm pleased neither has tried to claim me. I'm not one to preach, I just try to give them another view, something they can face the future with."

By the mid-1980s Brady's songwriting skills were widely recognized, and his songs were being covered by a number of other artists, including Santana, Dave Edmunds, and Tina Turner. He wrote "Paradise Is Here" especially for Turner's *Break Every Rule* album of 1986 and was a favorite songwriter among such pop superstars as Bob Dylan and Grammy-winner Bonnie Raitt, who sings a duet with Brady on his 1991 LP, *Trick or Treat.* Brady, in turn, wrote a couple of songs for Raitt's album *Luck of the Draw,* including the title track.

Debut Solo Album

Brady's *Trick or Treat* was not his first solo album, but it was his first for a major label—Fontana/Mercury—that received a lot of promotion. As a result, most critics considered it his debut. A *Rolling Stone* reporter asked Brady if he thought *Trick or Treat* would bring him the same sort of belated fame that his friend and fan Bonnie Raitt experienced. Brady replied, "In a way I relate to Bonnie, but in another way I don't. Whereas she's been here all this time and she's been part of the furniture, I haven't even been in the house yet. But my feeling is that as long as I'm producing work that is good and impassioned, it can happen any time." Critics noted that *Trick or Treat* benefits from the expertise of great studio musicians as well as producer Gary Katz, who worked with the rock group Steely Dan.

Rolling Stone, after praising Brady's earlier but little-known solo efforts, called *Trick or Treat* Brady's "most compelling collection." And the general critical acclaim for this album helps put into perspective such praise by Bonnie Raitt, and perhaps more remarkably, Bob Dylan, who calls Brady "a secret hero." With the release of *Trick or Treat* by a major label, Paul Brady, from the small town of Strabane, Northern Ireland, seems on the verge of becoming a public hero.

Selected discography

(Contributor) *Oisin,* Tara, 1976.
(Contributor) Tommy Peoples, *The High Part of the Road,* Shanachie, 1976.
(Contributor) *Matt Molloy, Paul Brady, Tommy Peoples,* Green Linnet, 1977.
It's a Hard Road to Travel: Traditional Music of Ireland, Shanachie, 1977.
Welcome Here Kind Stranger, Green Linnet, 1978.
(Contributor) Kevin Burke, *If the Cap Fits . . .,* Green Linnet, 1978.
(Contributor) Andy Irvine, *Rainy Sundays . . . Windy Dreams,* Tara, 1980.
The Green Crow Caws, EMI, 1980.
Hard Station, Polydor, 1981.
Andy Irvine & Paul Brady, Green Linnet, 1981.
(Contributor) Kevin Burke and Jackie Daly, *Eavesdropper,* Green Linnet, 1981.
True for You, Atlantic, 1983.
Full Moon, Demon Fiend, 1984.
(With Mark Knopfler) *Cal* (soundtrack), Mercury, 1984.
Biograph, 1985.
Back to the Centre, Mercury, 1986.
Trick or Treat, Fontana/Mercury, 1991.
Andy McGann & Paul Brady.
Bealoideas, Tara.
First Month of Spring, Shanachie.
The Gathering, Shanachie.

Paul Brady and John Vesey, Shanachie.
Primitive Dance, Mercury.

With the Johnstons

The Johnstons Anthology, Transatlantic, 1978.
The Johnstons, Transatlantic.
Give a Damn, Transatlantic.
The Barleycorn, Transatlantic.
Bitter Green, Transatlantic.
Colours of the Dawn, Transatlantic.
If I Sang My Song, Transatlantic.
Streets of London (compilation), Sonas.
Ye Jacobites by Name (compilation), Contour.

Sources

Books

Schaeffer, Deborah, *Irish Folk Music,* Greenwood Press, 1989.

Periodicals

Melody Maker, February 1, 1975; July 22, 1978; December 30, 1978; March 1, 1980; July 18, 1980.
Rolling Stone, December 4, 1986; July 11, 1991.

—*Tim Taylor*

Garth Brooks

Singer, songwriter

Garth Brooks is not just one of the most popular recording artists in the country music field; he is one of the most popular recording artists in any field. In the first week after his 1991 album, *Ropin' the Wind*, was released, it "made music history by becoming the first album to enter both *Billboard*'s country and pop charts at No. 1," reported *People* magazine. Because of his broad popular appeal, "Brooks has moved more records with greater velocity than anyone ever in Nashville," wrote *People*'s Jim Jerome. After releasing just three albums, his combined record sales "[approached] a staggering 10 million units."

Brooks was born in Tulsa, Oklahoma, in 1962 but was raised in small-town Yukon, Oklahoma. His father, Troyal, an oil company engineer, and mother, Colleen, had six children. Family life was very modest—"downright poor" Brooks's sister Betsy told Jerome—on Troyal Brooks's $25,000 annual salary. Brooks and his brothers and sister learned how to pick guitars and sing with their mother, who had a brief career as a country singer in the 1950s.

In high school, Brooks's major passion was sports; he was a four-sport athlete, participating in football, basketball, baseball, and track and field. Eventually his athletic talent won him a track scholarship to Oklahoma State University. Despite his heavy involvement in sports, however, Brooks maintained an interest in music and still found time to play in a band during his high school years.

Inspired by George Strait

Brooks's musical influences include traditional country music stars George Jones and Merle Haggard, pop singers Billy Joel, James Taylor and Dan Fogelberg, and the world of rock and roll in general. But a short time before starting college, Brooks "heard [country singer George] Strait do 'Unwound' on [his] car radio, and that's the exact moment it all changed," he told *People*'s Jerome; Brooks was profoundly affected by the neo-traditionalist country musician, and by his own admission "became a George wannabe and imitator for the next seven years."

As a track star at Oklahoma State, in Stillwater, the 6'1", 225-pound Brooks was a javelin thrower. In the classroom, he studied advertising, "hoping to adapt his original music to jingles and creative copy," revealed *Entertainment Weekly* contributor Alanna Nash. Brooks also played his music around campus, performing duets with roommate Ty Englund and, for a while, performing in a bluegrass band.

He also worked odd jobs to help support himself. One

of these was as a bouncer at a club called Tumbleweeds. It was there that Brooks met his future wife, Sandy Mahr. She had gotten into a brawl in the Tumbleweeds ladies' room one night; when Brooks rushed in, he found her with her fist through the wall. "All she said was, 'I missed,'" recalled Brooks to Jane Sanderson of *People.* "I thought, 'Man, this is nuts.' Then I told her she had to leave, but as I was takin' her outside, I kept thinkin' about how good-lookin' she was." Sandy was a fellow student, and she and Brooks soon began dating. Before long, romance blossomed.

Pursued Music When Athletic Career Foundered

While in college, however, athletics were still the driving force in Brooks's life—he wanted to be the best in the javelin throw. As *People's* Jerome noted, "His dreams then were more likely about gold medals and the Olympics than gold records and the Opry." But Brooks's dreams of athletic glory were dashed when he failed to

make the Big Eight Conference finals his senior year. "A coach came by and said, 'Well, now you can get on with what matters in life,'" Brooks told *People.* "I wondered, 'What the hell could that be?'"

After graduation in 1985, Brooks decided to head for Nashville to take his shot at country music stardom. He lasted only a short time in the country music capital. "I had thought the world was waiting for me," he told *People* contributor Sanderson, "but there's nothing colder than reality." Garth went back to Stillwater, and he and Sandy worked various jobs while he polished his musical skills. They married in 1986 and, a year later, put together their last $1,500 to try Nashville a second time. Once again, however, Nashville was not eager to have Brooks. He struggled to get his music heard, pitching his songs all over town for months. He finally got his big break when he was added to a newcomer showcase at a club when another act failed to show. Brooks was noticed by a talent scout from Capitol Records and was soon signed to a recording contract.

Lightning Struck

His debut album, *Garth Brooks,* was released in 1989. The album generated four Number One country singles and "raised Brooks from honky-tonker to concert headliner almost overnight," wrote Sanderson, who called the tunes on *Garth Brooks* a mixture of "soft laments and raucous cowboy rock." Citing the singer's "gift for finding something fresh in the familiar, something timely in the predictable and timeworn," Jay Cocks of *Time* explained that Brooks makes "a direct assault on the heartstrings, singing in a kind of simonized tenor suitable for both serenades and bust-outs." Other country stars were also impressed with Brooks's talent. "There are lots of artists who can sing but who can't impart the emotion and personality that make an entertainer shine," country singer Reba McEntire said to *People.* "Garth pulls it off."

Brooks's first Number One hit, "If Tomorrow Never Comes," was a ballad reminding people to appreciate their loved ones while they have them. "That song means a lot to me because of friends I've lost," he told Sanderson. "There's a million things you can say that need to be said," Brooks explained about his songs, "messages that are of common sense, of values, things people have to be reminded of."

In 1990 Brooks won the Country Music Association's Horizon Award for most promising newcomer. He also won a Video of the Year award for his song "The Dance." Also that year, he released his second album,

No Fences. Sales of this follow-up recording zoomed, launching more Number One country singles and reaching as high as Number Four on *Billboard's* pop chart. In the spring of 1991 Brooks won an unprecedented six Academy of Country Music awards—top male vocalist, single, song, album, video, as well as entertainer of the year. Later that year, Brooks's debut album passed two million copies in sales, *No Fences* passed 4 million, and the rising star's expected third album brought in advance orders of 2 million copies.

Topped the Pop Charts

When, in the fall of 1991, Brooks's album *Ropin' the Wind* performed the amazing feat of opening at the top of the *Billboard* pop charts—unheard of for a country act—Brooks was indisputably hailed as the new champion of the music business. *Entertainment Weekly* contributor Nash proclaimed him "the most popular male singer of any kind in the country today." *Stereo Review* called *Ropin' the Wind* "his best yet." The magazine allowed that *No Fences,* "with its provocative mix of styles and subjects, went a long way toward making [Brooks] stand out. But it [was the] third album that [told] the tale, primarily through the breadth of Brooks's songwriting in a program that ranges from bluegrass . . . to Western-swing . . . and pop." Discussing his third release with Celeste Gomes of *Country Song Roundup,* Brooks said, "I am the kind of person that can be happy with it if the people are. The purpose of *Ropin' the Wind* is to hopefully convince people that *No Fences* was not a fluke. And hopefully to convince people that if they buy a Garth Brooks product, it's 10 songs, not three singles and filler."

Brooks admitted to Nash that he is quite surprised at the enormity of his success. "I really don't have a clue why it happened to me," he said. "Because what I deserve and what I've gotten are totally off balance. . . . All I can say is that it's divine intervention." Nash, however, noted that there are "earthly explanations." Among the new generation of country stars, "Brooks is the performer who most understands common folk. A chubby, balding Everyman with boy-next-door appeal, he has exceptional taste in songs—both his own and those of others. It's real-life music to which nearly everyone . . . can relate."

Kills 'Em in Concert

An exuberant stage performer—more rock and roll on the boards than traditional country style . . . Analysts called

Brooks "an electrifying showman who choreographs his act with a unique, kick-ass abandon." *Entertainment Weekly* described his concert performance as "equal parts John Wayne and Mick Jagger." The comparison to John Wayne is an apt reflection of Brooks's love for the legendary star's movies. "I'd like to carry the same messages in song that he did in his movies," Brooks said to Sanderson. "He stood for honesty."

Brooks's road entourage includes close friends and family. His lifelong friend Mick Weber is his road manager, old college roommate and partner Ty Englund his guitarist, and sister Betsy his bass player. Brooks's brother Kelly, who is an accountant, handles tour financing and the star's investments. "I surrounded myself with people who knew me long before I happened," explained Brooks to *People* contributor Jerome. "So if I start acting different, man, they'll square me in a minute."

Despite his rocket to superstardom, praise for Brooks has not been universal. Nash reported that one critic called the singer "a calculating fake . . . a clone of George Strait." And for all his success, Brooks's post-stardom life has not been without it's difficulties. During

---

"I had thought the world was waiting for me, but there's nothing colder than reality."

---

his first six months on the road, in 1989, Brooks found women all around him, and the married man fell prey to temptation—wife Sandy told Jerome that "an informant" confirmed her suspicions. "Garth has always been a very sexual person," said Brooks's understanding spouse. "It was his ego: proving he could look out, point and conquer. What made it easier to cope with was that it wasn't someone special. It didn't mean anything." Sandy, who didn't tour with Brooks then, called him the night of November 4, 1989, to confront him and lay down the law. Brooks came home and begged her not to leave. "Garth has said to me a million times that was probably the best thing that ever happened to him," friend Englund said to Jerome. "It took a helluva human being to forgive me," Brooks himself said. "I had to promise I'd make this marriage work. It ain't a bed of roses now, but we bust our asses, and it works unbelievably well. For the first time in my life, I feel good about being a husband and a partner."

Controversy Over Video

A drop of rain fell on Brooks's professional parade in the spring of 1991 when the video for his song "The Thunder Rolls" was banned by America's two biggest country-music cable networks. The video depicted a wife abuser who gets gunned down by his desperate spouse. The Nashville Network (TNN) would not air the video without a trailer from Brooks denouncing domestic abuse and vigilantism. Country Music Television (CMT) pulled the video when viewer response became negative. The bans were "a total shock," Brooks said to *People.* Calling most videos "the same old crap," he stated "I refuse to make a no-brainer. I would have never, ever done something TNN and CMT couldn't use, but I'm not going to change what I do to fit their standards."

In the fall of 1991, he did, however, give television a whirl; Brooks appeared on the NBC situation comedy *Empty Nest*—playing himself. "They filmed me, that's about it," he told the *Detroit Free Press.* "There were actors there, but I wasn't one of them. To tell the truth, I feel lucky to be where I'm at in country music. I think I'll just stay here." Though Brooks may not have a second career as an actor, *Entertainment Weekly* reported in March of 1992 that the singer was close to endorsing a multimillion-dollar agreement to pen his official biography. The magazine further disclosed that Brooks's literary effort would be packaged with an upcoming record.

Feeling as fortunate as he does, Brooks insists on keeping his ego in check. "I'm still a bum, I'm no different," he said to Jerome. "I hate to take out the trash and clean my room. Sandy makes me do that stuff. I don't wake up and say, 'I cannot believe I am in the middle of all this.' I just wake up and say, 'You're a bum, go do something worthwhile today.'"

Selected discography

Garth Brooks (includes "If Tomorrow Never Comes"), Capitol, 1989.
No Fences, Capitol, 1990.
Ropin' the Wind, Capitol, 1991.
Beyond the Season, Capitol, 1992.
The Chase, Capitol, 1992.

Sources

Country Music, September/October 1991.
Country Song Roundup, December 1991.
Detroit Free Press, October 3, 1991; October 28, 1991.
Entertainment Weekly, September 20, 1991; March 20, 1992; March 27, 1992.
People, September 3, 1990; May 20, 1991; October 7, 1991.
Stereo Review, November 1991.
Time, September 24, 1990.

—*Greg Mazurkiewicz*

Dave Brubeck

Pianist, composer, bandleader

According to Robert Rice of the *New Yorker,* the combo led by jazz pianist Dave Brubeck during the 1950s and 1960s was "the world's best-paid, most widely travelled, most highly publicized, and most popular small group." While Brubeck may be considered the world's most widely acclaimed musician of his period, he is also quite possibly its most criticized, having been described as everything from mystical to methodical. Stanley H. White wrote in *Jazz Journal* in 1958 that Brubeck's "ability to improvise fluently on almost any given theme, and his ability to swing with both drive and imagination make him a jazz musician of singular merit"; two years later Joe Goldberg declared in *Jazz Review* "that jazz is not [Brubeck's] natural form of expression, but he is determined to play jazz, as if a man who knew five hundred words of French were to attempt a novel in that language."

Perhaps Rice's statement on the importance of Brubeck's music, that "it is impossible to make a comment—pro, con, or merely factual—that would not be disputed by a majority of the people who habitually play, listen to, or write about jazz," sums up the critical commentary that surrounds Brubeck's body of work. What can be asserted is that Brubeck, beyond the praise and fault-finding, beyond even the unexamined end result of his music, has always been an intelligent musician thoughtful of the process, an artist constantly seeking a new and justifiable means of creative expression.

"Perhaps the most significant contribution made by the Brubeck Quartet has been the integration of jazz and classical elements," Al Zeiger noted in *Metronome.* But Brubeck's precarious marriage of these two divergent styles has frequently offended stylists and aficionados of the pure jazz form. "He cannot always maintain the balance between jazz and classical music without forsaking an element vital to either one form," White appraised in *Jazz Journal.* More often than not, Brubeck's improvisations slip from jazz into classical colors, bringing up "a little canon a la Bach or some dissonant counterpoint a la Bartok or even a thrashing crisis a la Beethoven," a reporter for *Time* pointed out.

Influenced by Classical Music

Brubeck's tendency toward peppering his jazz speech with classical tones is rooted in his childhood. His mother, a classically trained piano teacher, was a believer in prenatal influence. "She practiced all through her pregnancies," Brubeck related, according to Len Lyons in *The Great Jazz Pianists: Speaking of Their Lives and Music.* "When we were born, we were all put near the piano to listen to her practicing. I heard Chopin, Liszt, Mozart, and Bach from infancy." While

For the Record. . .

Born David Warren Brubeck, December 6, 1920, in Concord, CA; son of Howard (a cattle rancher) and Elizabeth (a piano teacher; maiden name, Ivey) Brubeck; married Iola Marie Whitlock, September 21, 1942; children: David Darius, Michael, Christopher, Catherine, Daniel, Matthew. *Education:* College of the Pacific (now University of the Pacific), B.A. in music, 1942; postgraduate study with Darius Milhaud, Mills College, 1946-49.

Began playing piano with local jazz groups in 1934; during college years played in local nightclubs; drafted into U.S. Army, 1942; sent to Europe to lead service band, 1944-46 (discharged); began recording career with the Dave Brubeck Octet, 1949; organized the Dave Brubeck Trio (with Cal Tjader and Norman Bates), 1949-51; added Paul Desmond on alto saxophone, forming the Dave Brubeck Quartet, 1951; Brubeck and Desmond joined by Joe Morello on drums (1956) and Eugene Wright on bass (1958), creating Dave Brubeck Quartet that lasted until 1967; performed with symphony orchestras and led several quartets, 1971—. Occasionally teaches at Yale University as the Duke Ellington fellow.

Selected awards: Jazz Pioneer Award, Broadcast Music, Inc. (BMI), 1985; Compostela Humanitarian Award, 1986; Connecticut Arts Award, 1987; American Eagle Award, National Music Council, 1988; honorary doctorates from Mills College, Niagara University, and University of the Pacific.

Addresses: *Home*—Wilton, CT. *Office*—c/o Derry Music Co., 601 Montgomery St., Suite 800, San Francisco, CA 94111; and c/o Sutton Artists Corporation, 119 W. 57th St., New York, NY 10019.

---

his brothers took to classical training, Brubeck rebelled against his mother's teachings, preferring instead to make up his own songs. "There can be little doubt that his original interest in jazz arose as a protest against the idea of playing notes that were written on paper instead of the notes that were in his head," Rice wrote in the *New Yorker.* It is noteworthy that Brubeck did not learn to read music until later in life. Because of his acute musical ear, he was able to fool his mother by reproducing any piece after listening to it once or twice.

Despite Brubeck's early protestations, classical music informed his subsequent musical approach. He attested to this in an article he wrote for *Down Beat* at the beginning of his career: "Because the jazz musician creates music, interprets music as he hears it, it is natural that his improvised compositions should reflect every kind of music to which he has been exposed." Further exposure to the classical realm came through studies with the French composer Darius Milhaud.

After graduating with a degree in music and serving in the U.S. Army during World War II, Brubeck studied composition under Milhaud at Mills College for three years. From this classical instructor, Brubeck learned one important point about composing, as he explained to Michael Bourne in *Down Beat:* "One lesson was never give up jazz. And he told me I would be a composer on my own terms. . . . He said, 'If you don't reflect your own country and use the jazz idiom, you'll never be a part of this culture.' And, of course, Copland used it, Bernstein used it. Most of the important American composers have used jazz." But it seems that jazz was just a tool used to build his compositions, for in addition, Brubeck learned from Milhaud the usage of modern European polytonal harmonies, on which he was to base his style.

"European Harmony and African Rhythms"

After his apprenticeship under Milhaud, Brubeck sought a group sound for his compositions in 1949, first with an octet, then pared down to a trio. He also helped form Fantasy Records, the label on which he first recorded. But his definition of jazz—"an improvised musical expression based on European harmony and African rhythms," as he described it in *Down Beat*—was not fulfilled until Brubeck added alto saxophonist Paul Desmond to the group in 1951. "Desmond's yearning lyricism proved the perfect foil for Brubeck's percussive approach," Amy Duncan pointed out in the *Christian Science Monitor.* Another indication of Brubeck's keen judgement was his decision at the time to forego the nightclub circuit in favor of college campuses. The 1954 recording of one such tour, *Jazz Goes to College,* was the quartet's breakthrough, selling over a million copies and earning Brubeck the cover of *Time's* November 8, 1954, issue.

In *Time's* accompanying profile Brubeck was described as "a wigging cat with a far-out wail" who produces "some of the strangest and loveliest music ever played since jazz was born." His music and approach, which the article proclaimed heralded a new jazz age, "is neither chaotic nor abandoned. It evokes neither swinging hips nor hip flasks. It goes to the head and the heart more than to the feet."

But accompanying the rising acclaim was also rising derision. The debate over the purpose and sound of jazz divided the critical camps. *Metronome's* Zeiger lauded Brubeck's technique: "his texture has a refinement and lightness to it which, at times, is characteristic of the grace and elegance of Mozart"; but *Jazz Journal's* White stressed that "the unavoidable lack of beat, the absence of the jazz spirit—these indispensable jazz attributes—bring defeat to an otherwise highly intelligent and musicianly artist." Dave Gelly, writing in his book *The Giants of Jazz,* summed up the reasons for critical disapproval: "Brubeck's studious manner, his copious references to Milhaud and Hindemith in press interviews, his little lectures at concerts on how very complicated and demanding the next number was going to be, his quotations from Bach, the galloping pomposity of his piano solos." The public, however, continued its almost unanimous approval of the quartet. "The fact that it is admired by the public may explain the fact that it is scorned by many of the adepts," Rice assessed in the *New Yorker.* "'Popular' is an extreme [negative] in certain jazz circles."

First Gold Jazz Album

With the substitution of Joe Morello on drums and Eugene Wright on bass in the late 1950s, Brubeck formed the classic Dave Brubeck Quartet, which performed unchanged for almost ten years. Len Lyons and Don Perlo, in their book *Jazz Portraits: The Lives and Music of the Jazz Masters,* described the basic elements of the quartet's music: "Fuguelike interplay among the instruments; clear (sometimes simplistic) thematic statements; excursions into polytonality; and a tight group sound." This definitive Dave Brubeck Quartet sound also bore the mark of irregular time signatures. Brubeck's belief that "new and complex rhythm patterns, more akin to the African parents, is the natural direction for jazz to develop," as he wrote in *Down Beat,* was fully realized on his famous 1959 recording *Time Out,* which featured the hits "Take Five" (in 5/4 meter) and "Blue Rondo a la Turk" (in 9/8 meter). "Take Five" was so well received that it even made the popular music charts, unheard of for an instrumental jazz recording. *Time Out* went on to become the first instrumental jazz album certified gold.

The quartet continued to record and tour successfully until 1967, when Brubeck decided to disband the group to fully concentrate on composing sacred music and jazz-influenced symphonic works. Among his compositions is the cantata *Truth Is Fallen,* commissioned in 1971 and dedicated "to the slain students of Kent State University and Jackson State, and all other innocent victims caught in the cross fire between repression and rebellion," Leonard Feather noted in his book *The Pleasures of Jazz.*

Returned to Quartet Format

But Brubeck couldn't stay away from the quartet format and the improvisational element of jazz. "Jazz stands for freedom," he told Duncan of the *Christian Science Monitor.* "It's supposed to be the voice of freedom: Get out there and improvise, and take chances." Since the early 1970s, Brubeck has recorded and toured, his quartet composed of various musicians, including a combination of his sons, and labeled Two Generations of Brubeck. Although not quite the force he was in the 1950s and 1960s, Brubeck continued to produce vital music, as *Stereo Review's* Chris Albertson attested to in a review of Brubeck's 1986 offering, *Reflections,* stating that "the album only partly reflects the past: the present is also strongly represented, and the blend is good. . . . There was always a lyrical side to Brubeck, and that—as several selections here demonstrate—is an aspect of his music that time has enhanced."

For over four decades Dave Brubeck has created music, both written and unwritten. He led one of the

> *"Jazz stands for freedom. It's supposed to be the voice of freedom: Get out there and improvise, and take chances."*

most successful quartets in the history of jazz without pandering to either popular or critical dictates, remaining "a paragon of obstinacy, and [playing], stolidly or not, as he pleases," Rice observed in the *New Yorker.* He has persisted in seeking a voice for his creations with an informed intellectual purpose. "Far from being a born jazz man, Brubeck is a creative artist, an artist who uses jazz as his means of self-impression and as a source of unbounded inspiration," wrote *Jazz Journal's* White, adding that "the fundamental reason for Brubeck's failure to convince the jazz masses is simply that he attempted to bring something new into jazz."

Selected compositions

The Light in the Wilderness (oratorio).
To Hope: A Mass for a New Decade (mass).
The Gates of Justice (cantata).
Truth Is Fallen (cantata).
The Real Ambassadors (musical, lyrics by Iola Brubeck).

Points on Jazz (ballet).

Also composed the jazz works "The Duke," "Blue Rondo a la Turk," "It's a Raggy Waltz," "In Your Own Sweet Way," "Balcony Rock," "Koto Song," and "Softly, William, Softly."

Selected discography

Octet, Fantasy, 1949.
Jazz at College of the Pacific, Fantasy, 1953.
Jazz at Oberlin, Fantasy, 1953.
Jazz Goes to College, Columbia, 1954.
Jazz: Red Hot and Cool, Columbia, 1955.
Brubeck Plays Brubeck, Columbia, 1956.
Jazz Impressions of Eurasia, Columbia, 1958, reissued, Columbia Jazz Masterpieces/Legacy, 1992.
Dialogues for Jazz Combo and Orchestra, Columbia, 1960.
Time Further Out, Columbia, 1961.
Jazz Impressions of Japan, Columbia, 1964.
Elementals for Jazz Combo, Orchestra, and Baritone Solo, Decca, 1970.
Adventures in Time, Columbia, 1972.
Two Generations of Brubeck, Atlantic, 1973.
All the Things We Are, Atlantic, 1974.
Quartet: 25th Anniversary Reunion, A&M, 1976.
Back Home, Concord Jazz, 1979.
Paper Moon, Concord Jazz, 1981.
Concord on a Summer Night, Concord Jazz, 1982.
For Iola (recorded 1984), Concord Jazz, 1985.
Reflections (recorded 1985), Concord Jazz, 1986.
Gone With the Wind, Columbia Jazz Masterpieces, 1987.
Time Out (recorded c. 1960; reissue), Columbia Jazz Masterpieces, 1987.
Moscow Night (recorded 1987), Concord Jazz, 1988.
Jazz Impressions of New York, Columbia Jazz Masterpieces, 1990.
New Wine: With the Montreal International Jazz Festival Orchestra, MusicMasters, 1990.
Quiet as the Moon, MusicMasters, 1991.

With others

1975/Duets, A&M, 1975.
Brubeck/Mulligan/Cincinnati Symphony Orchestra With Jack Six, Alan Dawson (recorded 1970), MCA Classics, 1990.
Dave Brubeck/Paul Desmond With Ron Crotty, Wyatt (Bull) Ruther, Lloyd Davis, Herb Barman, Joe Dodge (recorded 1952-54), Fantasy, 1990.
Last Set at Newport, Atlantic.
Reunion (recorded 1957), Fantasy.
Take Five Live 1967, Jazz Music Yesterday.
We're All Together Again for the First Time, Atlantic.

Sources

Books

Feather, Leonard, *The Pleasures of Jazz,* Horizon, 1976.
Gelly, Dave, *The Giants of Jazz,* Schirmer Books, 1986.
Lyons, Len, *The Great Jazz Pianists: Speaking of Their Lives and Music,* Morrow, 1983.
Lyons, Len and Don Perlo, *Jazz Portraits: The Lives and Music of the Jazz Masters,* Morrow, 1989.

Periodicals

Christian Science Monitor, January 18, 1989; August 17, 1989.
Down Beat, January 27, 1950; February 10, 1950; February 6, 1957; October 1982; March 1991.
Jazz Journal, February 1958.
Jazz Journal International, December 1988.
Jazz Review, February 1960.
Metronome, August 1955.
New Yorker, June 3, 1961.
New York Times, July 1, 1990.
Stereo Review, February 1980; November 1986.
Time, November 8, 1954.

—*Rob Nagel*

Lindsey Buckingham

Singer, songwriter, guitarist

Multitalented musician Lindsey Buckingham first came to the attention of millions of music fans when he joined the rock and roll group Fleetwood Mac with his then girlfriend, Stevie Nicks, in 1975. With his revered compositions, vocals, guitar playing, and production skills, he made a major contribution to the band's extraordinary success in the years that followed. Buckingham provided Fleetwood Mac with such trademark songs as "Go Your Own Way," "Second Hand News," "Tusk," and "Big Love," in addition to venturing out with solo albums, including 1981's *Law and Order*, 1984's *Go Insane*, and his critically acclaimed release of 1992, *Out of the Cradle*.

Buckingham was born on October 3, 1949, in Palo Alto, California. He grew up listening to his older brother's recordings of Little Richard, Buddy Holly, and Elvis Presley. As a child, Buckingham practiced playing on a plastic Mickey Mouse guitar until his parents bought him a real one. Afterwards, he further honed his skills on the instrument by playing along with the albums of the folk group Kingston Trio and was greatly influenced by the music of the Beach Boys. Before Buckingham left high school, he began to play and sing for a rock group called Fritz. In this band, he was later joined by singer-songwriter Stevie Nicks.

Buckingham and Nicks eventually got involved romantically as well as musically, and when Fritz disbanded in 1971, the duo moved from the San Francisco Bay area to Los Angeles to work as a musical team. On their own, their style was more folksy than the harder rock music they had made with Fritz. After struggling for a few years, Buckingham and Nicks were signed by Polydor Records, and they released an album titled *Buckingham/Nicks*. Though this album was not a big seller, it inadvertently brought them to the attention of the rock band Fleetwood Mac, which was looking for a recording studio. The studio that had produced *Buckingham/Nicks* played the album for them as an example of its handiwork. The band's members not only liked the technical aspects of the LP, but were also intrigued by the duo they heard. Since Fleetwood Mac member Bob Welch had recently departed, they sought out Buckingham and Nicks to fill out their group in 1974.

A "Lesson in Adaptation"

Buckingham and Nicks's first work with Fleetwood Mac turned out to be another self-titled album. *Fleetwood Mac* marked the emergence of the band—which now consisted of Buckingham, Nicks, Christine and John McVie, and Mick Fleetwood—as a popular success, yielding hits such as Nicks's "Rhiannon" and Christine McVie's "Don't Stop." Buckingham acknowledged in

Rolling Stone, though, that even from the beginning, there were differences among the band's members. "Fleetwood Mac was one big lesson in adaptation for me. . . . There were five very different personalities, and I suppose that made it great for a while. . . . But the problems really kicked in when you started adding five managers and five lawyers to the equation."

Buckingham took a larger role both in the songwriting and production aspects of the group's 1977 album, *Rumours.* Extremely successful, *Rumours* climbed the charts, remaining there for years. Buckingham's "Go Your Own Way" was one of the first smash singles from the album. Unfortunately, however, *Rumours* was also a chronicle of the dissolution of Fleetwood Mac's two love relationships—the McVies' marriage and the long-time partnership of Buckingham and Nicks. Michael Goldberg of *Rolling Stone* called the album a "pop-rock soap opera." Despite personal differences, the band members decided to stay together musically, and Buckingham and Fleetwood Mac received a Grammy Award for *Rumours.*

Fleetwood Mac's next project saw Buckingham's creative control of the group increase dramatically. The result, the 1979 two-album set *Tusk,* was an immediate best-seller, but due to the fact that it was a departure from the style of *Fleetwood Mac* and *Rumours,* it only spawned two minor hits, Buckingham's title track and Nicks's "Sara." But Buckingham's experimentation on the LP won critical acclaim. "Tusk" combined unorthodox African rhythms with the impressive sound of the University of Southern California marching band. And *Rolling Stone* reviewer Christopher Connelly praised "the spare, threatening whomp of the album's undiscovered treasure, 'Not That Funny.'"

Launched Solo Career

Buckingham recounted what it was like to work on *Tusk* for Goldberg: "I would bring tunes in, and everyone [in the band] would go, 'Oh, that's great.' When Mick [Fleetwood] took the *Tusk* album down to Warner Bros., everyone was jumping up and down, going, 'Oh, this is really one of the neatest things we've ever heard'— although I have subsequently heard that when a lot of those people . . . heard that album, they saw their Christmas bonuses flying out the window. I do think there was a time when everyone in the band was quite carried away with the spirit of experimentation. But when it began to become apparent that it wasn't going to sell 15 million copies [like *Rumours*], then everyone from the band looked at me and went, 'Oh, you blew it, buddy.'"

In the same year that *Tusk* was released, Buckingham also busied himself producing records for other artists, most notably folk-rocker John Stewart's album *Bombs Away, Dream Babies.* The effort yielded Stewart's first pop hit, "Gold." Releasing his own album in 1981— titled *Law and Order*—Buckingham scored a hit with the single "Trouble," and after being disappointed with Fleetwood Mac's 1982 album *Mirage,* the musician increasingly concentrated on his own projects. An especially successful one was the 1984 solo album *Go Insane.* The title track became a hit for Buckingham, and the accompanying video received much airplay on MTV.

Rolling Stone's Connelly raved about *Go Insane,* calling it "the richest, most fascinatingly tuneful album of the year." He summed up Buckingham's work starting with *Tusk:* "This songwriter, singer and guitarist has struggled to combine the wildest possibilities of new music with the folk-fostered melodies that have marked his most commercially fruitful efforts." Like *Rumours,* however, *Go Insane* was a deeply personal creation for Buckingham, taking its inspiration from his relationship and breakup with longtime companion Carol Ann Harris.

Buckingham stayed with Fleetwood Mac until the completion of their 1987 album, *Tango in the Night.* "I would not have wanted to leave the group on the ambiguous note that *Mirage* sounded," he told Robert Hilburn in the *Los Angeles Times.* "This band has done some remarkable things and *Mirage* was no way to say goodbye. I think we had something to prove and we did it in the new album." Though Buckingham's "Big Love" was one of the most popular hits from *Tango in the Night,* artistic differences prompted the musician to leave Fleetwood Mac, foregoing its subsequent tour. In 1990, however, he took the stage with his former bandmates for the farewell concert of Nicks and Christine McVie. According to Steve Pond of *Rolling Stone*, Buckingham "wound up stealing the show" on this occasion.

Raves for *Out of the Cradle*

Five years after the release of *Tango in the Night*, three of which he spent 12 hours a day in the studio, Buckingham released *Out of the Cradle*, an album *Rolling Stone*'s J. D. Considine considered the place "where Buckingham's solo career grows up." Referring to his bittersweet departure from Fleetwood Mac, Buckingham admitted to David Wild in *Rolling Stone*, "I guess it's obvious that making [*Out of the Cradle*] hasn't been an especially speedy process. . . . But I had to let a lot of emotional dust settle." Such songs as "Wrong" and "Don't Look Down" contain subtle commentary on quitting Fleetwood Mac—an event he feels was wrongly portrayed in Mick Fleetwood's 1990 book *Fleetwood*—and on his decision to concentrate on solo ventures.

Calling *Out of the Cradle* "a wildly impressive coming-out party," Wild felt that "the album is an artfully crafted song cycle whose romantic lushness is effectively balanced by a healthy dose of ripping guitar." Further accolades came from *People* reviewer Craig Tomashoff, who declared that "nobody in pop music these days creates better feel-good melodies than Buckingham."

A truly respected and innovative figure in pop music, Buckingham was touring the United States in 1992, playing at clubs and on various radio stations in an effort to gain exposure for *Out of the Cradle* and his burgeoning solo career. He also indicated that he would be open to recording some new songs with Fleetwood Mac for a compact disc box set that was in the planning stages. Commenting on his productive career, Buckingham told Gary Graff of the *Detroit Free Press*, "See, making music with [Fleetwood Mac] was always a bit like making movies, I would imagine. It was a verbalized political process in many ways, to get from point A to point B. Working solo, playing most of the stuff myself, is always more like painting . . . a far more intuitive process."

Selected discography

With Fleetwood Mac; on Warner Bros. Records

Fleetwood Mac, 1975.
Rumours (includes "Go Your Own Way"), 1977.
Tusk (two album set; includes title track and "Not That Funny"), 1979.
Live, 1980.
Mirage, 1982.
Tango in the Night (includes "Big Love"), 1987.

Other

(With Stevie Nicks) *Buckingham/Nicks*, Polydor, 1973.
Law and Order (includes "Trouble"), Asylum, 1981.
Go Insane, Elektra, 1984.
Out of the Cradle, Reprise, 1992.

Sources

Books

Helander, Brock, *The Rock Who's Who*, Schirmer Books, 1982.
Stambler, Irwin, *The Encyclopedia of Pop, Rock, and Soul*, St. Martin's, 1989.

Periodicals

Detroit Free Press, July 10, 1992.
Detroit News, July 23, 1992.
Entertainment Weekly, July 17, 1992.
Musician, July 1992; August 1992.
People, July 6, 1992.
Rolling Stone, August 30, 1984; October 25, 1984; February 7, 1991; June 25, 1992; July 9, 1992.

—*Elizabeth Wenning*

The
Byrds

Rock band

Originators of folk-rock and pioneers of acid- and country-rock, the Byrds were one of the most influential bands in rock history. They left their mark on the sounds of the Eagles, Tom Petty, R.E.M., and hundreds of less well-known artists. The Byrds reclaimed rock and roll as an American music form in the wake of the Beatles-led British Invasion of English bands and brought a previously unimagined level of lyricism and artistic experimentation to pop music.

The Byrds were formed in 1964—when the British Invasion was at its height and the early 1960s folk scene that had built an intellectual wing onto American popular music was fading. Byrds founder Roger McGuinn was a moderately successful folksinger who had backed up his then-more-famous colleague Judy Collins, playing 12-string guitar and banjo on her recordings of the classic Pete Seeger compositions "Turn! Turn! Turn!" and "The Bells of Rhymney," among others. He had also played with Bobby Darin, the Chad Mitchell Trio, and the Limeliters. In 1964 McGuinn was playing coffeehouses in Los Angeles. He recalled of those days in Mike Jahn's book *Rock,* "I knew folk music was on its last legs. I loved folk music. . . . But [by 1964] it was obvious it was dying."

Actually, McGuinn had never been a folk purist. "I started with rock," he told *Guitar Player.* "I started with Elvis, and I was heavily into Carl Perkins, Gene Vincent, the Everly Brothers, and Johnny Cash—that whole rockabilly, Memphis sound." The Beatles showed McGuinn the way back to rock and roll. He began playing Beatles songs during his sets at the Los Angeles folk club the Troubador, but—though still using an acoustic 12-string guitar—he added a rock-like beat to the folk material. As he told *Rolling Stone* in 1990, "I came out and started blending Beatles stuff with the folk stuff, and the audience hated it. I used to get mad at 'em because I thought it was good. . . . Later on I ran into [original Byrds vocalist] Gene Clark at the Troubador. He was one of the few people who understood it. He asked if I wanted to write some songs with him. Then [original Byrds guitarist] David Crosby came in and started singing harmony."

Clark and Crosby Joined McGuinn

Clark, like McGuinn, was a midwestern folkie who had relocated to Los Angeles. He had spent two years with the very commercial folk group the New Christy Minstrels and in 1964 was frequenting folk clubs, writing Beatleseque songs, and looking for a partner. "He was looking for somebody else to go with him in [the folk-rock] direction, and I just happened to be going that way," McGuinn recounted in *Rolling Stone.*

For the Record. . .

Original members included **Gene Clark** (born November 17, 1941, in Tipton, MO; died May 24, 1991, in Los Angeles, CA; left group, 1966), vocals; **Michael Clarke** (born June 3, 1944, in New York, NY; left group, 1968), drums; **David Crosby** (born August 14, 1941, in Los Angeles; left group, 1967), guitar; **Chris Hillman** (born December 4, 1942, in Los Angeles; left group, 1968), bass; and **Roger McGuinn** (born Jim McGuinn, July 13, 1942, in Chicago, IL, [changed name, 1968]), guitar.

Later members included **Skip Battin** (born February 2, 1934, in Gallipolis, OH; joined group, 1969), bass; **John Guerin** (joined group, 1972), drums; **Kevin Kelly** (born in 1945 in California; joined group, 1968), drums; **Gene Parsons** (born in 1944 in Los Angeles), drums; **Gram Parsons** (born Cecil Connor, November 5, 1946, in Winter Haven, FL [changed name, c. 1960]; died September 19, 1973, in Joshua Tree, CA; joined and left group, 1968), guitar; **Clarence White** (born June 6, 1944, in Lewiston, ME; died July 14, 1973), guitar; and **John York** (left group, 1969) bass.

Group formed in 1964 in Los Angeles; originally named the Jet Set; signed with Elektra Records, released first single as the Beefeaters; signed with Columbia Records, released "Mr. Tambourine Man," 1965; released three LPs; released several LPs with various lineups, 1967-73; group disbanded, 1973; original members reunited to make one album, *The Byrds,* Asylum, 1973.

Awards: Inducted into the Rock and Roll Hall of Fame, 1991.

Crosby, a Los Angeles native, had met McGuinn in 1960. In the intervening years Crosby had played the coffeehouse circuit, sung with Les Baxter's Balladeers, and become part of a group of musicians who would create the California folk- and acid-rock scenes in the following few years. Crosby had also become friends with a recording engineer named Jim Dickson, a jazz buff who had become interested in folk music and made private tapes of folksingers in his spare time.

Dickson took McGuinn, Clark, and Crosby into the studio to make an audition tape. He recalled the sound of that tape in Crosby's autobiography, *Long Time Gone:* "Because of the British Invasion thing that was happening, they're singing with these English accents. It's marvelous, really, and funny. But they had a sound. There's no question about it. The Byrds . . . The fledgling

group hadn't yet hit on that name, however. McGuinn named them the Jet Set, and when Elektra Records signed them, it released their first single under the name the Beefeaters, trying to appeal to the craze for all things English. The single flopped, and Elektra dropped them.

Rocky Early Musicianship

The Jet Set were still playing acoustic guitars—and as such, were not really considered a rock band—but when they saw the Beatles film *A Hard Day's Night,* they decided true rock and roll was the way to go. Crosby tried to play bass, but found it impossible to sing when he did. Dickson knew a bluegrass mandolin player named Chris Hillman who was looking for something new; he agreed to join on bass, though he had never played the instrument before. Drums were a bigger problem, but Crosby remembered Michael Clarke, whom he had met while living on the beach in California's Big Sur in 1962. Clarke had never played rock and roll trap drums, only congas and bongos, and couldn't afford a drum kit—he showed up at the first rehearsal with an assortment of cardboard boxes.

Dickson rehearsed McGuinn, Clark, Crosby, Hillman, and Clarke intensely for several months, taping every session and forcing the musicians to listen to the playback. Crosby remembered it in his autobiography as a painful experience. "It was truly terrible. Michael Clarke, when he started out, was the only drummer who could, without any awareness of it at all, turn the beat around, back to front, three times in one song. And none of the rest of us were that much better. Roger was the only one who could really play." But the constant rehearsal paid off, and it was only a few months before the group—by then the Byrds—were ready for their first gig, a $50 lunch-hour set at Los Angeles City College.

The Byrds caught on quickly, with Dickson, as the group's manager, hustling furiously to get them into the new clubs that were opening on Hollywood's Sunset Strip. There they would play four or five sets a night for dancing teenagers, filling out their repertoire with cover versions of current hits. At Ciro's—one of the Strip's biggest clubs—the Byrds finally made their breakthrough in the spring of 1965.

"Mr. Tambourine Man" Attracted Attention

By then they already had a recording contract with Columbia and had released a single, "Mr. Tambourine

Man." Dickson had insisted they record the now-classic Bob Dylan song, but producer Terry Melcher decided that the Byrds' musicianship was not up to professional studio standards and used session musicians on the instrumental tracks, though McGuinn did contribute his twelve-string. "Mr. Tambourine Man" was released in March of 1965 and initially moved slowly, not entering the charts until May. Once there, however, it jumped quickly to Number One and stayed in the Top Ten for 13 weeks. Film- and music-business celebrities began showing up at Ciro's to catch the Byrds, and the *Los Angeles Times, Variety,* and *Time* wrote about them. Beatle John Lennon sang their praises, and Dylan himself joined them onstage. Somewhere along the way, someone coined the term "folk-rock" to describe the Byrds' unique approach to rock and roll.

What the Byrds had done was truly revolutionary: "Bringing Bob Dylan and the hit parade together," wrote *The Map* author Paul Williams more than 20 years later, "with a gorgeous twelve-string guitar sound that had nothing to do with either Dylan or 1965 pop, yet somehow served perfectly to unite the two." In a *Los Angeles Free Press* article quoted in John Stuessy's *Rock and Roll,* Mike Jahn's *Rock,* and the liner notes to *Mr. Tambourine Man,* among other sources, Paul Jay Robbins wrote: "Their singular method is to unite, in a dynamic and irresistible adventure, the techniques and honesty of folk music, the joy and immediacy of r & r, and the virtuosity of jazz. . . . What the Byrds signify . . . is a concept deeply applied to unification and empathy and a rich joy of life. . . . Dancing with the Byrds becomes a mystic loss of ego and tangibility; you become pure energy someplace between sound and motion and the involvement is total." Bud Scoppa, in *The Rolling Stone Illustrated History of Rock and Roll,* elaborated, writing, "The Byrds pioneered a new approach to rock. It all had to do with the sound. . . . [The Byrds' sound], with its 12-string symphony and massive chorale was new in rock, . . . as diamond-sharp cascading guitar notes intertwined with the Byrds' gothic vocal harmonies."

"Mr. Tambourine Man" was followed that summer by an album of the same name, on which the Byrds played their own instruments. That release in turn was copied by a host of imitators, emulators, and like-minded creators. It was reported that Dylan made up his mind to move toward rock only after hearing the Byrds; the Lovin' Spoonful came out with their own folk-rock sound; and Sonny and Cher, Barry McGuire, Donovan, and Simon and Garfunkel, among others, all rode the folk-rock wave, many of them to greater commercial success than the Byrds had enjoyed.

Moved Beyond "Dylanized Beatles"

Though Crosby told *Newsweek* in September of 1965, "We put reality in music. It's better than June-Foon-Boon-Spoon," the Byrds—who rarely sang Dylan-style protest songs—were not content to remain pigeonholed as "Dylanized Beatles." Their second album, *Turn! Turn! Turn!,* was much like their first, but the band's third outing, *Fifth Dimension,* moved well beyond folk-rock—and beyond the conventions of commercial radio in 1966. Crosby had discovered Indian sitarist Ravi Shankar and jazz saxophonist John Coltrane and played tapes of them incessantly while the Byrds were on tour. By the time the band next went into the studio, they had new songs, McGuinn had a new approach to the 12-string, and the Byrds were ready to revolutionize rock once more.

"Eight Miles High," the first single from *Fifth Dimension,* was unlike anything pop radio had ever seen. With no chorus or lyrical hook, surrealistic lyrics, Hillman's ominous, throbbing bass, and the unconventional counter-

> "It was truly terrible. Roger was the only one who could really play."
> —David Crosby

point of McGuinn's jazzy Indian-inspired solo, it was the first psychedelic rock song; despite common misperceptions, however, the song was not about drugs, but the Byrds' first, disastrous tour of England. The title referred to the transatlantic flight: "I said 'Six Miles High,' being more technologically oriented than Gene Clark," *Rock* author Jahn quoted McGuinn as saying. "Gene said, 'It doesn't sound right poetically, eight miles high sounds better.'" Enduring suspicions about the song's meaning, however, led some radio stations to ban it. Though "Eight Miles High" reached Number 14 on the charts, it was the last Byrds single to make the Top Twenty.

Clark First to Depart

Soon after the release of *Fifth Dimension,* personality conflicts began to take their toll on the group. The liner notes to the previous album had referred to "fistfights and great mouthfuls of awful abuse" in the recording studio; artistic and personal differences seemed to intensify with each record. Gene Clark was the first to go, driven out by clashes with McGuinn and Crosby and his own fear of flying, which made touring difficult. He teamed up with bluegrass musician Doug Dillard for two albums of country-rock, then went on to make several highly regarded solo records but never equalled the success he had had as a Byrd.

Younger Than Yesterday took the Byrds further from the pop mainstream and deeper into the eclecticism that once led Crosby to describe their music as "rock, folk, bossa nova, jazz, Afro." Of this style Sandy Pearlman wrote in *Crawdaddy!,* "The Byrds give us magic, science, religion, psychedelic sounds, lots of electronic stuff and technological tongues, love songs, Dylan . . . rock and roll, science fiction, some Southern California local lore, an African trumpet guy, a country and western guitar guy, a little bit of raga. . . . Yet after a while. . . . they make themselves very familiar." Though Hillman and Crosby became more prominent as singers and songwriters with songs like "Everybody's Been Burned" and "Thoughts and Words," McGuinn's guitar work continued to dominate the Byrds sound.

The first single off *Younger Than Yesterday,* "So You Want to Be a Rock 'n' Roll Star," satirized the music business; the second, "My Back Pages," was a Dylan song and, in Crosby's opinion, a step backwards. "It was 'Oh, let's make "Tambourine Man" again,'" he told *Rolling Stone's* Ben Fong-Torres in 1970. "It was a formula record. . . . Had all the life and commitment of a four-day old mackerel." It was also the last Byrds single to make it into the Top Forty, peaking at Number 30 as the Byrds became too hip for AM radio and more of a force in the growing "underground" rock scene. As Pearlman observed, "Only the Byrds, amongst modern rock stars, have managed to change their status from stardom to cultural heroism."

Crosby was kicked out of the band during the recording of *The Notorious Byrd Brothers.* Mike Clarke finished the record, but left before it was released. McGuinn unveiled the "new Byrds" in the spring of 1968; the major addition was Gram Parsons who, McGuinn told Jerry Hopkins of *Rolling Stone,* "added a whole hunk of country" to the Byrds sound. This new direction was confirmed with the release of *Sweetheart of the Rodeo,* the album that many credit with starting the country-rock movement of the late 1960s and early 1970s.

Sweetheart of the Rodeo

Sweetheart was the first Byrds album that did not feature McGuinn's guitar. As he told *Guitar Player* in 1991, "I guess I was kind of tired by then. Gram was a strong musical force. I just let him go and went along

with it." Response to the record was mixed; Richard Goldstein of the *Village Voice* called it "a gentle, moving work, and the most authentic piece of nostalgia in a year when every folkie worth his *Little Sandy Review* is going Nashville." Barry Gifford, in *Rolling Stone,* was more ambivalent, describing *Sweetheart of the Rodeo* as "interesting" but "uninvolved" and suggesting that it was a weak imitation of genuine country music. But Geoffrey Stokes, writing 18 years later in *Rock of Ages,* called the release "the Byrds' last perfect album, . . . free from condescension . . . with a skewed passion as genuine as that of the originals."

Though country music had been an element of the Byrds' style since 1965 and Hillman and Parsons wanted to further pursue country-rock, McGuinn considered *Sweetheart of the Rodeo* a one-time excursion. Parsons made continued discussion of the point moot when he quit the group rather than tour racially segregated South Africa (a tour McGuinn undertook on the advice of South African singer-activist Miriam Makeba). A few months later, Hillman left to join Parsons in the Flying Burrito Brothers; he later joined guitarist-vocalist Stephen Stills in Manassas, J. D. Souther and Richie Furay in the Souther-Furay-Hillman Band, and eventually made a series of solo albums before ultimately finding a niche in mainstream country music as leader of the Desert Rose Band.

McGuinn, the only remaining original Byrd, hired sidemen to fill out the band. At first the results were good: *Dr. Byrds and Mrs. Hyde* was praised by *Rolling Stone,* and with Clarence White on guitar and Gene Parsons on drums, McGuinn was able to declare, "For the first time, the Byrds are better live than on record." But the records became less consistent. Legendary rock scribe Lester Bangs, reviewing *(Untitled)* in *Rolling Stone,* remarked, "Some of it is fantastic and some is very poor . . . and between the stuff that will rank with their best and the born outtakes lies a lot of rather watery music. . . . Roger McGuinn and all Cos. have been plowing pastures in the same admittedly verdant American valley for just a season too long now. Their old riffs have run dry." Mixed reviews also greeted *Byrdmaniax* and *Farther Along,* and in 1973 McGuinn decided to call it quits.

That decision coincided with the reunion of the five original Byrds in the recording studio. It took several months of negotiation to settle both business and personal issues, but the album was made, and all the Byrds were enthusiastic about it. A tour was considered. Critical response, however, was mostly negative: "Unfocused," *Rolling Stone's* judgment, was one of the kinder assessments. McGuinn decided it was time to abandon the Byrds name and launch a solo career.

McGuinn Solo

The solo path turned out to be harder than he had expected. "When you've been in a group," he told *Guitar Player*'s Alan di Perna in 1991, "there's something that happens psychologically to the public, and I guess to the individual. If you step out of the group, it's almost like you're a traitor. . . . It's tough to do." Even when the music was good—Robert Christgau, in his *Record Guide,* called McGuinn's solo debut "more coherent than any Byrds album since *Sweetheart of the Rodeo*"—sales were not. Even a stint touring with Bob Dylan's Rolling Thunder Revue failed to ignite much interest in Roger McGuinn without the Byrds. After five solo albums and three collaborations with other ex-Byrds, he found himself entering the 1980s with neither a band nor a recording contract.

By then, the sound that McGuinn and the Byrds had created had become a major influence on musicians as diverse as Tom Petty, R.E.M., the Bangles, and dozens of British post-punk bands. Ironically, while they copied the jangling guitar sound of the early Byrds records, the man who developed it played solo acoustic sets in small clubs.

Nonetheless, McGuinn did not complain: "Doing solo gigs without a contract was really rewarding," he told Dave DiMartino in *Spin.* "I almost got to the point of saying who needs to record. . . . [I] just loved going out and touring. And audiences were so responsive—we just had such a good time all the time." The tide began to turn in the late 1980s with the release of *Never Before,* a collection of Byrds outtakes and alternate takes that was greeted by Steve Simels of *Stereo Review* as a reminder that "the Byrds were not only the premier American band of the day, but one of the most innovative and influential bands ever."

Legend Status Confirmed

As 1990 approached, and thus the Byrds' eligibility for induction into the Rock and Roll Hall of Fame, Columbia Records prepared a four-CD boxed set covering the Byrds' career; McGuinn, Hillman, and Crosby went into the studio to record four new tracks for that collection. And McGuinn found himself in demand elsewhere—he appeared on the Nitty Gritty Dirt Band's *Will The Circle Be Unbroken, Vol. 2,* and played guitar on Elvis Costello's album *Spike.*

The culmination of this activity was a contract for McGuinn with Arista Records and a new album, *Back From Rio.* The album hit Number 45 on the Billboard chart, and the video of the single "King of the Hill" got consider-

able play on MTV. John Milward of *Rolling Stone* wrote, "*Back From Rio* evokes the commercial pop rock of [the Byrds'] 1967 album *Younger Than Yesterday.* McGuinn's twelve-string shimmers . . . like sunlight on the ocean. . . . And on terrific tunes by Costello and Jules Shear . . . the sound meets the songs to create interpretive magic. . . . McGuinn is hardly the future of rock & roll, but he's an important part of the past on which that future rests, a past that will not fade away."

In January of 1991, the Byrds were inducted into the Rock and Roll Hall of Fame. McGuinn remarked to *Musician*'s Jon Young, "Everybody says it's the most prestigious honor in rock 'n' roll, but that's kind of a contradiction in terms, isn't it?" Of the momentous occasion, *Rolling Stone* concluded: "The Byrds were among the most liberating forces in American rock & roll history, . . . rooted partly in age-old folk tradition but with an eye toward unprecedented experimentalism. . . . This adventurous spirit—this playful mix of old forms, new concerns and spacey improvisation—would help to transform the entire style and context of West Coast rock & roll. And combined with the breakthroughs made by British rock, it would . . . transmogrify pop music's cultural purpose. . . . The Byrds helped turn rock & roll into something dreamy, daring and open-hearted, and because of those ambitions, modern pop music is all the richer."

Selected discography

Mr. Tambourine Man, Columbia, 1965.
Turn! Turn! Turn!, Columbia, 1966.
Fifth Dimension (includes "Eight Miles High"), Columbia, 1966.
Younger Than Yesterday (includes "So You Want to Be a Rock 'n' Roll Star" and "My Back Pages," Columbia, 1967.
The Byrds Greatest Hits, Columbia, 1967.
The Notorious Byrd Brothers, Columbia, 1968.
Sweetheart of the Rodeo, Columbia, 1968.
Dr. Byrds and Mrs. Hyde, Columbia, 1969.
Preflyte, Together, 1969.
(Untitled), Columbia, 1970.
Farther Along, Columbia, 1971.
Byrdmaniax, Columbia, 1971.
The Best of the Byrds: Greatest Hits Volume II, Columbia, 1972.
The Byrds, Asylum, 1973.
Never Before, Murray Hill, 1988.
The Byrds (boxed set), Columbia, 1991.

Solo LPs

(Chris Hillman) *Cherokee,* ABC, 1971.
(Hillman) *Slippin' Away,* Asylum, 1976.
(Hillman) *Clear Sailin',* Asylum, 1977.
(Hillman) *Morning Sky,* Sugar Hill, 1982.

(Hillman) *Desert Rose,* Sugar Hill, 1984.

(Souther-Hillman-Furay Band) *The Souther-Hillman-Furay Band,* Asylum, 1974.

(Souther-Hillman-Furay Band) *Trouble in Paradise,* Asylum, 1975.

(Gene Clark) *White Light,* A&M, 1971.

(Clark) *Roadmaster,* A&M, 1973.

(Clark) *No Other,* Asylum, 1974.

(Clark) *Two Sides to Every Story,* RSO, 1977.

(Clark) *Firebyrd,* Takoma, 1984.

(Doug Dillard and Clark) *The Fantastic Expedition of Dillard and Clark,* A&M, 1969.

(Dillard and Clark) *Through the Morning Through the Night,* A&M, 1969.

(Clark and Carla Olson) *So Rebellious a Lover,* Demon, 1987.

(Roger McGuinn, Clark, and Hillman) *McGuinn, Clark & Hillman,* Capitol, 1979.

(McGuinn, Clark, and Hillman) *City,* Capitol, 1980.

(McGuinn and Hillman), *McGuinn & Hillman,* Capitol, 1980.

Solo LPs by McGuinn; on Columbia, except as noted

Roger McGuinn, 1973.

Peace on You, 1974.

Roger McGuinn & Band, 1975.

Cardiff Rose, 1976.

Thunderbyrd, 1977.

Back From Rio, Arista, 1990.

Born to Rock 'n' Roll, 1991.

Sources

Books

Christgau, Robert, *Christgau's Record Guide,* Ticknor & Fields, 1981.

Cohn, Nik, *Rock From the Beginning,* Stein & Day, 1969.

Crosby, David, *Long Time Gone,* Doubleday, 1988.

Denselow, Robin, *When the Music's Over,* Faber & Faber, 1989.

The Encyclopedia of Pop, Rock and Soul, edited by Irwin Stambler, St. Martin's, 1989.

Goldstein, Richard, *Goldstein's Greatest Hits,* Prentice-Hall, 1970.

Jahn, Mike, *Rock: From Elvis Presley to the Rolling Stones,* Quadrangle/New York Times, 1973.

Marsh, Dave, *The Heart of Rock and Soul: The 1001 Greatest Singles Ever Made,* New American Library, 1989.

The Penguin Encyclopedia of Popular Music, edited by Donald Clarke, Viking, 1989.

Rock of Ages: The Rolling Stone History of Rock & Roll, edited by Ed Ward, Rolling Stone Press, 1986.

Rock On: The Illustrated Encyclopedia of Rock and Roll, vol. 2, edited by Norm N. Nite, Harper & Row, 1978.

The Rolling Stone Illustrated History of Rock and Roll, edited by Jim Miller, Random House/Rolling Stone Press, 1980.

The Rolling Stone Interviews, edited by Jann Wenner, Straight Arrow, 1971.

Roxon, Lilian, *Lilian Roxon's Rock Encyclopedia,* Grosset & Dunlap, 1969.

Stuessy, Joe, *Rock and Roll: Its History and Stylistic Development,* Prentice-Hall, 1990.

Williams, Paul, *The Map: Rediscovering Rock & Roll, A Journey,* And Books, 1988.

Williams, Paul, *Outlaw Blues,* Dutton, 1969.

Periodicals

CD Review, January 1, 1992.

Crawdaddy!, July/August, 1967; September/October, 1967; May 1968.

Down Beat, May 1, 1990.

Gentlemen's Quarterly, March 1, 1991.

Guitar Player, April 1, 1991.

Musician, April 1991; May 1991.

New York Times, January 30, 1966.

Newsweek, September 20, 1965.

Rolling Stone, April 27, 1968; May 11, 1968; April 5, 1969; May 17, 1969; November 26, 1970; August 19, 1971; March 16, 1972; January 4, 1973; December 6, 1973; December 15, 1977; March 24, 1988; August 23, 1990; February 7, 1991; July 11, 1991.

Spin, April 1, 1991.

Stereo Review, June 1, 1988.

Additional information for this profile was obtained from album liner notes to *Turn! Turn! Turn!,* Columbia, 1966.

—*Tim Connor*

David Byrne

Singer, songwriter, composer, filmmaker

More than almost any other popular musician, the multitalented David Byrne is at home in many worlds: rock music, "art" music, ballet, film music, photography, and filmmaking. His solo musical work, begun while he was still guitarist and lead vocalist for Talking Heads—a defunct new wave band formed in New York City in 1974—reflects his wide-ranging interests. Byrne has also experimented extensively with world beat music, implementing African and Latin rhythms. The Talking Heads albums of the 1980s—including *Remain in Light, Naked,* and *Speaking in Tongues*—show a substantial blending of international styles. By the end of his time with the band, Byrne's work with them and on his own was deeply influenced by world beat, featured cerebral, angst-ridden lyrics, and was heralded in the music world as eclectic and original.

Acknowledged as an intellectual rock star, Byrne, as frontman of Talking Heads, was an innovator in the emerging new wave rock scene of the late 1970s. A native of Scotland, Byrne immigrated to the United States and during his teens and early twenties played in small rock bands. Seeking the company of art students, he enrolled in several classes at the Rhode Island School of Design, where he eventually met up with his future Talking Heads bandmates.

"[I was] fascinated by conceptual art," Byrne told Jerome Davis, author of *Talking Heads.* "In particular, there was some that just used language. They'd just write a statement on the wall." He called such work "the ultimate in refining and eliminating all the superfluous stuff in art and being left with nothing but the idea." Friends grew familiar with the young Byrne's quirky concepts, including his song "Psycho Killer," a notorious ballad that later became one of the Heads' first recordings.

For the Heads, whose members included Tina Weymouth, Chris Frantz, and Jerry Harrison, Byrne wrote songs in praise of gainful employment, buildings, and television, but his words and his voice conveyed such underlying hysteria that the result verged on satire. But if Byrne criticized society, he did so indirectly, for his lyrics were characterized by their strange wording and absurdist humor. As Christopher Connelly observed in *Rolling Stone,* the songwriter "took cultural cliches—on everything from true love to civic pride—out of their customary contexts" and mixed them into dreamlike, ominous new statements, "whose odd juxtapositions and things left unspoken were rich with wit and insight."

For the Record. . .

B orn May 14, 1952, in Dumbarton, Scotland; immigrated to United States, 1958; British citizen; son of Thomas (an electrical engineer) and Emily Anderson (a teacher and activist; maiden name, Brown) Byrne; married Adelle Lutz (a designer and actress), 1987; children: Malu Abeni Valentine. *Education:* Attended Rhode Island School of Design, 1970-71, and Maryland Institute, College of Art, 1971-72.

Vocalist and guitarist with Talking Heads, 1974-88; solo artist, 1981—; conceived stage performance for film *Stop Making Sense,* 1984; co-wrote and directed film *True Stories,* 1986; producer of rock videos and recordings; actor appearing in television programs, including *Surviving a Family Tree,* c. 1985; formed own label, Luaka Bop, at Warner Bros. Records; illustrator, including art for Talking Heads albums and cover of *Time,* October 27, 1986; composer; photographer. Charter member of the Texas Accordion Association, 1987—.

Member: Musicians Union, Screen Actors Guild.

Selected awards: Film Critics Award for best documentary, for *Stop Making Sense,* and Video Vanguard Award from MTV, both 1985; Academy Award, Grammy Award, Golden Globe Award, and Hollywood Foreign Press Association Award, all for best original score, 1987, for *The Last Emperor.*

Addresses: *Agent*—Steve Davis, William Morris Agency, Inc., 1350 Sixth Ave., New York, NY 10019. *Record company*—Luaka Bop/Sire, 75 Rockefeller Plaza, New York, NY 10019.

Popular Among the Avant-Garde

Byrne's first major solo endeavor—which appeared after the release of four Talking Heads albums by Sire Records—was a collaboration with longtime Talking Heads producer Brian Eno on a 1981 album entitled *My Life in the Bush of Ghosts.* Demonstrating Byrne's growing interest in music of other cultures, the LP includes rhythms of Africa and the Middle East. Some critics found fault with such cross-cultural musical borrowings. John Pareles of *Rolling Stone,* for example, wrote that *My Life in the Bush of Ghosts* "raises stubborn questions about context, manipulation and cultural imperialism."

Also in the early 1980s, Byrne was becoming a popular figure among New York's avant-garde artists, some-

times joining them on projects outside the band. He provided music and lyrics for *The Catherine Wheel,* a dance production by choreographer Twyla Tharp, and later wrote music and texts for *The Knee Plays,* interludes in an epic opera by experimental dramatist Robert Wilson, with whom he later wrote the 1988 stage performance piece *The Forest.*

Byrne's intellectual approach to popular music and his desire to do more than play with sounds comes up again and again in interviews. When asked by *Rolling Stone* why he was interested in African music, Byrne stated that at first he just liked the music. Then, "later on, when I started breaking the beats down and putting them back together again, I saw how African and Afro-American songs were put together in similar ways. I saw there were social parallels to the music and a kind of sensibility and philosophy and even metaphysics that's inherent in the way the music's constructed and the attitude in which it's played."

Byrne's interest in African and Caribbean music has led him to a study of those areas' religions, but he never loses sight of the music. He commented in *Rolling Stone,* "Artistically, you notice that this is the route where a lot of music and sensibility and attitude finds its way into popular music and popular culture. So it's a pretty natural thing to want to find out where all this came from: Let's get back to whatever it is."

Solo Work

Since his interest in African music, Byrne's world musical tastes have moved closer to home: On 1989's *Rei Momo* he collaborated with Latin musicians and songwriters. Critics seemed to like the music, but only after they imagined Byrne out of it. A *Down Beat* correspondent wrote that Byrne just didn't understand the musical style he was using and that his effort was merely a pastiche. In a review that was even less forgiving, a *Melody Maker* critic accused Byrne of voyeurism on another culture and its music, of hiring authenticity rather than being true to himself. Byrne finds such criticism difficult to understand; he remarked in *Musician,* "Musically, you can't really ask musicians to sit still and not try to work with music that they enjoy. Most of the time, I work with the people, I'm friends with them. It's not like I just hear something on a record and go, oh, I'll cop that. But I don't see the press jumping all over Rod Stewart 'cause he stole Jorge Ben's song for 'Da Ya Think I'm Sexy?'"

Byrne's interest in Latin music wasn't a passing fad, or at least it hasn't passed yet. He compiled some albums featuring Brazilian music here and poems to want to be a participant in the constant definition and redefinition, appropriation and re-appropriation of African music that Latin musicians have been engaged in for centuries. Byrne's infatuation for Latin music eventually shifted to the rhythms of Cuba, and he has released two anthologies of Cuban music: *Cuba Classics* and *Cuba Classics 2: Dancing With the Enemy.*

Byrne's second solo album, *Uh-Oh,* released in 1992 by Luaka Bop/Sire Records, features some of the Latin musicians who appeared on *Rei Momo* and again displays Byrne's wide musical interests as well as his themes of alienation and social injustice. Well received by critics, *Uh-Oh* is a collection of mostly up-tempo songs with an undercurrent of sarcasm and irony. "Twistin' in the Wind," for example, "is a chipper diatribe about dirty dealings in Washington, D.C., and Everytown, U.S.A.," according to Josef Woodard in *Rolling Stone.* Rating the record an A-, *Entertainment Weekly*'s Stephanie Zacharek noted that "Byrne integrates musical genres with still more confidence. . . . And nearly every arrangement has been burnished to a luster."

Music for Plays and Films

Byrne's orchestral music to *The Forest,* a theatrical piece by the avant-garde performance artist Robert Wilson, continues many of Byrne's earlier concerns with identity and disaffection. In the liner notes accompanying the 1991 album, Byrne wrote that "*The Forest* is less a piece than a process. A process of discovering what it is we are made of. What kinds of ideas, what prejudices, what propaganda fills us up, what we think is beautiful and what we think is ugly, what we consider Nature and what we think is God." *The Forest,* like most of Byrne's work, tackles the musician's interest in life's larger questions as well as the enduring aspects of the industrial age. Set in the mid-1880s, the piece features probably the most classical of all musical styles Byrne has ever employed.

Byrne has also composed music for films, most notably for *True Stories* of 1986—a motion picture he also co-authored and directed—and 1987's *The Last Emperor*—a Stephen Spielberg creation. Despite the fact that *The Last Emperor* score, co-written with Rhuichi Sakamoto and Cong Su, garnered Byrne an Academy Award, it is his least discussed endeavor. *True Stories,* on the other hand, was Byrne's project and displayed many of his familiar concerns—about truth, identity, and post-modern alienation. The film and music were criticized by some as voyeuristic and exploitative, while others praised their quirkiness and humor.

Byrne's artistic activities are myriad, as displayed by his musical interests. His albums offer bold amalgamations of African, Latin, Middle Eastern, rock, and classical music, and he indicated in the early 1990s that he is planning to release LPs featuring Japanese and Indian music. Maybe Byrne's goal is not, as former bandmate Tina Weymouth once said of the Talking Heads, to change the face of music; his aim is perhaps to change the face of contemporary American culture.

Selected writings

(With Robert Wilson) *The Knee Plays* (play comprised of interludes in Wilson's epic opera *The CIVIL WarS*), 1984.
The Tourist Way of Knowledge (performance art), 1985.
(With Beth Henley and Stephen Tobolowsky) *True Stories* (screenplay), released by Warner Bros., 1986.
(With others) *What the Songs Look Like: The Illustrated Talking Heads* (lyrics), illustrations by Byrne and others, Harper, 1987.
Stay up Late (lyrics; for young people), illustrations by Maria Kalman, Viking, 1987.
(With Robert Wilson) *The Forest* (stage performance), 1988.

Selected discography

Solo albums

(With Brian Eno) *My Life in the Bush of Ghosts,* Sire, 1981.
The Complete Score From "The Catherine Wheel," Sire, 1982.
Songs From the Broadway Production of "The Catherine Wheel," Sire, 1982.
Music for "The Knee Plays," ECM, 1982.
Score for "Something Wild," MCA, 1986.
(With Rhuichi Sakamoto and Cong Su) *Music for "The Last Emperor,"* Virgin, 1987.
Score to "Married to the Mob," Reprise, 1988.
Rei Momo, Luaka Bop/Sire, 1989.
The Forest, Luaka Bop/Sire, 1991.
Uh-Oh, Luaka Bop/Sire, 1992.

With Talking Heads; on Sire Records

Talking Heads: 77, 1977.
More Songs About Buildings and Food, 1978.
Fear of Music, 1979.
Remain in Light, 1980.
The Name of This Band Is Talking Heads, 1982.
Speaking in Tongues, 1983.
Stop Making Sense, 1984.
Little Creatures, 1985.
True Stories, 1986.
Naked, 1988.
Popular Favorites, 1992.

Sources

Books

Davis, Jerome, *Talking Heads,* Vintage Books, 1985.
Rockwell, John, *All American Music: Composition in the Late Twentieth Century,* Knopf, 1983.
Tamm, Eric, *Brian Eno: His Music and the Vertical Color of Sound,* Faber and Faber, 1989.

Periodicals

Down Beat, January 1990.
Entertainment Weekly, March 13, 1992.
Melody Maker, October 14,1989.

Musician, April 1992.
The Nation, May 20, 1990.
Pulse!, February 1992; June 1992.
Rolling Stone, November 3, 1977; October 19, 1978; November 15, 1979; November 29, 1979; October 16, 1980; October 30, 1980; June 9, 1983; October 27, 1983; October 25, 1984; November 6, 1986; April 2, 1981; April 21, 1988; March 19, 1992.
Spin, March 1992.
Time, October 27, 1986.

Additional information for this profile was obtained from a Luaka Bop/Sire Records press release on *The Forest,* 1991.

—*Tim Taylor*

John Cage

Composer

John Cage is undeniably one of the most important composers of the twentieth century. He has broadened the definitions of music to include all types of sound. In a 1962 interview with composer Roger Reynolds in *Contemporary Composers on Contemporary Music,* Cage said, "If, in our dealings with our composition of music, we find that it distorts our daily life, then there must be something wrong with the way we're composing, it seems to me. Whereas, if the way we compose is applicable to our daily life, and changes it, then it seems to me that there is something useful in the way we're composing music."

John Milton Cage, Jr., was born on September 5, 1912, in Los Angeles, California. As a child he took piano lessons from his aunt. He attended Los Angeles High School, establishing the highest scholastic average in the school's history, and was valedictorian at his class's graduation in 1928. He enrolled in nearby Pomona College in Claremont, California, where he remained for two years. After withdrawing from Pomona, Cage traveled extensively in Europe and North Africa. He dabbled in architecture and painting and began composing music, using a complex mathematical system he designed to approximate the style of the eighteenth-century German composer Johann Sebastian Bach.

Studied With Schoenberg

In 1931 Cage returned to California with no money or job. He supported himself by giving lectures on modern art and music. Through these lectures, he developed an interest in the music of Austrian-born composer Arnold Schoenberg. Cage studied with Richard Buhlig—the first American pianist to perform the music of Schoenberg—and then in New York City with Adolph Weiss, a former student of Schoenberg. He also attended classes taught at New York City's New School for Social Research by the composer Henry Cowell. In 1934, Cage began studying with Schoenberg privately in Los Angeles and attending his classes at the University of Southern California and the University of California, Los Angeles.

In the 1930s Cage began writing percussion music, and in 1938 he was asked by dancer Syvilla Fort to write the music for her dance, *Bacchanale.* Because of space limitations, a percussion ensemble could not be used. Unhindered, Cage was able to achieve the effect he desired by placing objects inside the piano, thus altering the sound of the strings. This innovation, influenced by Henry Cowell's work in which piano strings were stroked or strummed, became known as the "prepared piano." Cage's *Sonatas and Interludes* of 1946 to 1948 remains his most famous work for prepared piano.

Born John Milton Cage, Jr., September 5, 1912, in Los Angeles, CA; died of a stroke August 12, 1992, in New York, NY; son of John Milton Cage (an engineer and inventor) and Lucretia Harvey; married Xenia Kashevaroff, 1935 (divorced, 1945). *Education:* Attended Pomona College, Claremont, CA, 1928-30; studied composition with Richard Buhlig and Adolph Weiss, 1933; studied harmony, contemporary music, and non-Western music with Henry Cowell at the New School for Social Research, 1933; studied composition, counterpoint, and analysis with Arnold Schoenberg both privately and at the University of Southern California and the University of California, Los Angeles, 1934.

Musical adviser, Merce Cunningham Dance Company, beginning in 1947; cofounded New York Mycological Society, 1962. Has taught and held fellowships at various colleges and universities, including Chicago Institute of Design, 1941; New School for Social Research, 1956-58 and 1959-60; University of Cincinnati, 1967; and Center for Advanced Study at University of Illinois, 1967-69.

Selected awards: Received grants from the Guggenheim Foundation, 1949, and National Academy of Arts and Letters, 1949; Commandeur de l'Ordre des Arts et des Lettres, France, 1982.

Member: American Academy of Arts and Sciences; American Society for Composers, Authors, and Publishers (ASCAP).

Addresses: *Home*—101 West 18th Street, New York, NY 10011. *Music publisher*—C. F. Peters Corporation, 373 Park Avenue S., New York, NY 10016.

In February of 1943 the League of Composers presented a concert of music written by Cage and others at the Museum of Modern Art in New York City. The concert was well received by critics and the public, and Cage's recognition as a leading avant-garde composer became widespread.

Eastern Thought and Chance Operations

After his divorce in 1945 from Xenia Kashevaroff, whom he had married ten years earlier, Cage took an interest in Eastern thought. He studied with Indian philosopher Gita Sarabhai and was instructed in Zen Buddhism by D. T. Suzuki, a leading authority on Zen who taught at Columbia University. The influence of Eastern philosophy on Cage resulted in his experimentation in the early 1950s with "chance operations," in which the means of composition are chosen at random. Cage began using chance operations in order to let music speak for itself, rather than imposing personal taste or desire onto it. American composer Christian Wolff, a former student of Cage, explained the method of composing in a 1982 National Public Radio interview, stating, "what you're listening for is sound in combinations that are not usual, though, when you get right down to it, are not that different from what you hear if you really listen to the world around you."

The first piece Cage wrote using chance operations was *Sixteen Dances,* composed for the Merce Cunningham Dance Company in 1950. Another chance piece, composed in 1951, was *Concerto for Prepared Piano and Chamber Orchestra.* After 1950 Cage's chance compositions were based on the use of the *I Ching,* or "Book of Change," an ancient Chinese text containing hexagrams used for making predictions by tossing coins. Cage's first piece composed by using the *I Ching* was similarly called *Music of Changes.*

In the early 1950s Cage became aware that absolute silence was an impossibility; even the supposedly sound-proof chamber he had visited at Harvard University revealed that he could hear his nervous system and circulation in operation. The result of this discovery was *4'33"* (four minutes and thirty-three seconds), a piece in which the performer appears but does not play an instrument. Instead, the audience is encouraged to listen to the sounds around them. *4'33"* was Cage's affirmation of the important role of nonintended sounds and remains perhaps his most famous work.

During the 1950s and 1960s Cage accepted teaching positions and visiting fellowships at several American universities. Meanwhile he composed *Atlas Eclipticalis,* an orchestral piece created by consulting astronomical charts he acquired at the Wesleyan University observatory, and *HPSCHD* (pronounced "harpsichord"), written in collaboration with University of Illinois composer Lejaren Hiller.

Works Since the 1960s

Since the late 1960s Cage has been devoted largely to eclecticism, either using elements from earlier works or combining previous ideas and methods with new ones. Perhaps most significant are the ambitious *Etudes Australes* for piano of 1974 to 1975, composed by tracing astronomical charts onto music paper; *Child of Tree* (1975) and its companion piece *Branches* (1976), in which contact microphones amplify the sounds of plants, and *Roaratorio, an Irish Circus on Finnegans*

Wake (1979), which features bits of text from James Joyce's novel *Finnegans Wake* accompanied by a collage of music, particularly traditional Irish music. In 1987, Cage's first opera, *Europera*, premiered in Frankfurt, Germany.

"Music is about changing the mind—not to understand, but to be aware," Cage expressed to Michael John White in the London *Observer*. The composer's music urges the audience to listen with new ears and pay attention to sound. "For any one of us," Cage wrote in his book *Silence*, "contemporary music is or could be a way of living."

Selected writings

Silence, Wesleyan University Press, 1961.
A Year From Monday, Wesleyan University Press, 1967.
Empty Words, Wesleyan University Press, 1979.

Selected compositions

Bacchanale, 1940.
Third Construction, 1941.
Credo in Us, 1942.
The Wonderful Widow of Eighteen Springs, 1942.
Amores, 1943.
The Perilous Night, 1944.
Sonatas and Interludes, 1946-48.
Sixteen Dances, 1950.
Concerto for Prepared Piano and Chamber Orchestra, 1951.
Music of Changes, 1951.
4'33", 1952.
Williams Mix, 1952.
Concert for Piano and Orchestra, 1957-58.
Aria, 1958.
Cartridge Music, 1960.
Atlas Eclipticalis, 1961.
(With Lejaren Hiller) *HPSCHD*, 1967-69.
Sixty-Two Mesostics re Merce Cunningham, 1971.
Etudes Australes, 1974-75.
Child of Tree, 1975.
Renga, 1976.
Freeman Etudes, I-XVI, 1977-78.
Roaratorio, an Irish Circus on Finnegans Wake, 1979.
Empty Words, 1981.
Ryoanji, 1984-85.
Europera, 1987.

Selected discography

Amores, Wergo.
Aria, Virgin Classics.
Cartridge Music, Mode.
Concerto, Elektra/Nonesuch.
HPSCHD, Nonesuch.
Indeterminacy: New Aspect of Form in Instrumental and Electronic Music (1959), Folkways.
Music of Changes, Wergo.
The Perilous Night, New Albion.
Sonatas and Interludes, Wergo.
Third Construction, Nexus.

Has also recorded works for piano and prepared piano on Wergo Records.

Sources

Books

Cage, John, *Empty Words*, Wesleyan University Press, 1979.
Cage, John, *Silence*, Wesleyan University Press, 1961.
Cage, John, *A Year From Monday*, Wesleyan University Press, 1967.
Contemporary Composers on Contemporary Music, edited by Elliot Schwartz and Barney Childs, Holt, Rinehart, and Winston, 1967.
Conversing With Cage, edited by Richard Kostelanetz, Limelight Editions, 1988.
Griffiths, Paul, *Cage*, Oxford University Press, 1981.
John Cage, edited by Richard Kostelanetz, Praeger Publishers, 1970.
Nyman, Michael, *Experimental Music: Cage and Beyond*, Schirmer Books, 1974.
Tomkins, Calvin, *The Bride and the Bachelors: Five Masters of the Avant-Garde*, Viking Press, 1965.

Periodicals

Baltimore Sun, November 19, 1982.
Horizon, December 1980.
New York, March 29, 1982.
New York Times, March 12, 1982; August 26, 1985; July 10, 1988.
Observer (London), September 26, 1982.
Washington Post, September 30, 1981; November 16, 1991.

Additional information for this profile was obtained from *The Sunday Show*, National Public Radio, September 5, 1982.

—*Joyce Harrison*

Belinda Carlisle

Singer

Belinda Carlisle first gained fame as the lead singer for the Go-Go's, a hugely popular all female group. The band's wholesome, fun image and light-hearted songs, including "We Got the Beat," "Our Lips Are Sealed," and "Head Over Heels," attracted legions of fans. But by 1985, the act had gone stale. The Go-Go's disbanded and Carlisle embarked on a successful solo career. "The Go-Go's was pretty much me when I was younger," she explained to Todd Gold of *People.* "But as I got older, I got kind of tired of being cute, bubbly and effervescent all day. I just didn't feel like being bouncy anymore."

Carlisle, the oldest of Walt and Joanne Carlisle's seven children, was raised in California's San Fernando Valley. After graduating from high school in 1976, she began frequenting Hollywood's new wave and punk rock music clubs, where she met Charlotte Caffey, Jane Wiedlin, Gina Schock, and Kathy Valentine. They formed the Go-Go's "for laughs," Carlisle told Gold. "I had never been in any other band. That was my first time singing." Eventually they acquired a manager and were booked to tour England. During the tour they recorded "We Got the Beat," a single that sold 50,000 copies in the United States. In 1981, the group signed with I.R.S. Records and later that same year released *Beauty and the Beat.* The debut album sold over two million copies and topped the charts for six weeks. Their next effort, *Vacation,* was less successful; *Talk Show,* released in 1984, flopped.

Wiedlin announced that she was leaving the quintet, and Carlisle and Caffey soon followed. The Go-Go's—immersed in conflict and succumbing to the pressures of fame—officially split up in May of 1985. Intent on pursuing a solo career, Carlisle decided to straighten out her personal life. While the Go-Go's enjoyed what Steve Pond of Rolling Stone called a "cotton candy image," several members of the group, including Carlisle had serious substance abuse problems.

Carlisle's plan for turning her life around included joining Alcoholics Anonymous, dieting, exercising regularly, and seeing a vocal coach three times a week. She also met the man who would become her husband, businessman and former White House staff member Morgan Mason, in 1984. The day after attending a concert together, Carlisle and Mason—the son of actors James and Pamela Mason—began sharing Mason's condo. The two embarked on an idyllic romance; married in 1986, they had their first child, James Duke, in 1992.

Inspired by her newfound love and her renewed physical state—she lost 60 pounds—Carlisle began work on her debut solo album, *Belinda,* which was released in 1986. An assortment of love songs, *Belinda* spawned the hit track "Mad About You," and also featured such tunes as "I Need a Disguise," "Shot in the Dark," and "I Feel the Magic." Former Go-Go's members Caffey and Wiedlin helped with the LP, which many critics found reminiscent of the band's early work. "If you liked the Go-Go's, you'll get a kick out of *Belinda,*" Jon Young noted in *Creem.* "Carlisle remains an optimistic bundle of energy, never less than charming."

Comparing Carlisle's solo efforts to her work with the Go-Go's, a *People* reviewer found that the songstress "sounds as peppy and wholesomely sexy on her own as she did with the band. . . . Producer Mike Lloyd helped Carlisle maintain another of the Go-Go's qualities, the ability to evoke the sound of early rock without seeming to parody it." *Belinda* was well received by audiences as well as critics.

Carlisle's career gained momentum in 1988, when the hit single "Heaven Is a Place on Earth" from her second solo effort, *Heaven on Earth,* was nominated for a Grammy Award. Another album firmly rooted in the pop tradition, it features, according to a *People* reviewer, "a sleeker and tougher" sounding Carlisle. The critic found that the songs on *Heaven on Earth* are "lacking such qualities as wit . . . and aural appeal," but praised Carlisle for providing a "more aggressive, focused delivery" than in her days with the Go-Go's.

Noting that Carlisle's "passion for fluffy dance music

has clearly hamstrung her," *Rolling Stone* critic Deborah Kirk summed up the lukewarm reception to the singer's 1991 LP, *Live Your Life Be Free.* The album reaffirmed Carlisle's reputation as "the high priestess of sugar pop," in Kirk's words, and had critics decrying her failure to offer meaningful lyrics and an innovative sound. *Entertainment Weekly's* Stephanie Zacharek found that the LP "ultimately chokes on its aggressively friendly sound and its dribbling sentiment." Though Carlisle—having made no plans for a tour to promote *Live Your Life Be Free*—had her own fears about becoming "passe," her work with the Go-Go's and during her early solo career secured her a spot in the annals of the ever-changing pop music genre. "As long as pop music has a sweet tooth," surmised James Wolcott in *Vanity Fair,* "there'll be a place for her on the car stereo."

Selected discography

With the Go-Go's

Beauty and the Beat (includes "We Got the Beat"), I.R.S., 1981.
Vacation, I.R.S., 1982.
Talk Show, I.R.S., 1984.

Solo albums

Belinda (includes "Mad About You"), I.R.S., 1986.
Heaven On Earth (includes "Heaven Is a Place on Earth"), MCA, 1988.
(With George Harrison and others) *Runaway Horses,* MCA, 1989.
Live Your Life Be Free, MCA, 1991.
Greatest Hits, MCA, 1992.

Also released video *Belinda Live!,* 1989.

Sources

Creem, October 1986.
Entertainment Weekly, October 25, 1991.
Interview, July 1985.
Los Angeles Times, May 13, 1985.
New York, February 5, 1990.
People, October 26, 1981; June 16, 1986; June 23, 1986; November 23, 1987; February 13, 1989; January 13, 1992; May 18, 1992.
Rolling Stone, July 5, 1984; July 3, 1986; August 28, 1986; November 6, 1986; July 14, 1988; January 23, 1992.
Vanity Fair, February 1992.
Variety, May 18, 1988.

—Denise Wiloch

José Carreras

Opera singer

The tenor voice "has always electrified operagoers more than any other kind of voice, male or female," José Carreras asserted, as quoted by Helena Matheopoulos in *Divo: Great Tenors, Baritones, and Basses Discuss Their Roles.* "Something about the physical qualities of this sound and of its vibrations, to say nothing of those high notes at the top of the register, seem to arouse an instant, visceral excitement in the audience." Judging from critical and popular reactions, since early in his career Carreras has easily validated this belief. In a 1978 article for the *New York Times,* John Gruen attested to Carreras's "aura of immediacy and theatrical credibility," a product of his "superior voice of lyric, verging on dramatic, quality [and] romantic good looks which invariably enhance any role he undertakes." But as Carreras's career and life progressed, his dominant human spirit, exemplified in his life story of triumph followed by tragedy followed by triumph again, informed his various stage personas and was communicated to his receptive audiences.

Carreras was born in 1946 in Barcelona, Spain, then a country ravaged by World War II and oppressed by the fascist Francisco Franco government. Carreras's family was poverty-stricken—his father had been a teacher before the Spanish Civil War but lost his position due to his Republican loyalties. When Carreras was seven years old, he saw a film about the great Italian operatic tenor Enrico Caruso that made a lasting impression on him. After listening to their son's constant imitation of Caruso, Carreras's nonmusical parents realized the young boy's potential and enrolled him in the Barcelona Conservatory where, for eight years, he studied music in addition to a traditional curriculum. Afterward, Carreras entered the University of Barcelona to pursue a career in chemistry, concurrently beginning voice lessons with a nonprofessional, Jaime Francisco Puig. Carreras left the university after only two years, however, deciding to return to the Barcelona Conservatory to continue musical studies. Puig remained his only vocal instructor.

Luck and Hard Work

These dramatic career moves might have proven unsuccessful for an average individual, but given Carreras's "talent, drive, ambition, and . . . professionalism," according to the *New York Times*'s Gruen, he was able to attain his goal of becoming a professional opera singer. Gruen also commented on the way luck and the friendship of the Caballes—the famous soprano Montserrat and her manager/brother Carlos—provided the young Carreras with opportunities to prove his talent. Montserrat Caballe was so impressed by Carreras's debut opposite her in the 1970 Barcelona production of Gaetano

Jr., explaining Carreras's sudden rise. "His voice had a lustrous sheen in the upper register, with flashes of fire that set it somehow, indefinably, apart." From recital recordings to operatic performances, Carreras continued his ascent.

More Dramatic Roles

Despite winning these accolades, however, Carreras explained to Matheopoulos in *Divo* that he "couldn't bear a boring career consisting of going around the world year after year with a repertoire of half a dozen roles even if I were to sing them near-perfectly." This desire for variety, coupled with a deepening change in voice that most tenors experience in their thirties, moved Carreras in the early 1980s into more dramatic roles. But a more important force that pushed him away from romantic hero parts to those in revolutionary, political settings, like Umberto Giordano's *Andrea Chenier,* was his father's political legacy. "Anything against justice—social justice, it is against myself. Anything against freedom or democracy, it is against myself, it's against society. So this is inside myself, this character," Carreras explained in *José Carreras: A Life Story,* a television biography produced for London Weekend Television.

Beginning in the mid-1980s, Carreras explored the repertoire of popular music, and it marked the first time he received widespread negative criticism. Although a commercial success, the 1985 recording of Leonard Bernstein's *West Side Story,* with its casting of opera stars Kiri Te Kanawa and Carreras in the lead roles, was faulted by critics. The *New Republic's* Edward Rothstein dismissed Carreras's venture, saying Carreras "lets nothing come through his singing other than the fact of his studied singing." While subsequent recordings by Carreras in the popular genre received mixed reactions as well, his operatic performances continued to earn almost unanimous support.

Diagnosed With Leukemia

But on July 15, 1987, when "he was at the height of his career, possessed of an instantly recognizable, warm and lustrous voice that he commanded with ravishing delicacy and musical intelligence," as Malitz noted in *Ovation,* Carreras stopped singing. He was diagnosed with acute lymphocytic leukemia. For almost a year, Carreras underwent chemotherapy and bone marrow manipulation in an attempt to stop the disease. The treatment was ultimately successful, but many in the opera community worried that the effects of the disease might prevent him from fulfilling his destiny as one of the world's great tenors. Carreras, quoted in his television

Donizetti's *Lucrezia Borgia* that she and her brother helped guide the young tenor's budding career.

In 1971 Carreras made his Italian debut singing the role of Rodolfo in Puccini's opera *La Boheme;* he also won the Giuseppe Verdi Competition held in Parma, Italy. The following year he made his American debut at the New York City Opera as Pinkerton in Puccini's *Madama Butterfly.* "Rodolfo, Cavaradossi, Alfredo, Edgardo, and the Duke in [Giuseppe Verdi's] *Rigoletto* followed. He then bowed at Covent Garden, Buenos Aires, and Vienna—all between 1973 and '74. Over the next two years came the Met [New York Metropolitan Opera] and La Scala [Milan], and his fortune was made," Nancy Malitz recounted in *Ovation.*

"His singing was natural, unaffected, disarmingly lyrical," wrote *New York Times* critic Theodore W. Libbey, biography, dismissed concerns about such issues: "You see the other dimension in life. And then you have time to think much more about your spirit, about the spiritual side of your life, about God, about religion, about faith. And you can arrive to certain conclusions."

Since his return to the stage in July of 1988, Carreras's voice has displayed few scars. Instead, it has carried a greater, deeper weight. Hilary Finch, writing for *Opera,* described a recital soon after his return: "The first sound of the raw, resurrected human voice leaping joyfully, two stairs at a time, up the rising lines of [Alessandro] Scarlatti's 'Gia il sole dal Gange' immediately cut through the cant. This was the *same* voice: highly strung in its inflection, lithe of movement, dusky in undertone, brilliant, if still driven, to the top. What had changed was the intensity of delivery and the urgency of communication."

In January of 1992 it was announced that Carreras would not only be embarking on his first major concert tour in the United States since his recovery, but that he would also serve as the music director of the 1992 Summer Olympics to take place in his hometown of Barcelona. His responsibilities included arranging the music to be played at the opening and closing ceremonies, which he promised in *Pulse!* would be "something new," adding that "instead of pulling marching music out of a file of band tunes, we will be adapting the works of important and famous Spanish composers not usually heard in this context." Carreras has not significantly slowed his pace since his return to performing, though much of his time is now taken up with business matters, a fact he attested to in *Pulse!,* stating, "Nowadays, I feel like an executive—who sings, sometimes."

Selected writings

Singing From the Soul: An Autobiography, Y.C.P., 1991.

Selected discography

Ave Maria, Philips.

Carreras, Domingo, Pavarotti, London.
José Carreras in Concert, SRO.
José Carreras in Recital, Legato Classics.
Early Live Recordings: 1972-1976, Legato Classics.
Lieder Recital, Arcanta.
Love Is. . ., Philips.
Merry Christmas, CBS Masterworks.
Neapolitan Songs, Philips.
Sings "Memory" From Cats & 15 Other Great Love Songs, Philips.
Sings Zarzuela Airs, Ensayao.
(With Kiri Te Kanawa and others) *West Side Story,* Deutsche Grammophon.
You Belong to My Heart, Philips.
(With Montserrat Caballe and Placido Domingo) *From the Official Barcelona Olympic Games Ceremony,* RCA Victor Red Seal, 1992.

Sources

Books

Carreras, José, *Singing From the Soul: An Autobiography,* Y.C.P., 1991.
Matheopoulos, Helena, *Divo: Great Tenors, Baritones, and Basses Discuss Their Roles,* Harper & Row, 1986.

Periodicals

Detroit Free Press, December 5, 1991.
Gramophone, January 1977.
New Republic, July 15 & 22, 1985.
Newsweek, June 10, 1985; July 22, 1991.
New York, November 2, 1987.
New York Times, February 26, 1978; November 22, 1981.
Opera, April 1983; May 1987; June 1989.
Ovation, August 1989.
Publishers Weekly, April 5, 1991.
Pulse!, May 1992.
Time, April 1, 1985.

Additional information for this profile was obtained from the television biography *José Carreras: A Life Story,* London Weekend Television, 1991.

—Rob Nagel

Carlene
Carter

Singer, songwriter

Few entertainers have come to Nashville with a richer musical heritage than Carlene Carter. A third generation singer-songwriter, Carter counts among her kin some of the best-loved country musicians, including the renowned Mother Maybelle Carter and June Carter Cash. With her infectious enthusiasm and wide-ranging mix of backwoods strains and contemporary rockabilly, Carlene Carter has brought her hillbilly roots into a new age. Her 1990 album, *I Fell in Love,* reached the country Top 20 and yielded a Number One hit, and her energetic live performances led a *Newsweek* correspondent to describe her as "every spunky inch the heir apparent to country music's most venerable dynasty."

Decades before Carlene was born, her grandmother Maybelle and her great aunt and uncle, Sara and A. P. Carter, formed a group called the Carter Family. By the mid-1930s the Carter Family was one of the nation's most famous acoustic country acts, releasing best-selling Victor recordings and becoming a staple on the radio. The original Carter Family achieved fame on the strength of traditional Appalachian mountain music with its reedy harmonies and fluent guitar-picking. When the group disbanded in 1943, Maybelle recruited her children and continued to perform as the Carter Sisters and Mother Maybelle. This Carter family incarnation was equally successful, appearing often on the Grand Ole Opry and touring together at a hectic pace.

Carlene's mother, June, eventually became famous in her own right as a singer and songwriter. During the 1950s June Carter married another Nashville performer, Carl Smith. They were the parents of Carlene, who was born in the mid-1950s and was more or less raised on the road. Growing up in an extended family of musicians, Carter almost subconsciously absorbed the style her grandmother and mother had popularized. She pointed out in *Newsweek,* however, that she was profoundly influenced by rock and roll music as well. While she admired her family's accomplishments, she said, "they were just my family. And then here came [the pop music group] the Monkees, and uh-oh."

"A Hitless Wonder"

In the mid-1960s June Carter married country star Johnny Cash. Carlene retains fond memories of her famous stepfather, recalling that he was especially generous with his money, doling out huge allowances to his children and stepchildren alike. The young performer offers few anecdotes on her teen years, however, which were particularly difficult. She ran away from home at age 15, and was married and divorced twice; each marriage yielded a child. Asked about that period of her life by a *People* reporter, Carlene merely responded, "Lots of girls marry at 16 in Tennessee. Everyone makes mistakes."

Carlene Carter was 22 when she stepped into the family line of work and signed a recording contract with Warner Bros. Records. All of Nashville had high hopes for the young descendent of country royalty, but somehow Carlene Carter albums failed time after time to yield any hits. *People* contributor Jim Jerome wrote that Carter's quest for a niche "drove her into country pop, [rhythm and blues] and ballads. Seemingly ready to sizzle, Carter remained a hitless wonder. She eventually left Warner Brothers Records after four LPs, but she kept her string of flops alive at five with one more at Epic."

Carter's best-known early work was the album *Musical Shapes,* produced by her third husband, British rocker Nick Lowe. The work was well received by critics, but it never found space on the airwaves. "Country radio wouldn't play it," Carter commented in *Newsweek.* "They said it was too rock." Rock stations would not play it either, citing its country influence. The failure of *Musical Shapes,* which sold only several thousand copies, was a blow to the fledgling artist. She moved to England, where she was more successful writing for other performers than recording.

Returned to Traditional Country

An Epic album released in the mid-1980s "didn't do nothin'," Carter admitted in *People.* "It was totally not me. Synthesizer pop, everything I hated. So I got discouraged and quit. I decided to take a rest, a long, very long rest." By that time Carter was in her late twenties and was well-battered by her fast-lane lifestyle—which included drug and alcohol abuse—and her lackluster record sales. She may have remained forever in obscurity but for a chance occurrence in 1986. That year her mother and aunts came to London on tour, and Carlene stepped in as a substitute when one of her aunts became ill. It was nothing less than a revelation for Carter, who had always taken her roots for granted. "I guess I had a sense of my own mortality," she noted in *People.* "It was time to learn about my heritage."

Carlene Carter toured with her mother and aunts for two years, absorbing the old Carter Family songs. June Carter explained in *People* that her daughter "began to feel whatever it is that you're born with that makes you a singing Carter and makes you love and sing that Appalachian mountain harmony. She'd found her way back to traditional country." Carlene's move toward her musical roots coincided with a general swing back to a more traditional sound common among her younger Nashville peers. She began to realize that she might have a more receptive audience for both her sassy and her sentimental tunes.

Carter returned to Nashville and settled into her grandmother's house to write new material. In 1990 she released *I Fell in Love,* an album that ranges from progressive country-rock to traditional Appalachian folk. The album was an immediate hit with critics, including *Stereo Review* correspondent Alanna Nash, who declared that the work "alternately delights, surprises, reaffirms [Carter's] independent musical stance, and reworks her family's musical legacy with songs of integrity, heart, and style." The title cut became Carter's first Number One country hit, but it was more notable for its giddy music video, described in *Newsweek* as "what would happen if [comedic actor] Pee-wee Herman took over Sun Records."

Took Success in Stride

At age 35, with two grown children, Carter had finally achieved country stardom. "I always thought that it would work out," she told a *People* correspondent. "But I didn't think it would work out so late in life. I'm just a little behind schedule." The attractive blonde entertainer is not rushing to catch up, however. she has sworn off alcohol and drugs and is taking her success in stride. "My excess now is feeling good and being chemically free," she said, according to *People.* "Playin' totally straight is a million times more fun than getting smashed on champagne."

In late 1991 Carter told a *Country Music* correspondent that she was at work on a follow-up to *I Fell in Love.* Pointing out that the album is similar to her successful 1990 release, the acclaimed singer-songwriter described it as "having a little more melancholy to it. I think this is a bit more of a grownup record. There was a certain high-spirited kind of frenzy to *I Fell in Love,* but now I'm more interested in opening up the direct channel from my heart to the tape recorder."

Selected discography

Musical Shapes, Warner Bros., 1979.
I Fell in Love (includes "I Fell in Love," "Come on Back," "The Sweetest Thing," "My Dixie Darlin'," "Goodnight, Dallas," "One Love," "The Leavin' Side," "Guardian Angel," "Me and the Wildwood Rose," "You Are the One," and "Easy From Now On"), Reprise, 1990.

Also recorded albums *C'est Si Bon* and *Blue Nun* and the single "Time's Up," a duet with Southern Pacific.

Sources

Country Music, November/December 1991.
Entertainment Weekly, August 31, 1990.
Houston Post, September 16-23, 1990.
Newsweek, August 27, 1990.
People, November 12, 1990.
Rolling Stone, November 1, 1990.
Stereo Review, November, 1990.
Time, December 3, 1990.
USA Today, November 12, 1990.

Additional information for this profile was obtained from Reprise Records press material, 1990.

—Anne Janette Johnson

Johnny Clegg

T hanks to the success of American pop star Paul Simon's Grammy-winning album *Graceland,* Western listening audiences have some notion of what South African popular music sounds like. But there were Westerners involved in making and producing African music long before Simon. White South African Johnny Clegg—known equally for his opposition to the racist apartheid government that has long blighted his adopted homeland—is one of these.

Born in England, Clegg moved with his family to South Africa when he was six. His mother was a cabaret singer and his father was a staunchly anti-apartheid journalist with an abiding interest in black culture. Clegg's own early interest in black culture was musical, but he did not begin his career as a musician. Clegg's interest in Zulu music and other aspects of Zulu culture led him to a junior lectureship in social anthropology at Johannesburg's University of the Witwatersrand, South Africa's leading institution of higher education.

Clegg left the university in the 1970s to pursue a career in music. He explained in *Rolling Stone:* "There's always been a hidden, invisible middle ground in South Africa of connections between people and cultures. That was being incinerated. Music was the most effective way I could work out my feelings." To learn how to play traditional Zulu music, he first approached Sipho Mchunu, a migrant worker employed as a gardener in Johannesburg who was also a street musician. Sipho has said that he was initially puzzled by the white man's interest in him, but that Clegg eventually won him over. In fact, some black South Africans refer to Clegg as the "white Zulu." Sipho taught Clegg traditional Zulu music and instruments, and they eventually formed a duo called Johnny and Sipho, later renamed Juluka—the Zulu word for "sweat." Along the way Clegg learned the Zulu language and an athletic style of Zulu traditional dance called *Indlamu,* which he performs as part of his act.

Juluka Stressed Traditional Sounds

Clegg spoke about the early days of Juluka in Jeremy Marre's film *Rhythm of Resistance:* "Originally, it was very difficult to play together in public, the laws being as they are: a black and a white not being allowed to play on a stage, or to a mixed audience. Things are starting to ease up slowly. . . . We've got a few sort of little hidden venues where everybody can come together and enjoy each others' music." In an interview with Chris Stapleton that appeared in *African All-Stars: The Pop Music of a Continent,* Clegg reflected on the group's success. "Juluka appeared at a time when black people were buying up records by the [American

For the Record. . .

Born October 31, 1953, in Rochdale, England; immigrated to South Africa, 1959; mother, Muriel Pienaar, was a cabaret singer, father was a journalist; children: Jesse (son). *Education:* University of the Witwatersrand, degree in anthropology, c. 1965.

Singer, songwriter, recording and performing artist. Junior lecturer in anthropology, University of the Witwatersrand, Johannesburg, South Africa, mid-1960s to late 1970s. Performed with Juluka, 1979-85; performed with Savuka, mid-1980s—.

Awards: Gold record (South Africa), for *African Litany;* gold or platinum records (South Africa and Europe), for *Third World Child* and *Shadow Man.*

Addresses: *Music publisher*—H.R. Music, Inc., 5430 Van Nuys Blvd., Ste. 305, Van Nuys, CA 91401.

pop-soul group the] O'Jays in the hundreds and thousands. . . . We went back to our roots. A cult fashion began, with people playing roots music. You had something similar in 1970, and again in 1976 with the black-consciousness movement, an attempt to recapture and to stress African roots and origins."

Juluka went from playing in small clubs and markets to become a top attraction, popular with both blacks and whites. Clegg and Sipho started out playing fairly traditional Zulu music with a political edge, but as they became more prolific and as other musicians joined them, their compositions began to display a more Western pop orientation. By the 1983 release of *Scatterlings,* several other musicians had permanently joined the band. Most of Juluka's albums, nonetheless, remained closely tied to *mbaqanga*—the black South African township music that became popular in the 1950s. Clegg told Stapleton that his music, widely referred to as "township pop," is "a new genre," elaborating, "It's a genre where reggae and mbaqanga meet, where soul and mbaqanga meet, where funk and mbaqanga meet."

Savuka Innovated

Sipho left Juluka in 1985 to return to his family farm in Zululand. Clegg went on to form a new band, Savuka—Zulu for "awakening"—comprised of three blacks and three whites. Savuka's music was more electronic than that of Juluka, but Clegg has remarked that he does not

feel authentic traditional styles should be preserved as museum pieces; he believes that musicians should feel free to experiment with styles and come up with new types of music. Clegg explained to *African All-Stars* author Stapleton that Savuka's "approach is that there should be a democracy of music: The new forms should get as much support as the old. There should be a balance. There is a growing resistance to people saying, 'This isn't groaners [male vocalists who sing the low parts in mbaqanga songs]; this isn't mbaqanga.' This isn't South Africa in 1950 . . . and many African musicians have spent a lot of time and energy trying to find a place for themselves in the new musical world." But even in this new musical world, whites who are involved in the music of black South Africans are often criticized from a variety of standpoints. Despite his political good intentions, Clegg's music has received all kinds of negative reviews. *Melody Maker* attacked Clegg for plundering African music, calling him a "cultural transvestite"; *Rolling Stone* criticized him for not being original enough.

The government of South Africa, uncomfortably aware of Clegg's untempered denunciation of apartheid and increasingly high profile, according to *Beats of the Heart* authors Jeremy Marre and Hannah Charlton, succeeded in banning a record that contained a song it construed as "an incitement against work" and questionable for its use of slang words like "sweetie" and "heavy." "Africa Kukhala Ambangcwele," from *Universal Men,* was a Number One hit before it was banned, and "Asimnonanga," Savuka's tribute to chief apartheid opponent Nelson Mandela, was proscribed as well. In *When the Music's Over,* Robin Denselow reported that Clegg and Savuka have regularly found themselves at the mercy of South African police; the band's van has been routinely searched and conflict over concert licenses has became the norm. Furthermore, according to *Rolling Stone,* Clegg has been arrested and spied upon by government authorities.

Simple Values Embroiled in Politics

Clegg has never hesitated to speak out on his music and politics. He told *Rolling Stone* that he and Sipho were "not revolutionaries, we're not a protest group," continuing, "We have certain general principles that are fundamental human values. It's basically, 'I want to be able to play to everybody.' That's all. . . . It's a simple thing. But in South Africa, it's a political issue."

Ironically, Clegg was expelled from the British Musicians Union in 1988 for performing in South Africa. The singer had experienced harassment from the union before, as well as the wrath of civil rights organizations outside South Africa. His explanation is that people outside South Africa view the country's racial issues simplistically. "The exile community," he told *Rolling Stone,* "has done the struggle [against apartheid] a disservice by trying to present the issue simply in terms of black and white." But Clegg is committed to beating apartheid and admits to being an idealist. "We're creating symbols of tomorrow, a nonracial future. We have to give people something that everybody can claim is his."

Selected discography

Universal Men (includes "Africa Kukhala Ambangcwele"), 1979.
African Litany, 1981.
Ubhule Bemvelo, 1982.
Scatterlings ("includes Asimnonanga"), Warner Bros., 1983.
Work for All, 1983.
Musa Ukungilandela, 1984.
The International Tracks, 1984.
The Good Hope Concerts, 1986.
Third World Child, Capitol, 1987.
Shadow Man, Capitol, 1988.
Cruel, Crazy, Beautiful World, Capitol, 1990.
The Best of Juluka, Rhythm Safari, 1991.

Sources

Books

Andersson, Muff, *Music in the Mix: The Story of South African Popular Music,* Ravan, 1981.
Bender, Wolfgang, *Sweet Mother: Modern African Music,* translated by Wolfgang Freis, University of Chicago Press, 1991.
Denselow, Robin, *When the Music's Over: The Story of Political Pop,* Faber & Faber, 1989.
Graham, Ronnie, *The Da Capo Guide to Contemporary African Music,* Da Capo, 1988.
Marre, Jeremy, and Hannah Charlton, *Beats of the Heart: Popular Music of the World,* Pantheon, 1985.
Stapleton, Chris, and Chris May, *African All-Stars: The Pop Music of a Continent,* Quartet, 1987.

Periodicals

Guitar Player, October 1988.
Melody Maker, March 10, 1990.
Rolling Stone, December 8, 1983; October 6, 1988; March 22, 1990; June 11, 1992.

Additional information for this profile was obtained from the film *Rhythm of Resistance: Black South African Music,* directed by Jeremy Marre, Shanachie, 1988.

—Tim Taylor

Jimmy Cliff

Singer, songwriter

Credited, along with Bob Marley, with playing a vital role in the introduction of reggae music to the world at large, Jimmy Cliff has never gained the kind of messianic reputation that his peer did. Despite the fact that Cliff's name is virtually a household word among reggae fans in the United States and Great Britain, very few of those fans really know much of his music beyond some standard selections. In addition, his tremendous energy and industriousness—which have produced over eighteen albums in as many years—have never produced consistent financial success.

Cliff's family descended from bands of fugitive Afro-Caribbean slaves called "Maroons," who eventually gave their name to what is now the Maroon country in Jamaica. Certain parts of the West Indian island—largely inaccessible because of mountains and thick rain forests—provided a haven for escaped slaves as early as the seventeenth century. The area began to function as a base of operations for Afro-Caribbean rebellion; consequently, it has for hundreds of years stood as a source of conflict for the English colonizers and a source of pride and strength for a struggling Afro-Caribbean population. James Chambers, whom we now know as Jimmy Cliff, grew up in the Maroon country with the Maroon spirit.

Born in 1948 in the rural village of Somerton in St. James Parish, Cliff was the second son of laborer parents. (The older son, Victor, would eventually become his brother's manager.) Because the children's mother left the family soon after Jimmy's birth, he and Victor were raised by their father, who worked nominally as a tailor but also supplemented his income as a farm hand. Beyond sustenance, he provided his sons with musical influence: "He was always singing. There wasn't TV, there wasn't radio. We played drums or guitars—that was the entertainment," Cliff revealed in a *Jet* interview.

Early Interest in Musical Career

Cliff quit school in 1961 at the age of 13. He soon left Somerton for Kingston, the major urban center of Jamaica, to seek some kind of training that would provide him with a trade. He knew, however, even before setting foot in the city that he wanted to make a living in music. The draw of a thriving music industry in Kingston in the early 1960s, which primarily produced rhythm and blues and ska, gave many black youths at least the fantasy of an opportunity to break out of a cycle of hopeless poverty. Ska, the roots of what would become reggae later in the 1960s, grafted the American mainland sound of R & B onto the syncopated calypso sound developed by Jamaican blacks. As ska grew into reggae, it would be adopted by a religion of black liberation—particular to Jamaica—embodied by the Rastafarians. Although Cliff never identified himself as a Rastafarian, most reggae musicians did, and the same musical roots offered him a ticket to success.

As an unskilled black youth plunged into the ghettos of a city where he knew no one, all Cliff had going for him was resourcefulness and staying power. Before he could even approach the city's music industry, he had to negotiate the dangers of the major slum of the city, Trench Town. Cliff displayed his usual bravado when he told *Reggae Bloodlines* author Stephen Davis about his experiences there as a teenager: "It was violent there, but I wasn't afraid because the environment of Somerton was also tough and I was used to it. You had to know how to defend yourself and fear is a thing you couldn't live with. In West Kingston we had political violence and they teargas my house all the time. . . . Dem raid and dem teargas the whole place." Because Cliff had the spirit necessary to handle this setting, he could hold out long enough to make himself known to the Kingston record producers.

Braved Local Music Scene

The local music industry was a thriving but extremely exploitative business, providing many young musicians with some degree of work. Small record producers participated in a kind of cottage industry, hiring local youths to write and record songs; the singles, called acetates, were played in dance halls where, depending on the response of the audience, the most popular would be chosen for sale in record shops. According to this system, an aspiring young musician could record a large number of acetates for a producer without ever releasing a single; if he or she did finally have a single, it was still a gamble as to whether or not the song would catch on and the musician would be paid to do more recordings.

Only a fraction of the talented individuals who put their energy into a vital Jamaican music industry have ever managed to make a living at it, or a name that goes beyond the island. Cliff expressed to Davis how even the possibility of success motivated him: "What was I supposed to do with my life? Work in a banana field? Cut cane? I came to Kingston to go to night school and learn a trade, but my intention was to sing." While he sought that break in the music industry, he supported himself by working on a vegetable truck; for the most part, he led a life of extreme poverty—often near to starving—typical in the ghettos of Kingston.

Soon after arriving in Kingston, Cliff—who had reportedly changed his name because he wanted something that expressed his ambition to reach the "heights"— began courting local record producers. He recorded his first single, "Daisy Got Me Crazy," and his first Jamaican hit, "Dearest Beverly," in 1962—only a year after his arrival in the city. The last song, combined with Cliff's ingenuity, even established Leslie Kong, the man who produced the single, as an important reggae producer.

Kong and his brothers owned a record store in Kingston called Beverley's. Although the brothers at this point only sold records and had never produced one, young Cliff wrote "Beverly" for the Kong brothers and then went so far as to suggest that they should produce it. Cliff described the evening to Davis: "I was alone and walking one night, and it was a night of frustrations. Go passed his record shop several times that night and I say, 'Beverley.' Right away think of a song called 'Beverly' and I walk in there to seduce him with my song that had the same name as his shop. Subliminal seduction, right?. . . So he liked the song and . . . said it was the best voice he had ever heard. . . . I was fourteen years old then. He didn't know anything about the business and so I gathered the musicians and two more singers, Monte Morris and Derrick Morgan, got them and bring them in and introduce them. We got a little hit out of 'Hurricane Hattie' and that was the beginning of Leslie Kong, too." With Kong established as a producer, Cliff was able to record as much as he liked; he turned out a series of island hits, including "Hurricane Hattie," "My Lucky Day," "Miss Jamaica," "Fat Man," and "Rudie in Court."

Gained International Exposure

At about this time, the Jamaican government put together a troupe of island musicians for a promotional tour to broaden the appeal of Jamaican culture and encourage tourism. Cliff went on the tour, planting the first seeds of his fame beyond the Caribbean in general and in the United States in particular. After the tour, in what seemed to be a major break for such a young new artist, Chris Blackwell, the president of Island Records, brought Cliff to London. In only two years, from 1961 to 1963, Cliff went from wandering the streets of Kingston to taking the first step in an international music career.

The move to London, however, first led Cliff into another period of poverty, struggle, and discrimination. He had to confront English racism: a government that tried to deport him and landlords who wouldn't rent to any nonwhite tenants. Furthermore, he ended up having to support his own musical interests with work as a back-up vocalist for English pop groups. Since ska was only then becoming palatable to English and American music audiences, Cliff couldn't build a career on the Jamaican sounds that were most familiar to him.

Already inclined to musical and cultural eclecticism, Cliff handled these circumstances by branching out into other forms of music, either recording strict R & B and soul or blending these other sounds with early reggae. As Davis noted, Cliff was "trying to shake off his musical patois and assume a more cosmopolitan soul style." Although his singles for Island at this time never had any notable success, he started to do well with a soul-based band that he had created in order to tour the European club circuit. In France and Scandinavia, he was especially well received; France has since remained one of his most loyal markets.

The next upturn in Cliff's career finally came in 1968, when the song "Waterfall" was accepted at a Brazilian music festival. Cliff was so taken by the culture in Brazil, which offers an incredible weave of diverse national and racial backgrounds, that he stayed for six months, working on the songs that would finally cement his international reputation. The album that he released in 1969, *Wonderful World, Beautiful People,* included the first release of "Many Rivers to Cross," which has since become one of the songs most often associated with Cliff's name. The album also introduced Cliff's first two

international hits, "Vietnam" and the title track. Although the British press, finding the album too commercial, gave it mediocre reviews, consumers loved it. *Wonderful World, Beautiful People* made Cliff money in markets ranging from the United Kingdom to South America. His next album, released in 1970, prompted precisely the opposite response: critics lauded *Another Cycle,* but Cliff's financial status waned due to slow record sales. To some degree, this vacillating condition would characterize the rest of Cliff's career, partly because his musical style would vary so much from one production to the next that critics and fans could not count on any single sound from him.

Film Debut

This trend, this limbo in which Cliff's career has generally suffered, was banished for a brief time in the early 1970s with the success of the low-budget cult film *The*

"What was I supposed to do with my life? Work in a banana field? Cut cane? I came to Kingston to go to night school and learn a trade, but my intention was to sing."

Harder They Come. Director Perry Henzell, a white Jamaican filmmaker who earned his living filming commercials, had an idea for a film that would introduce audiences to the harsh realities of Jamaican life. After seeing Cliff on an album cover, he determined that this was the face that he wanted for Ivan, his lead character. Ivan, a black youth not unlike Cliff, tries to make it in the music industry in Kingston only to end up forced into a kind of Robin Hood-gangster existence by the oppressive island government. Henzell approached Cliff about the film in 1970, produced the film in 1971, and released both the film and the soundtrack in 1972.

The Harder They Come had a powerful cultural effect. It introduced Cliff to international audiences and cemented his reputation with small but loyal reggae audiences in the United States and Britain well into the future; it also introduced reggae to international audiences, initiating its importance as a musical force with British and American audiences in general. The songs that Cliff wrote and performed for the film, "You Can Get It If You

Really Want," "Many Rivers to Cross," and "Sitting Here in Limbo," have remained Cliff's best known pieces and have positions in the history of reggae as vital as any of Bob Marley's most memorialized songs.

"Misunderstood Reggae Master"

Although Cliff's financial reward for the movie never amounted to more than $10,000, it did establish his popularity to such a degree that he had a chance to launch a lucrative career in reggae music. He chose, however, to prioritize his social and spiritual values over his wallet and engaged in a firsthand study of Africa in order to discover his racial roots and study the Muslim religion. Although he continued to produce albums at a rate of almost one each year, they rarely satisfied the expectations of the most commercial markets in the United States and Britain. This move in many ways typifies Cliff's career. He pursued African culture as an affirmation of his racial roots, but many critics have interpreted his quest as a rejection of Afro-Caribbean culture. To some degree, this and similar choices have cost him financial success and injured his reputation among Jamaican cultural forces and reggae purists.

Davis summed up the conflict as it prevailed in the late 1970s: "Jimmy Cliff is the most misunderstood of the reggae masters. He has been vilified for abandoning his roots and the Jamaican styles that nourished him. . . . In Jamaica, Cliff is respected as an artist who opened doors for reggae that might otherwise have remained shut. Others contend that Cliff moved to England so long ago he's lost contact. Critics point to the smoothness of some of his . . . albums, [which seems to represent a denunciation of] the fundamentally raw reggae sensibility. [In addition,] his religion gets him into trouble with the Rastafarians. In a weird incident late in 1975 Cliff was spit upon during a Wailers concert in Kingston by Rastas indignant at Cliff's ardent embrace of Islam."

Cliff has, however, established respect and success where he has most seemed to want it: in his own eyes and with untraditional—particularly Third World—markets. He told Lee Wohlfert-Wihlberg in *People* in 1982: "I realize that the world is set up on publicity and propaganda, and the wise thing for my career was to use it. But if I hadn't gone to Africa, I probably would have gone crazy. I don't regret it." Furthermore, he discovered in 1974 that he had a large following in Africa. Wohlfert-Wihlberg noted that "Cliff's biggest following is in Nigeria. He's also popular in Brazil, Sweden, the Soviet Union and South Africa." So, although he hasn't ever seemed to discover the proper

formula for British and American commercial success, his multinational-based career has been kept very much alive.

Critics Unkind in the 1970s

Greil Marcus, writing for *Rolling Stone,* called the 1978 effort *Give Thankx,* the most popular of Cliff's late seventies releases, "the first satisfying album Jimmy Cliff has made since the soundtrack to *The Harder They Come* in 1972." Sadly, this comment dismisses the numerous albums Cliff produced between 1972 and 1978. Marcus characterized the work of those six years very harshly: "Cliff, apparently confused by the stardom he'd wanted so long, took a new contract with Warner Bros. and proceeded to make music so dull you couldn't even blame it on an attempt to compromise, to 'reach a broader audience,' to sell out." In a 1984 review for *High Fidelity,* Steven X. Rea cast a condemning glance back through Cliff's career: "The quality of his work . . . has fluctuated dramatically. Most of his late '70s albums are ludicrously overproduced, zealously optimistic, rife with homilies and cornball sentiment."

By 1984, Cliff had returned to Jamaica, where he maintained homes in Montego Bay, Kingston, and Somerton. He continued with his eclecticism, mixing the ethics of Rastafarian life with his adoption of Muslim ideals, living between Jamaica and England, cultivating strong markets in South America, Africa, and continental Europe. His 1984 release *The Power and the Glory,* did better in the States than any album since *The Harder They Come;* it prompted some particularly optimistic statements from Rea, who claimed that it would "bode well for the future of reggae, and the future of popular music," adding, "Cliff appears to be widening his parameters toward a global pop context."

But even this album did not do well enough for Cliff to include any U.S. stops in his 1984 concert tour. The tour took him on 41 stops in Europe over the course of two months, during which he was embraced and encouraged by European audiences. One single from the album, "Reggae Nights," went gold in France, anticipating the excitement that French audiences would display at his concerts.

After another run of albums in the late 1980s, mostly produced with Columbia records, Cliff came on tour again in the United States to promote his 1990 release *Images.* He received favorable reviews for his performances, particularly since he combined his style and reputation with the growing popularity of an important African musician, Fela Anikulapo Kuti. Expectations that this album might be a change for Cliff were based on a change in production; Cliff stopped trying to work under the auspices of large record companies and formed his own company, Cliff Sounds and Films, in order to control the production entirely. But *Images,* where it even received notice, prompted reactions as tepid as his previous albums. Gene Santoro, writing in *Nation,* raved about the *Images* concert, but dismissed the album itself as "uneven."

Ultimately, the sense of unfulfilled critical promise that had hovered over Cliff in 1972 remained two decades later. Still, he is recognized as a leading voice in reggae music and a vital figure in the genre's explosion on the international scene. Of his 1992 release, *Breakout, Pulse!* contributor Doug Wendt wrote, "Cliff is obviously proud to leave the quest for the 'great American crossover album' behind and concentrate on just making great music."

Selected discography

Hard Rock, Island, 1968.
Wonderful World, Beautiful People (includes "Wonderful World, Beautiful People," "Vietnam," and "Many Rivers to Cross"), A&M, 1969.
Another Cycle, 1970.
The Harder They Come (movie soundtrack; includes "Sitting Here in Limbo," "Many Rivers to Cross," and "You Can Get It If You Really Want"), Island, 1972.
Unlimited, Reprise, 1973.
Music Maker, Reprise, 1974.
The Best of Jimmy Cliff/Live in Concert, Reprise, 1976.

Give Thankx, Warner Brothers, 1978.
I Am the Living, MCA, 1981.
Give the People What They Want, MCA, 1981.
Special, Columbia, 1982.
The Power and the Glory (includes "Reggae Nights"), Columbia, 1984.
Cliff Hanger, Columbia, 1985.
Hanging Fire, Columbia, 1988.
Images, Cliff Sounds and Films, 1990.
Breakout, JRS, 1992.

Sources

Books

Davis, Stephen, *Reggae Bloodlines: In Search of the Music and Culture of Jamaica,* Anchor Press, 1979.
The Rolling Stone Encyclopedia of Rock & Roll, edited by Jon Pareles and Patricia Romanowski, Rolling Stone Press/Summit Books, 1983.

Periodicals

High Fidelity, February 1984.
Jet, November 10, 1986.
Nation, August 13-20, 1990.
People, May 24, 1982; August 6, 1984.
Pulse!, August 1992.
Rolling Stone, December 14, 1978.

—*Ondine E. Le Blanc*

Bruce Cockburn

Singer, songwriter, guitarist, activist

Canadian singer-songwriter and virtuoso guitarist Bruce Cockburn is, according to *Maclean's* writer Nicholas Jennings, "a rocker with a mission—a troubadour for the common man." For more than two decades he has written articulate, insightful songs that point out the political and social injustices and inadequacies of the world. "To his credit," remarked Darren Ressler in *Pulse!,* "[Cockburn's] public visage has remained enigmatic as he eschews trends and flash-in-the-pan pop fashionability."

Critics have tried to pigeonhole Cockburn with such labels as folksinger, mystic, and environmentalist prophet. But he has defied definition, just as he has resisted the pressure to make his music conform to popular demand. By sticking uncompromisingly to his own inner truth throughout two decades of recording, by refusing to dilute his angry lyrics and—perhaps costlier in today's pop-rock world—his Christianity, Cockburn has developed an intensely loyal following and great respect within the music industry. But for most of his career he has stood stubbornly on the outskirts of fame.

A dedicated political activist, Cockburn is beginning to reap the rewards that many feel are his due from 20 years of sticking to his convictions. Worldwide sales of his more than 20 records total more than ten million, and his concerts in Australia, South America, and Europe usually draw sell-out crowds. His sudden rise in status, especially in Canada, must seem ironic after years of putting up with comparisons to popular American singers.

Journeyed to Central America

Cockburn, divorced, lives modestly in downtown Toronto with his one daughter. Born on May 27, 1945, he was raised in Ottawa, Ontario. After high school he traveled throughout Europe as a street musician, then studied at Boston's Berklee School of Music. Dropping out after a few years, Cockburn returned to Ottawa to play organ in a Top Forty cover band and harmonica in a blues band; he also began writing songs seriously. "About 1969," the singer recalled to Ressler, "I was in a state where I was so choked up with my songs that I just wanted to record them to forget them. When I hooked up with the means to do that, it didn't have the effect of allowing me to forget—people wanted to hear the songs that they liked from the album all of the time!"

Cockburn's writing, tending to the folky and romantic at first, has taken on an increasingly serious, often angry and militant quality over time. He is not only involved with political issues—frequently visiting Third World countries and speaking out on their behalf—but also with such environmental causes as stopping the destruction of tropical rain forests and cleaning the Exxon oil spill off the Alaskan coast. He has expressed that his activism was heightened after the birth of his daughter. "When my daughter was born, it sort of forced me to step back and look around," he told Ressler. "I mean, the first headline that you see is bound to threaten this precious life. . . . At the time, everything seemed very urgent and I started thinking about the world and the future. For me, that was really the beginning to take the need to act politically seriously."

Cockburn perhaps garnered the most attention for his four trips to Central America in the 1980s. After his first journey, during which he observed a Guatemalan military attack on a refugee camp in Mexico, the musician wrote one of his most popular, politically volatile anthems, "If I Had a Rocket Launcher." Subsequent visits to such countries as Nicaragua and Guatemala prompted Cockburn's "growing disdain for U.S. policy in Central America," according to Jennings. In addition to meeting with a Canadian foreign affairs minister to discuss that country's Central American policies, Cockburn, whose Juno Awards—the Canadian equivalent of the Grammys—began accumulating, increasingly addressed political issues on his albums, including *Stealing Fire* of 1984 and *World of Wonders* of 1986.

Proponent of Change

But Cockburn can also show a gentler side in his music. When not outraged, he writes songs about the simple day-to-day experiences common among all people. Scott Alarik of the *Boston Globe* described this marriage of emotions: "The presence of topicality in his love songs, and of personal love in his political songs gives Cockburn's work a total vision rare among political songwriters. . . . Through it all is a raw anger . . . the real anger of a feeling heart."

Despite the serious message of Cockburn's songs, they are written in the easygoing manner of a storyteller. The *Washington Post's* Geoffrey Himes noted, "Without any overt pleas for sympathy, he simply sets a scene, tells a story and lets listeners draw their own conclusions. . . . Cockburn's songs are marked by a powerful sense of place. In a few verses, he draws a vivid picture of a muddy road through the Amazon, a crowded street in Tibet or a bird-laden jungle as he weaves Asian, Latin and Dixieland motifs into his propulsive folk-rock."

Cockburn feels that songs can be a catalyst for social change. "What's important to remember," he expressed to Andrew Watt of Australia's *In Press,* "is that [as a singer/song-writer] you're either doing something to change the status quo, or you're reinforcing the status quo and as a human being it's your choice to make." Cockburn, who indicated to Ressler that "change is the theme that runs through all of my albums," has worked tirelessly to promote reform through his music.

Recorded First Album in the U.S.

Two years after touring to promote his 1989 album *Big Circumstance*—a work filled with songs contemplating such topics as rain forest depletion, Central American violence, and the Chernobyl nuclear accident in the former Soviet Union—Cockburn released the acclaimed *Nothing But a Burning Light.* The singer had been wanting to record an album somewhere other than his hometown of Toronto and headed for Los Angeles, hooking up with producer T-Bone Burnett and organist Booker T. Jones. Cockburn commented on the content of the LP in *Pulse!:* "In some ways it's a return to a rootsier, more direct style of songwriting that's folksier than my last few albums. . . . The songs are much more concrete than ones I'd written back in the old days."

Richard C. Walls of *Musician,* pointing out Cockburn's tendency toward political and social preachiness, found *Nothing But a Burning Light* to be "still dripping slightly, from the slough of moral goopiness." Nevertheless the reviewer declared, "Cockburn demonstrates once again that he's an excellent guitarist." Labeling the musician "one of the undersung heroes in the fading art of the well-tuned song," *Down Beat's* Josef Woodard found the album Cockburn's "most satisfying collection to date."

Although in the early 1990s Cockburn was concentrating more on songwriting than his political involvements, there is no doubt that the Canadian rock star will continue to play an activist role, giving voice to the hearts and consciences of those who care about the fate of their planet and fellow human beings. Acknowledging the interconnectedness of his activism and his music career, Cockburn told Ressler, "To me, all of my songs spring from the same place—they're the product of some kind of life experience."

Selected discography

Bruce Cockburn, Epic, 1970.
High Winds White Sky, 1971, reissued, Columbia, 1991.
Sunwheel Dance, Epic, 1972.
Night Vision, True North, 1973.
Salt, Sun and Time, 1974.
Joy Will Find a Way, 1975, reissued, 1988.
In the Falling Dark, Island, 1976, reissued, 1988.
Circles in the Stream, 1977.
Further Adventures Of, 1978.

Dancing in the Dragon's Jaws, Millenium, 1979, reissued, Columbia, 1991.
Humans, 1980, reissued, 1988.
Mummy Dust, 1981.
Resume, 1981.
Inner City Front, 1981, reissued, 1988.
The Trouble With Normal, 1983, reissued, Gold Castle, 1989.
Stealing Fire, 1984, reissued, Columbia, 1991.
World of Wonders, 1986.
Waiting for a Miracle, 1987, reissued, Gold Castle, 1989.
Big Circumstance, 1989, reissued, Columbia, 1991.
Bruce Cockburn Live, Gold Castle, 1990.
Nothing But a Burning Light, Columbia, 1991.

Sources

Atlantic Journal, April 22, 1989.
Boston Globe, March 4, 1989.
Down Beat, February 1992.
In Press, June 14, 1989.
Kingston Whig Standard, May 26, 1990.
Maclean's, February 27, 1989.
Metropolis, January 26, 1989.
Musician, December 1991; February 1992.
Pulse!, December 1991.
Sun-Times (Chicago), March 17, 1989.
Washington Post, April 6, 1989.

—*Heather Rhodes*

Bootsy Collins

Singer, bass guitarist, producer

"**M**y whole thing is like a fantasy cartoon," funk rocker extraordinaire Bootsy Collins told Mikal Gilmore in *Rolling Stone.* "It's like Caspar the Friendly Ghost. The kids loved the cat. He didn't want to scare nobody. All he wanted to do was help out." Having played bass guitar with the "Godfather of Soul" James Brown while still in his teens, Collins found his audience in the "geepies"—his term for his six- to twelve-year-old fans—when he joined George Clinton's rising groups Parliament and Funkadelic (collectively known as P-Funk). In 1976 the singer went solo with his own group, the Rubber Band, an extension of P-Funk. Collins is renowned for the appealing whimsy of his live performances and his trademark—star-shaped, rhinestone-studded mirror glasses. As he explained to John Leland in *Vogue,* "It's not just about doing records. It's got to be a circus, with a three-headed man and everything."

Born in Cincinnati, Ohio, on October 26, 1951, William "Bootsy" Collins followed in the footsteps of his older brother, Phelps "Catfish" Collins, who played guitar. Phelps introduced Bootsy to rock and roll when he brought home a recording of Lonnie Mack. During adolescence, both brothers played sessions at Cincinnati's King Records studio. In 1969 James Brown entered King Records in search of a bass player. After he heard the teenaged Bootsy, Brown used him on the cut "Lickin' Stick." In *Interview* magazine, Greg Goldin recounted Collins's "laying down a legendary groove" on the song. Brown hired Bootsy to fill the bass guitarist spot in his back-up band, the JBs, along with Bootsy's brother Phelps. "It had something to do with being in the right place at the right time," Collins told Goldin.

From the late 1960s to early 1970s, Brown pioneered the shift from "negro" to "black" music, reflecting the change in racial perceptions in the United States and the growing diversity of black artists' audiences. "He was in control of everything that was going down with him, and I dug him for that," Collins explained to Gilmore. Brown and the JBs were the masters of the new electric music known as "funk." Membership in the JBs fostered long-term relationships between Bootsy and fellow musicians, including trombonist Fred Wesley and saxophonist Maceo Parker.

Instigated P-Funk Whimsy

Bootsy left the Brown organization in 1971. Rather than back the Spinners, he decided instead to join bandleader Clinton's funk groups Parliament and Funkadelic. "I thought, 'Wow . . . Funkadelic . . . acid trip. . .!' That's where we was at," Collins related to Gilmore. Promoting his musical growth, Clinton let Bootsy write songs and

For the Record. . .

Born William Collins, October 26, 1951, in Cincinnati, OH.

Funk singer, songwriter, bass guitarist. Joined brother Phelps "Catfish" Collins playing sessions at King Records, Cincinnati, during the late 1960s; discovered by James Brown while at King Records, 1969, and joined Brown's band, the JB's; joined George Clinton's bands Parliament and Funkadelic, 1971; solo contract, Warner Brothers, 1976; formed the Rubber Band, 1976; producer for musicians, including James Brown, Sly Stewart, Johnnie Taylor, the Sweat Band, Zapp, Malcolm McLaren, Iggy Pop, Herbie Hancock, and Keith Richards; sideman for musicians, including Maceo Parker.

Addresses: *Record company*—Warner Bros. Records, 3300 Warner Blvd., Burbank, CA 91510. *Agent*—Triad Artists, Inc., 10100 Santa Monica Blvd., 16th floor, Los Angeles, CA 90067.

arrangements. "When we were doing funk . . . it was a nasty word," Collins explained to Goldin. "It wasn't legal then. It wasn't the thing to play on the radio." Collins was the coauthor of most of Parliament's material when the pivotal album *Mothership Connection* was recorded.

Post-Jimi Hendrix but influenced by acid rock replete with sexual imagery, Clinton's group played party music with more message than the tracks of the disco scene. The pounding funk beat and dazzling electronic effects enhanced the musical scenarios the band created with their bizarre stage personalities. "In the prevideo epoch," summarized Goldin, "the band was outrageous on stage—sometimes garbed in diapers, their mothership flying saucer descending—playing funk, funk, funk. It was danceable psychedelics long before Prince, Oingo Boingo, or the Sex Pistols broke through the conformity, and the *uniform*-ity, of the disco 1970s."

Concocted "Bootzilla"

Collins commanded the crowds during Funkadelic concerts as his stage persona "Bootzilla," a sci-fi cartoon character with an outrageous wardrobe. He sported his trademark "Bootzilla" sunglasses—the frames were cut-outs of stars decorated with rhinestones. An additional rhinestone star adorned the center of his forehead. Collins's finery was influential enough to reach

the Orient in the mid-seventies, where Japan boasted a Bootsy nightclub frequented by dreadlocked Japanese males clothed in Bootsy regalia.

When Clinton signed a recording contract with Warner Brothers for Parliament/Funkadelic in 1976, he negotiated an independent, solo contract for Collins. Collins continued working with Funkadelic, and Funkadelic band members Wesley and Parker, among others, recorded with him as his back-up group, the Rubber Band. That same year, Bootsy released his first album, *Stretchin' Out in Bootsy's Rubber Band.* Gilmore assessed the two albums that followed, *Ahh . . . the Name Is Bootsy, Baby!* and *Bootsy? Player of the Year*, in *Rolling Stone* as honing "Bootsy's sense of the absurd into a more sensually playful and childlike jargon."

Disillusioned Midway Through Career

Though Collins netted several hit singles and gold albums with the Rubber Band—which eclipsed Funkadelic in popularity—he quit performing in the early 1980s. "I got stuck in a role and I couldn't get out," he divulged to Leland. Bootsy lived with his mother and relaxed with his hunting dogs for eight years. When he released the album *What's Bootsy Doin'?* in 1988, Collins told Leland, "Now, I think I know how to hang Bootsy up when I get off the stage." Goldin noted, however, that Collins had not given up his "quirky, humorous approach" since his return to recording. "I look at it like this," Collins disclosed to Goldin: "They say it couldn't be done. I say if we ain't at the party, there is none. It's putting the fun back into what is supposed to be gone, what is not supposed to be around here now."

Throughout his musical career, he has continued to find opportunities to serve as sideman and producer for an impressive list of diverse musicians, including Sly Stewart, Johnnie Taylor, the Sweat Band, Zapp, Iggy Pop, Malcolm McLaren, Herbie Hancock, and Keith Richards. In the early nineties, he joined JB cohort Fred Wesley and other musicians to back up their fellow JB alumnus Maceo Parker on his highly touted album *Roots Revisited.* "Everybody's got [some] kid in them, and that's where I've placed my head," Collins disclosed to Gilmore. "When it's time to be a man, I'll be a man. But other than that, I'm a geepie at heart." Mindful of his image, Collins shuns booze and drugs, but his style remains the substance of fun.

Selected discography

(With Parliament) *Mothership Connection*, Casablanca, 1975.
Stretchin' Out in Bootsy's Rubber Band, Warner Bros., 1976.

Ahh . . . the Name Is Bootsy, Baby!, Warner Bros., 1977.
Bootsy? Player of the Year, Warner Bros., 1978.
Ultra Wave, Warner Bros., 1980.
The One Giveth and the Count Taketh Away, Warner Bros., 1982.
What's Bootsy Doin'? (includes "Party On Plastic"), Columbia, 1988.
Jungle Bass.
Talk Is Cheap.

Contributed bass and guitar tracks to Deee-lite's *World Clique,* Elektra, 1990, and appeared in the Deee-lite video "Groove Is in the Heart." Also contributed to Material release *The Third Power,* Axiom/Island, 1991, and to Maceo Parker's *Roots Revisited.*

Sources

Books

Rose, Cynthia, *Living in America,* Serpent's Tail, 1990.

Periodicals

Down Beat, October 1990.
Interview, November 1988.
Rolling Stone, April 6, 1978; November 3, 1988.
Stereo Review, March 1991.
Vogue, December 1988.

—Marjorie Burgess

Alice Cooper

Rock singer

Alice Cooper—the "King of Shock Rock," "Prince of Splatter," and "Godfather of Trash Heavy Rock"—appeared on the Los Angeles music scene just as the national passion for the flower power of the late 1960s began to wane; his arrival was nothing less than an explosive changing of the pop-music guard. In 1968, the year Cooper relocated from Phoenix, Arizona, to Los Angeles, the stages of Hollywood's Sunset Strip nightclubs were populated by laid-back, well-groomed bands featuring a jangly guitar sound. As might be expected, the decidedly un-jangly Alice Cooper band—named, according to *The Rolling Stone Encyclopedia of Rock & Roll,* for a 17th-century witch whom a Ouija board had revealed was reincarnated as the group's lead singer—was at first poorly received; in *Prime Cuts,* a Cooper video documentary, the former bandleader said, "It used to be the hip thing to walk out on us." Of the group's early reception, he added, "No one could clear a room faster than the Alice Cooper band."

Cooper and his cohorts were the antithesis of what was expected from rock bands at the time—owing more to loud, crude, Detroit groups like Iggy and the Stooges and the MC5 than anything sunny California had to offer. From the beginning the group displayed a theatrical bent, emphasizing visual aspects as well as musical: An early video of the band from *Prime Cuts* shows Cooper dressed as Satan—complete with horns and pitchfork. Not surprisingly, the band is often cited as the origin of shock rock. It was manager Shep Gordon's idea of cultivating this negative image that ultimately led to Cooper's success. Cooper and his early band were among the first to exaggerate the androgynous aspects of the rock and roll image; they looked almost as much like women—though nightmarishly so—as they did guitar warriors. One need only look at groups like Motley Crue and Poison to realize the impact Cooper has had on rock style.

Gallows and Guillotines

In 1971, after releasing two albums on musician Frank Zappa's Straight label, the Alice Cooper band signed to Warner Bros. Records. The label provided the group with a substantial budget to further explore their theatrical leanings. Stage settings became as extensive as those of a Broadway show. One notorious effect was the gallows the Cooper band brought along on the tour supporting their 1971 album *Killer:* At the culmination of the song "Dead Babies," Cooper would slip his head into a noose and hang himself. Two years later, in support of the *Billion Dollar Babies* album, Cooper outdid the gallows effect by utilizing a guillotine; a roadie dressed as an executioner would parade around the stage afterwards with the bloody head of the pop

For the Record. . .

B orn Vincent Damian Furnier, December 25, 1945 (one source says February 4, 1948), in Detroit, MI; son of a protestant minister; married, two children.

Began career during high school as member of the Earwigs; group relocated to Los Angeles, 1968, and changed name to the Spiders, then the Nazz, then Alice Cooper; released first two records on Frank Zappa's Straight Records label; signed to Warner Bros., 1971; launched solo career and released first solo album, *Welcome to My Nightmare*, 1975; moved to MCA records; moved to Epic Records, and released *Trash*, 1989. Appeared in films *Sgt. Pepper's Lonely Hearts Club Band*, 1978, *Sextette*, 1979, *Roadie*, 1980, *Monster Dog*, 1982, *Decline of Western Civilization Part II*, 1988, *Wayne's World*, 1992, and *Nightmare on Elm Street Part VI*, 1992.

Addresses: *Home*—Scottsdale, AZ. *Record company*—Epic Records, 51 West 52nd St., New York, NY 10019.

troversial singer—much to the audiences mixture of delight and repugnance. Cooper would emerge soon after his "beheading" dressed in a white suit with tails to sing the song "Elected."

With the Alice Cooper band, Cooper earned chart success many times. There were two hit singles from 1970's *Love it to Death* album, the psychedelic "Caught in A Dream" and "I'm Eighteen," which *Creem* magazine said was "like a [rock and roll pioneer] Chuck Berry poem, timeless as far as anthems were concerned." The following year's *Killer* was an even greater sensation, boasting "Under My Wheels" as it's main selling point. Celebrated rock critic Lester Bangs in *Rolling Stone* called the song "a [Rolling] Stones classic translated into Alice Cooper's obsession with machines and technology." In *Stairway to Hell,* a book notating the top-500 best heavy metal records of all time, author Chuck Eddy called *Killer,* "faux Detroit." Indeed, of all the Cooper band LPs, *Killer* is perhaps the most indebted to the raunchy guitar-drenched sound made famous in the Motor City.

"School's Out" a Hit

It was the 1972 release, *School's Out*, however, that culled the Cooper band's biggest hit—the anthem-like title cut "School's Out." Describing this paean to youth rebellion, *Rolling Stone* contributor Ben Gerson called it "an instant classic as well as an instant manifesto."

Melody Maker deemed the song "rough as a ropeburn." Continuing the hit parade, 1973 saw the release of *Billion Dollar Babies,* which featured the chart-toppers "Elected" and "Hello, Hooray." The tide turned somewhat, however, in 1974, when the Cooper band released what would be their last album, *Muscle of Love.* Though ambitiously packaged in an oversized cardboard box, even perennially ardent fans like *Rolling Stone* scribe Lenny Kaye thought it a mediocre effort. "It's not a bad collation," wrote Kaye, "but the very safety that *Muscle of Love* implies makes me apprehensive for the band's creative future. Has success spoiled Alice Cooper?"

Although the Cooper band reached the mid-1970s rich and famous—having by the end of 1973 earned, according to *Spin* magazine, upwards of 17 million dollars—all was not well within the group. In *Billion Dollar Baby,* a book documenting the final tour of Alice Cooper—the band—Chicago journalist Bob Greene revealed that the rest of the band resented Cooper's star treatment and what they felt was their relegation to backup status. Though the group disbanded amicably in 1975, Cooper's girlfriend from that period, Cynthia Lang, sued Cooper four years later, according to *Variety,* for three million dollars, money he had earned during the tenure of their relationship.

Launched Solo Career

The groundwork laid by the Alice Cooper band helped build the foundation for Cooper's solo career, which has spanned nearly two decades and boasts more than 20 albums. In an attempt to market his solo image, Cooper appeared on the game show *Hollywood Squares* and on the Pro-Am golf circuit. He also made certain to publicly insist that Alice Cooper was strictly an onstage character, a rock and roll alter ego. Of Cooper's solo image, *Rolling Stone* contributor Chris Holdenfield offered, "Although Alice uses sex, confusion, and death as crowd pleasers, it's only a variation on the Hot Shot Singer formula, popular from [Frank] Sinatra to [Jim] Morrison. Alice Cooper is believable because he doesn't believe."

The release of Cooper's first solo album, 1975's *Welcome To My Nightmare*, was accompanied by a successful prime-time television special. The album contained an unlikely hit, the ballad "Only Women Bleed." Other cuts demonstrated Cooper's still-sharp penchant for theatrics, including the sinister "Black Widow"—which in concert featured human-sized spiders crawling across a giant web suspended across the stage—and the surreal "Escape," where in live performance Cooper was chased by a ten-foot-tall one-eyed monster.

In keeping with the punk/new-wave era of the late 1970s and early 1980s, Cooper in 1980 released *Flush the Fashion*. *Flush* is best remembered for the single "Clones (We Are All)"; its liberal use of the Moog synthesizer and monotone vocal style were both indicative of the popular "cold wave" style of the day. David Fricke of *Rolling Stone* reported that *Flush the Fashion* "wisely scrapped the flatulent vaudeville trappings and tragicomic pretensions of [Cooper's] late seventies work and reassumed the punk mantle he wore when the original Alice band was cutting a [Civil War Union] General Sherman-like swath."

First Substantial Film Role

1982 was a banner year for Cooper. *Zipper Catches Skin* got good reviews; *Melody Maker* contributor Steve Sutherland called the record "if not a 'School's Out'-style renaissance, at least a gloriously ghoulish lapse from the wimpy ex-lush confessional back to the ham homicidal." The "ex-lush" characterization made reference to Cooper's 1978 treatment for alcoholism, which he chronicled in that year's *From the Inside*. Nonetheless, Sutherland seemed to have been letting up on Cooper after calling 1981's *Special Forces* "too inoffensive to turn many heads." 1982 was also the year Cooper took his first substantial film role, portraying a vampire in a Brazilian gore flick called *Monster Dog*. Though Cooper later condemned the film—expressing in *Rolling Stone* his disappointment with the film's producers for not keeping it's circulation limited to Brazil—he admitted his excitement at the prospect of satisfying his longtime acting bug.

Although Cooper's impact on the music scene has been strong and fairly consistent throughout his career, reviews of his work have been mixed; there exists an enduring debate over the value of Cooper's solo work versus his material with the Alice Cooper band; a *Melody Maker* review of the 1986 LP *Constrictor* remarked, "One does not instinctively judge Alice with regard to competition from outside, he is judged simply by his own standards, in competition only with himself." A review of the same record in *Creem* more explicitly held the singer up for comparison to his group work: "I find *Constrictor* pretty unlistenable, it probably meets the heavy metal standard of today, but there's about as much similarity between old and new Alice Cooper here as there is between Elvis Presley and ['lite' metal rocker] Jon Bon Jovi." Like comments—this time about 1989's *Trash*—came from Melody Maker's John Wilde, who lamented, "There's something unconvincing being

ic about the fact that Alice Cooper will still be puking blood out into the front row of seats when he's 80, but he'll never write a 'School's Out' again." Perhaps *Rolling Stone* contributor Tom Carson, in longing for a time Cooper had moved beyond, best illuminated the issue in his review of 1979's *From the Inside*: "Alice Cooper was our last great juvenile delinquent, and that's what kids loved him for. The trouble with his recent work . . . isn't so much a failure of imagination as it is of showmanship. Cooper's still pushing anarchy, but now he wants to do it politely. And who ever listens to a polite anarchist?"

All-Star Collaborations

Trash, Cooper's first release for Epic Records, started a tradition of extensive collaboration with other prominent artists. Steven Tyler of Aerosmith accompanied Cooper on "Hell Is Living Without You," a ballad co-written by Jon Bon Jovi and guitarist Richie Sambora, and "Poison," the smash single from the album, the video of which was broadcast regularly on MTV, featured the

---

> *"It used to be the hip thing to walk out on us. No one could clear a room faster."*

---

backing vocals of Bon Jovi. 1991's *Hey Stoopid!* boasted a stellar studio lineup that included metal elder statesman Ozzy Osbourne, who sang, and Slash from Guns and Roses, who played guitar on the title track. Guitar aces Joe Satriani and Steve Vai lent dueling guitars to "Feed My Frankenstein," and Motley Crue guitarist Mick Mars contributed licks to "Die For You." *Hard Force* magazine called *Hey Stoopid!* "the best since *Welcome to My Nightmare,* a vicious guitar record."

Promotion for *Hey Stoopid!* was characteristically spectacular. Cooper took to the streets, turning up in various public places to perform songs from the album and generally wreak havoc. Dubbing the September, 1991, tour the "Nightmare on Your Street," he performed at 8:45 in the morning in the parking lot of Los Angeles radio station KLOS, causing a standstill in rush-hour traffic. In New York City, Cooper tempted fate by playing in Times Square on Friday the 13th. Confused onlookers in Detroit were treated to a concert on the roof of the local Sound Warehouse record store, and in Towson, Maryland, Cooper held forth on the steps of the county courthouse.

Further promotion for *Hey Stoopid!* came in the form of a cameo role in director Penelope Spheeris's blockbuster *Wayne's World*. In the film, Cooper performed the song "Feed My Frankenstein" and offered the starstruck protagonists an impromptu backstage lesson on the history of Milwaukee worthy of the best high school geography teacher. Commenting in *Rolling Stone* on the head-banging community-access television hosts portrayed in the film, Cooper said, "I like Wayne and Garth, I meet people like them all the time, they are my audience."

And because—or in spite—of his over-the-top image, Cooper's fans seem to be able to relate to Alice as well. Cooper has endured because he consistently plays the type of villain or monster that audiences can't help but cheer. By innovating a diabolic, yet charismatic, character back in the seventies, he has become a legendary figure in rock music. *Melody Maker* commented aptly on the universal appeal of Cooper's persona, allowing, "There has to be an Alice Cooper just like there has to be a Father Christmas.

Selected discography

With the Alice Cooper band

Pretties for You, Straight, 1969.
Easy Action, Straight, 1970.
Love It to Death, Warner Bros., 1971.
Killer, Warner Bros., 1971.
School's Out, Warner Bros., 1972.
Billion Dollar Babies, Warner Bros., 1973.
Muscle of Love, Warner Bros., 1974.
Alice Cooper's Greatest Hits, Warner Bros., 1974.
Live at the Whisky, reissue, Bizarre/Straight/Rhino, 1992.

Solo LPs

Welcome to My Nightmare, Atlantic, 1975.

Alice Cooper Goes to Hell, Warner Bros., 1976.
Lace and Whiskey, Warner Bros., 1977.
The Alice Cooper Show, Warner Bros., 1977.
From the Inside, Warner Bros., 1978.
Flush the Fashion, Warner Bros., 1980.
Special Forces, Warner Bros., 1981.
Zipper Catches Skin, Warner Bros., 1982.
Da Da, Warner Bros., 1983.
Constrictor, MCA, 1986.
Raise Your Fist and Yell, MCA, 1987.
Trash, Epic, 1989.
Hey Stoopid!, Epic, 1991.

Sources

Books

Eddy, Chuck, *Stairway to Hell,* Harmony Books, 1990.
Greene, Bob, *Billion Dollar Baby,* Signet, 1975.
The Rolling Stone Encyclopedia of Rock & Roll, edited by Jon Pareles and Patricia Romanowski, Rolling Stone Press/Summit Books, 1983.

Periodicals

Creem, March 1987.
Hard Force, October 1991.
Melody Maker, January 7, 1978; September 19, 1981; October 2, 1982; October 25, 1986; April 16, 1988; November 7, 1987; August 19, 1989.
Rolling Stone, January 6, 1972; March 30, 1972; September 28, 1972; August 21, 1980; October 31, 1991; March 19, 1992.
Spin, November 1989.
Variety, June 22, 1977.

Additional information for this profile was obtained from the videocassette *Prime Cuts,* Epic Video, 1991.

—*Barry C. Henssler*

Robert Cray

Singer, guitarist

In the 1960s a young Robert Cray, snooping through his parents' record collection, discovered the music of Chicago bluesmen Buddy Guy, Magic Sam, and Otis Rush. Cray was immediately captivated by the sound, and his music bears the distinct mark of the blues of that era. After graduating from high school, he formed the Robert Cray Band and began playing the blues in clubs and at festivals all over the Pacific Northwest. Taking the early blues music that originated in the impoverished Mississippi Delta region of the southern United States, and blending it with soul, jazz, and rhythm and blues, Cray has developed a style that appeals to a wide range of listeners—to which the popularity of his albums can attest.

Cray's comfortable, middle-class upbringing stands in sharp contrast to the lifestyle of the original blues singers, many of whom eked out a living working by day on farms and plantations in the South during the Great Depression. Cray was born to a relatively well off family in Columbus, Georgia, but being an Army "brat" he moved frequently as a youth before the family settled in the Pacific Northwest. Earlier, during a stay in Germany, Cray studied classical piano. Unable to understand German television, he entertained himself by exploring his parents' varied record collection, which included a wide range of black artists from Sam Cooke to Ray Charles.

Cray soon persuaded his mother to buy him a guitar, which he practiced faithfully. To the shy, often uprooted teen, music offered one of the few constants in his life. In high school, Cray joined his first band. They performed an eclectic mix of rock and roll and rhythm and blues. The Cray family then moved to Tacoma, Washington, where Cray joined another band.

Became a Blues "Fanatic"

Around the same time, Cray went rummaging through his father's record collection looking for some new influences. He discovered the music of Muddy Waters and Howlin' Wolf. "Then and there is when I became a fanatic," Cray revealed to J. O. Considine in *Musician.* "Nobody could tell me that anything was better than blues." The young musician even convinced his high school classmates to invite blues musician Albert Collins to play at their graduation party.

In 1969, Cray met Richard Cousins, another local musician. Over the years a musical relationship developed, and they started playing in local bars while studying the blues. "We became re-educated," Cray told Mikal Gilmore in *Rolling Stone.* "We began figuring out who people like Sonny Boy Williamson, Robert Johnson and

Tampa Red were. I mean, it's embarrassing to admit, but at one time we'd thought these songs were written by the Allman Brothers. It was kind of funny to be learning this stuff in reverse." In 1974, they went to Eugene, Oregon, hoping to get more gigs in the progressive college town.

The Robert Cray Band featured Cousins on bass and Tom Murphy on drums. The shy Cray was on guitars and vocals. "When I realized I had to be the frontman, I was scared to death. I couldn't look at anybody, and my teeth would chatter so bad, Richard had to do all the announcing of songs," Cray admitted in *Rolling Stone.* The band got their big break when Albert Collins asked them to open for him on his Pacific Northwest tour. Collins "showed us the ropes—how to collect money, and how to deal with the bar owners. He's like our father," Cray told Considine. Cray was also noticed by John Belushi, who happened to be in the area during the filming of the 1978 frat-house spoof *Animal House.* Belushi gave him a small part in the movie and shortly after formed the Blues Brothers act on *Saturday Night Live.*

Landed First Recording Contract

The year 1978 turned out to be a pivotal one for the fledgling band. Playing at the San Francisco Blues Festival, they caught the eye of Bruce Bromberg, a promoter for Tomato Records. Bromberg wanted to produce the band on his own label, but mounting financial problems led to the completion of their recording project on the Tomato label. The resulting album, *Who's Been Talkin'*, was finished in 1978 but not released until 1980. Shortly afterward, Tomato Records folded and the recording vanished.

The Robert Cray Band went back to playing blues festivals and clubs for a while until they ran into Bromberg again and agreed to have him produce their next album. *Bad Influence* was finished in 1983 and released on Bromberg's HighTone label. The recording won the band some notoriety, as well as tours in England and Japan and a few dates with Eric Clapton. Gilmore praised the work in *Rolling Stone,* indicating that "with its emphasis on evocative melodies and well-drawn characterizations, the album came across as the first major effort at revitalizing and advancing the blues song form in many, many years." The album won four W.C. Handy awards and became a hit in England.

In 1985, Cray released *False Accusations* with a line-up of Cray, Cousins, Peter Boe on keyboards, and David Olson on drums. Cray broke ground by including only original material on this album instead of covers of blues classics. The album was quite popular, ending up in the top 200 for the year.

Success continued to follow the band. Their 1986 album, *Strong Persuader,* went platinum, won a Grammy, and was in the top 20. Cray continued to stray from blues tradition by adding other influences to the music. "Our music is a combination of blues, rhythm and blues, jazz, and rock and roll. I think it's kind of hard to put a label, an exact tag on it. I think that's made it a lot more accessible to a lot of people," Cray commented in *EM.* Dan Forte of *Guitar Player* praised the album's deviation from standard blues form, saying, "On the one hand, *Strong Persuader* doesn't contain a single stock blues tune, but on the other, it's all blues—the blues of the '80s. The singer/guitarist is true to the genre's spirit without resorting to its standard form."

Acclaim for New Sound

Cray scored again with *Don't Be Afraid of the Dark* in 1988. In spite of the band's success, though, they failed to reach a large black audience. "We're not getting that much air play on urban radio stations," he commented in *EM.* "I can understand why, it's not too modern of a sound. But still I'm a little disappointed." In 1990, Cray decided to shake things up within his band by recruiting the Memphis Horns to join the group and adding keyboardist Jimmy Pugh, drummer Kevin Hayes, and guitarist Tim Kaihatsu to the lineup. Cray debuted the new group on *Midnight Stroll,* a recording he described in the *Detroit Free Press* as "extremely funky."

Bill Milkowski in *Down Beat* was thrilled with the new sound, commenting that "Robert Cray is capable of rising above polite radioplay fare and delivering an honest-to-goodness soul-stirring performance. . . . [He] digs deep on *Midnight Stroll* and comes up with the genuine goods." With a string of successful albums, Cray no longer has to worry about getting money from bar owners. Being in a classic genre like the blues has helped him allay fears about the fickleness of fame. "I don't have to worry about trying to slip into Spandex," he commented to Steve Hochman in the *Los Angeles Times.* "You know what I look at? I look at my friend John Lee Hooker and the success he's having now. He's 73. He doesn't have to act like he's in his 20s."

Selected discography

Who's Been Talkin', Tomato, 1978.
Bad Influence, HighTone, 1983.
False Accusations, HighTone, 1985.
(With guitarists Albert Collins and Johnny Copeland) *Showdown,* Alligator, 1985.
Strong Persuader, HighTone/Mercury, 1986.
Don't Be Afraid of the Dark, HighTone/Mercury, 1988.
Midnight Stroll, PolyGram, 1990.
I Was Warned, Mercury, 1992.

Sources

Books

Newsmakers 1988, Gale, 1989.

Periodicals

Detroit Free Press, March 30, 1987; November 7, 1990.
Down Beat, March 1984; August 1984; March 1987; May 1988; January 1991.
Ebony Male, February 1989.
Guitar Player, May 1987.
Living Blues, March/April 1990.
Los Angeles Times, December 5, 1990.
Musician, April 1987.
People, April 13, 1987.
Pulse!, March 1992.
Rolling Stone, December 4, 1986; June 18, 1987; November 16, 1989; June 27, 1991.

—Nancy Rampson

Rodney Crowell

Singer, songwriter, producer

In 1988 Rodney Crowell began to emerge from his image as a songwriter and producer for other country stars. After releasing four relatively unsuccessful albums for Warner Bros. and Columbia, the talented Crowell finally found his niche with the release of *Diamonds and Dirt,* a work that scored four consecutive Number One country singles and garnered numerous award nominations. Since then, Rodney Crowell has achieved a dream he long held dear—to perform his own songs and be recognized as a singer and entertainer in his own right.

As Alanna Nash noted in *Stereo Review,* Crowell had been "one of the most respected songwriters and producers in the business for at least a decade." The list of stars Crowell has assisted with songs or production work is impressive: Emmylou Harris, Waylon Jennings, the Oak Ridge Boys, the Nitty Gritty Dirt Band, Sissy Spacek, Bob Seger, and Crowell's second wife, Roseanne Cash. Unfortunately Crowell watched in frustration as these other performers scored Number One hits with songs he had composed and often recorded himself on his own albums. In *Behind Closed Doors: Talking With the Legends of Country Music,* Crowell told Nash that he has finally overcome the dissatisfaction that plagued him before he became known as a singer. "I want to know how to enjoy the successes I *do* have, no matter how big or small they are," he said. "I think that's the key. That's the ultimate thing to me."

Headed for Nashville

Crowell was born in Houston, Texas. His family was full of musicians—his grandfather played banjo, his grandmother was a guitarist, and his father made pocket change as a sideman in the city's numerous honky tonks. "My dad had [musical] talent, but he went for something else," Crowell related to Nash. "He went for that construction job, where he could make some money, and that kept him there. So he never did really pursue his dream to be a singer, or a country music star. But I know that he really wanted to, had circumstances been different. So I think he enjoys it through me."

By the time he was 11 years old, Crowell was playing in his father's band, banging drums in Houston's portside bars. Unlike his father, however, Crowell was determined to earn a living as a musician, and he was strongly influenced by such rock and roll artists as Elvis Presley and the Beatles. Crowell originally wanted to play pure rock music, but he gravitated to the country-rock style just as the movement was gaining strength. In the early 1970s Crowell bid his family farewell and left

Born in 1950 in Houston, TX; son of a James Crowell (a construction worker and part-time musician); married second wife, Rosanne Cash, 1979 (divorced, March, 1992); children: (second marriage) Hannah, Caitlyn, Chelsea. *Education:* Attended Stephen F. Austin College, Nacogdoches, TX.

Singer, songwriter, producer, and guitarist, 1965—. Moved to Nashville, c. 1970; performed on writer's night at Bishop's American Pub and worked briefly as a songwriter for Jerry Reed's Vector Music Company. Joined Emmylou Harris's Hot Band, 1974, as songwriter, backup guitarist, and vocalist. Solo artist, 1977—. Signed with Warner Bros. Records, 1977; released first album, *I Ain't Livin' Long Like This,* 1978. Had first Top Ten country hit with "It's Such a Small World," 1988, a duet with Rosanne Cash. Has written and/or produced songs for numerous country stars, including Rosanne Cash, the Nitty Gritty Dirt Band, Emmylou Harris, the Oak Ridge Boys, Bob Seger, and Waylon Jennings.

Addresses: *Agent*—Bill Ruff, William Morris Agency, Inc., 1350 Sixth Ave., New York, NY 10019. *Record company*—Columbia Records, 1801 Century Park West, Los Angeles, CA 90067.

for Nashville with some songs he had written. "I wasn't worried about keeping a job," he divulged in *Behind Closed Doors.* "I didn't mind moving to Nashville and sleeping in my car for a while. That was an adventure to me. The first time I moved to Nashville, in [1972], I slept in my car for the first two months I was here. And I was having a ball. I wasn't worried about security at all. The world was my oyster."

Crowell supported himself by washing dishes in restaurants, and he also worked briefly for Jerry Reed's music publishing company. By 1973 he was sharing living quarters and creative ideas with some other budding Nashville writers, including Townes Van Zandt, Steve Young, and Richard Dobson. Also during that period, Crowell cut a demo tape that drew the attention of Brian Ahern, Emmylou Harris's manager.

Joined the Hot Band

In 1974 Harris invited Crowell to join her backup group, the Hot Band. She also recorded several Crowell songs, including "Amarillo," "Till I Gain Control," "Tulsa Queen," and "I Ain't Livin' Long Like This." Gaining exposure for

himself as Harris became a major country star, Crowell told Nash in *Behind Closed Doors,* "I would have to say I owe one of my biggest debts of gratitude to Emmylou for taking me around with her, and letting me gather up a lot of experience for myself while she was forging her own career. With her generosity, and her belief in my talents that were, at that time, really way down deep, and not really surfacing, she thrust me into a situation where I could grow. She let me get in touch with my talents. A lot of people wouldn't have done that. But she knew that there was a writer in there somewhere, and I think that's why she did it."

Crowell left the Hot Band in 1978 under the most cordial of terms. Ahern, in fact, produced Crowell's debut album for Warner Bros., *I Ain't Livin' Long Like This.* Though the album sold less than 20,000 units, it earned Crowell a cult following for its rock- and new wave-influenced country sound. Subsequent Crowell albums offered more of the same—hard-edged sentiments presented with musical twists and poetic turns of the lyric. "Ashes by Now," a single from his second LP, went to Number 37 on the country charts, but what baffled Crowell was the success others had with his songs. Three works from his debut album sold a million singles for other artists, and a particular Crowell favorite, "Leaving Louisiana in the Broad Daylight," was a Number One hit for the Oak Ridge Boys.

The artist had little time to reflect on his peculiar status, however. In 1979 Rosanne Cash asked him to help her with a new album being produced in Germany. The finished album was a disappointment to both artists, but they were able to persuade Columbia Records to give them more creative freedom on their next project. That work turned out to be *Right or Wrong,* the 1980 LP that more or less launched Cash's career. By the time the album was released, she had married Crowell.

Crowell kept quite busy producing his wife's albums and writing songs for other artists, but he also continued to release his own work. His Warner Bros. output includes *What Will the Neighbors Think* and *Rodney Crowell.* Though it also released the 1984 album *Street Language,* the company refused to market the LP, stating that it had no potential for producing a hit. Undaunted, Crowell took the finished product to Columbia. The album was not a big seller but drew favorable reviews for being musically adventurous.

By 1985 Crowell had come to realize that his marriage and his creative ability were both being undermined by his drug abuse. He and Cash both quit taking drugs, and their relationship improved measurably. "Drugs keep you from growing emotionally," Crowell admitted in *Behind Closed Doors.* "And since I've been straight, I think my emotional growth is starting to catch up with me." One discovery Crowell made paved the way to his stardom. "I had such a high opinion of myself as a songwriter," he said, "that I failed to realize I needed to deliver that much as a performer. But with the time that I've had away from that, and with growing personally and spiritually and every other way that you grow as you get older, it became obvious to me that I wasn't being really honest with myself about all of my talents."

Moved to Pure Country

Crowell's 1988 release, *Diamonds and Dirt,* literally put him over the top. He became the first country musician to amass four Number One hits for self-written songs from a single album. He also scored a major hit with "It's Such a Small World," a duet with his wife. *Diamonds and Dirt* marked a return to a more country-oriented style for Crowell, and he continued in this vein with his 1989 release, *Keys to the Highway,* an LP containing songs written in remembrance of his deceased father, James Crowell. Pointing out that Crowell's "recent records indicate a maturing and more sharply focused self-image," Nash wrote that the singer's "long suits have always been the descriptive narrative and the ability to capture complex emotion in simple language. . . . Crowell continues to insist on eloquent, nononsense playing and on stretching his limits as an expressive, emotive vocalist."

For his 1992 album, *Life Is Messy,* released shortly after his March divorce from Rosanne Cash, Crowell had "set out not to do anything in the same way," he expressed in a Columbia Records press packet. "I took voyages into as many places as I could. I was digging for something deeper in myself in terms of how I dealt with realizing the potentials of the songs." The dissolution of his 12-year marriage to Cash, he continued, "brought challenges on all kinds of levels—physical and emotional;" it also inspired "Alone But Not Alone," a song termed "achingly beautiful" by Ken Tucker in *Entertainment Weekly.*

Spawning the Top Ten country hit "Lovin' All Night," *Life Is Messy* drew a lukewarm reception from *Rolling Stone*'s David McGee as well as Alanna Nash, who commented in *Entertainment Weekly:* "Crowell's keening tenor . . . is a constant pleasure, but too many of his songs splinter into nebulousness with the occasional joltingly bad line ('Life is messy/I feel like Elvis Presley')." Tucker, however, lauded Crowell for his effort. Citing some of the singer's influences as Miles Davis and Frank Sinatra, the reviewer found that "as has been true since he released his first album in 1978, Crowell creates songs that tackle classic country themes—

lovin', leavin', and honky tonkin'—without the musical and verbal cliches."

As far as he has come from his Houston roots, Crowell has never forgotten the reasons he became a singer. "Music was a big part of both sides of my family," he acknowledged in *Behind Closed Doors.* "It was a real escape valve. They worked hard all week long, and the way they celebrated and rejoiced in life was by making music on weekends. And the music was country music." As for himself, Crowell says he no longer chases the elusive element of superstardom. "I can't sit here and say I'm gonna be a pop artist, or I'm gonna be anything," he told Nash. "I'm just gonna be a songwriter, a singer, and a performer. And I'm gonna do that as good as I can. I want to do something that is poignant and that expresses a reality that comes from your heart, as opposed to your mind. And then the results of that will be seen."

Selected discography

I Ain't Livin' Long Like This, Warner Bros., 1978.
What Will the Neighbors Think?, Warner Bros., c. 1981.
Rodney Crowell, Warner Bros., c. 1982.
Street Language, Columbia, 1984.
Diamonds and Dirt, Columbia, 1988.
Keys to the Highway, Columbia, 1989.
Life Is Messy, Columbia, 1992.
Collection, Warner Bros.

Sources

Books

Nash, Alanna, *Behind Closed Doors: Talking With the Legends of Country Music,* Knopf, 1988.
Vaughan, Andrew, *Who's Who in New Country Music,* St. Martin's, 1989.

Periodicals

Country Music, May/June 1992; July/August 1992.
Entertainment Weekly, May 22, 1992; June 26, 1992.
Rolling Stone, August 6, 1992.
Stereo Review, January, 1990.

Additional information for this profile was obtained from Columbia Records press material, 1992.

—Anne Janette Johnson

The Dorsey Brothers

Bandleaders, instrumentalists

Jimmy and Tommy Dorsey, two talented and energetic brothers from a small coal mining town in Pennsylvania, produced a music that lifted and unified a depressed American consciousness, providing "an alluring escape from the often distressing real world—into that other world of dancing feet, twirling bodies, and tapping toes," Gunther Schuller noted in his study *The Swing Era: The Development of Jazz, 1930-1945.* Although illusory in nature, the world created by the music and the shared identity of the listeners "is perhaps the happiest and most significant aspect of the Swing Era," Schuller declared. That facet of swing faded, however, when the American consciousness was permanently changed by World War II. *Stereo Review*'s Peter Reilly consequently dismissed the Dorsey brothers' music for modern listeners: "It doesn't have enough vitality or true style to bridge the years." But Schuller contended in 1989 the music should not be measured by the subjectivity of timelessness, for swing's important qualities are "impossible to recapture now, and, for those who did not actually experience it, difficult to savor in retrospect."

Born in Shenandoah, Pennsylvania, in 1904 and 1905, respectively, Jimmy and Tommy Dorsey were both playing instruments by 1910 under the strict tutelage of their father, a music teacher and bandmaster, who, to be certain his sons practiced, hid their shoes so they couldn't play outdoors. After starting out as cornetists, both Dorseys quickly switched to instruments for which they would later become known: Jimmy to alto saxophone and clarinet, Tommy to trombone. By the time they were 17 years old, they were musically proficient enough to leave Shenandoah and tour with various bands. By 1925 both had ventured to New York City to work as free-lance section players and as soloists. "Despite the oncoming Depression, radio was expanding rapidly," Jeff Scott recounted in the liner notes to *Big Bands: Tommy Dorsey.* "The networks and radio stations insisted on live music, so there were plenty of studio jobs. . . . The Dorseys made good livings as freelancers because they were known to be reliable, as well as virtuoso players and expert sight readers."

Orchestrated Swinging Dance Tunes

In 1928, using various studio musicians, the Dorsey brothers began recording under the name the Dorsey Brothers Orchestra for special engagements and studio work. A permanently functioning orchestra was not formed, however, until early in 1934. "The repeal of Prohibition [a ban on the manufacture and sale of alcoholic liquors] in 1933 led to the proliferation of city clubs, roadhouses, and dance pavilions," Scott wrote. Despite the hard times, prospects for a good band

For the Record. . .

Jimmy Dorsey born James Francis Dorsey February 29, 1904, in Shenandoah, PA; died June 12, 1957, in New York City; **Tommy Dorsey** born Thomas Francis Dorsey November 19, 1905, in Shenandoah, PA; died November 26, 1956, in Greenwich, CT; sons of Thomas Francis (a coal miner, then music teacher and bandmaster) and Theresa (Langton) Dorsey; Jimmy Dorsey married Jane Porter; children: Julie Lou; Tommy Dorsey married Mildred Kraft (first wife), Pat Dane (second wife), Janie (third wife); children: (first marriage) Thomas Francis III, Patricia. *Education:* Both brothers studied in public schools and under their father.

The Dorsey brothers formed first band, Dorseys' Novelty Six, then Dorseys' Wild Canaries, c. 1920; brothers then performed with the Scranton Sirens and the California Ramblers in the early 1920s; both worked as free-lance and studio musicians, 1925-34; began recording sessions under Dorsey Brothers label with studio groups, 1928-34; formally organized Dorsey Brothers Orchestra and recorded, 1934-35; brothers split up and formed separate bands, 1935; Jimmy led Jimmy Dorsey Orchestra (original Dorsey Brothers Orchestra), 1935-53; Tommy led Tommy Dorsey Orchestra, 1935-46 and 1948-53; Tommy was director of popular music for the Mutual Radio Network, 1945-46; brothers reunited to form the Tommy Dorsey Orchestra Featuring Jimmy Dorsey, 1953-57; had CBS television series featuring the orchestra, 1955-56. Both brothers' orchestras appeared in numerous films; the brothers also appeared in and were the subject of the semi-biographical film *The Fabulous Dorseys,* 1947.

looked promising." As a group the Dorsey brothers and their orchestra turned out "a light, airy, bouncy style in which the arrangement was primary, solos and improvisation secondary and incidental, but which at its instrument best nevertheless achieved a pleasant danceable kind of swing jazz," Schuller observed.

The group was never able to realize its full potential, though. The brothers' constant harassing and challenging of each other—a characteristic honed in their childhood—prevented a harmonious coalescing of the group. In May of 1935, while playing at the Glen Island Casino in New Rochelle, New York, the Dorsey Brothers Orchestra came to an end when Tommy, admonished by Jimmy for setting a tempo too fast, walked off the stage and never returned.

Fraternal Fragmentation

Jimmy Dorsey's preference would have been to remain in the sax section, but after his brother departed, he was forced out in front. At this time, Jimmy's musical technique was highly regarded. "His execution was impeccable, his choruses either demonstrations of effortless command or examples of modern thinking, full of whole tone scales, unusual chordal voices, wide intervals, and other innovations," Richard M. Sudhalter wrote in the liner notes to *Big Bands: Jimmy Dorsey.* But Jimmy was not an overbearing bandleader. George T. Simon stated in his book *The Big Bands* that Jimmy Dorsey's temperament allowed him to be "dedicated to high musical standards but less blatantly devoted to ruling the roost." His easygoing manner helped create a "disciplined spirited ensemble and made it a resounding commercial success without exercising an authoritative hand. Dorsey's men respected and loved him," Sudhalter explained.

The Jimmy Dorsey Orchestra achieved commercial success by playing for motion pictures and for such radio broadcasts as Bing Crosby's *Kraft Music Hall.* With the addition of singers Bob Eberly and Helen O'Connell, the orchestra reached the top of the popularity polls in the late 1930s and early 1940s with songs such as "Amapola," "Green Eyes," "Maria Elena," and "Tangerine." Sudhalter placed this success in historical perspective: "Since popular-music tastes had shifted from the instrumental pyrotechnics of the thirties to something more subdued and sentimental, it seemed almost inevitable that Jimmy Dorsey's band, playing arrangements that spotlighted the boy-and-girl-next-door attractiveness of Eberly and O'Connell, should catch the public fancy."

In an overall assessment of the Jimmy Dorsey Orchestra, Schuller maintained that while the ensemble was important for its period, it failed to reach high enough, that the combination of "commercialism, financial competitive survival, and the seductions of mass popular appeal. . . undercut much of what the orchestra was actually capable of."

Tenacity Evoked Sentimental Mood

Tommy Dorsey, on the other hand, was constantly trying to extend his capabilities and those of his musicians. He was among those leaders who "approached their jobs with a rare combination of idealism and realism," Simon observed. "Well-trained and well-disciplined, they knew what they wanted, and they knew how to get it. Keenly aware of the commercial competition, they drove themselves and their men relentlessly, for only through achieving perfection, or the closest possible state to it, could they see themselves realizing their musical and commercial goals."

Tommy's fierce drive was evident in his horn playing. "As a lyric player and a romantic balladeer [Tommy] Dorsey had no equal. Indeed, he virtually invented the genre," Schuller proclaimed, adding that "Dorsey was clearly the creator and master of this smooth 'singing' trombone style, so seemingly effortless, largely because of his virtually flawless breath control." Tommy's technique helped him become "a master of creating moods—warm, sentimental, and forever musical moods—at superb dancing and listening tempos," Simon opined.

Although Tommy's single-mindedness worked for him as an individual, the approach lost meaning when translated to his musicians. "His big trouble, one which earned him a number of impassioned enemies, was his lack of tolerance of others' mistakes and his lack of tact when they were made," Simon pointed out. Tommy was quick to fire any musician who didn't live up to his ideals, whether in the studio or on the bandstand during a performance. Because of the sudden change in personnel that occurred at any moment, Schuller contended, "the sections in the [Tommy] Dorsey band and the orchestra as a whole never developed cohesive ensembles."

When everything did fall into place, the Tommy Dorsey Orchestra exemplified the most favorable qualities of a quintessential big band of the Swing Era. Utilizing members of the Joe Haymes Band, Tommy formed his orchestra in the fall of 1935. "Virtually from the beginning, the band was a huge success," Scott explained. "Tommy's primary objective was to play music for dancing, and he and his men did exactly that with enormous skill." The orchestra was immediately given a recording contract and appeared on several radio shows in the first few years after its formation, establishing its sound with a highly receptive public. "I'm Getting Sentimental Over You"—Tommy Dorsey's theme song—"Marie," "Song of India," and "Boogie Woogie" solidified the orchestra's top standing in the late 1930s.

Singers Stole the Show

In 1940 Tommy Dorsey signed Frank Sinatra away from the Harry James Orchestra. The 24-year-old crooner soon began his ascent under Tommy's direction. Simon quoted Sinatra on Tommy's influence: "There's a guy who was a real education to me in every possible way. I learned about dynamics and style from the way he played his horn." This relationship was extremely

beneficial for Sinatra, but ultimately destructive for Tommy's orchestra and big bands in general. "Indeed, the effect of Sinatra's phenomenal success . . . was such that singers everywhere began to dominate popular music, even more than before, until eventually most big bands became strictly accompanimental and secondary to the vocalists," Schuller pointed out.

The rise of vocal musicians and the demise of big bands was further prompted in 1942 by a thirteen-and-a-half-month recording ban issued by the American Federation of Musicians (AMF). While the AMF renegotiated contract terms with record companies, singers, because they were not members the union, continued to

---

Jimmy and Tommy Dorsey produced a music that lifted and unified a depressed American consciousness.

---

record and remained in the public eye. Consequently, "with wartime and postwar prosperity everyone was trying for 'the big popular hit'—via the singers," Schuller contended. "As a result, jazz—and even its most popular manifestation, swing—was driven to the sidelines or stifled altogether."

Brothers Briefly Reunited

Both Dorseys' musical careers declined in the late 1940s. Jimmy formed and reformed his own big bands; Tommy disbanded his orchestra in 1946, only to reorganize in 1948. The brothers were brought back together briefly to work on the 1947 film *The Fabulous Dorseys,* but in light of the times, the film seemed retrospective at best. In 1953 they were finally reunited musically as the Tommy Dorsey Orchestra Featuring Jimmy Dorsey, regaining national exposure when Jackie Gleason had them appear regularly on his television show.

Despite new publicity, their era was over; a new one had arrived, as poignantly expressed when the Dorsey brothers introduced a young Elvis Presley on Gleason's show. After Tommy died unexpectedly in 1956, Jimmy took over the band. Before his own death less than a year later, Jimmy recorded "So Rare," a song he had introduced 20 years earlier. Unexpectedly, the record went to the top of the charts and became the biggest hit of his career. "Its popularity was a reminder of just how potent a musical force Jimmy Dorsey had been," Sudhalter concluded, "but the record sounded less like a hit than a requiem."

In the end the music the Dorseys created didn't change; the country that listened to it had changed. The brothers' work helped establish and define a specific period in American music and history. Tommy Dorsey is still regarded as one of the greatest trombonists of all time, and his orchestra "must be recognized as the greatest all-around dance band of them all," Simon asserted. "Others may have sounded more creative. Others may have swung harder and more consistently. Others may have developed more distinctive styles. But of all the hundreds of well-known bands, Tommy Dorsey's could do more things better than any other could." The value of the Dorseys' music, as a reviewer for *People* explained, lies in its defining quality of a bygone innocent time: "When everything meshed, when the talents, egos, and circumstances came together, they all produced music that was as good as any of its era."

Selected discography

Singles; Dorsey Brothers Orchestra

"My Melancholy Baby," Okeh, 1928.
"Praying the Blues," Okeh, 1929.
"Oodles of Noodles," Columbia, 1932.
"Fidgety," Brunswick, 1933.
"Shim Sham Shimmy," Brunswick, 1933.
"Stop, Look, and Listen," Decca, 1934.
"Sandman," Decca, 1934.
"Tailspin," Decca, 1935.
"Dippermouth Blues," Decca, 1935.

Singles; Jimmy Dorsey Orchestra

"Parade of the Milk Bottle Caps," Decca, 1936.
"John Silver," Decca, 1938.
"Dusk in Upper Sandusky," Decca, 1939.
"My Prayer," Decca, 1939.
"Contrasts," Decca, 1940.
"Amapola," Decca, 1941.
"Green Eyes," Decca, 1941.
"Maria Elena," Decca, 1941.
"Blue Champagne," Decca, 1941.
"Embraceable You," Decca, 1941.
"Tangerine," Decca, 1941.
"Brazil," Decca, 1942.

Singles; Tommy Dorsey Orchestra

"I'm Getting Sentimental Over You," Victor, 1935.
"Marie," Victor, 1937.
"Song of India," Victor, 1937.
"Boogie Woogie," Victor, 1938, reissued, 1943.
"Hawaiian War Chant," Victor, 1938.
"Music, Maestro, Please," Victor, 1938.
"I'll Be Seeing You," Victor, 1940.
"I'll Never Smile Again," Victor, 1940.
"Yes, Indeed!," Victor, 1941.
"Well, Git It!," Victor, 1941.
"On the Sunny Side of the Street," Victor, 1944.
"Opus No. 1," Victor, 1944.

Reissues and compilations

The Dorsey Brothers: 1934-1935 Decca Sessions, MCA.
Jimmy Dorsey and His Orchestra: 1939-1940, Circle.
The Dorsey/Sinatra Sessions, Bluebird, Vol. 1, 1940, Vol. 2, 1940-41, Vol. 3, 1941-42.
Big Bands: Tommy Dorsey, Time-Life Music, 1983.
Big Bands: Jimmy Dorsey, Time-Life Music, 1984.
Best of Big Bands, Columbia/Legacy, 1992.
The Best of Jimmy Dorsey, MCA.
The Best of Tommy Dorsey, MCA.
Sentimental Dorsey, Pair.

Sources

Books

Schuller, Gunther, *The Swing Era: The Development of Jazz, 1930-1945,* Oxford University Press, 1989.
Simon, George T., *The Big Bands,* Macmillan, 1967, revised, 1974.

Periodicals

New York Times, June 13, 1957.
People, November 1, 1982.
Saturday Review, January 17, 1970.
Stereo Review, January 1983; March 1983; April 1984.

Other

Scott, Jeff, liner notes to *Big Bands: Tommy Dorsey,* Time-Life Music, 1983.
Sudhalter, Richard M., liner notes to *Big Bands: Jimmy Dorsey,* Time-Life Music, 1984.

—Rob Nagel

Michael Doucet

Violinist, singer, songwriter

Michael Doucet and the band Beausoleil have been getting the world up to dance since 1975. And although Doucet traces the growing popularity of Cajun music in the United States to when "some big guy from New Orleans [Chef Paul Prudhomme] burned the fish" and started the Cajun food craze of the 1980s, according to the *Kitchener-Waterloo Record,* it is more likely an outcome of South Louisiana's own peculiar mix of music styles. Beausoleil has been the premier ambassador of that mix, offering music that is usually melodic and harmonically interesting, in addition to its riveting rhythmic drive. Doucet's vocal style copies the nasal quality of early Cajun musicians, but overall the band is slick in its transformation of the different meters and spontaneous chord changes of the old Cajun masters.

The name of the band acknowledges the history of the Cajun people. The Cajuns are descendants of French-Canadians who were deported from Acadia, Nova Scotia, by British colonists in 1755 and settled in southern Louisiana. Beausoleil was the name of one of the leaders of a rebellion against the forced deportation of the Acadians, from which the word Cajun is derived. Once the French-Canadians were in Louisiana, their culture became intermingled with that of Native Americans, African-Americans, Spaniards, and Britons. As Doucet explained in *Dirty Linen,* "Cajun music has been the definitive 'World Music' for a long time. If you look at the history, not only does it have French folk songs in it, but it's always had Afro-Caribbean sounds as a big influence."

Embraced Traditional Cajun Style

Doucet's own roots reveal much about the music he and the band play. He grew up on his father's farm about five miles west of Lafayette, Louisiana. His father's side of the family was steeped in traditional Cajun music, and his mother's family had been classically trained and played jazz. Doucet played the trumpet as well as the guitar in elementary and high school. He didn't seriously take up his signature instrument, the violin, until 1972.

By 1974 Doucet was playing in local hangouts to the approval of an older audience that was appreciative of his return to traditional Cajun roots. At one of these performances a French promoter asked him and his band to come to France for two weeks to play at a folk festival. The two weeks stretched into six months. "So we went to France," Doucet related in *Sing Out!* "Wow! They know about this music. I remember being woken up with about ten hurdy-gurdies and a bunch of fiddle players playing 'Jolie Blonde' under our window. Where guitars became popular, and Cajun music became increasingly tinged with country and western sounds.

Influenced by Rock and Roll

Though Doucet was mainly drawn to the older styles and has continued to play them both as a member of Beausoleil and with other musicians, he has also always been influenced by rock and roll. His early band, Coteau, until its dissolution in 1977, fused Cajun and rock. That same year marked Beausoleil's first release in the United States, *The Spirit of Cajun Music.* Appropriately, the band's first album had been recorded in France the year before. Since then, Doucet has been involved in projects with the ultratraditional Savoy-Doucet band as well as other Cajun and non-Cajun musicians. Though he has also embarked on some solo efforts, he has spent most of his time with Beausoleil since the band's inception in 1975.

Beausoleil's different record companies reflect the band's changes throughout the years. Their albums released by the Louisiana-based Swallow Records as well as their recordings with the traditional Arhoolie Records are usually old-time Cajun numbers or contemporary compositions in the same vein, often recorded without over-dubbing and thereby capturing the intimacy of live performance. Their move to Rounder Records in the late 1980s was accompanied by a return to the more rock-oriented sounds of Doucet's earlier band, Coteau. Later issues from Rounder have included a variety of styles as the band continued to expand its horizons.

The composition of Beausoleil changed over the years, though Doucet's brother, David, long played guitar for the group, and the percussion section for a considerable time included washboard player Billy Ware and drummer Tommy Alesi, both of whom have jazz backgrounds. For their 1991 album, *Cajun Conja,* the band also featured Doucet's school friend Tommy Comeaux on bass and mandolin, Al Tharp on banjo, and Jimmy Breaux on accordion. The group continued to tour worldwide, performing in the Middle East in 1990 and frequently holding gigs in Europe and the Americas.

Beausoleil has been involved in numerous projects over the years. In 1986 the band composed and recorded the sound track for the movie *Belizaire the Cajun,* and they did the title song for the 1987 romantic thriller *The Big Easy.* Their influence even can be heard on Frito-Lay snack food commercials, on which the band actually played to the work of Paul Simon and John Cougar Mellencamp. Doucet has collaborated with Richard Thompson, and the band has made several

were we? Died and gone to heaven, you know. It was amazing. It was like speaking to people of our great-grandfathers' era who were our age. It was the turning point of my life."

It was also when Doucet realized the importance of correlations between old French songs from the Middle Ages and modern Cajun music. Upon his return to the United States in 1975, he received a grant from the National Endowment for the Arts to study the music styles of such living Cajun music legends as Dennis McGee.

Cajun music had developed over time from the old French ballads to dance tunes played by two fiddles. The accordion, introduced to Louisiana by German immigrants from Texas, replaced the fiddles in the 1920s. But by the 1930s, fiddles had returned and appearances on Garrison Keillor's radio show *Prairie Home Companion.* Keith Richards asked Doucet to play on his solo release *Talk is Cheap,* and in 1990, Beausoleil celebrated Mardi Gras with the Grateful Dead for 17,000 fans at Oakland Coliseum.

Resisted Commercialization

Despite their success the band continued to resist commercializing their tradition. This does not mean, however, that they remained static. In fact, they had four different accordion players in a period of 15 years. In a 1989 *Rolling Stone* review, Steve Pond described Beausoleil's 1988 Grammy-nominated album, *Bayou Cadillac,* as "rooted in tradition but far from traditional." Pond wrote further that Doucet and Beausoleil, "after proving themselves masters of traditional music, have in the past few years grown looser and more eclectic, drawing on pop, rock, and R & B songs and riffs. What distinguishes their recordings from the pop covers performed by some of their Cajun and Zydeco colleagues is that Doucet and Beausoleil are clearly not trying to get a crossover radio hit or make their music more palatable to the masses, but rather add fun and spice to what was already a rich musical sauce."

Doucet summed up the band's direction in his 1990 interview with Mike Greenberg in *Sing Out!:* "We've always dug up old songs, songs that were forgotten, just to revive them—not to play them exactly alike but just to show what kind of music we had. I think people respect that. We're at a very nice point where we don't have to prove ourselves with anything, because nobody knows what to expect from us next."

Selected discography

Solo albums

Beau Solo, Arhoolie.
Cajun Fiddle, Beausoleil Productions.

With Beausoleil

La Nuit, Pathe Marconi, EMI, 1976.
The Spirit of Cajun Music, Swallow, 1977.

Les Amis Cadjins, Modulation, 1979, reissued as *Zydeco.*
Dit Beausoleil, Arhoolie, 1981.
Parlez-Nous a Boire, Arhoolie, 1984.
Belizaire the Cajun (original motion picture soundtrack), Arhoolie, 1986.
Gris-Gris, Swallow, 1986.
Bayou Cadillac, Rounder, 1988.
Live! From the Left Coast, Rounder, 1989.
DeJa Vu, Swallow, 1990.
Cajun Conja, Rhino, 1991.
Hot Chile Mama, Arhoolie.
Bayou Boogie, Rounder.

With others

Michael Doucet and Cajun Brew, Rounder, 1988.
Christmas Bayou, Swallow.
(With Savoy-Doucet) *Les Harias Home Music,* Arhoolie.
(With Savoy-Doucet) *Two-step d'Amede,* Arhoolie.
(With Danny Poullard) *Cajun Jam Session,* Arhoolie.
(With Canray Fontenot) *Allons A Lafayette,* Arhoolie.
(With Savoy-Doucet) *With Spirits,* Arhoolie.

Sources

Books

Ancelet, Barry Jean, *Cajun Music: Its Origins and Development,* Center for Louisiana Studies, 1989.
Ancelet, Barry Jean, *The Makers of Cajun Music,* University of Texas Press, 1984.
Broven, John, *South to Louisiana: The Music of the Cajun Bayous,* Pelican Publishing Co., 1987.

Periodicals

Dirty Linen, Summer 1989.
Eugene Register (Oregon), January 11, 1991.
Frets, September 1987.
Kitchener-Waterloo Record (Ontario, Canada), August 31, 1990.
Rolling Stone, June 16, 1988; September 21, 1989; February 6, 1992.
Sing Out!, fall 1990.

—John Morrow

Brian Eno

Composer, producer, keyboardist, singer

Brian Eno, who initially earned fame playing synthesizers for the British pop band Roxy Music, has made his greatest artistic impact with his theory of "ambient" music and his tutelage of such pop musicians as David Bowie, Talking Heads, Devo, and U2. For someone who describes himself as a nonmusician, Eno has mastered diverse musical skills: composing, singing, playing the synthesizer, and editing and producing music for other groups.

Eno originally planned a career in art, studying painting in the late 1960s at art schools in Ipswich and Winchester, England. He felt his art resembled avant-garde music, particularly because he considered the execution of the work more important than the finished product. Eno told *People* contributor Arthur Lubow, "I found that I was considering the paintings more like performance pieces." Eno once directed an artist colleague to paint a picture in his absence and then remove it from the studio; Eno then attempted to recreate the picture with the information at hand, such as the paint splashes on the floor and the testimony of bystanders. Ultimately, the paintings were displayed together. Despite the affinity Eno felt for avant-garde music, however, he did not seriously consider a musical career at that time because he did not play an instrument.

Joined Roxy Music

In 1971 Eno was invited by a musician friend to record music by a band led by Bryan Ferry; the art student's manipulations of the band's music with a tape recorder and a borrowed synthesizer led to his inclusion in the new group, Roxy Music. Eno first performed his manipulations in the audience, but when he began to sing backup he was such a distraction that the group decided to move him onto the stage. To overcome his unobtrusiveness there, he wore flamboyant sequined clothing with feathers, which magnified his small movements at the keyboard. Eno began to rival Ferry as the group's focal point, which perhaps led to the former's departure from the group in 1973.

Eno immediately launched a solo career, releasing several successful pop albums in the following few years. He also demonstrated his now well-established desire to create new sounds, experimenting with tape-echo and delay techniques in his collaboration with Robert Fripp on *No Pussyfooting* and anticipating punk rock with his 1974 single "Seven Deadly Finns." At this time Eno also collaborated with John Cale and Nico, previously of the Velvet Underground, and Kevin Ayers, ex-Soft Machine member, on the live album *June 1, 1974.*

When Eno's lung collapsed in 1974 on what was to be his last concert tour, the performer expressed relief that his frantic lifestyle as an up-and-coming rock star had been interrupted. Never comfortable on stage, Eno decided to concentrate on studio work. His next albums, *Taking Tiger Mountain (by Strategy)* and *Another Green World,* were influenced by the work of minimalist composer John Cage. *Tiger Mountain* in particular received critical acclaim.

Convalescence Spawned Ambient Music

Struck by a car in 1975, Eno once again used his convalescence to reassess his career; while inadvertently listening to records someone else was playing, Eno developed his theory of "ambient" music, or subtle instrumentals that blend with the environment. Although sometimes referred to as glorified Muzak—elevator music—Eno's ambient music is considered quite complex by many critics and thus worthy of close listening. *Music for Airports,* which played temporarily at La Guardia Airport in New York City, achieved the most widespread popularity of Eno's ambient albums, selling over 100,000 copies worldwide.

Although Eno had always been considered an experimentalist in the music world, his work on ambient music led him even further toward the periphery of pop. Nonetheless, Eno's influence on pop music perhaps increased during this period due to his production work with mainstream stars David Bowie, Devo, and Talking Heads, all of whom were inspired by Eno's theories and techniques. His hallmarks can be heard on David Bowie's *Heroes,* Talking Heads' *More Songs About Buildings and Food,* and Devo's *Q: Are We Not Men? A: We Are Devo!,* all of which Eno helped produce.

Eno has always made great use of tape recorders—employing them to manipulate recording tracks that vary from traditional vocals to stones rubbing against metal. Talking Heads' David Byrne told *People* contributor Lubow, "He doesn't approach music in a traditional way—'We need a hook line here and eight bars there.' He takes concepts often expressed in nonmusical terms and applies them to music." Eno himself explained to Lubow, "Tape makes music into a plastic material, which is why someone like me can make music. Once it's on tape, I can rearrange things, and I can make sounds that aren't available from any instrument."

Bush of Ghosts Presaged Worldbeat Craze

Eno elaborated on this technique in the African-inspired *My Life in the Bush of Ghosts,* a 1981 collaboration with Byrne. By stripping various vocal recordings of their context and combining them with instrumentals produced by everyday materials like ashtrays and lampshades, Eno and Byrne created what Kurt Loder of *Rolling Stone* called "the most compelling example to date of what might truly be called one-world music." Loder also commented that "a major marvel of *My Life in the Bush of Ghosts* is the way percussion and melody have been melded into a single, unifying force." The African influence apparent on *Bush of Ghosts* prefigured a craze for what would several years later be termed "Worldbeat" music.

In the 1980s Eno concentrated primarily on his ambient music, which he released through Opal, a label he and his wife, Anthea Norton-Taylor, created. He was associated at this time with a variety of musicians, including his guitarist brother Roger and pianist Harold Budd, both of whom worked with Eno on *The Plateaux of Mirrors.* After glasnost—the Soviet Union's late 1980s policy of cultural openness toward the West—Opal also issued works by Soviet avant-garde musicians.

Fruitful Collaboration With U2

Eno has continued to influence pop and rock groups through his production efforts, most notably his collaboration with producer Daniel Lanois on U2's popular releases *The Unforgettable Fire, The Joshua Tree,* and

Achtung Baby. Some musicians who have worked with Eno have complained that he focuses too narrowly on creating individual sounds—one instrumentalist told *People*'s Lubow that Eno "spent three days twirling hoses." But in an article Eno wrote for *Rolling Stone* about his work on 1991's *Achtung Baby,* he said, "It's easy to get stuck in the detailed work of overdubbing, fiddling, and tweaking, but it often doesn't get you far from where you started. Bigger jumps take a type of nimbleness, the agility to switch back and forth from detail to big picture, from zoom to wide angle." Of *Achtung Baby,* Eno revealed that Berlin—where much of the record was recorded—was used as its conceptual backdrop: "The Berlin of the Thirties—decadent, sensual and dark—resonating against the Berlin of the Nineties—reborn, chaotic and optimistic—suggested an image of culture at a crossroads. In the same way, the record came to be seen as a place where incongruous strands would be allowed to weave together."

Eno's own release from that period, 1990's *Wrong Way Up,* was a collaboration with John Cale that featured Eno's first songs in 13 years. This return to mainstream rock seemed unusual for a musician so determinedly experimental, but Eno revealed that he had been recording songs for several years and simply not releasing them. In *Down Beat* Marc Weidenbaum described Eno's singing on the record as "deadpan, nearly nasal, . . . reminiscent of [his] '70s pop albums." Still, Weidenbaum allowed, "For all its affinity with both Eno and Cale's early solo work, [*Wrong Way Up* is] also uproariously contemporary, and sounds fine on a party tape right alongside the Fine Young Cannibals."

Although Eno has not achieved the same fame as some of the groups for whom he has done production work, he has played a pivotal role in rock music's evolution. As Mark Sinker explained in *Spin,* "Sound-as-pleasured-complicity and sound-as-violent-refusal became the poles of the universe he birthed; the universe that all of us live in, from [U2 lead singer] Bono victims to world-beat converts—Eno invented U2 *and* Africa, of course."

Selected discography

(With Roxy Music) *Roxy Music,* Reprise, 1973.

(With Roxy Music) *For Your Pleasure,* Reprise, 1973.
(With Robert Fripp) *No Pussyfooting,* Island, 1973.
Here Come the Warm Jets, Editions EG, 1973.
(With John Cale and Nico, and Kevin Ayers) *June 1, 1974,* Island, 1974.
Taking Tiger Mountain (by Strategy), Editions EG, 1974.
Another Green World, Editions EG, 1975.
(With Fripp) *Evening Starr,* Editions EG, 1975.
Discreet Music, Obscure, 1975.
Before and After Science, Island, 1977.
Cluster and Eno, 1977.
Music for Films, Polydor, 1978.
(With Moebius and Rodelius) *After the Heat,* Sky, 1978.
Music for Airports, Editions EG, 1979.
(With John Hassell) *Possible Music,* 1980.
(With Roger Eno and Harold Budd) *The Plateaux of Mirrors,* Opal, 1980.
(With David Byrne) *My Life in the Bush of Ghosts,* Sire, 1981.
Music for Airplay, Editions EG, 1981.
On Land, Editions EG, 1982.
More Blank Than Frank, Polydor, 1986.
Desert Island Selection, Polydor, 1987.
(With Cale) *Wrong Way Up,* Opal/Warner Bros., 1990.
Nerve Net, Warner Bros., 1992.

Also recorded *Apollo* and *Thursday Afternoon,* Editions EG, and *My Squelchy Life,* Opal/Warner Bros.

Sources

Books

Hardy, Phil, and Dave Laing, *The Faber Companion to 20th-Century Popular Music,* Faber & Faber, 1990.
The Penguin Encyclopedia of Popular Music, edited by Donald Clark, Viking, 1989.

Periodicals

Down Beat, January 1991.
High Fidelity, April 1988.
People, October 11, 1982.
Rolling Stone, March 5, 1981; November 28, 1991.
Spin, December 1990.

—*Susan Windisch Brown*

Bela Fleck

Banjo player, composer

Bela Fleck is an acknowledged master of the five-string banjo. An unassuming artist whose virtuoso performances fuse jazz, rock, Irish balladry, and bluegrass, Fleck fronts a band that cannot possibly be classified as strictly bluegrass or even "new grass." His is an original style, a hip, urban sound that just happens to come from a backwoods instrument. *Time* magazine contributor John Elson called Fleck "the Paganini, or maybe the Jimi Hendrix," of the banjo, noting that the three-time Grammy Award nominee has taken "this jangling folk instrument into jazz, classical music, and beyond."

Fleck never touched a banjo until he was fourteen, but by the time he was in his mid-twenties, he was cutting solo albums and picking with the New Grass Revival, a premier bluegrass band. His later work, with the Flecktones, is more likely to be heard on jazz radio stations than on country shows. "I wanted to play like [pianist] Chick Corea," Fleck disclosed in *Down Beat* magazine. "I could look up and down the banjo neck and everything was there that you needed to play the notes, but no one had come up with the technique to play it. I started working on things most musicians work out on for most instruments, like working on scales, finding a way to play the chords. There was nothing remarkable about the things I did except that they were on the banjo."

Bela Fleck was born and raised in New York City, an unlikely environment from which to pull a love of the banjo. He and his brother lived with their mother, a public school teacher. "I never met my father," Fleck declared in *Time*. "He taught German for a living but was crazy about classical music. He named me after Bela Bartok, the Hungarian composer. He named my brother Ludwig after Beethoven. It was rough. The torture started in kindergarten."

Fleck was just about ready to start kindergarten when he had his first brush with the banjo. Like many Americans, he initially heard the instrument in the theme music of the 1960s television series *The Beverly Hillbillies.* Fleck recalled in *Time* that he and his brother were watching the show at his grandparents' house. "The theme music started, and I had no idea it was the banjo," he said. "It was Earl Scruggs in his prime. I only remember hearing something beautiful. It called out to me."

Other musical influences intervened, however. Fleck learned to play guitar and was influenced by pop and rock as a youngster. Then, at 14, he saw the film *Deliverance,* with its "Duelling Banjos" bluegrass theme. "The sound of the banjo just killed me," he remembered in *Time.* "It's like hearing mercury."

The shy and overweight teenager bought a banjo and began to spend up to eight hours a day locked in his room, experimenting with the instrument. He was accepted into Manhattan's High School of Music and Art, but since the banjo was not considered a serious instrument there, he played guitar and studied music theory. He took private banjo lessons with three teachers, Tony Trischka, Erik Darling, and Mark Horowitz. He also learned, as most bluegrass musicians do, from listening to and imitating such bluegrass pioneers as Scruggs and J. D. Crowe.

As soon as he graduated from high school in 1976, Fleck moved to Boston and took a job with the bluegrass band Tasty Licks. In 1979 he moved south to Lexington, Kentucky, to help form the group Spectrum. Fleck confessed to a *Time* correspondent that his first exposure to Southern bluegrass was a "big culture shock." He added: "I was a little cocky, but down South, they didn't think I sounded so great because I lacked tone and I didn't have a great sense of rhythm. They were right."

Fleck perfected his technique and cut his first solo album, *Crossing the Tracks,* in 1980. Two years later he joined Sam Bush, John Cowan, and Pat Flynn in the New Grass Revival. Throughout the 1980s the New Grass Revival offered a benchmark for experimental bluegrass. *Stereo Review* correspondent Alanna Nash proclaimed the band "the ultimate progressive supergroup" with "its own unique, indescribable, and innovative blend of jazz, rock, reggae, gospel, [rhythm and blues], and whatever else strikes its fancy."

Almost every New Grass Revival album features an instrumental with Fleck as principal performer and composer. Among these are the Grammy-nominated "Seven by Seven," "Big Foot," and the popular "Metric Lips." Nash commented that some of Fleck's riffs on the New Grass albums are so hot that the artist "probably had to cool off in the shower between takes."

The New Grass Revival disbanded in 1991, each member going his own way but holding out the option for a reunion in the future. In Fleck's case, the split offered an opportunity to play more jazz-oriented material. He formed the Flecktones in 1990 with a pair of brothers, Victor and Roy Wooten, on bass and Drumitar, and added Howard Levy on keyboards and harmonica. The group's albums have sold well to jazz enthusiasts, while Fleck continues to appear at the more progressive bluegrass festivals—especially the annual affair in Telluride, Colorado.

In *The Big Book of Bluegrass,* Fleck discussed his artistic goals and his position in the music business. "I think I just have to follow the path where the music leads me and play as many different kinds of things as I can," he said. "Basically, I try not to take it all too seriously. As Alan Munde once said, 'It's only a banjo.' I mean, how seriously can you take it? It's like being the best kazoo player in the world."

Critics have taken it seriously indeed. Elson concluded that Fleck's work "is pure revelation. . . . His technique is always at the service of a sophisticated musical imagination that can make the [banjo] sound as if it were born to play jazz."

Selected discography

Solo albums

Crossing the Tracks, Rounder, 1980.
Natural Bridge, Rounder, 1982.
Daybreak, Rounder, 1987.
(With Jerry Douglas, Mark O'Connor, and others) *Inroads,* Rounder, 1987.
Places, Rounder, 1988.
Double Time, Rounder.
Drive, Rounder.

With Tasty Licks

Anchored to the Shore, Rounder.
Tasty Licks, Rounder.

With Spectrum

Opening Roll, Rounder.
Spectrum Live in Japan, Rounder.
Too Hot for Words, Rounder.

With the New Grass Revival

Deviation, Rounder, 1985.
On the Boulevard, Sugar Hill, 1985.
New Grass Revival, EMI America, 1986.
Hold to a Dream, Capitol, 1988.
Friday Night in America, Capitol, 1989.
The New Grass Revival Live, Sugar Hill, 1989.
New Grass Anthology, Capitol, 1990.

With the Flecktones

Bela Fleck and the Flecktones, Warner Bros., 1990.

Flight of the Cosmic Hippo, Warner Bros., 1991.
UFO Tofu, Warner Bros., 1992.

Sources

Books

Kochman, Marilyn, editor, *The Big Book of Bluegrass,* Morrow, 1984.

Periodicals

Bluegrass Unlimited, November 1978.
Chicago, December 1986.
Down Beat, July 1986; July 1988; August 1991.
Guitar Player, February 1989; July 1990.
People, May 25, 1992.
Rolling Stone, July 13, 1989.
Stereo Review, May 1985; January 1988; November 1988; September 1990.
Time, June 11, 1990.
Variety, July 4, 1990.

—Anne Janette Johnson

Gang
of
Four

Rock band

"**G**ang of Four are probably the best politically motivated dance band in rock & roll," declared *Rolling Stone's* David Fricke in 1980. Emerging in the waning days of the British punk revolution, the group set intensely analytical lyrics—usually about the omnipresence of political forces in everyday life—to a hard, spare music consisting of dissonant, edgy guitar patterns and a funk-influenced beat. The Gang's distinctive sound and unconventional messages raised the hopes of critics and discerning listeners, though many felt that the group never lived up to the promise of their first recordings and performances. After a series of personnel changes, the band broke up in 1984; two founding members reunited for a 1991 Gang of Four album, *Mall,* and a new tour. Both garnered impressive reviews. According to some critics, the music world had taken a decade to catch up with Gang of Four; the band's dance-oriented message music seemed as timely as ever.

Singer Jon King and guitarist Andy Gill had been friends for years before deciding to form a band. The

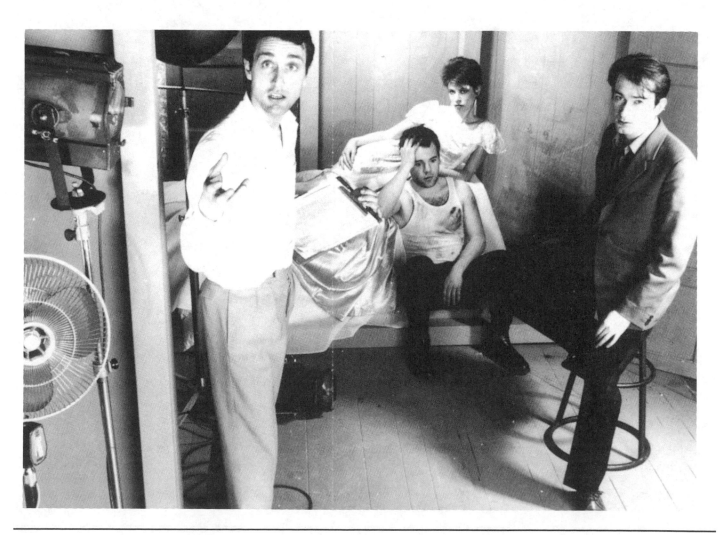

two studied in the fine arts department of the University of Leeds in northern England as did a circle of postpunk musicians who would later comprise such bands as the Mekons and the Delta 5. Gill was a devotee of sixties guitar giant Jimi Hendrix, whose psychedelic blues, hard rock, and noise were decidedly unhip in the punk days. King told *Melody Maker* that "Andy wore a black armband at school the day Hendrix died," an admission that clearly embarrassed Gill.

Leftist Intellectuals

Drummer Hugo Burnham was an English major at Leeds who at one point formed a theater group influenced by the writings of Karl Marx—the nineteenth-century German philosopher and cofounder of communism—but grew tired of "preaching to the converted," as he was quoted as saying in *Melody Maker*. Gill and King, leftist intellectuals themselves, had been collaborating on songs for some time before they decided to put their group together; they found Burnham and a bass player—a hippie named Wolfman—and began performing in 1977. They took their name from a political faction associated with the widow of Chinese Communist leader Mao Tse-Tung. Although they knew little about Maoism, King admitted in a 1982 interview with *Musician,* "it was suggested because it was a good name for a band."

Wolfman never quite fit into the band's tensely political groove, his tendency to meditate during sound checks caused the band to consider a replacement. Salvation

came in the form of Dave Allen, an experienced professional who had been transformed by the musical atmosphere: "Until the New Wave [music movement] happened, I was looking for a band that was like [rhythm and blues musician] Stevie Wonder turned heavy," Allen admitted to *Melody Maker's* Mary Harron. Allen gave up a comfortable living as a session player to travel to Leeds and find a place on the burgeoning new wave scene.

Allen's bass playing proved a supple foil for Gill's guitar playing, though at first Allen's approach created conflicts: "During the first gigs," the bassist told Harron, "Gill kept saying, 'Can't you tone it down? You're playing too many notes.'" The result of the band's synthesis, however, was a distinctively funky rhythmic structure that provided a counterpoint rather than support for the guitar and King's vocals and melodica—a toy-like combination of harmonica and keyboard.

Dialectical Dissonance

After the raw energy and unfocused rebellion of the punk years—most famously represented in England by the Sex Pistols—the scene was ripe for music that expressed the anger and intensity of punk in a more subtle and musically sophisticated form. As Jon Pareles noted in the *Village Voice,* Gill had been forced "to rethink his role" to help the group find its rhythmic focus. "As propounded by the early Ramones [an American punk band], punk was utterly redundant: power-chorded guitar doubletiming the bass and drums and voice. Gill recognized that continuous strumming merely doubles what's already implicit in bass and drums while swaddling the band in constant harmony. His solution: liquidate most of the harmony, and—in true dialectical style—strengthen the groove by defying it."

By "dialectical" Pareles meant the Marxist ideal of bringing opposing forces together, something the Gang attempted both musically and lyrically. The dialectical process also came through in their interviews: the band constantly argued, debated, and pondered virtually everything. Chris Brazier of *Melody Maker* enthused that "it's so good to come across a group that is unequivocally socialist, intelligently and openly so, and that sees the importance of rock as a direct communicator." The disagreements between band members made for stimulating interviews, but would lead to more serious conflicts later.

Marxist Rock for a Corporate Label

After playing around and recording some singles for a small label, the Gang did something that seemed in conflict with their politics: they signed a contract with a major record label, Britain's EMI. In 1979—after waiting for Gill to complete his exams at Leeds—the group recorded their first LP, *Entertainment!* The ironic title referred to a line from the song "5:45," in which a viewer of television news observes that "guerilla war struggle is a new Entertainment!" The album was filled with bitter and incisive sentiments. Songs like "At Home He's a Tourist," "I Found That Essence Rare," "Contract," and "Damaged Goods" presented what *Rolling Stone's* Greil Marcus called "cut-up situational accounts of the paradoxes of leisure as oppression, identity as product, home as factory, resident as tourist, sex as politics, history as ruling-class private joke." The album— released in the United States on the Warner Bros. label—was carefully produced by Gill, King, Rob Warr, and Rick Walton, with a spare, driving sound. *Rolling Stone's* Jon Savage called the record "an impressive, efficient and provocative debut, with at least one classic, the superb 'I Found That Essence Rare.'" *Rolling Stone* would include *Entertainment!* on a 1989 list of the top one hundred records of the eighties.

Gang of Four spent most of 1980 on tour in the United States and Europe. Their performances—intense and physical bouts with moody lighting—impressed some critics even more than did the recordings. Tom Carson of the *Village Voice* concluded that "live, this young English band comes up with rock and roll urgency to match their intellectual commitment." Fricke, reviewing a New York show in *Rolling Stone,* admired the Gang's "highly developed rhythmic muscle." After the tours, the quartet returned to Leeds and wrote some new songs. They released a single, "To Hell With Poverty"/ "Capital (It Fails Us Now)," and Warner Bros. put out an EP, *Gang of Four,* which contained four tunes recorded between 1978 and 1980.

Antidote to Feel-Good Rock

In 1981 the Gang put out a second album, *Solid Gold.* Like *Entertainment!* the album was uncompromising, spare, and analytical; such songs as "Cheeseburger," "He'd Send in the Army," and "In the Ditch" exposed the paradoxes of warfare, work, and leisure. Van Gosse's *Village Voice* review described the record as a difficult but necessary antidote to feel-good rock: "Gang of Four embody a new category in pop, which illuminates all the others, because the motor of their aesthetic is not a 'personal creative vision.' It is a social theory and world view which expresses itself organically in their sound. *Solid Gold* informs us about us: it is profoundly political because its style is critical." Adam Sweeting of *Melody Maker* found the LP "lower key and more considered than *Entertainment!*" and remarked that "with *Solid Gold,* Gang of Four have deliberately steered away from the abrasive polemics of their earlier material. They've gone instead for more of a cohesive feel."

The tour following *Solid Gold* exhausted the band; the rigors of travel took a particularly large toll on Allen, who left the group during the tour. Subsequent press suggested animosities between Allen and his former bandmates, particularly King, whom Allen described as having become politically "liberal," that is, more moderate. The remaining members found a temporary replacement in American bassist Busta "Cherry" Jones, a sometime player with such respected American funk-rock collectives as Parliament and Talking Heads. Jones learned the Gang's songs in a marathon week of rehearsals. "That week was very intense; we got very close," Jones revealed in *Rolling Stone.* "Playing those tracks and hearing the lyrics, I fell in love with the music. And the guys got a glimpse of being broader in ambiance—a whole new idea of what their songs could do." King noted that by the end of the tour "it was like we'd been playing with him for years. Now the [Rolling] Stones are trying to steal him from us." The Stones—a legendary British band mounting a typically enormous and expensive tour—succeeded. Jones was therefore unavailable for the Gang's next project.

Moved Toward Streamlined Sound

King, Gill and Burnham enlisted Sara Lee, an old friend of King and Gill and veteran of British guitarist Robert Fripp's musical project the League of Gentlemen. "We did want a woman" to help put the band's feminist politics into practice, King told *Musician's* J. D. Considine. Lee turned out to be a good vocalist as well as a talented bassist, and her vocals helped to give the tunes on the group's next effort—*Songs of the Free*—a melodic and accessible quality. "Call Me Up" and "I Love a Man in Uniform" were the first radio-friendly songs the Gang had put on vinyl, and though the latter was banned from British radio shortly after its release— because England was at war in the Falkland Islands— the group enjoyed some commercial success. *Songs of the Free* received mixed reviews. Sweeting called it "an uncomfortable album of transition," but Pareles, writing for *Rolling Stone,* felt it was "by no means a pop sellout." King admitted to Considine that the group "definitely wanted to move towards using melody more in the songs," and this approach no doubt seemed to some listeners like a musical version of the softening that had worried Allen.

In 1983 King and Gill fired Burnham, much to the drummer's surprise and disappointment, before recording a new LP. *Hard* was an attempt to create an even more commercially viable sound; though Burnham was succeeded by Steve Goulding on stage, the group utilized drum machines along with banks of keyboards and the harmonies of several female backup singers on the album. The single "Is It Love" fared reasonably well in clubs and as a rock video. This time, however, the critics didn't pull any punches. "*Hard* is largely a string of wasted opportunities," opined *Melody Maker*'s Lynden Barber, who added that "the Gang simply sound *old*." For Greg Tate of the *Village Voice*, *Hard*'s compromises in sound, though substantial, were less offensive than the compromises in content; Tate noted that the band's "insincerity" this time led to "insufferable meaninglessness." Fricke called the album "a bland offering of Manhattan disco with dashes of postpunk cool."

Breakup, Hiatus, and Reunion

"The Gang of Four have called it a day, due to musical differences," *Melody Maker* reported in March of 1984. The group held a farewell performance at London's Hammersmith Palais, a show that Barber found disappointing except for the Gang's brief reunion with Allen and Burnham during one of the encores. In 1984 Mercury released a live album, *Gang of Four at the Palace,* which memorialized the *Hard* tour's stop in Hollywood. 1986 saw the release of *The Peel Sessions Album,* a collection of rawly rendered material recorded from 1971 to 1981 for British radio. *Melody Maker* dubbed the album "a perfect and classic nostalgia trip into the world of gaunt cynicism."

Andy Gill spent the next few years producing—he worked with American funk-rockers the Red Hot Chili Peppers on their debut—and writing music for films like *The Karate Kid.* But the revival of funk rock and the monster success of rap in the late eighties suggested to Gill and King that a new Gang of Four project might be well suited to the times. The Gang of Four had finally become available on compact disc (CD) after the 1990 Warner Bros. release of a collection entitled *A Brief History of the Twentieth Century;* in 1991 Gill, King, and some new collaborators put out an album of new material for Polydor records entitled *Mall.* The record manages to bring the hard political funk of classic Gang records into sync with the sound of the rap era without the mid-eighties compromises of *Hard.* "Don't Fix What Ain't Broke" was a driving dance anthem, while "Satellite" was an edgy but tuneful ballad. In addition, *Mall* contained songs about communication problems, the Vietnam war, and the paradoxes of consumer culture

Guitar Player declared *Mall* "a stunning album recapturing the best aspects of [the group's] past incarnations," while Dave Levesque of *Rhythm & News* called it "a thoroughly enjoyable piece of funk-drenched rock 'n roll." The band's tour for the album, on a bill with rap superstars Public Enemy, was also well received: *Variety* called the Gang set "a pleasantly surprising mix of old and new" and noted that "Gang of Four's sociopolitical point of view remains relevant some seven years after first breaking up." Even so, the low sales of *Mall* led Polygram to drop the group. Whatever its eventual fate, though, Gang of Four have achieved an important niche in the annals of alternative music for their powerful social criticism and skillful mix of funk, punk, and rock.

Selected discography

Entertainment! (includes "5:45," "At Home He's a Tourist," "I Found That Essence Rare," "Contract," and "Damaged Goods"), EMI/Warner Bros., 1979.

"To Hell With Poverty"/"Capital (It Fails Us Now)" (single), EMI, 1980.

Solid Gold (includes "Cheeseburger," "He'd Send in the Army," and "In the Ditch"), EMI/Warner Bros., 1981.

Songs of the Free (includes "Call Me Up" and "I Love a Man in Uniform"), EMI/Warner Bros., 1982.

Hard (includes "Is it Love"), EMI/Warner Bros., 1983.

Gang of Four at the Palace, EMI, 1984.

The Peel Sessions, Strange Fruit (U.K.), 1986.

A Brief History of the Twentieth Century, Warner Bros., 1990.

Mall (includes "Don't Fix What Ain't Broke" and "Satellite"), Polygram, 1991.

Sources

Guitar Player, June 1991; October 1991.

Melody Maker, May 26, 1979; October 6, 1979; November 3, 1979; February 28, 1981; March 7, 1981; August 8, 1981; May 22, 1982; July 10, 1982; June 25, 1983; September 17, 1983; March 3, 1984; April 21, 1984; December 6, 1986.

Musician, October 1982; October 1991.

Rhythm & News, July 1991.

Rolling Stone, May 29, 1980; July 24, 1980; September 3, 1981; July 8, 1982; October 27, 1983; November 16, 1989.

Variety, July 29, 1991.

Village Voice, October 1, 1979; May 19, 1980; April 29, 1981; July 27, 1982; November 8, 1983.

—*Simon Glickman*

David Geffen

Record company executive

Recording executive David Geffen is a phenomenon even by Hollywood's inflated standards. The wealthiest man in the entertainment industry, Geffen has displayed an uncanny assessment of musical talent and sharp business maneuvers. Though his list of money-making projects includes comedy films and real estate, Geffen remains best known for his work in the music industry. He has proven pivotal in the careers of a diverse group of artists, from folk artists to album-oriented rock acts to modern metal groups.

Geffen became a precocious *wunderkind* in the late 1960s, when he earned his first million dollars at the age of 25. He became successful because he could identify, advise, and guide potential superstar musicians. In later years he has retained his hold on an industry that caters to young people by delegating the responsibility for signing new talent to a small group of younger subordinates. *Vanity Fair* contributor Annie Leibovitz suggested that the difference between Geffen and traditional recording industry executives is that Geffen understands the artistic as well as the financial aspects of the business. "He really is friends with the talent that made him his fortune," Leibovitz wrote. "He can talk music and movies and theater with creative artists, and he understands their process."

Just a Poor Brooklyn Boy

Geffen has fondly called himself "just a boy from Brooklyn who wishes he were six feet tall, with blond hair and blue eyes," as quoted in *Vanity Fair.* Fantasizing was certainly important to the son of Russian immigrants who grew up in a three-room apartment. Geffen was born on February 21, 1943, in Brooklyn, New York. His father, a pattern maker, was often unemployed; his mother, Batya, supported the family by making corsets and brassieres and selling them from her home. Batya was so successful that she was eventually able to buy a building big enough for her store and several other tenants as well. "My mother in her own tiny, little way was entrepreneurial," Geffen stated in the *New York Times Magazine.* "Everything that I've ever applied in my life I learned hanging around her store. . . . I grew up learning my mother's ideas about integrity and business and negotiating. It never occurred to me I'd be anything but a businessman."

Another world lured Geffen, however. He haunted the Brooklyn movie theaters, drawing inspiration from the lavish lifestyles of the stars, especially studio bosses like Louis B. Mayer and Jack Warner. In a *Forbes* profile, Geffen said: "I looked at these moguls and the world they created and figured it would be a fun way to make a living."

His ambitions notwithstanding, Geffen was an indifferent student who graduated from Brooklyn's New Utrecht High School in 1960 in the bottom ten percent of his class. The same day he earned his diploma, Geffen ventured west where he hoped to enter the University of California, Los Angeles (UCLA). He was denied admission on the basis of poor grades, but was able to enroll at the University of Texas at Austin; he lasted only a semester before flunking out. He returned home to New York for an equally short stint at Brooklyn College.

Early jobs as an usher at the CBS television studios and as a receptionist for a television production company also ended disastrously—Geffen was fired both times. In 1964 he landed a job in the mail room at the William Morris Agency. In order to be considered for the position he had to lie about his college background. He told personnel at William Morris that he had graduated from UCLA. When he discovered that the agency planned to contact UCLA to corroborate his story, the resourceful Geffen kept watch in the mailroom for four months, until he was able to retrieve the college's reply. He steamed the letter open, took it to a printer, had the letterhead forged, and created his own academic credentials. Geffen told a *New York Times* reporter: "It was either

give William Morris what they wanted or give up my dreams. . . . I just don't believe in taking no for an answer."

From Agent to Executive

Taking advice from the head of the William Morris music office, Geffen began scouting talent among his own age group—especially musicians. He proved to have a good ear, and the agency promoted him to junior agent after 18 months. In 1968 Geffen moved to the less staid Ashley Famous Agency, where he worked with such powerhouse groups as the Doors and Peter, Paul, and Mary. Leibovitz noted that Geffen quickly became a "Talent Scout Extraordinaire" with "the best instincts about people."

Those instincts blossomed in the early 1970s, when Geffen and partner Elliot Roberts formed a record label, Asylum Records, supported by their own management company. They produced records with such artists as Joni Mitchell, Jackson Browne, the Eagles, and Linda Ronstadt, all of whom enjoyed great success with the label. In 1971 Geffen sold Asylum to Warner Communications for $7 million but kept his position as director of the company. Two years later, Warner asked him to head the struggling Elektra subsidiary. Geffen dropped two-thirds of Elektra's artists and signed new talent. Soon both Asylum and Elektra were thriving.

Hiatus and Triumphant Return

A brief and less-than-successful stint as vice-chair of Warner Brothers Pictures convinced Geffen that he was not suited for the standard bureaucracy of Hollywood filmmaking. His career came to an abrupt halt in 1976 when he was misdiagnosed with bladder cancer. Convinced he was fatally ill, he left the business for the less taxing work of teaching at Yale University and UCLA. Four years passed before doctors in New York City reversed the prognosis on his illness. Relieved, Geffen resumed working in the recording industry.

Geffen subsequently founded Geffen Records, an independent label promoted and distributed by Warner Communications. Artists on the starting roster at the company's founding in 1980 included Donna Summer, Elton John, and John Lennon and Yoko Ono. An album by the latter couple, *Double Fantasy,* went triple platinum and won a Grammy Award for album of the year. Geffen was back in the game.

Always keen to good business, Geffen made a decision. "At the age of thirty-three I stopped signing acts," he disclosed in *Vanity Fair.* "I don't hold myself out to be a talent scout any longer. I'm too old." Despite Geffen's personal doubts, younger Geffen employees with somewhat radical tastes helped their leader stay at the forefront in pop music, signing acts like Guns N' Roses, Whitesnake, and Aerosmith. In the meantime, Geffen branched into musical theater, producing some major Broadway hits, including *Cats, Little Shop of Horrors, Dreamgirls,* and *M. Butterfly. Cats,* which opened on Broadway in 1982, is still running.

By March of 1990 Geffen was responsible for 50 gold and 31 platinum albums. In a surprise move, he sold his label to MCA, Inc., for 10 million shares of stock. The decision proved momentous. Eight months later, MCA was sold to a Japanese company, Matsushita, for $6.1 billion. Geffen reaped a $170 million profit on the deal.

Vanity Fair's Leibovitz called David Geffen "the man who can fix things, who can smooth things over. The man who can get people placed and replaced. The man whose phone call has the effect of a corporation." An equally fitting tribute comes from the lyrics of Joni Mitchell's hit "A Free Man in Paris," written about Geffen. According to Mitchell's song, the tempestuous Geffen spends his days "stoking the starmaker machinery behind the popular song."

Sources

Esquire, February 1975; November 1982.
Forbes, April 14, 1980; December 24, 1990.
GQ, March 1991.
Los Angeles Times, November 15, 1991; March 3, 1992.
Newsweek, November 20, 1972.
New York, May 17, 1982; January 24, 1983.
New York Times, October 3, 1982; October 31, 1982.
New York Times Magazine, July 21, 1985.
Rolling Stone, May 15, 1980; January 22, 1981; March 5, 1981.
Time, February 25, 1974.
Vanity Fair, March 1991.
Washington Post, May 6, 1982.

—*Anne Janette Johnson*

The Gipsy Kings

Flamenco band

From the obscurity of playing parties and festivals in the south of France, the Gipsy Kings have moved up to the prominence of performing on *Saturday Night Live* and the *Johnny Carson Show*. Their music has been used in a range of different projects, including the soundtrack to pop star George Michael's Diet Coke commercial and cover material for salsa and merengue band recordings. They have developed a style of music that has been described variously as gypsy rock and salsa-flamenco fusion. The Gipsy Kings are not only adaptable but are internationally accessible, as 15 gold and platinum albums worldwide bear witness.

The six-member group formed in 1976 when musicians from two French Gypsy families joined together. Nicolas and Andre Reyes—the sons of Jose Reyes, the famed flamenco singer for Manitas de Platas—along with Tonino, Paco, and Diego Baliardo and Chico Bouchikhi—all of whom are either cousins or brothers-in-law of the Reyes—are steeped in the Gypsy lifestyle. All of the Gipsy Kings live in an 80-trailer Gypsy caravan near Arles, France, for at least part of the year.

For the Record. . .

Members include **Diego Baliardo** (guitar), **Paco Baliardo** (guitar), **Tonino Baliardo** (solo guitar), **Chico Bouchikhi** (guitar and background vocals; retired in 1989, replaced by **Canut Reyes**), **Andre Reyes** (guitar and background vocals), and **Nicolas Reyes** (lead vocals and guitar).

Band formed c. 1976 in Arles, France; as Los Reyes, released album *Gitan Poete,* 1977; changed name to the Gipsy Kings and released album *Allegria,* 1982; performed throughout Europe and North Africa; released *Gipsy Kings,* Elektra, 1987.

Awards: 15 gold and platinum records worldwide; nominated for best world music artist, *Billboard,* 1989.

Addresses: *Manager*—Shep Gordon, Alive Entertainments, Inc., 8912 Burton Way, Beverly Hills, CA 90212. *Record company*—Elektra, 75 Rockfeller Plaza, New York, NY 10019.

Only three of the members have permanent houses elsewhere in France. "Our music is ageless and its roots are in the family and in caravan life," Chico Bouchikhi was quoted as saying in the *New York Times.* "Our mothers were listening to this music when we were still in their wombs and now our children are born with it. That's how integral it is to our lives."

Originally called Los Reyes, the group recorded under that name on their first album, *Gitan Poete,* in 1977. This record was the first of the Gipsy Kings' efforts to put flamenco music into pop song structures. From the start they were followed by devoted fans to every *feria* (festival) in the south of France. From St. Tropez to Italy, thousands of men and women danced the night away to the rhythm of the six guitarists dressed in flashy dress shirts, black peg-leg pants, and shiny boots.

Played for the Rich and Famous

In 1982 the band changed their name to the Gipsy Kings, preferring the uncommon alternate spelling with an "i," and released their second album, *Allegria,* a folk record featuring more traditional songs. The lyrics, sung in a patois called *Gitane*—a mixture of French, Spanish, and Gypsy languages—cover the subjects of love, freedom, and the celebration of life.

The Gipsy Kings recorded another acoustic album entitled *Luna de Fuegos* in 1983. The music was characterized by the cascade of five rhythm guitarists strumming and was punctuated by the passionate, raspy wails of Nicolas Reyes and the daring solo lines of lead guitarist Tonino Baliardo. Baliardo's agile playing drew comparisons to another French Gypsy guitarist, the jazz master Django Reinhardt. Over the next three years the band established themselves as a popular live act in clubs throughout Europe and North Africa. They became a favorite of the French jet set, even receiving an invitation from sultry screen actress Brigitte Bardot to play at her birthday party.

Things really took off for the Gipsy Kings in 1986, however, when the group caught the attention of French record producer Claude Martinez. Martinez, who later became their manager, offered the band a recording opportunity using modern pop production and arrangements. After a year of careful work the Gipsy Kings managed to match folk melodies with a contemporary rhythm section that included bass, synthesizer, and percussion. "The change came pretty smoothly," Chico Bouchikhi commented in the *Washington Post.* "We all agreed on it. The only thing that we were afraid of is that if we were to invite new musicians, that we would lose our essence. But actually it worked very well and we all thought it was perfect timing to do it."

Rocketed to International Stardom

Indeed the setting was ripe for the Gipsy Kings' induction into international stardom. *Gipsy Kings* was released in 1987 on Elektra and became a surprise Top 10 hit in continental Europe. Both "Bamboleo" and "Djobi Djoba" became hit singles in more than half a dozen countries. Although *Gipsy Kings* entered *Billboard's* pop album chart at Number 199, the recording sold more than 150,000 copies in America alone. At last the band had cracked the U.S. market.

The Gipsy Kings spent the next two years touring extensively and promoting the new album. Life on the road suited the group very well; they spent all of their time, both on and off the stage, together. True Gypsies, the nomadic way of life was in their blood as well as in their music. As Chico Bouchikhi stated in the *Washington Post:* "It was very important to us not to be a big group but to be together as a family. It was one way to stay together and also explore a career."

The Gipsy Kings' music was soon touching the lives of many people. In July of 1988 the group performed at a benefit concert for *SOS Racisme,* a French human rights organization that has sponsored concerts in Africa, Europe, and New York City. In the same year

French fashion designer Christian Lacroix came out with a line of clothing he said had been inspired by listening to the Gipsy Kings' music. In the United States the adult contemporary video channel VH-1 chose the single "Bamboleo" as a Pick of the Week.

Nominated for Best World Music Artist

Although the Gipsy Kings' previous effort had done very well, a doubt arose as to whether or not *Gipsy Kings* had been too acoustic for American discotheques. The sextet responded in 1989 by introducing a mix of electronic and acoustic percussion that blended polyrhythmic styles ranging from salsa to the Islamic popular music of *rai* on their next major label recording. Salsa superstar Ruben Blades collaborated with the Gipsy Kings on the album and co-wrote "Caminando por la Calle." The result, *Mosaique,* was an exotic, toe-tapping flamenco crossover and earned the group a nomination for *Billboard's* best world music artist. Later that year Joan Baez did a Spanish version of "May Way" with the Gipsy Kings on her own album, *Speaking of Dreams.*

During one of their infrequent rests from touring, Chico Bouchikhi retired. He was replaced in 1989 by yet another relative from Arles, Canut Reyes. The new lineup of Gipsy Kings recorded *Este Mundo* in the spring of 1991. Like previous releases, the album contained both traditional songs and flamenco tunes amidst a variety of *cantes,* or ballads, *bailes,* or dance music, and *toques,* solo guitar instrumentals. The album, however, contained very different rhythmic ideas from the disco-oriented *Mosaique.* Mideastern influences were explored with the use of two percussion instruments, the darbouka and the tabla. The unique sounds of *Este Mundo* proved to be another winner for the band.

The Gipsy Kings' successes continued into the 1990s, prompting the group to deliver a live album in 1992.

Before he left the band, Chico Bouchikhi, as quoted in *People,* expressed a sentiment that may well explain the reason behind the Gipsy Kings' great popularity: "We played for Charlie Chaplin before he died and the music made him cry. It's for a reaction like that that we work so hard."

Selected discography

(As Los Reyes) *Gitan Poete,* Tudor, 1977.
Allegria, CBS France, 1982.
Luna de Fuegos, CBS France, 1983.
Gipsy Kings, Elektra, 1987.
Mosaique, Elektra, 1989.
Este Mundo, Elektra, 1991.
Live, Elektra, 1992

Sources

Books

Manuel, Peter, *Popular Musics of the Non-Western World: An Introductory Survey,* Oxford University Press, 1988.

Periodicals

New York Times, July 21, 1988; July 24, 1988; March 6, 1989; December 6, 1989.
People, February 13, 1989; January 29, 1990.
Spin, November 1991.
Time, January 2, 1989.
Washington Post, December 28, 1988; March 4, 1989; January 28, 1990.

Additional information for this profile was obtained from Elektra Records press releases, January 1988, February 1989, and June 1991.

—*Christian Whitaker*

Herbie Hancock

Pianist, composer

Virtuoso pianist Herbie Hancock is, in a sense, a musical chameleon whose compositions and recordings change direction as unceremoniously and effortlessly as the lizard's skin changes color. But with Hancock, the transformations are not designed for camouflage and self-defense; rather they are the outgrowth of a mind that resists stagnation and harbors a deep love of all music—a love that would be compromised if it were hostage to a particular style of song. In playing acoustic bebop jazz as well as electronic fusion, in composing sweeping film scores alongside playful advertising jingles, Hancock knowingly risks disappointing those camps that wish to claim him as their darling. But only by straddling so many styles and interests can Hancock tap his copious talent for versatility and allow his moods and feelings to find their truest expression in music.

Herbert Jeffrey Hancock was born in Chicago, Illinois, on April 12, 1940, to Wayman Hancock, a grocery store clerk and future federal meat inspector, and Winnie Griffin Hancock, a secretary in whom a love of music and appreciation for education had been instilled as a young child. When Herbie was a baby, his parents discovered that he would stop crying when music was played. And as a toddler, he would respond ecstatically when a piano was near. This ecstasy was finally put to use when his parents bought an old upright piano for 25 dollars. Instead of playing sports and running about with his schoolmates in the back alleys of Chicago, the studious seven-year-old preferred to stay home learning piano and nurturing a fascination with science and electronics. He skipped two grades, an academic feat that was fostered by his parents' promotion of discipline and that he would later say helped forge his identity as a high achiever. Similarly prompted by his mother's love of music and by enthusiastic public school instructors, young Hancock listened to opera on the radio and excelled at the piano, winning a scholastic contest at age 11, the award for which was a concert performance of a Mozart concerto with the Chicago Symphony Orchestra.

Drawn to Jazz Improvisation

Throughout high school, Hancock enjoyed listening to the rhythm and blues music that was echoing in the city, but he never considered trying to play these soulful, animated songs. The free-form phrases of jazz were even more remote. But then he heard a classmate perform an improvisational piece at a talent show, and he was so fascinated with the spirit of it, so mesmerized by the honesty of its expression, that he decided to learn everything he could about this music, which he had never really understood. "So he closeted himself

For the Record. . .

Born Herbert Jeffrey Hancock, April 12, 1940, in Chicago, IL; son of Wayman Edward and Winnie (Griffin) Hancock; married Gudrun Meixner, August 31, 1968. *Education:* Attended Grinnell College, 1956-60; Roosevelt University, 1960; Manhattan School of Music, 1962; and New School for Social Research, 1967.

First performed with Chicago Symphony Orchestra, 1952; pianist with Donald Byrd group, 1960-63, and with Miles Davis Quintet, 1963-68; formed band Mwandishi, and released breakthrough fusion album of same name, 1971; formed acoustic jazz ensemble V.S.O.P.; host of programs appearing on television, including *Coast-to-Coast,* *Showtime,* and *Rockschool.*

Selected awards: Citation of Achievement, Broadcast Music Club, 1963; Jay Award, *Jazz* magazine, 1964; talent deserving wider recognition, 1967, first place in piano category, 1968, 1969, and 1970, composer award, 1971, and jazzman of the year, 1974, *Down Beat* critics' polls; All-Star Band New Artist Award, *Record World,* 1968; named top jazz artist, *Black Music* magazine, 1974; Grammy Award for best rhythm and blues instrumental performance, 1983 and 1984, and for best jazz instrumental composition, 1987; received five awards on First Annual MTV Video Music Awards show, including best concept video and most experimental video, for "Rockit," 1984; Academy Award for best original score for *'Round Midnight,* 1986.

Addresses: *Publicist*—Hanson & Schwam, 2020 Avenue of the Stars, Suite 410, Los Angeles, California 90067. *Record company*—Columbia, 51 West 52nd St., New York, NY 10019.

for hours alone with Oscar Peterson and George Shearing records," noted Lynne Norment in *Ebony,* "committed to paper their notes and then reproduced them. This tedious exercise led to his ability to analyze and dissect harmonic structures, rhythmic patterns and choral voicings."

In 1956, again at the urging of his mother, Hancock enrolled at Grinnell College in Iowa, at first studying engineering—the knowledge of which would later help him launch electronic jazz fusion—but soon turning to a field closer to his heart: music composition. In 1960, armed with an analytical understanding of music, Hancock returned to Chicago, where he gigged as a free-lance pianist with several jazz combos and visiting bands, playing with, among others, Coleman Hawkins.

In the winter of 1960 a blizzard delayed the pianist for trumpeter Donald Byrd's group, which was scheduled to play in Chicago, and a local club owner suggested Hancock as a substitute. After that performance Byrd became the first professional jazz mentor for Hancock, bringing the young pianist to New York City, introducing him to those within the jazz establishment, and laying the groundwork for Hancock's 1962 debut album, *Takin' Off.* The LP featured the accompaniment of jazz greats Dexter Gordon and Freddie Hubbard and introduced Hancock's composition, "Watermelon Man;" the piece was made a hit by Mongo Santamaria a year later and was subsequently recorded by over 200 artists.

Although he would continue playing conventional jazz for the next few years, Hancock joined briefly with the experimental avant-garde instrumentalist Eric Dolphy in the first of what would be many trailblazing forays. "I played things that were almost blasphemous and sounded grotesque," Hancock was quoted as saying in *People* in 1987. "But they had a certain beauty that we could feel even if nobody in the audience could. Sometimes it was good and sometimes it wasn't, but I had to stand up for all of it or else I couldn't play any of it. I learned how to be courageous from that experience."

Played With Miles Davis Quintet

In 1963, on the recommendation of Byrd, Hancock was invited to join the quintet of jazz giant Miles Davis, a pioneering trumpeter who was credited with ingenuously nurturing young talents. Along with Wayne Shorter, Ron Carter, and Tony Williams—the *wunderkind* drummer who would help Hancock develop his signature percussive piano style—the young pianist was given comfortably broad guidelines for playing. The Davis group became one of the most influential jazz combos in the 1960s, fostering an environment in which the musicians were given free reign to instrumentally express their emotions and moods. Outside of the group, Hancock continued to perform with such luminaries as Phil Woods, Oliver Nelson, Wes Montgomery, Quincy Jones, and Sonny Rollins.

In the mid-1960s, jazz was beginning to lose some of its audience, in part because purist fans resented the movement away from traditional bebop; even Davis, one of the standard bearers of this tradition, began to steer his combo in the direction of a more funky, rock-driven style. Jazz was also competing with rock and soul music for the attention and dollars of young listeners. Throughout this financially troubled period, Hancock proved his resiliency and flexibility by writing commercial jingles for Chevrolet, Standard Oil, and

Eastern Airlines; composing the soundtrack for the film *Blow Up;* and penning "Fat Albert Rotunda" for comedian Bill Cosby's television special *Hey, Hey, Hey, It's Fat Albert.*

Also during this time, an era of explosive change in politics and social dynamics, Hancock, a self-described jazz snob, began flirting with music beyond that of the narrowly defined jazz world. He had always enjoyed rhythm and blues, but considered it somehow inferior to the pure jazz he had embraced. In the 1950s and mid-1960s, "I tried to pretend that I was liberal, musically tolerant," the musician divulged in *Down Beat* in 1988. "But I really wasn't. Actually the first record that turned me on to R & B—and pop music in general—was [James Brown's] 'Poppa's Got a Brand New Bag.' That made me start listening to R & B, because I liked that kind of beat. . . . Later on, I liked Sly Stone's 'Thank You Falettinme Be Mice Elf Agin' a lot. It was like the funkiest thing I ever heard, and I still like it."

Expanded Musical Interests

After leaving Davis in 1968, Hancock, always eager to take new musical steps, formed his own quintet, which departed from the acoustic status quo and welcomed the emerging age of electronics. Under Davis he had started playing the electric piano; though providing a less personal sound, the instrument tapped into Hancock's long-held fascination with technology and further stretched the limits of music and Hancock's own virtuosity. In 1971 Hancock helped usher in the era of jazz fusion with the album *Mwandishi*—a Swahili word for composer—which featured state-of-the-art technology, and was named one of the year's ten best LPs by *Time* magazine.

Although *Mwandishi* disappointed jazz purists who believed Hancock had squandered his talent and forsaken his inimitable piano style, it served as the springboard for the artist's love affair with cutting edge music. What made the criticism bearable for Hancock, above and beyond his revelry in experimentation, was his growing adherence to Nichiren Shoshu Buddhism. "Buddhism has helped me toward gaining control over my own destiny, and given me the courage to follow directions I believe in," he expressed in *Ebony* in 1987. "Over the years I've made decisions about things, especially music, and have been scoffed at and ridiculed and opposed, but I knew I had to do these things."

Venturing further into unknown territory, Hancock released the watershed *Headhunters* in 1973, an album using synthesizers and other gadgetry, which essentially defined the jazz/funk/pop hybrid and sold more than a million copies. This crossover LP played off the burgeoning disco craze and, predictably, further piqued Hancock's critics. The musician continued affirming his individuality, though, playing with pop artists Stevie Wonder and the Pointer Sisters, and—to the delight of traditionalists who thought they had lost him—forming the acoustic jazz group V.S.O.P. with several members of the old Davis quintet.

Dance Music and Film Scores

The 1983 release *Future Shock* once again confirmed Hancock's successful formula of using new sounds and high technology to frame popular music. The song "Rockit," spun off from the album, reached Number One on the dance and soul music charts, became the biggest selling twelve-inch single in Columbia Records history, and garnered a Grammy Award for best rhythm and blues instrumental. The key to this hard-

---

"Over the years I've made decisions about things, especially music, and have been scoffed at and ridiculed and opposed, but I knew I had to do these things."

---

driving dance song, which surprised even those listeners who had become accustomed to Hancock's musical wanderings, was the use of record scratching—rubbing the needle the wrong way while an LP is playing—a technique that had been gaining popularity with fans of rap music. Further inventiveness with the song's video, featuring the gesticulations of dismembered robots, led to Hancock's accrual of five MTV awards.

Other 1980s releases also included an amalgamation of styles. On his 1984 album *Sound-System,* which also won a Grammy, Hancock explored the sounds of street funk music, integrating African and Latin American undertones. The 1988 release *The Perfect Machine* was similarly rooted in the rhythms and beats of contemporary urban life.

Hancock's ability to adjust to and even create musical trends is an outgrowth of an ear brilliantly attuned to the modulation and changeability of individual pieces. In a review of a Hancock quartet performance in 1990, Jon

Pareles of the *New York Times* wrote, "When a pop-jazz tune threatened to get too sweet, Mr. Hancock would come up with a lilting, melodic solo but attack the notes just off the beat, giving them an intransigent edge, or he would skew the harmony with a disturbing hint of dissonance." In another case, while performing at a 1986 jazz festival, Hancock noticed that a string on the piano had broken. Instead of avoiding the key or demanding a new piano, he chose to use the metallic twang as percussive accompaniment to a ballad.

Hosted Instructional Series

Hancock's interest in telling stories musically has translated into his prolific compositions of film scores. He won an Academy Award and a Grammy for his soundtrack to *'Round Midnight,* the celebrated 1986 film based loosely on the life of expatriate bebop musician Bud Powell in Paris in the late 1950s. Hancock has also composed music for *Colors, A Soldier's Story, Death Wish, Livin' Large, Action Jackson,* and *Jo Jo Dancer, Your Life Is Calling.* In pursuing the love of education that his mother instilled in him as a youngster, Hancock hosted the instructional television series *Rockschool,* which taught viewers about jazz history and the playing of jazz instruments, and a cable series, *Coast-to-Coast,* a show featuring concerts and interviews with established and promising musical personalities.

It is a credit to Hancock's talent that he has so successfully balanced commercial success with artistic integrity. In stepping out of the role of "pure jazzman," a classification that traditionalists were eager to impose on him, he has risked being seen as a fickle sell-out. But he has stuck by his belief that all music is equally valid. When asked in a 1988 *Down Beat* interview what he thought of the view that pop music should not be considered on a par with jazz and classical, he was reported to have said, "My opinion is that a hamburger and a hot dog deserve an equally important place in history as caviar and champagne, because we can't do without any of it. . . . On a human level, the garbage man is just as important as the teacher or a rock star or a president, because you have to have them. The world would have been dead a long time ago without garbage men."

Selected discography

Takin' Off (includes "Watermelon Man"), Blue Note, 1962, reissued, 1987.

(With others) *My Point of View,* Blue Note, 1963.
Herbie Hancock, Blue Note, 1964.
Empyrean Isles, Blue Note, 1964, reissued, 1985.
Inventions and Dimensions, Blue Note, 1965.
Maiden Voyage, Blue Note, 1966.
Speak Like a Child, Blue Note, 1968.
Mwandishi, Warner Bros., 1971.
Crossings, Warner Bros., 1972.
Sextant, Columbia, 1972.
Headhunters, Columbia, 1973.
Man-Child, Columbia, 1975.
Secrets, Columbia, 1976.
Feets Don't Fail Me Now, Columbia, 1979.
Lite Me Up, Columbia, 1982.
Future Shock (includes "Rockit"), Columbia, 1983.
Sound-System, Columbia, 1984, reissued, 1985.
The Prisoner, Blue Note, 1987.
The Perfect Machine, Columbia, 1988.
The Best of Herbie Hancock, Columbia, 1988.
(With Chick Corea) *Corea and Hancock,* Polydor, 1988.
(With V.S.O.P.) *The Quintet: V.S.O.P. Live* (recorded 1976), Columbia, 1988.
(With Coleman Hawkins and Sonny Rollins) *All the Things You Are* (recorded 1963-64), Blue Note, 1990.
(With others) *A Jazz Collection,* Columbia Jazz Contemporary Masters, 1991.
Mr. Hands, Columbia.
Monster, Columbia.
Quartet: Hancock, Marsalis, Carter, Williams, Columbia.
Thrust, Columbia.

Has performed on more than a dozen albums with the Miles Davis Quintet.

Composer of film scores, including *Blow Up,* GB, 1966; *Death Wish,* Paramount, 1974; *A Soldier's Story,* Columbia, 1984; *'Round Midnight,* Warner Bros., 1986; *Jo Jo Dancer, Your Life Is Calling,* Columbia, 1986; *Action Jackson,* Lorimar, 1988; *Colors,* Orion, 1988; and *Livin' Large,* Samuel Goldwyn, 1991.

Sources

Down Beat, July 1986; June 1988.
Ebony, March 1987.
New York Times, July 2, 1990.
People, January 19, 1987.
Rolling Stone, October 25, 1984.

Additional information for this profile was obtained from a Hanson & Schwam Public Relations biography, 1992.

—*Isaac Rosen*

Screamin' Jay Hawkins

Singer, songwriter

One of rock's true wild men, Screamin' Jay Hawkins burst on the music scene with a 1956 hit called "I Put A Spell On You" and a frenzied stage show that included a coffin, a skull on a stick, and mock voodoo shrieks. Born Jalacy J. Hawkins in Cleveland, Ohio, on July 18, 1929, the singer was one of several children (the number varies, even according to Hawkins's own account). He was placed in an orphanage as an infant and adopted at the age of 18 months. By the time Hawkins was four he showed an interest in the piano and soon learned to read and write music. He admired singers Paul Robeson and Enrico Caruso and studied opera at the Ohio Conservatory of Music. As a boy, he played piano in Cleveland night spots for tips. And in his teens, Hawkins made successful boxing appearances in local Golden Gloves competition.

In 1944 Hawkins dropped out of high school and joined the military. Accounts of his years in the service differ; the most accepted version is that he joined the Special Services and entertained U.S. troops at home and in Germany, Japan, and Korea. Hawkins himself, however, has claimed that he fought in the Pacific. "I got caught on the island of Saipan" he told Karen Schoemer of the *New York Times*. "Our drop zone was right in the middle of the enemy compound. . . . Before we could get the straps of the parachutes off, we were in the enemy's hands. We never got a chance to fire a shot. . . . It was 18 months before we got rescued." Aside from entertaining the troops, Hawkins worked as a boxer throughout the 1940s, even winning the middleweight championship of Alaska in 1949.

First Recording Stint Nearly Ended Career

After leaving the army in 1952, Hawkins took a job as musician and chauffeur with jazz bandleader Tiny Grimes. According to Gerry Hirshey's book *Nowhere to Run,* Hawkins didn't much like the jazz music or Grimes's car—in which he had to sleep most nights. What he really wanted to do was play the new post-War blues. It was these blues, a raw, danceable music, that was on Hawkins's mind in 1953 when he accompanied Grimes to a recording session for Atlantic Records. The fledgling label had already scored hits with Ruth Brown, Big Joe Turner, and Ray Charles and was cultivating a smooth mixture of pop and rhythm and blues. Grimes had agreed to let Hawkins sing a couple of his own tunes if the main recording session went well.

Hawkins did get his chance, but when he launched into a raucous version of a tune he had written called "Screamin' Blues," pop-minded Atlantic chief Ahmet Ertegun found his vocals too raw and tried to get Hawkins to sing smoothly—like popular 1950s crooner

Born Jalacy J. Hawkins (changed name c. 1954), July 18, 1929, in Cleveland, OH. *Education:* Studied opera at the Cleveland Conservatory of Music.

Singer, songwriter, pianist. Boxer, 1940s; middleweight champion of Alaska, 1949. Performed with Tiny Grimes band, 1952-54; performed with Fats Domino, 1954-55, at Small's Paradise, Harlem, NY, and in Atlantic City, NJ, clubs; began solo career, signed with Okeh records, and released "I Put a Spell on You," 1955; performed on radio, beginning 1956; performed at clubs in Hawaii and military bases in the Far East, 1960s, and in Hawaii, New York, and Europe, 1970s; recorded with Rolling Stone Keith Richards, 1979, and opened for the Rolling Stones, 1980; toured the U.S., mid 1980s—; made commercials in Japan for Sony. Film appearances include *American Hot Wax,* 1978, *Mystery Train,* 1990, and *A Rage in Harlem,* 1991. *Military service:* U.S. Army/Air Force, Special Services Division, 1945-52.

Addresses: *Record company*—Bizarre Records, 740 North La Brea Ave., 2nd floor, Los Angeles, CA 90038-3339. *Management*—Glitter Management Company, 833 North Orange Grove Ave., Los Angeles, CA 90046.

Fats Domino. In the ensuing argument Hawkins nearly ended his career by trying to strike Ertegun. Needless to say, "Screamin' Blues" was never released.

Shortly after the Atlantic fiasco, Hawkins split with Grimes and began drifting between bands—even spending time in Domino's group—before getting his first solo gig at Small's Paradise in New York City's Harlem. It was at Small's, and later at clubs in Atlantic City, New Jersey, that Jalacy J. Hawkins transformed himself into Screamin' Jay Hawkins.

"I Put a Spell on You"

In 1955 Hawkins signed with Okeh Records. Okeh producer Arnold Maxim wanted Hawkins to record "I Put A Spell On You," a song Hawkins had written the previous year and had already recorded for the Grand label. The earlier version of the song that would become Hawkins's signature was subdued; Maxim wanted it wild. "[Maxim] got everybody drunk," Hawkins told the *Los Angeles Times,* "and we came out with this weird version, I don't even remember making the record. Before, I was just a normal blues singer. I was just

Jay Hawkins. It all sort of just fell in place. I found out I could do more destroying a song and screaming it to death."

"Spell" was a sensation; at first it was banned. "They said it was 'cannibalistic,' that it sounded like a man eating somebody," Hawkins told the *Washington Post.* So Okeh edited the offensive portions and the song became a hit. In fact, Hawkins exploited the cannibal controversy for all it was worth. "I stuck the bone in my nose," he told the *Post,* "put on white shoe polish, combed my hair straight up and got naked with a piece of cloth around my loins, had a spear and shield. . . . So what's wrong with acting like a wild warrior? The NAACP [National Association for the Advancement of Colored People] and CORE [Congress of Racial Equality] didn't like it, said I was making fun of the black people. . . . I said . . . I'm making a living. I'm not breaking the law. How dare you?'"

In 1956 Hawkins began appearing in New York disc jockey Alan Freed's legendary package shows. Freed liked Hawkins and persuaded him to begin making his entrance in a coffin. According to *Nowhere to Run,* Hawkins was at first reluctant to get into the coffin, but after Freed offered him $2,000 for the stunt, he agreed to make it a part of the act. Though the untamed stage antics, coffin routine, and "I Put A Spell on You" kept Hawkins's career going for many years, the "savage" persona also proved to be a liability. Mike Boehm of the *Los Angeles Times* reported that Hawkins "fell into a pre-show ritual of imbibing while listening to favorite records to psyche himself up for the transformation into Screamin' Jay." Hawkins told Boehm, "I figured I couldn't sing the song unless I was drunk."

Transition Beyond 1950s Difficult

Like many 1950s rockers, Hawkins had a difficult time in the following decade. He worked clubs in Hawaii and toured military bases in the Far East. His biggest successes came in Europe, where he continued to enjoy wide popularity. In England, he found imitators in Screamin' Lord Sutch, Arthur Brown, and the rock band Black Sabbath. In 1967 Hawkins released *Feast of the Mau Mau,* an album that made no impression on the pop charts but which the *Los Angeles Times* called "fine, fun-house horror stuff."

During the 1970s Hawkins split his time between Hawaii, New York City, where he played in local clubs, and Europe, where he remained a popular attraction. He quit drinking in 1974 and found he could do "Spell" just as well sober as he could drunk. He also collected royalties from the many cover versions of his songs

Artists from jazz singer Nina Simone to rockers Creedance Clearwater Revival recorded "Spell" and other Hawkins-penned tunes. In 1978 the singer appeared in *American Hot Wax,* the film biography of disc jockey Freed. The following year Hawkins went into New York's Blue Rock Studio with Rolling Stone Keith Richards, who lent his guitar to "Armpit #6" and a new version of "Spell." The collaboration was such a success that in 1980 Hawkins opened for the Rolling Stones at Madison Square Garden.

Interest in Hawkins mounted in earnest in 1984 when film director Jim Jarmusch used "I Put a Spell on You" as the centerpiece of his cult hit *Stranger Than Paradise*; a wider audience began to appreciate Hawkins's talents, and he began touring the United States regularly. Before a Boston show he told the *Boston Herald,* "I am going to reach into . . . [spectators'] chests, grab their hearts, fumble with their emotions, and have them walking sideways and eating chop suey with chopsticks out of their ear[s] while wearing a gas mask."

Film Career Proved Fruitful

In 1990 Hawkins appeared as the sardonic night manager of a seedy Memphis hotel in Jarmusch's film *Mystery Train,* a performance that Karen Schoemer of the *New York Times* called "wonderfully subdued." The 1991 film *A Rage in Harlem* featured a Hawkins performance of "I Put A Spell on You," among other tunes, in one of its pivotal scenes. In Japan, where Hawkins is extremely popular, he has made commercials for Sony. Royalties from the many remakes of his songs bring in a tidy sum every year, and he continues to tour Japan, Europe, and the U.S. regularly.

At times Hawkins continues to be frustrated by the persona he has created for himself; he told the *New York Times,* "For once I want to go out and sing 'Stardust' or 'Feelings' and I want to sing it straight. I want to show that I can do it." But on the whole, Hawkins seems satisfied with his position in the rock and roll stratosphere; "I don't want nothin' else from this world," he told the *Los Angeles Times.* "I stuck to the roots, and it carried me this far. I have no complaints."

Selected discography

Feast of the Mau Mau, 1967.
Real Life (recorded 1983), EPM, 1989.
Voodoo Jive: The Best of Screamin' Jay Hawkins (1954-1969), Rhino, 1990.
Black Music for White People, Bizarre, 1991.
Cow Fingers & Mosquito Pie, Epic/Legacy, 1991.
The Night & Day of Screamin' Jay, 52 Rue Est, 1992.

Sources

Books

Hirshey, Gerry, *Nowhere to Run,* New York Times Books, 1984.

Periodicals

Boston Herald, December 18, 1987.
Living Blues, Spring 1982.
Los Angeles Times, April 12, 1991.
New York Times, April 5, 1991.
Washington Post, February 3, 1990.

—Jordan Wankoff

John Hiatt

Singer, songwriter

Singer-songwriter John Hiatt has been an important and enduring figure in rock music, a flipside to many rock artists who live by the guitar and the groove. Rock audiences, no less than their Broadway counterparts, value the perfect line of lyric that flashes with wit or cuts to the bone of a painful story. Over the last several years, wordsmith John Hiatt has gradually risen to prominence by converting his personal tragedies into a lengthy catalogue of recordings.

Hiatt's raspy, blues-based singing has been compared with that of Bruce Springsteen. Dabbling in several styles of music, including what *Rolling Stone* critic Ira Robbins cited as "heartland rock, Philly soul, stately folk [and] countrified swing," Hiatt has consistently assembled fine backup groups featuring such rock stalwarts as Ry Cooder and Nick Lowe. Ultimately, however, Hiatt's skill as a lyricist is the thread that ties his music together.

Hiatt turned to writing during a traumatic childhood in Indianapolis, Indiana; within a two-year span his father died, and his older brother committed suicide. Hiatt eventually sought fame and fortune in the country music capital of Nashville, Tennessee, where he worked his way up from a $25-a-week staff songwriting job at Tree Publishing, one of the city's largest musical enterprises. With the exception of a stint in Los Angeles in the early 1980s, Hiatt has always maintained his base of operations in Nashville. He credited the country songwriting environment for influencing his later compositions and adding directness and sincerity to his innate storytelling tendencies.

Hiatt passed through a southern-fried-rock phase while recording for Epic and MCA in Nashville in the late 1970s, then veered from folkish restraint to punk-influenced anger in Los Angeles. In the early 1980s he was dropped by Geffen Records following the commercial failure of 1983's *Riding With the King,* and its 1985 successor, *Warming up to the Ice Age*—both of which were critically lauded. All of Hiatt's early releases, though favorably received by many critics, failed to catch the attention of the music-buying public. He did not hit his stride commercially until signing with A&M Records in 1987, a success due in part to the strength and honesty of his songwriting.

Propelled by Anguish

Hiatt's creative activity has often been fueled by personal crises. "The night [his daughter] Lilly was born, I was in a Mexican restaurant barfing on my shoe," Hiatt told *Rolling Stone* reporter Steve Hochman. As Hiatt descended into the final depths of a long alcohol addiction in 1985, his estranged wife committed suicide, leaving him with the responsibility of caring for one-year-old Lilly. Hiatt permanently renounced alcohol and drugs and once again began the long process of putting his life back together. Fleeing Los Angeles for the comparative tranquillity of Nashville, Hiatt met his third wife, Nancy, also a single parent and a recovering alcoholic.

Thus fortified, Hiatt returned to songwriting with a vengeance, reaching a new plateau of commercial success in the late 1980s and early 1990s. *Slow Turning* rose to Number 98 on *Billboard's* charts in 1988, staying on the charts for an impressive 31 weeks; *Bring the Family* and *Stolen Moments,* from 1987 and 1990 respectively, also had consistent sales. These three recordings elicited strong praise from rock music's critics. Kevin Ransom of the *Metro Times* described the albums as "arguably the smartest, most compelling pop-music trilogy released by a single artist over the last three years." In *Musician,* Dan Martino wrote that "Hiatt has bared more of himself on *Bring the Family* than he ever has before. And it's his best album ever." All three recordings were notable for their concentration of autobiographical material: harrowing, howling scenes of alcoholic despair, reminiscences of Hiatt's own youth, and serene love songs that reflected his newfound stability.

Enlivened the Mundane

As Peter J. Smith of the *New York Times* suggested, Hiatt's narrative songs are reminiscent of "good, short car rides with the top down." Hiatt has long specialized in fast-moving, vivid stories that often conclude with some type of ironic twist, a technique for which he has been compared to acclaimed short story writer Raymond Carver. In the song "Trudy and Dave" on *Slow Turning,* for example, two spaced-out, small-town criminals have riddled an automatic-teller machine with gunfire in order to get money to do their laundry. In the end, the song wryly recounts, the twosome "drove away clean." Hiatt likewise has excelled at drawing small, intense pictures of everyday encounters: "Icy Blue Heart," also from *Slow Turning,* sketched a sad, defensive barroom conversation between a man and a woman. The song's male narrator muses, "Should I start / To turn what's been frozen for years / Into a river of tears?"

In early 1992 Hiatt reunited with band members from his five-year-old breakthrough album *Bring the Family:* guitarist Ry Cooder, bassist Nick Lowe, and drummer Jim Keltner. They formed a group called Little Village and put out a self-titled work. While the band recaptured the spontaneity that marked *Bring the Family,* Hiatt's contributions continued to mine territory already traversed on his solo recordings. "Performance over perfection. That's totally what this album is about," Keltner commented in the *Virginia Pilot.*

Revered by Honky-Tonk Buddies

Hiatt seems likely to continue widening his circle of admirers. Country musicians have been drawn to his outrageous rhymes, and several of the most prominent artists in the country field, including Rodney Crowell, Earl Thomas Conley, and Rosanne Cash, have taken Hiatt's songs to the top of the country charts. More popular than any of Hiatt's own recordings is his witty rock composition "Thing Called Love," which went a long way toward insuring the runaway success of Bonnie Raitt's 1989 *Nick of Time* album; American airwaves resounded with Hiatt's lines, "I ain't no porcupine, take off your kid gloves. / Are you ready for this thing called love?" for months.

Hiatt's songwriting mastery stems from years of practice and intense musical pursuits. "I've always written songs, whether I was making records or not, he told *Musician's* Josef Woodard. "It serves a lot of purposes for me. I'm good at working by myself; it's therapeutic. It's a means of focusing my world, my views, and explaining some things to myself."

Selected discography

Hanging Around the Observatory, Epic, 1974, reissued, Epic/Legacy, 1991.

Overcoats, Epic, 1975, reissued, 1991.

Slug Line, MCA, 1979, reissued, 1990.

Two-Bit Monsters, MCA, 1980, reissued, 1990.

All of a Sudden, Geffen, 1982.

Riding With the King, Geffen, 1983.

Warming up to the Ice Age, Geffen, 1985.

Bring the Family, A&M, 1987.

Slow Turning (includes "Trudy and Dave" and "Icy Blue Heart"), A&M, 1988.

Stolen Moments, A&M, 1990.

Y'all Caught?: The Ones That Got Away, 1979-1985, Geffen, 1989.

(With Little Village) *Little Village,* Reprise, 1992.

Sources

Down Beat, September 1990.

Metro Times (Detroit), August 1, 1990.

Musician, May 1985; August 1987; March 1992.

New York Times Magazine, March 12, 1989.

Rolling Stone, September 10, 1987; July 12-26, 1990; October 18, 1990.

Time, April 18, 1988.

Village Voice, March 12, 1985.

Virginia Pilot (Norfolk, VA), October 25, 1991.

—*James M. Manheim*

Whitney Houston

Singer

Since her debut on the music scene in the mid-1980s, Whitney Houston has established herself as an American pop institution. Born into a musical family—her mother, Cissy, is a gospel singer and backup artist, and the sultry-voiced Dionne Warwick is her cousin—Whitney knew at an early age that she wanted to be a professional singer. After years spent as a backup vocalist on her mother's acts, she met Arista Records executive Clive Davis, who saw her star potential. Houston's first two albums sold millions, demonstrating her popular appeal to a large and diverse audience. But while a majority of critics acknowledge the singer's technical finesse, some find her songs lacking in real depth and emotion.

Houston began her singing career in the basement of her parents' home, belting out Aretha Franklin songs while pretending to perform in Madison Square Garden. By the time she got out of elementary school, she had decided on a career in music, even though her mother wanted her to be a teacher. Cissy Houston conceded to young Whitney's decision, however, and began to personally coach her daughter. "My mom has been my biggest influence," Houston commented in the *New York Times.* "Everything she knows physically and mentally about singing she has passed on to me, and she taught me everything I know about the technology of the recording studio and about the business."

Displayed Talent Early

Houston began singing with the church choir that her mother ran. As a high school student, she was singing backup for her mother and a variety of other artists including Lou Rawls and Chaka Khan. With a pretty face and a slim figure, the hardworking Houston also launched a successful modeling career, appearing in *Vogue, Seventeen,* and *Cosmopolitan.* She wanted to quit high school and devote more time and energy to her career, but her mother advised her to complete her education first. After graduation, Houston signed with a talent management agency and continued to model and sing.

When Houston was 19, she gave a special concert at a Manhattan nightclub to showcase her talents to industry executives. It was there that she met one of the most influential people in her life, Arista Records president Clive Davis. He had significantly boosted the careers of other artists, including Air Supply, Aretha Franklin, and Dionne Warwick. After careful consideration, Houston signed with him. Over the course of two years the shrewd executive showcased Houston at selected venues and carefully selected material for her debut

Born August 9, 1963, in Newark, NJ; daughter of John (head of a music management company) and Cissy (a singer; maiden name, Drinkard) Houston; married Bobby Brown (a singer), July 18, 1992. *Education:* Graduated from parochial high school in New Jersey.

Backup vocalist on recordings of various artists, including Lou Rawls, Chaka Khan, Paul Jabara, Cissy Houston, and the Neville Brothers, 1975—; singer of commercial jingles; fashion model, 1979—; singer and recording artist with Arista, 1985—. Started companies in publishing, video, and other related fields. Has appeared on several television programs, including *The Merv Griffin Show, Silver Spoons,* and *Gimmie a Break;* actress in feature film *The Bodyguard,* Warner Bros., 1992.

Awards: Grammy awards, 1986, for best female pop performance, for "Saving All My Love for You," and for "I Wanna Dance with Somebody (Who Loves Me)"; MTV Video Music Award for best female video, 1986, for "How Will I Know"; Emmy Award, 1986; seven American Music awards for album *Whitney Houston;* four American Music awards for *Whitney;* three People's Choice awards; honorary doctorate from Grambling State University; United Negro College Fund Award for long-standing support and commitment to the black community.

Addresses: *Home*—Mendham, NJ. *Record company*—Arista Records, 6 West 57th St., New York, NY 10019.

album. This recording, titled *Whitney Houston,* cost Arista an unprecedented $250,000—a very rare expenditure for a first album.

Debut Album Topped Charts

Whitney Houston features songs from some of the top names in the recording industry. After debuting a single in Europe, the album was released in the United States. It contains duets with Jermaine Jackson and Teddy Pendergrass as well as the hit singles "You Give Good Love," "Saving All My Love for You," "How Will I Know," and "The Greatest Love of All." The album remained at the top of the charts for forty-six weeks.

"This is infectious, can't-sit-down music," wrote Richard Corliss of the release in *Time.* Other critics were impressed by the catchiness of Whitney's songs and her professional delivery but complained about the lack of originality of her selections. Gary Gratt summed

up these complaints in the *Detroit Free Press,* noting, "Critics . . . uniformly praised her exceptionally trained voice but attacked the unapologetically mainstream approach of her music and her stiff stage performances." Nevertheless, *Whitney Houston* sold over 13 million copies and launched the singer into superstardom almost overnight.

Houston's next album was delayed for half a year because of the resurgence in popularity of her first effort. In 1987, the follow-up LP, *Whitney,* was finally released. "We intentionally sought a waiting period," manager Davis told *Newsweek.* "We didn't want a saturation of the market." *Whitney* was the first album by a female singer to debut on the top of the *Billboard* charts. Corliss reported that "the new album showcases a Whitney Houston who sings bolder, blacker, badder," and added, "*Whitney* marks graduation day for the prom queen of soul."

Against charges that the album's songs were trite and hackneyed, *Whitney* became an overnight hit. Part of the reason for this was the singer's popularity with a wide range of listeners. "She can get the kids on the dance floor," said Narada Michael Walden in *Time,* "then turn around and reach your grandmother." This was Houston's intention all along. "We wanted that mass appeal," she commented in the *Detroit Free Press.* "I wanted to appeal to everybody—moms, kids, dads. . . . It's great we achieved that."

Became Tabloid Target

After the completion of her second album, Houston stepped out of the limelight to assess her career. She established friendships with gospel singers and started a few businesses. By the early 1990s, however, Houston became the victim of rumors about her personal life. She was purported to be involved in a lesbian relationship with her personal assistant, but she was also romantically linked with comedian Eddie Murphy and actor Robert De Niro. Controversy within the music industry also plagued her. Several rhythm and blues enthusiasts suggested that she was "too white" to succeed as a black artist, while the television show *In Living Color* satirized her in a sketch called "Whitney Houston's Rhythmless Nation." (*In Living Color*'s producers apparently felt that Houston's dancing prowess failed to match that of chart-topper Janet Jackson, who showcased her expertise in skillfully choreographed videos from her hit album *Janet Jackson's Rhythm Nation 1814.*)

Houston, however, bounced back in 1990 with the release of *I'm Your Baby Tonight.* The new album was proclaimed by Davis to be more mature and funky than her previous works. Although Houston's name alone seemed to be enough to sell the albums, Davis commented in a *Detroit Free Press* interview: "We don't approach this with any sense of aggressiveness or cockiness. We worked hard to make this . . . as great as we can. Hopefully, everyone who liked or loved her before will be happy, and she will also make a giant number of new fans."

Entered New Phase

I'm Your Baby Tonight sold over 6 million copies worldwide, which was a slight disappointment compared to sales of her first two albums. Commenting on speculation that the star was losing popularity, Graff suggested: "What's really happening is that, after a sizzling start, Houston's career is cooling down and settling in at a level that's impressive by any standard—except when measured against her prior accomplishments."

Houston also scored with U.S. audiences with the release of her stirring rendition of the "Star Spangled Banner," which she belted out at the start of the 1991 Super Bowl. Proceeds from that recording went to the American Red Cross Gulf Crisis Fund. The next year she again grabbed the spotlight with news of her marriage to singer Bobby Brown—her wedding dress reportedly cost $40,000—and her feature film debut opposite Kevin Costner in *The Bodyguard.*

"Like all of us in the family, Whitney was singing from the moment she came out, " Dionne Warwick commented in *Time.* Houston has parlayed this family legacy into an amazingly successful career. And with her breakthrough superstardom, Houston has not only carved a nice niche for herself, but has made it easier for other talented young female singers to get into the business. "Here I come with the right skin, the right voice, the right style, the right everything," commented Houston to Corliss in *Time.* "A little girl makes the crossover and *VOOOM!* It's a little easier for the others."

Selected discography

Whitney Houston, Arista, 1985.
Whitney, Arista, 1987.
I'm Your Baby Tonight, Arista, 1990.

Sources

Books

Greenberg, Keith Elliot, *Whitney Houston,* Lerner Publications, 1988.

Periodicals

Chicago Tribune, July 1, 1991.
Detroit Free Press, November 5, 1990; June 30, 1991.
Ebony, June 1990; May 1991.
Harper's, September 1986.
Jet, June 20, 1988; September 11, 1989; July 16, 1990.
Ladies' Home Journal, March 1988; March 1989.
Newsweek, July 21, 1986; July 13, 1987.
New York Times, November 11, 1990.
New York Times Biographical Service, October 1985.
People, May 19, 1986; December 22-29, 1986.
Vogue, July 13, 1987.

—*Nancy Rampson*

The Isley Brothers

Rhythm and blues group

Inducted into the Rock and Roll Hall of Fame in 1992, the Isley Brothers are an enduring rhythm and blues band known to several generations of music fans for a multitude of hits, beginning in the late 1950s. Their biggest single, "It's Your Thing," was released in 1969 and rose to Number Two on *Billboard*'s pop charts. Young audiences in the sixties knew the band for their rollicking "Shout" and "Twist and Shout," the latter of which was later recorded by the Beatles. During the 1970s, the Isley Brothers scored big with their expanded lineup, and in 1990, pop-rocker Rod Stewart revived their 1966 Motown version of "This Old Heart of Mine" in a duet with Ronald Isley to score a top ten pop hit.

When O'Kelly Isley, Sr., first married Sallye Bernice Bell, he announced that he wanted to have four sons who would replace the Mills Brothers, a World War II-era pop group that got their start in Cincinnati, Ohio. The Isley patriarch got his wish when the young Isley Brothers, all born in Cincinnati, began as a trio consisting of brothers O'Kelly, Jr. (known as Kelly), Rudolph,

and Ronald. (A fourth brother, Vernon, died tragically in 1954 when he was knocked off his bike while riding to school.) In the early 1950s, the brothers were singing gospel music in the churches of southern Ohio and northern Kentucky with their mother accompanying them on piano. Around 1973 they added two younger brothers, Ernie (on guitar and drums) and Marvin (on bass and percussion), and their brother-in-law Chris Jasper (on keyboards) to form the "3+3" lineup.

Set Out for New York City

In 1956 Kelly, Rudolph, and Ronald set out for New York City. When they arrived, they worked odd jobs for fast cash and tried to break into the music business. By the beginning of 1957 they had demonstrated enough talent to land a spot on a bill at the Apollo Theater in Harlem. They made their first record that year, "Angels Cried" on the Teenage label, and toured the East Coast circuit of black theaters from the Howard Theater in Washington, D.C., to the Uptown in Philadelphia.

After making several records in New York for George Goldner, who owned the Mark X, Cindy, and Gone labels, they were searching for their first hit when they found what they were looking for at D.C.'s Howard Theater. According to Marvin Isley as quoted in *Goldmine,* "They'd see things that won and got them what you call 'house' when they were performing with the other acts on the show. And that's how 'Shout' was written." Influenced by rhythm and blues pioneer Jackie Wilson's ability to get a crowd going, Ron Isley wrote the song that became their first hit when it was recorded by RCA and released in the summer of 1959.

The Isley Brothers developed a reputation for a rousing stage show. One such show was described by singer James Brown in his autobiography: "We saw the Isley Brothers coming from the back of the theater, swinging on ropes, like Tarzan, onto the stage. They hardly had to sing at all. They'd already killed 'em."

After releasing a couple of songs that went nowhere, the Isleys came up with "Twist and Shout" in 1962. It received airplay in England, and the Beatles recorded their version of the song in January of 1963 with John Lennon on lead vocals. The Beatles met the Isley Brothers in person when the Isleys were touring England in 1962, but it wasn't until 1964 that the Beatles' version of the song went to Number Two on the U.S. charts.

From Motown to T-Neck

Over the next couple of years the group formed their own label, T-Neck, named after Teaneck, New Jersey, where the family had settled after "Shout" became a hit. In 1964, a young guitarist named Jimmy (later Jimi) Hendrix joined the group for a brief time before skyrocketing to fame on his own. By late 1965 the Isley Brothers had signed with Berry Gordy's Motown Record Corporation. Gordy had high hopes for the band and assigned them right away to his top songwriting-production team of Holland-Dozier-Holland (H-D-H). Their first Motown release—on the Tamla label—was the H-D-H composition "This Old Heart of Mine (Is Weak For You)." They also released an album featuring ten other H-D-H songs.

Some of Motown's other acts were reportedly jealous of the treatment given to the Isleys, and they were soon assigned to other producers there. They left the label in 1968 and the next year released their biggest hit, "It's Your Thing," on the T-Neck label. Appearing on the record were the Isleys' younger brothers Ernie and Marvin and brother-in-law Chris Jasper. The success of the song enabled the Isleys to record other groups on their label, and in the summer of 1969 they organized and headlined one of the biggest live performances of their career at New York's Yankee Stadium.

New Pop Sensibility

With their new 3+3 lineup, the Isley Brothers opted for a new pop-rock sound. In June of 1971 they covered Stephen Stills's "Love the One You're With," which featured Ernie's acoustic guitar playing. It became a top 20 hit and was included on the album *Givin' It Back,* on which the Isleys chose to record the pop-rock songs of several other artists.

With the younger members of the group studying for their fine arts degrees in music, the group's sound expanded to include a range of musical ideas. According to Marvin, they began to incorporate a jazz idiom based on their studies with jazz pianists Billy Taylor and Ramsey Lewis. The 3+3 lineup became official in 1973 when the group signed with CBS/Epic for distribution of their T-Neck releases and recorded their *3+3* album.

The Isleys were heavily influenced by Stevie Wonder's self-produced 1972 album, *Music of My Mind.* Rather than containing one or two good songs and a lot of filler material, Wonder's was a concept album in which all of the songs were significant. When the Isleys discovered *Music of My Mind* had been recorded in Los Angeles, they decided to go there to record *3+3.* The recording facility was state of the art and allowed them to use a Moog synthesizer and phase shifter, a pedal that Ernie used to alter his guitar sound.

Marvin Isley also noted another influence: "Marvin Gaye and Ronald definitely had influence on each other, because they kind of admired the same people. . . . When Marvin put that *What's Going On* album out [1971], that became the way of, 'Let's approach our album like these artists are doing now.'"

3+3 was a landmark album for the Isley Brothers, both from a commercial standpoint and from a creative one. The album balanced cover songs of other artists with a selection of original compositions. It made the Isleys one of the first black groups to go platinum, selling over two million units.

3+3 Go Separate Ways

The Isley Brothers were one of the top rhythm and blues acts of the 1970s, along with their two main competi-

tors, Earth, Wind, and Fire and the Commodores. Their 1975 hit, "Fight the Power," went to Number Four on the pop charts, and their live performances were held in 20,000-seat arenas such as the Forum in Los Angeles and Madison Square Garden in New York.

In 1984 the six-member 3+3 group split up. Ernie, Chris, and Marvin stayed with CBS to record for them as Isley/Jasper/Isley. Ronald, Rudolph, and Kelly signed with Warner Bros. T-Neck Records closed, marking the end of an era. In 1986 Kelly died of a heart attack in his sleep in Teaneck, New Jersey.

In addition to the Beatles' version of "Twist and Shout," other songs written by the Isleys became hits for various groups in the 1960s and 1970s. The Outsiders, known mainly for their 1966 hit "Time Won't Let Me," made the Isley Brothers' "Respectable" a top twenty hit later that same year. In addition, the brothers wrote "Work to Do," recorded by the Average White Band, and their earliest hit, "Shout," was revived by Otis Day and the Knights in the film *Animal House.*

"We saw the Isley Brothers coming from the back of the theater, swinging on ropes, like Tarzan, onto the stage. They hardly had to sing at all. They'd already killed 'em."
—James Brown

The breakup of the six-man lineup was not the end of the Isley Brothers. Aside from Ronald's solo successes, Marvin, Ernie, and Ronald reformed a band in 1990, and by 1992 they released an album titled *Tracks of Life.* "[We] see ourselves as the next generation of Isley Brothers, in touch with the past but looking to the future," Ronald was quoted as saying in a Warner Bros. press release. "It feels fantastic . . . like getting up to speed."

Selected discography

Singles

"Angels Cried," Teenage, 1957.
"Shout," RCA Victor, 1959.
"Twist and Shout," Wand, 1962.
"This Old Heart of Mine," Tamla, 1966.

"It's Your Thing," T-Neck, 1969.
"Fight the Power," T-Neck, 1975.
"Who Loves You Better," T-Neck, 1976.
"Don't Say Goodnight (It's Time for Love)," T-Neck, 1980.
(Recorded by Rod Stewart and Ronald Isley) "This Old Heart of Mine," Warner, 1990.

Albums

Shout!, RCA Victor, 1959.
Twist and Shout, Wand, 1962.
Twisting and Shouting, United Artists, 1963.
This Old Heart of Mine, Tamla, 1966.
Soul on the Rocks, Tamla, 1967.
It's Our Thing, T-Neck, 1969.
The Brothers Isley, T-Neck, 1969.
Live at Yankee Stadium, T-Neck, 1969.
Get Into Something, T-Neck, 1970.
In the Beginning, T-Neck, 1971.
Givin' It Back, T-Neck, 1971.
Brother, Brother, Brother, T-Neck, 1972.
3+3, T-Neck, 1973.
Live It Up, T-Neck, 1974.
The Heat Is On, T-Neck, 1975.
Harvest for the World, T-Neck, 1976.
Go for Your Guns, T-Neck, 1977.
Showdown, T-Neck, 1978.
Timeless, T-Neck, 1978.
Winner Takes All, T-Neck, 1979.
Go All the Way, T-Neck, 1980.

Grand Slam, T-Neck, 1981.
Inside You, T-Neck, 1981.
The Real Deal, T-Neck, 1982.
Between the Sheets, T-Neck, 1983.
Greatest Hits, Volume 1, T-Neck, 1984.
Masterpiece, Warner Bros., 1985.
Smooth Sailin', Warner Bros., 1987.
Spend the Night, Warner Bros., 1989.
Tracks of Life, Warner Bros., 1992.

Sources

Books

Brown, James, and Bruce Tucker, *James Brown: The Godfather of Soul,* Macmillan, 1986.
Heat Wave: The Motown Fact Book, edited by David Bianco, Pierian, 1988.
Joel Whitburn's Top Pop Singles, 1955-1990, Record Research, 1991.

Periodicals

Goldmine, November 29, 1991.
Rolling Stone, August 10, 1978.
Sepia, December 1980.

Additional information for this profile was obtained from a Warner Bros. press release, 1992.

—*David Bianco*

Mahalia
Jackson

Gospel singer

Throughout her celebrated career, gospel singer Mahalia Jackson used her rich, forceful voice and inspiring interpretations of spirituals to move audiences around the world to tears of joy. In the early days, as a soloist and member of church choirs, she recognized the power of song as a means of gloriously reaffirming the faith of her flock. And later, as a world figure, her natural gift brought people of different religious and political convictions together to revel in the beauty of the gospels and to appreciate the warm spirit that underscored the way she lived her life.

The woman who would become known as the "Gospel Queen" was born in 1911 to a poor family in New Orleans, Louisiana. The Jacksons' Water Street home, a shotgun shack between the railroad tracks and the levee of the Mississippi River, was served by a pump that delivered water so dirty that cornmeal had to be used as a filtering agent. Jackson's father, like many blacks in the segregated south, held several jobs; he was a longshoreman, a barber, and a preacher at a small church. Her mother, a devout Baptist who died when Mahalia was five, took care of the six Jackson children and the house, using washed-up driftwood and planks of old barges to fuel the stove.

As a child, Mahalia was taken in by the sounds of New Orleans. She listened to the rhythms of the woodpeckers, the rumblings of the trains, the whistles of the steamboats, the songs of sailors and street peddlers. When the annual festival of Mardi Gras arrived, the city erupted in music. In her bedroom at night, the young Mahalia would quietly sing the songs of blues legend Bessie Smith.

"The Little Girl With the Big Voice"

But Jackson's close relatives disapproved of the blues, a music indigenous to southern black culture, saying it was decadent and claiming the only acceptable music for pious Christians were the gospels of the church. In gospel songs, they told her, music was the cherished vehicle of religious faith. As the writer Jesse Jackson (not related to the civil rights leader) said in his biography of Mahalia, *Make a Joyful Noise Unto the Lord!,* "It was like choosing between the devil and God. You couldn't have it both ways." Mahalia made up her mind. When Little Haley (the nickname by which she was known as a child) tried out for the Baptist choir, she silenced the crowd by singing "I'm so glad, I'm so glad, I'm so glad I've been in the grave an' rose again. . . ." She became known as "the little girl with the big voice."

At 16, with only an eighth grade education but a strong

ambition to become a nurse, she went to Chicago to live with her Aunt Hannah. In the northern city, to which thousands of southern blacks had migrated after the Civil War to escape segregation, Jackson earned her keep by washing white people's clothes for a dollar a day. After searching for the right church to join, a place whose music spoke to her, she ended up at the Greater Salem Baptist Church, to which her aunt belonged. At her audition for the choir, her thunderous voice rose above all the others. She was invited to be a soloist and started singing additionally with a quintet that performed at funerals and church services throughout the city. In 1934 she received $25 for her first recording, "God's Gonna Separate the Wheat from the Tares."

Tempted by the Blues

Though she sang traditional hymns and spirituals almost exclusively, Jackson continued to be fascinated by the blues. During the Great Depression, she knew she could earn more money singing the songs that her relatives considered profane and blasphemous. But when her beloved grandfather was struck down by a stroke and fell into a coma, Jackson vowed that if he recovered she would never even enter a theater again,

much less sing songs of which he would disapprove. He did recover, and Mahalia never broke that vow. She wrote in her autobiography, *Movin' On Up:* "I feel God heard me and wanted me to devote my life to his songs and that is why he suffered my prayers to be answered—so that nothing would distract me from being a gospel singer."

Later in her career, Jackson continued to turn down lucrative requests to sing in nightclubs—she was offered as much as $25,000 a performance in Las Vegas—even when the club owners promised not to serve whisky while she performed. She never dismissed the blues as antireligious, like her relatives had done: it was simply a matter of the vow she had made, as well as a matter of inspiration. "There's no sense in my singing the blues, because I just don't feel it," she was quoted as saying in *Harper's* magazine in 1956. "In the old, heart-felt songs, whether it's the blues or gospel music, there's the distressed cry of a human being. But in the blues, it's all despair; when you're done singing, you're still lonely and sorrowful. In the gospel songs, there's mourning and sorrow, too, but there's always hope and consolation to lift you above it."

Reigned as "Gospel Queen"

In 1939 Jackson started touring with renowned composer Thomas A. Dorsey. Together they visited churches and "gospel tents" around the country, and Jackson's reputation as a singer and interpreter of spirituals blossomed. She returned to Chicago after five years on the road and opened a beauty salon and a flower shop, both of which drew customers from the gospel and church communities. She continued to make records that brought her fairly little monetary reward. In 1946, while she was practicing in a recording studio, a representative from Decca Records overheard her sing an old spiritual she had learned as a child. He advised her to record it, and a few weeks later she did. "Move On Up a Little Higher" became her signature song. The recording sold 100,000 copies overnight and soon passed the two-million mark. "[It] sold like wildfire," Alex Haley wrote in *Reader's Digest.* "Negro disk jockeys played it; Negro ministers praised it from their pulpits. When sales passed one million, the Negro press hailed Mahalia Jackson as 'the only Negro whom Negroes have made famous.'"

Jackson began touring again, only this time she did it not as the hand-to-mouth singer who had toured with Dorsey years before. She bought a Cadillac big enough for her to sleep in when she was performing in areas with hotels that failed to provide accommodations for blacks. She also stored food in the car so that when she visited the segregated south she wouldn't have to sit in the backs of restaurants. Soon the emotional and resonant singing of the "Gospel Queen," as she had become known, began reaching and appealing to the white community as well. She appeared regularly on famous Chicagoan Studs Terkel's radio show and was ultimately given her own radio and television programs.

On October 4, 1950, Jackson played to a packed house of blacks and whites at Carnegie Hall in New York City. She recounted in her autobiography how she reacted to the jubilant audience. "I got carried away, too, and found myself singing on my knees for them. I had to straighten up and say, 'Now we'd best remember we're in Carnegie Hall and if we cut up too much, they might put us out.'" In her book, she also described a conversation with a reporter who asked her why she thought white people had taken to her traditionally black church songs. She answered, "Well, honey, maybe they tried drink and they tried psychoanalysis and now they're going to try to rejoice with me a bit." Jackson ultimately became equally popular overseas and performed for royalty and adoring fans throughout France, England, Denmark, and Germany. One of the most rewarding concerts for her took place in Israel, where she sang before an audience of Jews, Muslims, and Christians.

Involved in Civil Rights Movement

In the late 1950s and early 1960s, Jackson's attention turned to the growing civil rights movement in the United States. Although she had grown up on Water Street, where black and white families lived together peacefully, she was well aware of the injustice engendered by the Jim Crow laws that enforced racial segregation in the South. At the request of the Reverend Martin Luther King, Jackson participated in the Montgomery bus boycott, the ground-breaking demonstration that had been prompted by Alabaman Rosa Parks's refusal to move from a bus seat reserved for whites. During the Washington protest march in 1963, seconds before Dr. King delivered his famous "I Have a Dream" speech, Jackson sang the old inspirational, "I Been 'Buked and I Been Scorned" to over 200,000 people.

Jackson died in 1972, never having fulfilled her dream of building a nondenominational, nonsectarian temple in Chicago, where people could sing, celebrate life, and nurture the talents of children. *Christian Century* magazine reported that at the funeral, which was at-

tended by over six thousand fans, singer Ella Fitzgerald described Jackson as "one of our greatest ambassadors of love . . . this wonderful woman who only comes once in a lifetime."

Jackson considered herself a simple woman: she enjoyed cooking for friends as much as marveling at landmarks around the world. But it was in her music that she found her spirit most eloquently expressed. She wrote in her autobiography: "Gospel music is nothing

---

> *"In gospel songs, there's mourning and sorrow, but there's always hope and consolation to lift you above it."*

---

but singing of good tidings—spreading the good news. It will last as long as any music because it is sung straight from the human heart. Join with me sometime—whether you're white or colored—and you will feel it for yourself. Its future is brighter than a daisy."

Selected discography

Amazing Grace, CBS Records, 1977.
Mahalia Jackson, Bella Musica, 1990.
Gospels, Spirituals, and Hymns ("Gospel Spirit" series), Columbia/Legacy, 1991.
Nobody Knows the Trouble I've Seen, Vogue, 1991.
Best Loved Hymns of Dr. Martin Luther King, Jr., Columbia.
Bless This House, Columbia.
Come On, Children, Let's Sing, Columbia.
The Great Mahalia Jackson, Columbia.
Great Songs of Love and Faith, Columbia.
I Believe, Columbia.
In the Upper Room, Vogue.
Let's Pray Together, Columbia.
Mahalia Sings, Columbia.
Mahalia Jackson—The World's Greatest Gospel Singer and the Falls-Jones Ensemble, Columbia.
Mahalia Jackson's Greatest Hits, Columbia.
Make a Joyful Noise Unto the Lord, Columbia.
Newport, 1958, Columbia.
The Power and the Glory, Columbia.
Silent Night, Columbia.
Sweet Little Jesus Boy, Columbia.
You'll Never Walk Alone, Columbia.

Sources

Books

Goreau, L., *Just Mahalia, Baby,* Pelican, 1975.

Jackson, Jesse, *Make a Joyful Noise Unto The Lord!,* G.K. Hall & Co., 1974.

Jackson, Mahalia, and Wylie, Evan McLeod, *Movin' On Up,* Hawthorne Books, 1966.

Periodicals

Christian Century, March 1, 1972.

Ebony, March 1972, April 1972.

Harper's, August 1956.

Reader's Digest, November 1961.

Saturday Review, September 27, 1958.

—Isaac Rosen

Elmore James

Blues singer, guitarist

E lmore James was a highly regarded blues musician who played regularly in the Mississippi Delta and later in Chicago. In 1992 he was inducted into the Rock and Roll Hall of Fame as a precursor of rock and roll. Although James never played rock and roll as such, his music was admired and performed by such rock bands as the Rolling Stones and the Yardbirds. Best known for his classic blues rendition of "Dust My Broom," James developed a distinctive electrified slide guitar sound that was influenced by fellow Delta blues musician Robert Johnson. Rock critic Greil Marcus, in his book *Mystery Train,* described James's rough and emotional vocal style as "a slashing vocal attack that traded subtlety for excitement."

James was born in 1918 on a farm near the Mississippi Delta town of Richland. His mother was 15-year-old Leola Brooks. Although James was born out of wedlock, he was raised by his mother and Joe Willie James, the man who was thought to be his father and whose name he took as his own. With Elmore as their only child, his parents supported themselves as sharecroppers, moving about from plantation to plantation in Holmes County, Mississippi.

James's interest in playing music reportedly began at an early age. According to Robert Palmer in *Deep Blues,* "Elmore taught himself to play by stringing broom wire on the wall of one of their cabins, and by the time he was nineteen, he was a reasonably competent young blues guitarist." According to other sources, his first "guitar" was fashioned out of strings and an old lard can when he was twelve. Like other young boys in rural Mississippi, he learned to play guitar on an instrument made from spare materials at hand.

Associated With Fellow Delta Bluesmen

As a young man James fell in with legendary blues musicians Robert Johnson and Sonny Boy Williamson, whose real name was Rice Miller. Williamson was a noted harmonica player who used several other names as well, including Little Boy Blue. Since another blues musician also used the name Sonny Boy Williamson, he became known as Sonny Boy Williamson #2. After World War II Williamson would play on a variety of radio shows sponsored by various patent medicines, and James would occasionally appear as a guest on those shows. And it was Williamson who would ultimately lead James to the recording session that spawned "Dust My Broom."

Influenced by Johnson, who is usually given credit for writing "Dust My Broom," James developed a distinctive sound using a slide guitar. Playing slide guitar involved putting a piece of glass or metal—often a pocket knife was used—on the frets of the guitar to create a special sound. It was a popular style of playing guitar among many Delta blues musicians, and it survived into the later Chicago blues styles of the 1950s.

As early as 1939 James was playing and singing with a full band that played for dances in the Delta. According to Palmer, "It was one of a number of early attempts to fit traditional Delta blues into a band context." Traditionally, Delta bluesmen were itinerant musicians who typically played and sang without accompaniment. Evidence exists, however, that some Delta bluesmen, notably Robert Johnson and Honeyboy Edwards, were experimenting with bands and performing with backup musicians in the late 1930s. Later, when the Delta sound, along with many of the Delta musicians, reached Chicago, it was necessary to adapt the traditional Delta blues to the electrified blues band sound the Chicago audiences demanded.

James served two years in the U.S. Navy during World War II, when he participated in the invasion of Guam. After the war he picked up again with Williamson. The two men played together over the next two years. When Williamson landed a local radio show in Belzoni, Mississippi, where both men were living, James would occasionally make guest appearances. "By this time," wrote Palmer, James "was a formidable electric bluesman, crying out traditional lyrics in a high, forceful, anguished-sounding voice over his screaming, superamplified slide guitar leads."

Recorded "Dust My Broom"

Palmer and others have noted that James was initially nervous or reticent about recording in the studio or performing over the radio. In 1951 James and a few other blues musicians accompanied Williamson to a recording session for Trumpet Records in Jackson, Mississippi. Trumpet was a recently established independent label that recorded blues, gospel, country, and rockabilly music. According to Palmer, James's version of "Dust My Broom" was "celebrated throughout the Delta by this time, and Lillian McMurry [who ran the label] asked him to record it. He wouldn't, but . . . he was tricked into rehearsing it in the studio with Sonny Boy . . . while McMurry surreptitiously ran a tape."

James didn't know he was making a record, and his nervousness in front of a recording microphone prevented him from recording a b-side. Trumpet put a song by another artist on the other side of the record and released it. "Dust My Broom" surprised everyone by becoming a national rhythm and blues hit in 1952. As a result, James was sought after by other record labels. He went to Chicago in 1952 at the behest of the Bihari brothers, who owned Modern Records, and recorded a thinly disguised version of "Dust My Broom" under the title "I Believe" for their subsidiary label, Meteor. "I Believe" also became a top ten rhythm and blues hit for James.

While in Chicago, James put together a four-piece band that became known as the Broomdusters. The group included saxophonist J. T. Brown, drummer Odie Payne, Jr., and pianist Johnny Jones. This quartet, with a few changes and additions over the years, remained together for most of the 1950s. James had successfully adapted the Delta sound to an ensemble format that featured keyboards and horns. As Palmer wrote, "The music didn't change much during this time, but it didn't really have to. The Broomdusters rocked harder than any other Chicago blues band."

Overcame Fear of Recording

As the 1950s progressed, James seemed to overcome his fear of recording, making numerous recordings with his band. These were heard on a variety of independent blues labels, including Chess, Checker, Meteor, Flair, and Chief. James and the Broomdusters also played the blues clubs of Chicago. When times were hard in Chicago, they went back to Mississippi and toured the South.

It was also during the 1950s that James developed a heart condition. Combined with his penchant for heavy drinking and fast living, it would eventually prove fatal. However, his music continued to progress from the rural sound that is evident on his first recording of "Dust My Broom." As reviewer Ron Weinstock wrote in *Living Blues*, "James didn't live to play to white audiences or record albums with rock heavyweights like Eric Clapton or Johnny Winter. . . . Unlike [Muddy] Waters, and more so than [Howlin'] Wolf, James was able to adapt his own down-home Delta blues to modern tastes." Quoting blues authority Mike Leadbitter, Weinstock continued, "Towards the end, he was becoming better known for his slow blues and had reached his peak as a musician. The great thing about Elmore is that he progressed. Though his basic style remained unchanged he was adding to it and improving it. He seemed to grow more powerful session by session."

Final Sessions

James suffered a mild heart attack in the late 1950s and had temporarily retired to Mississippi. Chicago disc jockey "Big" Bill Hill contacted James and persuaded him to come back to Chicago to do some radio broadcasts. On his first day back in Chicago, James played in a small blues club and was heard by record producer Bobby Robinson. As Robinson told *Living Blues* magazine, "I was lucky, because Leonard Chess [co-owner of Chess Records] would have certainly grabbed him, no question about it."

Robinson and James got together the very next day and recorded James's band in the living room of the house where James was staying. As Robinson described the session, "It was raining that day, very nasty day outside. . . . I think the weather influenced us somehow. Elmore and I came up with the idea of doing a song called 'The Sky Is Crying.' And it was just a spontaneous kind of a thought and we started to kick it around a little bit there and I got a pencil and a pad, and we sat down by the window and we wrote it out." "The Sky Is Crying" was released in 1960 on Robinson's Fire label and became a top twenty rhythm and blues hit.

Robinson recorded James with a variety of backup musicians from 1959 until James's death in 1963. Robinson told *Living Blues*, "Of course, Elmore being such a dominant kind of a personality and artist, it was the Elmore James sound wherever we recorded, but the background music was different in each place." James recorded for Robinson with a band in Chicago, a larger ensemble with horns, in New York, and with his Mississippi band, which included harmonica, in New Orleans. Songs recorded at those sessions were released on Robinson's Fire and Enjoy labels.

Heart Attack Ended World of Trouble

In the early 1960s James was in trouble with the musicians union in Chicago. When he didn't pay his union dues, he was blacklisted. He was also very ill, and his heart condition appeared to worsen. In the spring of

---

"The great thing about Elmore is that he progressed. He seemed to grow more powerful session by session."
—Mike Leadbitter

1963 James was in Chicago to perform at the opening of Big Bill Hill's new establishment, the Copa Cabana Club. He was staying with his older cousin, Homesick James, and his family when he suffered a fatal heart attack on the night of May 24.

Selected discography

Singles

"Dust My Broom," Trumpet, 1951.
"I Believe," Meteor, 1952.
"The Sky Is Crying," Fire, 1960.
"It Hurts Me Too," Enjoy, 1965.

Albums

Original Folk Blues (includes early sessions recorded 1952-56 for Meteor and Flair), Kent, 1964, reissued, United, 1975.
The Legend of Elmore James (includes early sessions recorded 1952-56 for Meteor and Flair), Kent, 1964, reissued, United, 1975.
The Resurrection of Elmore James (includes early sessions recorded 1952-56 for Meteor and Flair), Kent, 1964, reissued, United, 1975.
One Way Out (includes 1951 recording of "Dust My Broom"), Charly, 1980.
The Complete Fire and Enjoy Sessions, Parts 1-4, Collectables, 1989.
The Last Session: 2-21-63, Relic, 1990.
Let's Cut It: The Very Best of Elmore James, Flair, 1991.
Elmore James—King of the Slide Guitar—The Fire/Fury/Enjoy Recordings (recorded from 1959-1963), Capricorn Records, 1992.
(With John Brim) *Whose Muddy Shoes*, Chess.
Anthology of the Blues, Crown.
Red Hot Blues, Intermedia.

Sources

Books

Finn, Julio, *The Bluesman,* Quartet Books, 1986.
Guralnick, Peter, *Listener's Guide to the Blues,* Facts on File, 1982.
Harris, Sheldon, *Blues Who's Who,* Da Capo, 1979.
Marcus, Greil, *Mystery Train,* Dutton, 1975 and 1982.
Palmer, Robert, *Deep Blues,* Viking, 1981.

Periodicals

Blues Unlimited, June 1970; September 1971; October 1971; November 1971.

Goldmine, March 20, 1992.
Guitar Player, April 1992.
Living Blues, number 54, 1982; number 66, 1985; number 67, 1986; January/February 1988; March/April 1989.
Rolling Stone, November 14, 1991; February 6, 1992.

Other

Liner notes, *The Complete Fire and Enjoy Sessions, Parts 1-4,* Collectables, 1989.

—David Bianco

Jethro Tull

Rock band

F rom modest beginnings in the late 1960s, Jethro Tull, led for nearly a quarter century by inimitable flutist-singer-songwriter Ian Anderson—has ascended to fame with a long string of hits, several dramatic comebacks, and a 1988 Grammy Award. The group's sound, a mixture of heavy rock, English folk music, blues, and jazz, has no parallel in contemporary music.

Tull was formed in Blackpool, England, in 1967; several of its early members—including Anderson—had played in the John Evan Band. When Anderson, lead guitarist Mick Abrahams, bassist Glenn Cornick, and drummer Clive Bunker teamed as a quartet, they found themselves at a loss for a name. The band performed under numerous monikers, finally settling on their agent's suggestion, Jethro Tull—the name of an 18th-century English inventor, agronomist, musician, and author. This namesake's various pursuits have led some to characterize him as an eccentric, if not a crackpot, and his slightly crazed, albeit imaginative, persona suited the band nicely.

Anderson started out exclusively as a singer but picked

hybrid sound and featured ten original songs, including "A Song for Jeffrey," which would become an early Tull standard, and a cover of jazz legend Roland Kirk's "Serenade to a Cuckoo." (*Creem's* Lester Bangs noted in 1973 that "Anderson has always trotted out old Roland Kirk riffs . . . and Anderson should admit the debt he owes him," though the band insisted from the outset on its utter originality.) *Rolling Stone's* Gordon Fletcher called *This Was* "uneven" and dubbed the band "an extremely crude outfit that occasionally came on like an amplified Salvation Army band." Nonetheless, the album reached Number Five on English album charts two weeks after its release.

Jethro Tull's debut appeared in the U.S. on Reprise Records early in 1969. Shortly thereafter, guitarist Abrahams left the band and founded his own group, Blodwyn Pig; Martin Barre took over lead guitar duties as the band rushed a follow-up album, 1969's *Stand Up,* through production. The inside of the record's gatefold cover featured a group photo that "popped" up—in reference to the LP's title—when the cover was opened. The LP went gold in the U.S. and included a number of refinements to Tull's sound. "Nothing Is Easy," a bluesy rocker graced by a soaring flute solo, was prototypical Tull, and the quartet's jazzy arrangement of Bach's "Bouree," complete with bass solo, further pushed rock's stylistic envelope. The previously dissenting Fletcher called *Stand Up* "magnificent."

Tull's stage show became increasingly unique and raucous, if a bit off-putting to the uninitiated. Of their appearance at the 1970 Rock and Roll Circus festival, *Rolling Stone's* David Dalton reported, "When Ian Anderson gets up on stage to do his act, he completely transforms. Jekyll and Hyde. He becomes a twitching werewolf, wildly scratching his hair, his armpits, and in his long shabby grey coat, part clown, part tramp. . . . The audience is mainly teenyboppers and have never heard of the group. 'Who is that?' they say to each other in disgusted tones."

up the flute because—according to a press release cited by Irwin Stambler in his *Encyclopedia of Pop, Rock, and Soul*—"When the others were playing, I found I was just gazing 'round the lofty halls. I thought I'd like to be playing something and moving 'round too, so I got hold of a flute and a harmonica and bluffed my way through." Anderson's bizarre stage presence, characterized by one-legged, breathy flute-playing and wild leaps, created a sensation early in the band's career. But it was Jethro Tull's innovative mixture of jazz, blues, and rock styles that caught the attention of critics and two young managers, Terry Ellis and Chris Wright.

Ellis and Wright got the band a recording contract with Chrysalis Records, and the first Tull release, *This Was,* debuted in 1968. The record showcased the group's

Developed Harder Edge

The band delivered a handful of singles before releasing *Benefit* in 1970. The Tull sound—augmented notably by John Evan's keyboards—was substantially refined, transformed from the psychedelic blues of the first two albums to a slicker, more rock-oriented feel. The hard crunch of Barre's guitar fueled the hit single "Teacher" as well as the cuts "To Cry You a Song" and "With You There to Help Me." The band was deemed "most promising new talent" in a 1970 musician's poll, according to Fletcher; indeed, Tull was only just beginning to show its potential.

In 1971 Jethro Tull released *Aqualung,* its "classic" LP—at least in the minds of "classic rock" radio programmers. The title cut, with lyrics by Anderson's wife Jennie, became the quintessential Tull anthem, its unmistakable guitar riff the most familiar piece of Jethro Tull music to non-fans. "Aqualung" describes a "dirty, wheezing old man," a beggar making his way through London, Ian Anderson told *Rolling Stone*'s Grover Lewis. The rest of the "Aqualung" side of the album describes other down-and-out characters, while side two, entitled "My God," attacks what Anderson perceived as the hypocrisy of organized religion—particularly the Church of England.

"The strongest thing that hit me was the fear tactics of the religion my parents attempted to have me enter into," Anderson told Lewis of his inspiration for side two of *Aqualung.* "For that and other reasons, I was estranged from my father for years, couldn't even bear to speak to him." The song "Hymn 43" typifies the record's message: "If Jesus saves, then He'd better save himself/From the gory glory-seekers who use his name in death." The album also featured the rock-radio standards "Locomotive Breath" and "Cross-Eyed Mary," alongside such Old English-style folk ditties as "Mother Goose." *Aqualung* was a Number One album in the U.K. and a Top Ten record in the U.S. Critics, for their part, had more reservations about the disc than fans. Ben Gerson's *Rolling Stone* review typified some of their objections: "Despite the fine musicianship and often brilliant structural organization of songs, this album is not elevated, but undermined by its seriousness." *Contemporary Pop Music* authors Dean and Nancy Turner, however, wrote in 1979 that "*Aqualung* was one of the few successful concept-story albums in rock music."

Solidified New Direction

By the time *Aqualung* appeared, Tull's lineup had changed. Cornick and Bunker were replaced by two of Anderson's Blackpool friends, bassist Jeffrey Hammond-Hammond and drummer Barriemore Barlow. Critics disappointed by the band's new message-heavy direction alleged that Anderson had purged his old rhythm section to tighten his control over the sound. The contrast between the old and new styles was heightened by the release in 1972 of the two-record retrospective *Living in the Past,* a compendium of singles, unreleased tracks, and live numbers from the bands first four years. *Rolling Stone*'s Fletcher referred to the new direction as "little more than amplified folksiness and moralistic non rock—a pale shadow of their earlier work."

Despite these grumbles, *Aqualung* had made Jethro Tull a supergroup; Anderson and company routinely sold out large halls and merited feature articles like Lewis's piece in *Rolling Stone.* Lewis described Anderson's stage demeanor—here during a performance of the song "My God"—in familiar terms: "Anderson . . . goes all but berserk as he raves against 'the bloody church of England,' hopping about on one leg, grimacing, twitching, gasping, lurching along the apron of the stage, rolling his eyes, paradiddling his arms, feigning flinging snot from his nose, exchanging the guitar for a flute, gnawing on the flute like corn on the cob, flinging it forward like a baton, gibbering dementedly." The group, which Lewis described as "more like a natural force, a wind or river," communicated their fervor to fans; a riot at a Denver concert led police to spray gatecrashers with tear gas, and a rush for tickets to a 1972 Tull appearance in Uniondale, New York, resulted in another violent clash between fans and police.

> *"Anderson goes all but berserk, hopping about on one leg, grimacing, gasping, feigning flinging snot from his nose, gnawing on the flute like corn on the cob, gibbering dementedly."*
> —*Rolling Stone*

If the conceptual ambition of *Aqualung* rankled many rock critics, the album-length song *Thick as a Brick,* released in 1972, was a downright provocation. Fletcher, for one, dismissed it as "emotionally vapid." *Rolling Stone*'s Gerson, by contrast, hailed the album as "one of rock's most sophisticated and groundbreaking products." *Melody Maker*'s Chris Welch compared it more or less favorably to The Who's smash rock opera *Tommy,* praising *Thick as a Brick* while admitting that it needed "time to absorb." Bangs described the LP in *Creem* as "a series of variations (though they really didn't vary enough to sustain forty minutes) on a single, simple theme, which began as a sort of wistful English folk melody and wound through march tempos, high energy guitar, glockenspiels, dramatic staccato outbursts like something from a movie soundtrack and plenty of soloing by Anderson." Bangs also ventured that the lyrics "set new records in the Tull canon of lofty sentiments and Biblically righteous denunciations of contemporary mores." The record's cover contained a

12-page mock newspaper full of Tull in-jokes and parodies of British tabloid stories; a three-minute "edit" of *Thick as a Brick* earned heavy radio play as the album soared to the top of the charts.

Satisfied Fans in Concert

Jethro Tull maintained its sizeable following by delivering shows that defined the over-the-top arena concert approach of the 1970s. Bangs, never really a fan of the band's sound, owned that "in terms of sheer professionalism, Jethro Tull are without peer. They stand out by never failing to deliver a fullscale show, complete with everything they know any kid would gladly pay his money to see: music, volume, costumes, theatrics, flashy solos, long sets, two encores. Jethro Tull are slick and disciplined; they work hard and they deliver."

What Tull delivered next was another album-length song, *A Passion Play.* Critics willing to indulge the band *Thick as a Brick* showed signs of impatience. Stephen Holden slammed the album in his *Rolling Stone* review, calling it "45 minutes of vapid twittering and futzing about, all play and no passion—expensive, tedious nonsense." Bangs confessed that "I have absolutely nothing to say about it. I almost like it, even though it sort of irritates me. Maybe I like it because it irritates me." The group's fans, however, remained loyal, flocking to concerts during which *A Passion Play* was performed in its entirety, along with the usual Tull hits.

Anderson's tireless band trotted out a series of successful albums throughout the 1970s. *WarChild,* released in 1974, yielded the hit single "Bungle in the Jungle," and 1975 saw *The Minstrel in the Gallery* garner respectable sales. Anderson was clearly following his muse, regardless of what critics might say. "From a very personal point of view," he told *Melody Maker's* Harry Doherty after the release of *Minstrel,* "I want to continue to justify the place on my passport where it says 'Occupation: musician.' I feel I've not yet really justified that. I am not fully and wholly a musician." To the group's devotees, however, he had more than justified himself. Even so, he hinted to Doherty that he might be leaving behind "that heavy show biz thing," despite his prediction that "Jethro Tull, in the latter half of '76, will become a much more hugely popular group."

Apparently Not "Too Old"

Anderson's prediction was accurate: the group's release of that year—*Too Old to Rock 'n' Roll, Too Young to Die!*—sold briskly thanks to the infectious title track's success on radio. If the album's title reflected some uneasiness about a rocker's longevity, its songs and garish comic-book cover showed a newfound lightness and embrace of a more traditional rock approach. Also in 1976, Chrysalis put out *M.U.: The Best of Jethro Tull* to capitalize on the band's hits; a second disc of greatest hits, *Repeat: The Best of Jethro Tull, Volume II* followed in 1977.

Bassist John Glascock, meanwhile, had replaced Hammond-Hammond and would stay with Tull for 1977's *Songs From the Wood* and 1978's *Heavy Horses.* These albums moved in the direction of folk-rock, with a heavy emphasis on Elizabethan-style minstrelsy. 1978 also saw the release of a feisty live double album, *Bursting Out.* Glascock died in 1979, the year the band released its next LP, *Stormwatch.* Anderson played most of the bass parts on the album as well as acoustic guitar and flute. David Palmer, who had arranged strings and horns for the band since its debut, became a full-fledged member in 1976 and took over keyboards on *Stormwatch* after Evan's departure. Despite these shake-ups, the band continued to keep their customers satisfied; as a *Los Angeles Times* concert review put it, "Tull's baroque rock hasn't been fresh for years, and its stage show is no longer novel; but if the spontaneity and surprises are gone, they've been replaced by a calm, easy-to-admire professionalism that is consistently entertaining."

During their 1979 tour, Tull was supported by another English progressive-rock band, U.K. That group's keyboardist-electric violinist, Roxy Music alumnus Edwin Jobson, so impressed Anderson that he recruited him to play on what he intended to produce as a solo album. The result, 1980's *A,* pleased Anderson so much that it was released as a Jethro Tull record. Once again the lineup had changed: Jobson replaced Palmer; Dave Pegg of the folk-rock ensemble Fairport Convention took over on bass; and youthful American Mark Craney served as the band's new drummer. *A's* sound was more electronic than past Tull efforts, though the flute and violin interplay between Anderson and Jobson hinted at a classical-progressive rock fusion.

Lampooned in *This Is Spinal Tap*

In 1982 Jethro Tull released *The Broadsword and the Beast;* the medieval iconography of the cover and featured tunes suggested that Tull had begun recycling the image for which it had been most soundly ridiculed. Indeed, that same year saw the release of Rob Reiner's satirical "rockumentary" *This Is Spinal Tap,* and the fictional Tap's mystical setpiece "Stonehenge" was a dead-on spoof of Tull's excesses.

Soon abandoning the Middle Ages for a more contemporary sound, Anderson debuted a solo album, *Walk Into Light*," in 1983. Assisted by keyboardist Peter-John Vettese, who had joined Tull for *Broadsword*, Anderson produced what *Stereo Review*'s Mark Peel called "a consistently interesting musical project." Tull released *Under Wraps* in 1984. The tour supporting this album was marred by several difficulties, including voice trouble for Anderson, about which he made news by chiding fans at a Los Angeles concert for hurting his throat with their marijuana smoking.

After the *Under Wraps* tour Anderson took some time off from Jethro Tull. A 1985 *People* article detailed his new business venture, a highly lucrative salmon farm on the Isle of Skye, near Scotland. The profile described the star "going from *Aqualung* . . . to aquaculture—and achieving equally impressive results." By 1987, however, Tull had a new release in the offing, *The Crest of a Knave,* which *Encyclopedia of Pop, Rock, and Soul* author Stambler dismissed as one of the band's "poorest offerings yet." The band's lineup had changed again, with drummer Doane Perry replacing Craney and the arrival of keyboardist Martin Allcock.

Snagged Grammy in '88

Far from defeated, Anderson and crew still had a few surprises left for the rock world: *Crest* went gold and, in a surprise to many, beat out heavy metal favorites Metallica for the Grammy Award for best hard rock/heavy metal performance of 1988. In a *Rolling Stone* profile Anderson defended Tull's win in the face of widespread criticism from industry pundits and Metallica fans, who—at the time—were new to the sport compared to Tull fans: "Metal we aren't. Hard rock, in a pinch, yeah, okay. If you ask the average kid in the street to sing a Jethro Tull song, he's gonna go . . .," explained Anderson, humming the guitar riff to "Aqualung."

In 1988 Chrysalis put a Jethro Tull boxed set on the market; stuffed with re-mastered classics, unreleased songs, and live takes of singular hits, *Twenty Years of Jethro Tull* earned a favorable review from *Rolling Stone*'s Parke Puterbaugh: "With its obsessive emphasis on unissued material, this boxed set is perhaps best described as a deluxe souvenir for serious fans only. Yet there are doubtlessly some recent Tull converts who will dive into this deep mother lode headfirst—and not come up disappointed." *Stereo Review* called Tull's next LP, 1989's *Rock Island*, "fodder for 'classic rock' stations that want to play something current without throwing their listeners too big a curve." By this new

ever, the Grammy had considerably expanded Jethro Tull's following.

Riding the momentum of their new success, the band unveiled *Catfish Rising* in 1991. Puterbaugh, writing for *Stereo Review*, allowed that "after twenty-four albums, it's safe to say you're either on the bus or off the bus insofar as Jethro Tull is concerned," but commended *Catfish Rising* as a record likely to leave fans "pleasantly smitten." *CD Review*, while less enthusiastic about this mix of folksy acoustic songs and trademark Tull hard rock, called it a "subtly accessible blend." Even so, the approval of rock critics undoubtedly mattered little to a band that has followed its highly independent flute-wielding leader for well over two decades. Whether they will ever grow "too old to rock and roll" will be up to their fans. And many of these fans are young, listeners Anderson described in *Rolling Stone* as "the kids who watched Muppets on TV and heard Jethro Tull coming from their parents' stereo. . . . They literally grew up with Jethro Tull. We're the teddy bear they didn't throw away."

Selected discography

On Chrysalis/Reprise

This Was, 1968.
Stand Up, 1969.
Benefit (includes "Teacher"), 1970.
Aqualung (includes "Aqualung," "My God," "Hymn 43," "Locomotive Breath," "Cross-Eyed Mary," and "Mother Goose"), 1971.
Thick as a Brick, 1972.
Living in the Past, 1972.

On Chrysalis

A Passion Play, 1973.
WarChild (includes "Bungle in the Jungle"), 1974.
The Minstrel in the Gallery, 1975.
Too Old to Rock 'n' Roll, Too Young to Die!, 1976.
M.U.: The Best of Jethro Tull, 1976.
Repeat: The Best of Jethro Tull, Volume II, 1977.
Songs From the Wood, 1977.
Heavy Horses, 1978.
Live: Bursting Out, 1978.
Stormwatch, 1979.
A, 1980.
The Broadsword and the Beast, 1982.
Under Wraps, 1984.
The Crest of a Knave, 1987.
Twenty Years of Jethro Tull, 1988.
Rock Island, 1989.
Catfish Rising, 1991.
A Little Light Music, 1992.

Solo albums by Ian Anderson

Walk Into Light, Chrysalis, 1983.

Sources

Books

Stambler, Irwin, *Encyclopedia of Pop, Rock and Soul,* St. Martin's, 1989.
Turner, Dean, and Nancy Turner, *Contemporary Pop Music,* Libraries Unlimited, 1979.

Periodicals

CD Review, December 1991.
Creem, May 1973; October 1973.
Los Angeles Times, November 15, 1979.
Melody Maker, March 11, 1972; September 27, 1975.
People, April 22, 1985.
Rolling Stone, March 19, 1970; July 22, 1971; May 25, 1972; June 22, 1972; February 15, 1973; August 30, 1973; December 1, 1988; September 21, 1989; November 10, 1989.
Stereo Review, April 1984; February 1990; December 1991.

—*Simon Glickman*

Booker T. Jones

Organist, producer

Booker T. Jones is best known as the leader of the instrumentalist group Booker T. and the MGs. In addition to providing background music for the other rhythm and blues recording stars of Memphis, Tennessee's Stax and Volt Records, Jones and his MGs had solo hits of their own, including the 1962 smash "Green Onions." They were a key element in what became known as the "Memphis sound" during the 1960s, a bluesy-sounding music that Geoffrey Stokes called in his book *Rock of Ages: The Rolling Stone History of Rock and Roll* "spiritually . . . midway between New Orleans and Detroit." After leaving the MGs in 1970, Jones produced records at A&M; released albums with his second wife, Priscilla, and as a solo act; and continued to work with other artists.

Jones was born into a middle-class family on November 12, 1944, in Memphis, Tennessee. He showed his considerable musical talent early; his mother recalled for Phyl Garland in *Ebony* that he was always playing with the family's old upright piano. "He would get up there with these two fingers and actually make harmony. When I got rid of [the piano], Booker's heart was broken." To cheer the young musician, his parents provided him with musical toys and later with instruments and lessons. He received occasional instruction on the piano and organ and took clarinet lessons when he was ten. By the time Jones entered high school, he was good enough to serve as pianist and organist for a group that performed at the school's dances.

Barely two years later, Jones auditioned with Stax, a local Memphis recording company, and won a spot as a studio musician. In addition to providing backup music for the likes of Carla Thomas and her father, Rufus Thomas, Jones and some of the other studio players, including drummer Al Jackson, guitarist Steve Cropper, and bass guitarist Donald "Duck" Dunn, formed their own group, Booker T. and the MGs—MG stood for Memphis Group. Their first major effort, 1962's "Green Onions," became a huge hit when Jones was only 18, first reaching Number One on the rhythm and blues charts and then climbing the pop lists, an extremely rare accomplishment for an instrumental record.

Notwithstanding such early success, Jones faithfully persisted in his musical education, enrolling at the University of Indiana to study applied music. While there, he served as trombonist for the university's symphony and made the dean's list. When he graduated in 1966, Jones had several offers to play with professional symphonies, but he turned them down to concentrate on his work with the MGs full time.

With the band, Jones continued to produce hits, not only backing acts like Otis Redding, Wilson Pickett, and Sam and Dave, but scoring with instrumental singles, including 1967's "Groovin'," 1968's "Soul Limbo" and "Hang'em High," and 1969's "Time Is Tight." The latter song represented a more personal triumph for Jones, because it came from the soundtrack of his first composed film score, for the motion picture *Uptight.* The soundtrack of *Uptight* was also the first album to feature Jones's vocal performance.

With the onset of the 1970s, Jones left the MGs and Stax/Volt to head for California, where he settled with A&M Records as an arranger and producer. He had already honed these skills while with Stax, and during his tenure with A&M, he supervised the recordings of such stars as Bill Withers and Rita Coolidge. Coolidge was related to Jones by marriage, being the sister of his second wife, Priscilla, and Jones produced Priscilla's recordings as well. He also made some duet albums— *Booker T. and Priscilla, Home Grown,* and *Chronicles*— with his wife for A&M during the 1970s.

Jones released a solo album on Epic Records, *Evergreen,* before having a brief reunion with the MGs— minus Al Jackson, who was tragically shot and killed while talk of the reunion was still in its early stages. Together they released *Universal Language* in 1977. Afterwards, Jones both continued with his solo career—recording albums that included *Try and Love Again, The Best of You,* and *Booker T. Jones* for A&M— and loaned his expertise to other recording artists. Another late 1970s project with Cropper and Dunn involved recording an album with Levon Helm, formerly

drummer for the Band; in the 1980s Jones toured as organist for John Fogerty's band after the success of the latter musician's *Centerfield* album.

Inducted into the Rock and Roll Hall of Fame on January 15, 1992, Booker T. and the MGs played a celebratory gig at the Lone Star Roadhouse in New York City on the following night. "From the one-heartbeat groove they unleashed in the opener, 'Green Onions,'" *Rolling Stone's* Steve Futterman observed, "it was obvious that whatever bond united Jones, Cropper and Dunn in the Sixties still coursed through their veins." Commenting on the group's momentous musical contribution, Futterman declared, "Their stripped-down sound was an inspiration to pragmatic rockers like the Band and Creedence Clearwater Revival; their insistence on funky substance over empty flash remains the essence of pure soul." Not one to rest on his laurels, however, Jones, according to *Rolling Stone* in July of 1992, was hard at work laying down keyboard tracks to enhance the usually "guitar-saturated" sound of the Minneapolis alternative-rock band Soul Asylum. Said Dave Pirner, the band's singer, "This record has a broader outlook on music. It's pretty all over the place. Booker T. kind of acted as the glue on a lot of the songs."

Selected discography

Singles; with the MGs; on Stax Records

"Green Onions," 1962.
"Boot-Leg," 1965.
"Hip-Hug-Her," 1967.
"Groovin'," 1967.
"Soul Limbo," 1968.
"Hang 'Em High," 1968.
"Mrs. Robinson," 1969.
"Time Is Tight," 1969.

Albums; with the MGs; on Stax Records, except where noted

Green Onions, 1962.
Soul Dressing, 1965.
And Now!, 1967.
Hip-Hug-Her, 1967, reissued, Rhino/Atlantic, 1992.
Doin' Our Thing, 1968, reissued, Rhino/Atlantic, 1992.
Soul Limbo, 1968.
In the Christmas Spirit, 1969.
Uptight, 1969.
Set, 1969.
McLemore Avenue, 1970.
Greatest Hits, 1970.
Melting Pot, 1971.
Universal Language, Asylum, 1977.

And Now!, Rhino/Atlantic, 1992.

Other

(With wife, Priscilla) *Booker T. and Priscilla,* A&M, 1971.
(With Priscilla) *Home Grown,* A&M, 1972.
(With Priscilla) *Chronicles,* A&M, 1973.
Evergreen, Epic, 1974.
(With Levon Helm, Steve Cropper, and Donald Dunn) *Levon Helm and the RCO All Stars,* ABC, 1977.
Try and Love Again, A&M, 1978.
The Best of You, A&M, 1980.
Booker T. Jones, A&M, 1981.
(Contributor) Carlos Santana, *Havana Moon,* 1983.
The Runaway, MCA, 1989.
(Contributor) Bruce Cockburn, *Nothing But a Burning Light,* Columbia, 1991.

Sources

Books

Helander, Brock, *The Rock Who's Who,* Schirmer Books, 1982.
Stambler, Irwin, *The Encyclopedia of Pop, Rock, and Soul,* St. Martin's, 1989.
Ward, Ed, Geoffrey Stokes, and Ken Tucker, *Rock of Ages: The Rolling Stone History of Rock and Roll,* Summit Books, 1986.

Periodicals

Ebony, April 1969.
Pulse!, June 1992.
Rolling Stone, February 6, 1992; March 5, 1992; July 9, 1992.

—*Elizabeth Wenning*

Nigel Kennedy

Violinist

When he sets foot onstage, Nigel Kennedy raises eyebrows. In his oversized shoes and "punk" attire, Kennedy looks more the waif than the classical violin virtuoso. But when he lifts his bow, it is Kennedy's technical finesse that leaves audiences stunned, dispelling any suspicion that he is anything but a musician of the highest caliber.

Kennedy's unconventional approach to music-making is more than superficial. One of a new breed of classical musician, he has developed a highly individualized style that draws on an eclectic musical background. Inspired by jazz and rock, Kennedy's classical technique is spontaneous and enhanced by his mastery of improvisation.

Born in Brighton, England, Nigel represents a third generation of Kennedys to pursue a career in classical music. Both his grandfather and father were professional cellists—his grandfather a well-respected chamber musician, his father a member of the Royal Philharmonic. Nigel began his musical training at the age of seven when Yehudi Menuhin awarded him a scholarship to attend his highly regarded school in Surrey. It was there that Kennedy turned to the violin and developed a preference for the informal performance style that has become his trademark.

Kennedy, as quoted in the *Detroit News,* elaborated on this development: "I had this really rigorous teacher who used to hang out backstage to make sure my tie was on straight and that I was wearing the right jacket. Well, I had a lot of trouble wearing a jacket and tie when I performed. So I would wait until she had closed the door behind me when I walked onstage. And then, in front of the audience, I'd take the jacket off, put it on the floor, loosen my tie, play the gig, get back into the jacket and go back offstage before she could find out. That worked out fine until she noticed that the applause went on a bit too long before I played, because a lot of the audience identified with what I was doing. The whole thing was a lesson to me in two ways: first, that I could get away with it, and second, that if you showed who you were, the audience was more likely to identify with you, which is what you want anyway."

Influenced by Menuhin and Grappelli

It was also at the Menuhin School that Kennedy discovered jazz. Yehudi Menuhin encouraged his interest by introducing him to the renowned jazz violinist Stephane Grappelli, with whom he would later make his Carnegie Hall debut at the age of 17. "Nigel didn't really get into the classical stride until after he had liberated himself in the improvised jazz world," Menuhin noted in the *New*

120 concerts worldwide each year. He has appeared with major symphony orchestras in North America, Great Britain, Europe, Australia, New Zealand, and the Far East, and performs regularly with the National Symphony and St. Paul Chamber Orchestra, which he also conducts. Kennedy has collaborated with such renowned conductors as Vladimir Ashkenazy, Neville Marriner, Antal Dorati, and Andre Previn.

Wherever he performs, Kennedy's technical virtuosity and "everyman" style rarely fail to delight audiences and critics alike. Fans are charmed by his habit of "chatting up" the audience between pieces, addressing its members fondly as "monster," "animal," and "mate." Critics are awed by his sheer artistry. A reporter for the *Detroit News* deemed him "easily the most refreshing, disarming, personal, intuitive, [impetuous] and unorthodox fiddler currently before the public." A *Boston Globe* reviewer described his playing as "technically assured, extremely musical, dashing, elegant, and sweet-toned," while a *Washington Post* critic assessed Kennedy as "gifted not only with an incredible pair of hands but also with a superb set of musical instincts. He is able to play not only with incredible speed, power, and accuracy . . . but also with a heart-on-sleeve romanticism when the music requires it."

Signed With EMI Records

In addition to maintaining a rigorous performing schedule, Kennedy has recorded extensively. He has an exclusive and unprecedented contract with EMI Records that includes a rock, classical, and jazz repertoire.

Kennedy's rock recordings include collaborations with Paul McCartney, Talk Talk, and Kate Bush, on her album *The Sensual World* and on her single "Experiment IV" from the album *The Whole Story.* He also composed his own progressive rock album *Let Loose* with keyboardist Dave Heath. "Writing rock music really helps me," Kennedy maintained in *Vogue.* "Being involved in compositional techniques yourself makes you appreciate the techniques of the classical composers."

Judging from the critical acclaim his classical recordings have received, Kennedy does indeed appreciate those techniques. His rendition of the Elgar Violin Concerto, recorded with the London Philharmonic, was named best classical recording at the British Record Industry Awards ceremony and was honored as record of the year by *Gramophone* in 1985.

Kennedy then recorded Bartok's Sonata for Solo Violin along with "Mainly Black"—an interpretation of Duke Ellington's orchestral suite "Black, Brown and Beige"

York Times. Together, Menuhin and Grappelli had great influence on the development of Kennedy's musical style. From Menuhin he gained technical assurance, and from Grappelli, a fondness for spontaneity and a sly sense of play. "Menuhin had the right spiritual approach, yoga before breakfast and all that," Kennedy contended in *Harper's Bazaar,* adding that "Steph likes to have a whiskey before going onstage, and then enjoy every second of playing. He had a great attitude."

After completing his studies at the Menuhin School, Kennedy became a student of Dorothy DeLay at the prestigious Juilliard School. While at Juilliard he continued to perform as a jazz musician, appearing at Greenwich Village nightclubs with such jazz greats as Stan Getz and Helen Humes.

Performed to Critical Acclaim

In 1977 Kennedy made his London debut at the Royal Festival Hall, where he appeared with the Philharmonia Orchestra, conducted by Riccardo Muti. Since that time, his performance schedule has grown to include two pieces that were also included on his *Strad Jazz* album. The inspired pairing of these two 1940s classics was hailed by critics for its innovation.

Pursuit of Rock and Jazz

By mid-1992 Kennedy had decided to form his own string quartet and concentrate chiefly on music in the rock and jazz arenas rather than classical. "Others might see it as a giant leap, but I don't," he explained in *Entertainment Weekly.* "If the true test of classical music is being remembered, [rock artists Jimi] Hendrix and Led Zeppelin are the classical artists of their age."

An accomplished musician at an unusually young age, Kennedy has not let success go to his head. When asked about his booming career by a correspondent for the *Baltimore Evening Sun,* as reprinted in the *Oakland Press,* he responded in characteristically humble fashion: "I'm pleased to have a career now because it means I can buy a violin and live in a place with more than one room. But you can't take the music for granted. . . . The best audience I played for was in a pub in Dublin, elbow to elbow with people and mugs of Guinness. I was playing with a local violinist and the audience was so quiet that you really could've heard a pin drop. That's what I'm after. As long as I get that, the career doesn't matter."

Selected discography

Classical releases

Bartok, Bela and Duke Ellington: *Sonata for Solo Violin* (Bartok); *Mainly Black* (Ellington), Angel/EMI, 1986.
Elgar, Sir Edward William: *Violin Concerto in B minor, Op. 61,* Angel/EMI, 1984.
Just Listen, EMI, 1992.

Mendelssohn, Felix and Max Bruch: *Violin Concerto in E minor, Op. 64* (Mendelssohn); *Violin Concerto in G minor, Op. 26* (Bruch), Angel/EMI, 1986.
Sibelius, Jean: *Violin Concerto, Symphony No. 5,* Angel/EMI, 1986.
Vivaldi, Antonio: *The Four Seasons,* Angel/EMI, 1989.
Walton, Sir William Turner: *Violin Concerto, Viola Concerto,* Angel/EMI, 1987.

Nonclassical releases

Nigel Kennedy: Let Loose, EMI.
Nigel Kennedy Plays Jazz, Chandos.
Once Upon a Long Ago, EMI.
Strad Jazz, Chandos.

Also contributed to Kate Bush's album *The Sensual World,* Columbia, 1989, and single "Experiment IV" from *The Whole Story,* EMI, 1987.

Sources

Books

Kennedy, Nigel, *Always Playing* (autobiography), St. Martin's, 1992.

Periodicals

Boston Globe, August 6, 1985.
Detroit News, April 11, 1991; April 19, 1991.
Entertainment Weekly, June 26, 1992.
Harper's Bazaar, February 1990.
New York Times, April 12, 1992.
Oakland Press (Pontiac, MI), April 19, 1991.
People, March 9, 1992.
Stereo Review, October 1985; January 1986.
Vogue, November 1987.
Washington Post, March 2, 1988.
Washington Times, March 3, 1988.

—Nina Goldstein

KRS-One

Rap singer

"In these cynical times," wrote *Rolling Stone's* Alan Light in 1991, "KRS-One is an inspiring example of the role pop music can play in social discourse." A self-described teacher whose Boogie Down Productions (BDP) has been an important influence on hardcore rap, KRS-One has survived street life, prison, homelessness, the murder of a close friend, and negative criticism to emerge as one of rap's most powerful figures. While many of his contemporaries have confined their raps to boasting and glorifying gunplay, KRS-One, Boogie Down Productions' MC, has always considered his time on the mike as an opportunity to enlighten his listeners both politically and socially. His booming voice and skillful rhyming have helped him achieve huge sales, and he has used his earnings to influence and finance projects that stress dignity, self-worth, the acquisition of knowledge, and otherwise advance his humanistic views.

The advent of Boogie Down Productions in the late 1980s has been responsible, in part, for giving rap music visibility as a viable teaching medium and for pioneering the hardcore sound that is characterized by graphic depictions of the downside of life on the streets. The success of BDP's first record fueled a string of smash releases, guest appearances by KRS-One on other musicians' albums, and an editorial by the rapper in the *New York Times.* Despite conflicts with some other rap groups over credibility—notably a skirmish with P.M. Dawn—and a move towards more politically oriented lyrics, KRS-One triumphed again in 1992 with *Sex and Violence,* a return to the hardcore rhymes and heavy beats of his early days.

On the Streets From Age 13

KRS-One was born around 1965 in Brooklyn, New York, the son of Jacqueline Jones, a real estate secretary, and Sheffield Brown, a Trinidadian handyman who—according to *People*—was deported the year of Kris's birth. Though given the name Lawrence at birth, the child's name was changed to Kris, a shortened version of Krishna. In 1970 Jacqueline remarried, and Kris and his brother Kenny received her husband's last name, Parker. Mr. Parker—a United Nations bodyguard—was given to violence, however, and Jacqueline and the boys fled in 1972. Jacqueline had a daughter by another man in 1975, but this relationship also collapsed within a couple years.

Kris remains "in constant contact," with his mother, according to *The Source,* and he described her to *People's* Steve Dougherty as "an education fanatic," though he admits he was interested only in rap music from a young age. Indeed, his brother Kenny recalled

For the Record...

Born Lawrence Parker c. 1965 in Brooklyn, NY; son of Jacqueline Jones (a real estate secretary) and Sheffield Brown (a handyman); married Ramona Scott (rap name, Ms. Melodie), 1987 (divorced). *Education:* Attended Grady High School, New York, NY; dropped out at age 13; received GED.

Recording and performing rap artist; formed Boogie Down Productions (BDP) with DJ Scott LaRock (born Scott Sterling; died in 1987), c. 1985; performed in New York City area and released *Criminal Minded* on B Boy Records, 1986; signed with Jive/MCA, 1988; founder of Edutainer Records and H.E.A.L. (Human Education Against Lies), 1990; lecturer; producer.

Awards: Four gold records.

Addresses: *Record company*—Jive Records, 137-139 W. 25th St., New York, NY 10001. *Other*—H.E.A.L., P.O. Box 1179, Murray Hill Station, New York, NY 10136.

to Jon Schechter of *The Source* that when he and Kris were 12 and 13 years old respectively—and dirt poor—they imagined what they'd do with a thousand dollars. "Kris was like, 'I'd make a record.' I was like, 'Are you out of your mind? We have nothing!' I thought he was crazy. But now it looks like I was crazy, actually."

Kris matured early; six-foot-two by the time he was in ninth grade at New York City's Grady High School, Kris admitted to *The Source* that he was "vicious" in school. At age 13 he left home. "No one told me leave, and I wasn't going to [go] back whining," he recalled to Dougherty. "I was going to stick it out until I got what I wanted." He lived on the streets and in homeless shelters, taking odd jobs, hanging out, and reading in public libraries. Independent reading formed the basis of his doctrine of self-education. In the meantime he was living hand to mouth; he served some jail time at age 19 for selling marijuana.

Formed BDP With Scott LaRock

After his release, while staying at the Bronx's Franklin Armory Shelter, Kris met Scott Sterling, a 22-year-old social worker and part-time DJ. Kris had been writing poems and raps for some time—"I beat out my songs on the bathroom wall," he remarked in *People.* He and Sterling formed a powerful bond. Sterling, who worked under the DJ name Scott LaRock, exercised a tremen-

dous influence on Kris. The two began working together, calling their rap duo Boogie Down Productions in honor of the "Boogie Down" Bronx. *Criminal Minded,* their trailblazing hardcore album detailing street life and violence, came out on B Boy Records in 1986 and sold impressively, attracting the attention of several major labels.

Kris's nickname, KRS-One, which had begun as graffiti he sprayed in his neighborhood and initially meant "Kris, Number One," became the acronym for "Knowledge Reigns Supreme Over Nearly Everyone," as he explained in the track "Elementary" on *Criminal Minded.* The album also featured hardcore jams like "9 mm Goes Bang" and "South Bronx." The twosome eventually signed on with Jive/RCA Records and was at work on a second album when Scott was killed while trying to break up a fight. Devastated, Kris nonetheless decided to keep BDP alive: "If I was to quit, Scott would really be dead," he explained to Dougherty.

Developed Personal Philosophy

Unfortunately, Jive/RCA wanted to drop the deal after Scott's death; only an extensive effort by Kris kept BDP signed. In 1988 Kris had a new deal with Jive and released his second record, *By All Means Necessary.* Dougherty noted that the album "uses the bold rhythms and raw rhymes of rap and hip-hop to call for social justice." Featuring raps that would become trademarks for Kris, most notably "My Philosophy," the album was another hit, combining the intellectual probing of Kris's lyrics with relentless beats and a militant stance—on the cover Kris emulated a famous picture of Malcolm X at a window holding a gun. The record also contained the landmark track "Stop the Violence," one of the earliest rap songs to address black-on-black killing. In "My Philosophy," KRS-One announced, "Rap is like a set-up / A lotta games / A lotta suckers with colorful names." Unlike the "suckers," this MC promised to focus upon the reality of the "intelligent brown man" while espousing vegetarianism, community activism, "what we call hiphop / And what it meant to DJ Scott LaRock."

The death of a young fan resulting from a fight during a 1988 BDP show with fellow rappers Public Enemy in Long Island, New York, led to widespread calls for censorship of rap and resulted in far fewer rap concerts around New York City. To repair some of the damage, Kris and several other rap heavyweights got together to form the Stop the Violence movement, recording a single called "Self-Destruction." The success of this record helped raise half a million dollars for the National Urban League, an organization dedicated to broadening opportunities for minorities and solving community problems of low literacy rates and substandard education. KRS-One, however, would later wonder, in an interview with *Rap Pages,* what had been done with the money.

In 1989 Kris took a new approach to BDP's sound, crafting a spare, intensely politicized album called *Ghetto Music: The Blueprint of Hip Hop.* The BDP crew now consisted of Kris's wife, Ms. Melodie, born Ramona Scott, whom Kris had married in 1987; D-Nice; Scottie Morris; Harmony, Ms. Melodie's sister; and eight others. KRS-One's goal, as quoted in Light's *Rolling Stone* profile, was "making intelligence the fad." *Ghetto Music* included raps like "Why is That?," Kris's lecture on black history traced through the Bible, and "Jack of Spades," the theme from the Blaxploitation parody film *I'm Gonna Git You Sucka.* David Fricke of *Rolling Stone* praised both the album and its creator: "KRS-One is actually a man of remarkable patience. By advocating higher learning and communal faith to rebuild the black spirit, he's embarked on the long road to change. But *Ghetto Music* shows that KRS-One has the mind and muscle to last the trip." KRS-One's liner notes to the album, in which he refers to himself as a "Metaphysician," declare the record's intention to "return to our roots— 'The Ghetto'—to insure purity, talent and intelligence often lost in trying to keep up with the Joneses."

Lecturer and Rap Spokesperson

Ghetto Music's intellectual focus caught the attention of the mainstream community, and in 1989 the *New York Times* asked Kris to write an editorial on education; he complied and explained his belief that "Rap music, stigmatized by many as mindless music having no artistic or socially redeeming value, can be a means to change." He also expressed that "it's no longer acceptable to strut around with big gold chains, boasting. That stereotype, that lifestyle, must be crushed." Soon thereafter constituents at Harvard and Yale universities asked him to lecture; his speaking tour spanned 40 U.S. cities. He also participated in a number of political causes and rallies, including an appearance at an Earth Day event in Washington, D.C.

KRS-One managed to release a new BDP album in 1990, *Edutainment,* featuring the hit single "Love's Gonna Get'cha (Material Love)." As the title of the album suggests, *Edutainment* combined Kris's teaching—more explicitly humanitarian in focus this time— with the irresistible BDP sound, which Light described " "a stripped down beat, a throbbing bass line maybe a dash of keyboards, with occasional forays into

reggae stylings." Like all the preceding efforts, the album was a smash.

KRS-One also put together a new organization in 1990, which he named H.E.A.L., or Human Education Against Lies. H.E.A.L.'s pro-education focus spawned an album, *Civilization vs. Technology,* on Kris's Edutainer label, featuring such rappers as Queen Latifah, Big Daddy Kane, L.L. Cool J., along with pop performers like Billy Bragg, Ziggy Marley and R.E.M.'s Michael Stipe. *Silence of the Lambs* director Jonathan Demme shot the video. H.E.A.L. published and distributed a free book at schools, shows, and by mail. "The H.E.A.L. project," Kris noted in *Rap Pages,* "simply says that before you are a race, a religion or an occupation you are a human being. Once we begin to act human, we can act African correctly. If you're thinking African and not human, you're not a correct African."

In 1991 Kris contributed a rap to "Radio Song" on *Out of Time,* the hit record by rockers R.E.M., and appeared on the little-known rock album *Cereal Killers* by Too

> *"I want to be remembered as the first ghetto kid to jump up for world peace. I came from the heart of the ghetto—there ain't no suburbia in me!"*

Much Joy. He remarked of such appearances that they make "rap look a little better. It's not that separatist, racist solo attitude that people think rap is about— which is an image rap has lived up to." The same year saw the release of *Live Hardcore Worldwide,* one of the first live rap albums ever, and—according to many critics—the most ambitious. Steven Volk of *Rolling Stone* noted that "Nonstop booty shakin'" is one option as BDP runs through 21 tracks in around 50 minutes, but listening to the words pays too. Parker has taken rap lyrics to a whole 'nother level of complexity." The live album contained a number of tracks from the hard-to-find *Criminal Minded,* as part of a royalty settlement with B Boy. He also produced other acts, including Queen Latifah and the Neville Brothers.

Returned to Hardcore

Kris's lecture tours, mainstream appearances, and outspoken humanism left him vulnerable to criticism from within the rap community about his hardcore credibility.

Black Nationalists and Muslims accused him of not following their path; the group X-Clan rapped on one of their records that they "got no time to be hangin' out with humanists"; and Prince Be from P.M. Dawn questioned KRS-One's status as a teacher. KRS-One and his crew responded by storming the stage during a 1992 P.M. Dawn concert, forcing the group off the stage and performing three BDP classics. "The crowd," noted Schecter, "was simultaneously shocked and rocked." Defending his motives to *USA Today*'s James T. Jones IV, KRS-One remarked, "I answered his question. 'A teacher of what?' I'm a teacher of respect." He added that he had a "hit list. Whoever dissed me in the past is on it." His "hits," though, would be in rhyme.

KRS-One was serious, as evidenced on his next album, 1992's *Sex and Violence,* which returned to the hardcore sound of early BDP. *Creem*'s Suzanne McElfresh declared that the record "delivers slamming beats and hooks galore, hit-hard lyrics and KRS-One's trademark execution, which varies between straight-on conversational, emphatic oratorical romping and a musical Jamaican lilt." Dimitri Ehrlich commented in *Spin* that "there is a sense of delight, confidence, creativity, and sheer pleasure that KRS-One has been unable to generate since *By All Means Necessary.*" Of the track "Like a Throttle" Ehrlich asserted that it "ranks among the best rap songs of all time." Among the other tracks on the album are "Duck Down," which contains a message to "Sucker MC's," "Build and Destroy," and the single "13 and Good." *Entertainment Weekly* took exception to the latter song, calling it "not only tacky but so inept you'd like to forget it's on the album at all," but otherwise deemed *Sex and Violence* "funky from beginning to end."

The BDP posse had changed again. Kris had divorced Ms. Melodie, and she and Harmony left the group, as did D-Nice. Kris's brother Kenny Parker, noted producer Prince Paul, Pal Joey, and D-Square were the crew for *Sex and Violence,* a record "my audience asked for," Kris told a *New York Daily News* correspondent. He explained that his core followers wanted him to reprise the hard-edged sound he had established on *Criminal Minded.* "So *Sex and Violence* for my audience is like, 'Here it is. He's given us what we want!' Now I can go back to raising consciousness for five more years. And I'm not contradicting myself. A TV set doesn't just have one channel, and neither do I."

His newfound contentiousness may have surprised journalists who knew only his "edutainer" side, but KRS-One's message has always been about fighting and taking unpopular stands. "World peace is the issue. I want to be remembered as the first ghetto kid to jump up for world peace, because the stereotype is that all ghetto kids want to do is sell drugs and rob each other, which isn't fact. I came from the heart of the ghetto—there ain't no suburbia in me!," the rapper exclaimed in *Stop the Violence: Overcoming Self-Destruction.* Though critics have confronted him with the contradictions of his violent raps in the context of the Stop the Violence movement, KRS-One refuses to be pinned down; as he told Schecter, "I got all kinda flavors. I got styles that I didn't even start doin' yet."

Selected discography

With Boogie Down Productions

Criminal Minded (includes "Elementary," "9 mm Goes Bang," and "South Bronx"), B Boy, 1986.
By All Means Necessary (includes "My Philosophy" and "Stop the Violence"), Jive, 1988.
Ghetto Music: The Blueprint of Hip Hop (includes "Why is That?" and "Jack of Spades"), Jive, 1989.
Edutainment (includes "Love's Gonna Get'cha [Material Love]"), Jive, 1990.
Live Hardcore Worldwide, Jive, 1991.
Sex and Violence (includes "Like a Throttle," "Duck Down," "Build and Destroy," and "13 and Good"), Jive, 1992.

With others

Stop the Violence, "Self Destruction," MCA, 1989.
H.E.A.L., *Civilization vs. Technology,* Edutainer, 1991.
R.E.M., *Out of Time* (appears on "Radio Song"), Warner Bros., 1991.
Too Much Joy, *Cereal Killers* (appears on "Good Kill"), Warner Bros., 1991.

Sources

Creem, May 1992.
Entertainment Weekly, March 27, 1992.
Ghetto Music: The Blueprint of Hip Hop (liner notes), Jive, 1989.
New York Daily News, April 2, 1992.
People, February 27, 1989.
Pulse!, August 1992.
Rap Pages, April 1992.
Rolling Stone, October 5, 1989; May 30, 1991; June 27, 1991.
The Source, April 1992.
Spin, April 1992; May 1992.
USA Today, March 6, 1992.

—*Simon Glickman*

Patti
LaBelle

Singer, songwriter, actress

atti LaBelle is a musical veteran who started singing in pop groups as a teenager. As the leader of Patti LaBelle and the Bluebells (known briefly as the Blue Belles in the early 1960s), she rose to some notoriety with a few hit singles. That group was renamed LaBelle in 1971, and with flashy outfits and wild hairdos, its three members soared to fame with the racy single "Lady Marmalade," which featured LaBelle's trademark screams and lung-bursting notes. After the trio's breakup, LaBelle launched her own solo career, which has turned her into a musical superstar.

LaBelle grew up in Philadelphia, Pennsylvania, and was part of the group the Ordettes while still a teenager. She formed Patti LaBelle and the Bluebells in 1961 with Nona Hendryx, Sarah Dash, and Cindy Birdsong (Birdsong left in 1967 to join the Supremes). The group had several hit singles, including "I Sold My Heart to the Junkman," 1962, "Danny Boy," 1964, and "You'll Never Walk Alone," 1964. They achieved some level of success, but overall, they lacked the kind of gimmicky trademark they needed to distinguish them from the multitude of female groups that flourished in the sixties.

That was to change in 1970 when an Englishwoman named Vicki Wickham took over management of the group and suggested they change their name to LaBelle. The adventurous woman encouraged them to don wild costumes, adopt extreme hairstyles, and put on outrageous stage shows. The group soon earned a cult following and had the distinction of being the first black band to play at the Metropolitan Opera House. It was in this venue that they introduced their only number one hit, "Lady Marmalade," a rousing screamer about a New Orleans hooker. One of LaBelle's more outrageous tactics while touring with this group was to be lowered on guy wires to the stage for her opening.

Rumors circulated that LaBelle and manager Wickham were constantly fighting and that it was tearing the group apart. In an article in the *Chicago Tribune,* Wickham commented, "We would fight, but we had great rapport. I remember in New York once when we were arguing about a song, Pat suddenly slammed the table and said, 'That's it. I can't do it. I'm going back to Philadelphia.' A few minutes later, the bell rang and there was Patti. I asked if that meant we could do the song. She said, 'No, but we can fight about it some more.'"

LaBelle Disbanded

Eventually, however, the group's artistic differences caused them to split. LaBelle insisted that it was an amicable break. "Each of us had those individual needs

For the Record. . .

Born Patricia Louise Holte, October 4, 1944, in Philadelphia, PA; daughter of Henry Holte; married Armstead Edwards, 1969; children: Zuri, Stanley Stocker, Dodd Stocker.

Sang in band the Ordettes as a teenager; formed group the Blue Belles, later called Patti LaBelle and the Bluebells, in the early 1960s, with Nona Hendryx, Sara Dash, and Cindy Birdsong (Birdsong left in 1967); renamed group LaBelle, 1971, and recorded hit single "Lady Marmalade"; disbanded, 1976, and began solo recording career. Starred in musical *Your Arms Too Short to Box With God* for two years; appeared in TV programs *Sisters in the Name of Love* with Dionne Warwick and Gladys Knight, HBO, July 18, 1986, *A Different World,* NBC-TV, and series *Up All Night,* 1992—; played part in film *A Soldier's Story,* 1984. Owner of boutique La Belle Amis in Philadelphia.

Awards: Winner in You went platinum, 1986; NAACP awards, 1986 and 1992; Grammy Award, 1992, for best female vocal performance.

Addresses: Agent—Armstead Edwards, PAZ Entertainment Management Co., 2041 Locust St., Philadelphia, PA 19103. *Record company*—MCA Records, 70 Universal City Plaza, Universal City, CA 91602.

about how things should go, and we were no longer jelling as a group," she confessed in *Ebony.* "If we had tried to stay together we would have been constantly clashing, and the audience would have noticed it. It was better for us . . . to break up the group while it was still popular." In 1976, the three women ended their 16-year-long collaboration.

Following the breakup, LaBelle was riddled with self-doubt. Although she wanted a solo career, she didn't know whether it was in the stars. "I sat around thinking about all those tales about 'three strikes and you're out' and 'the third time is the charm' and, you know, all the negative things," she told *Ebony.* Although this lack of self-confidence didn't show in her disarming stage performances, it began to weigh her down.

LaBelle's family also felt the strain of this change in her career, and she and her husband were not communicating well. After a tough decision to seek professional help, the couple began to mend their relationship. As a result, LaBelle's husband, Armstead Edwards, began to help manage his wife's career. A big contract was negotiated with Epic Records, as well as a concert tour

to get her solo career started. LaBelle related in *Ebony* that she knew she "had to get back on that stage. I confronted all of that self-doubt and the other negative things."

Launched Successful Solo Career

LaBelle's solo career was marked by performances to packed audiences. She began to tone down her costumes from her LaBelle days. Although she worked steadily, it was not until the 1986 album *Winner in You* that she attained truly mainstream appeal. That, along with "New Attitude," a rousing tribute to self-determination included on the *Beverly Hills Cop* soundtrack, put LaBelle in the spotlight once again. She was well on her way to a comeback enjoyed by such performers as Aretha Franklin and Tina Turner. In fact, LaBelle commented in *Newsweek,* "When I saw Tina finally getting what she deserved, it *did* give me more confidence. I did think, maybe I can do that."

A stirring duet with ex-Doobie Brother Michael McDonald, "On My Own," also won much airwave play. "The contrast between Mr. McDonald's creamy soulfulness and Miss LaBelle's rugged, spontaneous effusions help to create the sense of an actual personal drama unfolding," Stephen Holden noted in a *New York Times* review.

Pursued Acting

LaBelle was also taking on different roles on the stage, screen, and television. In 1982 she starred in the Broadway hit *Your Arms Too Short to Box With God.* A television special and roles in the feature film *A Soldier's Story* and the hit series *A Different World.* By 1992, she was cast as a club owner/landlady in her own television series, *Up All Night.* The singer continued to be known for her energetic concerts, which some likened to a revival meeting. And her wild hairdos were back, this time with an angular, lacquered, wigged-out look.

LaBelle had another breakthrough album with *Burnin'* in 1991. The pop diva used her strong, nasal-edged voice to perfection on such songs as "Feels Like Another One" and "Somebody Loves You Baby." To her complete surprise, LaBelle captured a Grammy Award for her work on the record—her first after being in the business for over 32 years. She dedicated the award to her mother and three sisters, all of whom had passed away.

Despite her rousing onstage performances, LaBelle is

an admitted homebody who is more comfortable on a stage with five hundred people than one-on-one. "Although I love my career," LaBelle explained in *Essence,* "long ago I realized I couldn't be happy if I weren't married, if I didn't have a man to take care of, a house to keep." The singer is admittedly a great cook and is often seen making her own dinners in hotels while she is on the road.

The two sides of LaBelle include the cozy homemaker and the complete showstopper. With an electrifying voice that seems to defy human boundaries, LaBelle continues to make her mark in the music world. "I could never give up performing," LaBelle claimed in *Essence.* "If I didn't sing, I'd be a crazy woman. Onstage is the one place where I can open up, vent my hostility, cry out my pain. And that has freed me to be a better wife and mother."

Selected discography

With LaBelle

(As Patti LaBelle and the Bluebells) *Dreamer,* Atlantic, 1967.
LaBelle, Warner Brothers, 1971.
(With Laura Nyro) *Gonna Take a Miracle,* Columbia, 1971.
Moonshadow, Warner Brothers, 1972.
Pressure Cookin', RCA, 1973.
Nightbirds, Epic, 1974.
Phoenix, Epic, 1975.
Chameleon, Epic, 1976.

Solo Albums

Patti LaBelle, Columbia, 1977.
Tasty, Epic.
It's Alright with Me, Columbia, 1979.
Released, Columbia, 1980.
Best of Patti LaBelle, Columbia, 1981.
Winner in You, MCA, 1986.
Burnin', MCA, 1991.

Also contributed backup vocals to comedian Eddie Murphy's single "Yeah."

Sources

Chicago Tribune, March 16, 1986.
Ebony, September 1978; April 1986; March 1989; May 1991.
Entertainment Weekly, October 18, 1991; May 29, 1992.
Essence, October 1985; May 1990; March 1991.
Harper's, August 1986.
Jet, June 26, 1989; July 16, 1990; December 24, 1990; January 21, 1991.
Musician, July 1986.
Newsweek, July 21, 1986.
New York Times, July 6, 1986; November 7, 1991.
People, June 16, 1986; July 21, 1986.
Premiere, February 1989.
Rolling Stone, June 19, 1986.

—*Nancy Rampson*

Daniel Lanois

Record producer

"I want to leave something behind that means something," Daniel Lanois told *Rolling Stone's* James Henke, explaining his singular approach to life and record making. "Am I going to follow my own ideas and philosophies, or am I just going to fall in the rut of doing rubbish for the sake of making a living?" Lanois's decision to follow a more meaningful approach led him from recording groups in a homemade studio in the 1970s to forging a partnership with avant-garde producer Brian Eno in the early 1980s to producing some of the best-known—even legendary—acts in popular music, including U2, Peter Gabriel, Robbie Robertson, the Neville Brothers, and Bob Dylan.

Lanois's record-producing capabilities are virtually unassailable: all productions have been hailed. Although Nicholas Jennings, writing for *Maclean's,* credited Lanois's success as a producer to his "reputation for a lighter touch and for bringing out the artist's best," it is perhaps Lanois's spiritual conviction to capture an artistic moment that has gone the furthest in reaching listeners. "I'm passionate about music," he emphasized to Richard Flohil in *Canadian Composer.* "I want to get committed, passionate music on a record, so that other people can understand the passion and the message."

Lanois began his recording career in 1970 in a small studio he and his brother Robert built in their mother's basement. "From the beginning," Flohil recounted, "the studio's reputation was strong; there was a nice atmosphere and a relaxed feeling; [the brothers] were good engineers and were able to help many artists sharpen their material in the studio." They recorded dozens of artists from the surrounding area throughout the 1970s. In 1980, because of increased demand, the Lanois brothers were forced to open the larger Grant Avenue Studio in nearby Hamilton, Ontario. Here Lanois's producing talents gained notice through work with such groups as Martha & the Muffins and the Parachute Club. With the arrival of rock experimenter Brian Eno to the Grant Avenue Studio in the early 1980s, however, Lanois's recording direction changed.

Atmospheric Influence

Looking for a studio out of the mainstream, Eno came to Lanois's to begin his self-termed "ambient music" series of records. The first of these experimental recordings, which were to become highly influential in the music industry, Lanois simply thought of as "badly recorded piano tapes," he admitted to Rob Tannenbaum in *Canadian Composer.* But after working on these carefully composed and recorded works, Lanois found he "just got into that pace. Really quiet and atmospheric music that paints a very strong picture with slow detail—almost like musical landscapes," he explained to Henke. The artistic view Eno opened up for Lanois was accompanied by an expanded technological understanding as well. "The challenge of evoking a strong emotion on an instrumental record without the benefit of lyrics forced Lanois to experiment with outboard effects, playing the studio as he would a guitar," Tannenbaum wrote.

The techniques and philosophies Lanois drew from Eno in their early partnership continued to evolve on their later collaborations and on Lanois's solo journeys during the 1980s. Although he learned to use the technology available in the studio to its maximum benefit, Lanois never let it overwhelm his tender approach to the artist. He explained to Henke that a producer's most important function is "keeping track of the big picture. Understanding the intentions of the artist from the beginning and carrying that through to the end. Obeying the ground rules. . . . Then I suppose another function—the most important, really—is drawing a performance."

Lanois's ability to do this, a talent considered his forte,

is achieved in part by eschewing the conventional distance between a producer and artist. "I don't spend much time in the control room," he told Jennings. "I try to get out there, listen to the songs and get to the bottom of the arrangements—and get involved. If you're standing right next to someone, a lift of an eyebrow will convey a message that would be lost behind a piece of glass." Lanois also began recording outside of the controlled studio environment, capturing the spontaneity, acoustic warmth, and human element of performances in such informal and comfortable settings as castles, dairy barns, and homes. He sold the Grant Avenue Studio in 1985 and since prefers to simply set up a portable studio where a performance is to be recorded.

Reverence for Magic

"With an approach that emphasizes tranquility and ingenuity over technology . . . Lanois contradicts the modern notion of a producer as a flesh-bound instruction guide," Tannenbaum observed. Indeed, Lanois approaches the musicians with whom he works as part artists, part mystics, and always human beings. He never leads them, but instead lets them explore, often bringing to light the artistic achievement that is already contained within them. Peter Gabriel, who worked with Lanois on the film soundtrack *Birdy* and his album *So*, told Stephanie Ortenzi of *Maclean's* that "Dan worked best in maximizing my performance. He has a reverence for the magic of the moment." This intuitive insight, an attention to the possibilities of what might already exist or could be, is also what collaborator Brian Eno values in Lanois. "Dan listens to feel, to the skeleton of the songs, and draws attention to the things everybody else has stopped noticing," Eno wrote in *Rolling Stone*.

The critical consensus of Lanois's work has been extremely favorable: he has helped musicians, especially the Neville Brothers and Bob Dylan, create some of their most acclaimed work. Of the Neville Brothers's *Yellow Moon* recording, David Fricke wrote in *Rolling Stone* that "their native brand of dance-floor *fiyo* is stroked by producer Daniel Lanois with a cool voodoo intensity. The result is like Mardi Gras meets [U2's] *The Joshua Tree*: French Quarter magic infused with spiritual urgency." For Dylan, Lanois "fashioned evocative, atmospheric soundscapes that elicit every nuance of meaning from Dylan's songs while never overwhelming them," Anthony DeCurtis declared in *Rolling Stone*. "Dylan's lyric style on *Oh Mercy*—a plain-spoken directness with rich folkloric and Biblical shadings—finds an ideal setting in the dark, open textures of Lanois's sonic weave."

Passion and Contrasts

The artistic vision Lanois extends when producing other musicians was evident on his own recorded work, *Acadie*. "Lanois's own album resonates with the kind of textual subtleties and artful treatments that don't present themselves on casual listening. . . . *Acadie* is an album with the muted glow of a reverie-at-dawn, the tail end of a long night's journey into day," *Down Beat*'s Josef Woodard maintained. Lanois's commitment to provide the most passionate vehicle for the message was also carried over from his previous productions to his own work. Flohil pointed out that "while [*Acadie*] may not sell the millions of copies racked up by his clients, it has a similar warmth, a similar integrity, a similar sense of care and concern."

Lanois's desire to create "'soul music,' born out of passion and commitment and need," as he conceded to Tannenbaum, is evidenced by the similarity that weaves through his various productions and his solo recording. Lanois explained to Henke that what binds his works together is "an undercurrent of tension that is created by various treatments and atmospheres that were applied. . . . You're presented with one angle, and then that is contrasted or undermined by something ominous, something that you feel more than you hear." That is his artistic predilection, an idea he further elucidated to Henke: "I gravitate toward a lyric that says something, that carries some kind of weight or substance and that a listener will be able to draw a positive meaning from. . . . I gravitate more toward the melancholy and serious. Darkness with optimism. . . . And if I can incorporate what I feel in my work, then that's my first choice."

Selected discography

Acadie, Opal/Warner Bros., 1989.

Producer

Martha & the Muffins, *This Is the Ice Age*, RCA, 1981.
The Parachute Club, *The Parachute Club*, RCA, 1983.
Martha & the Muffins, *Danceparc*, RCA, 1983.
(With Brian Eno) Brian Eno, *Apollo Atmospheres and Soundtracks*, Editions EG, 1983.
M + M, *Mystery Walk*, RCA, 1984.
(With Eno) U2, *The Unforgettable Fire*, Island, 1984.
(With Peter Gabriel) *Birdy* (film soundtrack), Geffen, 1985.
Roger Eno, *Voices*, Editions EG, 1986.
(With Gabriel) Peter Gabriel, *So*, Geffen, 1986.
(With Robbie Robertson) Robbie Robertson, *Robbie Robertson*, Geffen, 1987.
(With Eno) U2, *The Joshua Tree*, Island, 1987.
Bob Dylan, *Oh Mercy*, Columbia, 1989.
The Neville Brothers, *Yellow Moon*, A & M, 1989.
(With Eno) U2, *Achtung Baby*, Island, 1991.

Also produced Eno's *The Plateaux of Mirror* and *On Land*.

Sources

Canadian Composer, January 1987; November 1989.
Down Beat, March 1986; April 1990.
High Fidelity, December 1984; March 1988.
Maclean's, July 21, 1986; March 14, 1988.
Nation, April 24, 1989.
New York Times, November 29, 1989.
Pulse!, July 1992.
Rolling Stone, December 17, 1987; September 21, 1989; November 30, 1989; December 14-28, 1989; November 28, 1991.
Stereo Review, February 1988.

Additional information for this profile was obtained from an Opal/Warner Bros. Records press release, 1989.

—*Rob Nagel*

Peggy Lee

Singer, songwriter, composer, actress

With her soft, rhythmic voice and purring sensuality, singer Peggy Lee has been intriguing audiences for more than half a century. Beginning as a vocalist with Benny Goodman's band in the early 1940s, she learned to sing everything from swing to blues, using her voice like an instrument—always with an emphasis on the beat. Considered one of the most jazz-oriented vocalists in popular music, Lee "swings as intensely and eccentrically as Billie Holiday," observed Witney Balliett in the *New Yorker*. Yet "she is a stripped-note singer," added the critic; she "keeps her vibrato spare and her volume low [and] . . . avoids long notes and glissandos." Balliett concluded that, unlike the many vocalists who "confuse shouting with emotion, . . . Lee sends her feelings down the quiet center of her notes." In a similar assessment, *People* interviewer J. D. Reed quoted an unnamed critic who wrote of Lee's silky stylings: "Never has so much been delivered from so little."

Lee was born Norma Dolores Egstrom in a North Dakota farm town in 1920. Raised by a stepmother who was abusive, Norma at least found approval when singing with the church choir or the high school glee club. She headed for Hollywood immediately after graduation to pursue a professional singing career, but after limited success she decided to try her luck a little closer to home. She found work as a singer with the Fargo, North Dakota, radio station, WDAY, where the program director renamed her Peggy Lee. Singing stints with bands led by Jack Wardlaw and Will Osborne brought Lee further recognition, and she began to appear in some major clubs. It was while performing at the Doll House, a noisy Palm Springs, California, jazz spot, that the vocalist forged her quiet, cool style: unable to sing above the din, she softened her voice, which resulted in riveting the audience. "I've been easy on my voice. . . . That's why I'm still around," Lee reflected in her 1984 interview with Reed. "Vocal chords wear out. Besides, if you shout, you can't converse with your audience, and that's what I do best."

Soon after the Doll House stint, swing bandleader Goodman discovered Lee while she was performing at Chicago's Buttery Room. Replacing singer Helen Forrest, Lee joined the ensemble in 1941, touring the United States when the band was at its peak of popularity. In 1942 she recorded her first big hit, "Why Don't You Do Right?," a song that sold more than one million copies and launched her into stardom. Though she left the band the following year—to marry Goodman guitarist Dave Barbour and start a family—Lee deemed her two years with the group invaluable, for she learned the importance of practice, discipline, and the interplay between singer and musician. During that time Lee also began to cultivate the seeds that would germinate into her second major career, that of songwriter. Sitting on the stage in her chair, waiting for her vocals with the band, she started to compose and form lyrics in her head.

Lee began her long association with Capitol Records in 1944, writing many of her songs with husband Barbour. Their numerous hits include "It's a Good Day" and "Manana," which sold more than two million copies; Lee also collaborated with such composing talents as Duke Ellington, Quincy Jones, Sonny Burke, and Victor Young. In addition, she supplied music and lyrics for motion pictures; her work included the theme music for *Johnny Guitar* and lyrics and several voices for the 1955 Disney animated classic *Lady and the Tramp.* (In 1991 the performer was awarded 3.8 million dollars as her share of the enormous profits the movie has earned in video-cassette sales, a decision that has other Disney vocal talents rushing to file suit.) Lee also had a

brief but distinguished acting career in the early 1950s, her performance as an alcoholic blues singer in *Pete Kelly's Blues* earning her an Academy Award nomination for best supporting actress in 1955. "I loved acting, but my agents never brought me another script," she recalled for Reed. "I was worth a lot more to them on the road."

Indeed, it was Lee's singular singing that ensured her legendary status. Her rhythmic croonings of tunes like "Lover," "Fever," and "Is That All There Is?"—which won her two Grammys in 1969—made such songs instantly identifiable with her. By 1960 Lee was considered a female equivalent of superstar Frank Sinatra; playing before sell-out crowds at home and abroad, she counted among her fans such twentieth-century luminaries as Albert Einstein and author Aldous Huxley. Also as prolific as Sinatra (by the mid-1980s she had recorded 59 albums and 631 numbers), Lee has always endeavored to remain musically current, performing the songs of contemporary composers or collaborating with them. Still, in these contemporary pieces the singer looks for the "haunting melodies and engaging word-pictures" that she was "trained to appreciate," according to Eliot Tiegel in *Down Beat;* these are qualities that, in Lee's words, make an audience "walk away humming."

Along with her meticulously chosen repertoire, Lee plans her performances with exacting precision. For decades she has detailed every appearance in a notebook: from lighting and props to the weather, her elaborate costumes, and the color of her nail polish. She even devises the arch of an eyebrow, a laugh, or the flip of a hand; eschewing the improvisatory nature of jazz, she plots every note. The result of this carefully crafted stage persona has been considered dazzling— and a bit larger than life. Lee's driving perfectionism has been blamed in part for the ill health that has plagued her most of her life. A diabetic, she was hospitalized for pneumonia in 1958 and 1961 and for a time had to travel from club to club with a respirator. Four failed marriages and a near-fatal fall in 1967 that left her temporarily blind, partially deaf, and unable to stand compounds her list of travails. (She recounted these personal tragedies in the musical autobiography *Peg,* which struggled on Broadway in 1983.) Limiting her performances in the early 1990s to a few club dates and recording sessions, Lee is being rediscovered by a new generation of listeners and appreciated anew by performers like Elvis Costello and k.d. lang. Discussing Lee's 1980 album *Close Enough for Love* in *Stereo Review,* Peter Reilly stated that her style is "still one of the seven wonders of the world of popular entertainment." Seconding that sentiment in a *Stereo Review* critique of the vocalist's 1990 album *There'll Be Another*

Spring, Roy Hemming wrote, "Lee sings with the same kind of sparkle, lilt, and sexily purring style that have been her trademarks for some five decades."

Selected writings

Softly, With Feeling (verse), 1953.
Miss Peggy Lee: An Autobiography, D. I. Fine, 1989.

Selected compositions

Has written and co-written numerous songs, including "It's a Good Day," "Manana," "Where Can I Go Without You," and "Fever"; collaborators have included Dave Barbour, Duke Ellington, Quincy Jones, and Paul McCartney. Composer of theme music for motion pictures *Johnny Guitar* and *About Mrs. Leslie,* both 1954; and of musical scores for cartoon features *Tom Thumb* and *The Time Machine,* both 1960. Contributed lyrics to Disney feature *Lady and the Tramp,* 1955; contributor to score of stage musical *Peg,* 1983.

Selected discography

Peggy Lee With David Barbour and Billy Jay Bands, 1948, Hindsight, 1985.
Peggy Lee Sings With Benny Goodman, Columbia, 1988.
Miss Peggy Lee Sings the Blues, Musicmasters, 1988.
Miss Peggy Lee (reissue), Columbia, 1988.
Mirrors (reissue), A&M, 1989.
All-Time Greatest Hits, Volume 1, Curb/CEMA, 1990.

Peggy Lee, Volume 1: *The Early Years,* Capitol, 1990.
(With George Shearing) *Beauty and the Beat!,* Capitol Jazz, 1992.
Close Enough for Love, DRG.
You Can Depend on Me, Glendale.
The Best of Peggy Lee, MCA.
Peggy Lee: Collector's Series, Capitol.
Peggy Lee Songbook: There'll Be Another Spring, Musicmasters.
Seductive!, Pair.

Sources

Books

Clarke, Donald, editor, *The Penguin Encyclopedia of Popular Music,* Viking, 1989.
Lee, Peggy, *Miss Peggy Lee,* Berkley, 1989.
Simon, George T., and others, *The Best of the Music Makers,* Doubleday, 1979.

Periodicals

Down Beat, June 1990.
New York, December 26, 1983.
New Yorker, August 5, 1985; July 18, 1988.
People, January 9, 1984; October 1, 1990; April 8, 1991.
Stereo Review, May 1980; September 1982; December 1988; July 1990.
Time, April 1, 1991.

—*Nancy Pear*

James Levine

Conductor, pianist

James Levine is a world-renowned conductor whose leadership at New York City's Metropolitan Opera (Met) has ushered in a new era of artistic creativity and musical excellence. After taking over the music directorship of the Met orchestra in 1976 and the opera company's artistic directorship in 1985, Levine transformed the ensemble into an entity that *Gramophone* magazine compared favorably to the celebrated Vienna Philharmonic of Austria. While modestly not taking credit for the opera's accomplishments, Levine wrote in *Opera News* in 1990, "Those singers, conductors, directors who work in opera houses around the world concur about one thing—the work that is done at the Met is more consistently serious, thoughtful, comprehensive, imaginative, professional, stylish and exciting, with greater combined musical, dramatic and technical resources, than in any other international theater in the world."

The oldest of three children, James Lawrence Levine was born into a musical family in Cincinnati, Ohio, on June 23, 1943. His father played the violin and, under the stage name Larry Lee, led a dance band during the 1930s; Levine's mother was an actress on Broadway before she married. Levine displayed an interest in music when—as a toddler—he began picking out melodies at the piano. He began formal piano lessons at age four and worked unflaggingly at the ivories throughout his childhood. The boy often attended local opera and symphony performances with his parents and, with a score open in his lap, "conducted" the pieces with a knitting needle. At age nine he staged his own operas at home with the help of a puppet theater and record player.

Professional Piano Debut at Ten

Levine made his professional piano debut at the age of ten with the Cincinnati Symphony Orchestra. His parents carefully managed his budding talent while he performed several times with the orchestra over the next few years. "I was not really anxious to be exposed early, and my parents were very anxious not to expose me," Levine told *New York Post* correspondent Fern Marja Eckman. "They turned down all offers which smacked of exploitation. I'm eternally grateful. . . . They always encouraged me to do what I wanted and what gave me pleasure. They never pushed me. They didn't give me a sense of having to succeed, but only of making myself happy."

During the summer of 1956 Levine studied piano with revered master Rudolf Serkin at Vermont's Marlboro Music Festival; the following year he spent the summer under the guidance of acclaimed pianist Rosina Lhevinne at the Aspen Music Festival in Colorado. To further his knowledge in harmony and theory, Levine also studied with Walter Levin, violinist of the La Salle Quartet. As a high school student, Levine dabbled in composition but did not see a future in it. The prospect of long and lonely tours as a piano soloist did not appeal to him either. Finally, the blossoming star realized that conducting should be his vocation: "I found that immersing myself in the task of communicating masterpieces was more rewarding for me than turning out bad compositions of my own," he revealed in *Opera News.*

After high school graduation in 1961, Levine was accepted at the prestigious Juilliard School in New York City. There he studied conducting with Jean Morel and piano with Lhevinne, finishing a five-year program in just two years. He spent his summers at Aspen, studying conducting with Wolfgang Vacano; it was there that he first conducted an opera, *The Pearl Fishers.* After placing as a finalist in the Ford Foundation American Conductors Project in 1964, Levine became an apprentice to George Szell, conductor of the Cleveland Symphony Orchestra. Szell taught Levine the nuts and bolts of conducting. Following his apprenticeship, Levine won offered the position of assistant conductor with the Cleveland orchestra, which he accepted without hesi-

tation. During this time Levine also founded, managed, and conducted a student orchestra at the Cleveland Institute of Music and in the summers taught at the Aspen Music Festival.

Named Principal Conductor of the Met

Levine left the Cleveland Orchestra in 1970 to guest conduct nearly every important orchestra in the United States, including the Philadelphia Orchestra, Chicago Symphony Orchestra, Los Angeles Philharmonic, Boston Symphony, Cincinnati Orchestra, and the National Symphony, as well as several prominent European orchestras. He also became the director of the Ravinia Festival, the summer home of the Chicago Symphony, and for several years was music director of the May Festival in Cincinnati. Levine made his debut with New York City's Metropolitan Opera in 1971 with a performance of *Tosca* by Giacomo Puccini. He was then offered a guest conducting contract for the 1972-73 season, during which he mounted Guiseppe Verdi's *Otello* and *Rigoletto* and Gioacchino Rossini's *The Barber of Seville.* The next season, Levine was named principal conductor of the Metropolitan Opera.

When Levine took the baton of the Met he found that the orchestra had suffered neglect from a long line of guest conductors. "Extraordinary orchestras were built by the conductor and the players working on every aspect of music-making day after day, year after year, until they understood each other musically in subtle and complex ways," Levine explained in *Opera News.* "It requires patience and dedication. This is the work we began in 1973." Thus Levine devoted much time to orchestra rehearsals, working resolutely on technique and details. "He cajoles, he compliments, he works in subtle ways. He's never destructive," Met violinist Toni Rapport stated in *Newsweek.* Although Levine's unbridled enthusiasm and talkative nature occasionally grated on musicians, performers and critics alike admit that Levine's efforts paid off. The orchestra is considered a superb, world-class ensemble. "I think today at the Met one can hear operas performed by an orchestra and chorus second to none and continuously improving," Levine observed in the *Opera News.*

Avoids Flamboyance

The image of the showy conductor does not appeal to Levine; during performances he prefers to stay in the background, a nearly impossible feat for a conductor. "I want to make myself obsolete in the concert itself," he told Stephen Rubin, author of *The New Met in Profile.* "I want to be able to have the conception known to time nate from the orchestra members who are, after all, the ones with the instruments, instead of from the crazy magician with a stick who is making all the gestures and telling the audience what they ought to be feeling and hearing. I want to get to the point where the audience would have the feeling they didn't see me."

In 1985 Levine was named the Metropolitan Opera's artistic director, a post that broadened his responsibilities to include working with stage managers, set designers, and others in the many positions that are needed to stage an opera. Under Levine's leadership the Met expanded its repertoire to include new productions of several twentieth-century operas, including Benjamin Britten's *Billy Budd* and *Death in Venice,* Kurt Weill's *Mahagonny,* Alban Berg's *Lulu,* Maurice Ravel's *L'Enfant et les Sortileges,* George Gershwin's *Porgy and Bess,* Arnold Schoenberg's *Erwartung,* and Bela Bartok's *Duke Bluebeard's Castle.* It also mounted the world premier of John Corigliano's *The Ghosts of Versailles,* a huge hit commissioned especially for the Met. New York City opera lovers have also seen revivals of standard works by Verdi, Puccini, Mozart, and Wagner, among others, and special treatment of other standards, including versions sung for the first time at the Met in their original languages, uncut renditions, and new English translations. Many of these productions were filmed for television and broadcast by PBS.

Renewed Recording at the Met

From the 1950s to the 1980s there had only been one recording project at the Metropolitan Opera, but interest was renewed in the late 1980s when performances were contracted by recording giants Deutsche Grammophon, Philips, and Sony. Levine finds the recording work exciting because it puts emphasis back on the vocals and music of opera, rather than on its visual elements. Levine hopes that Metropolitan Opera recordings will encourage listeners to attend live performances. Orchestra-only recordings are also planned. In addition to these projects, the maestro has conducted the Metropolitan Opera Orchestra in productions of non-operatic works, including a successful three-city concert tour in 1990.

Although the Metropolitan Opera already employs a roster of the best singers in the world, it has created a young artists development program to provide a training ground for promising young vocalists. Levine maintains that such a program is necessary because the style and technique that created the operatic form are no longer passed from generation to generation. With the development program, the Met's management hopes

to improve the chances for it and other opera theaters' long-term survival.

To accept artistic directorship of the Met, Levine cut his annual conducting schedule from 90 to 60 performances. He is in residence at the Metropolitan Opera during 85 percent of its season but still regularly conducts the Chicago Symphony at the Ravinia Festival, the Vienna Philharmonic at the Salzburg Festival, and the Berlin Philharmonic at the Wagner Festival in Bayreuth, Germany. The conductor feels that his time away from the Met enriches him artistically, allowing him to return renewed. A brilliant pianist, Levine also performs at chamber recitals with other members of the Metropolitan Opera Orchestra and with the La Salle Quartet and mezzo-soprano Christa Ludwig.

Pleased with the fruits of his efforts and those of countless others at the Metropolitan Opera who make opera come to life, Levine related in *Opera News,* "I'm enthusiastic . . . because I see us as an artistic collective

---

> *"I found that immersing myself in communicating masterpieces was more rewarding than turning out bad compositions of my own."*

---

gathering momentum in potential and esprit. . . . The positive attitude of the company, the feeling of 'family,' the ever increasing possibility to do serious work unencumbered by much of the nonsense that is so prevalent in society today, are things remarked upon over and over by visiting artists, and things we ourselves feel more and more strongly." The conductor went on to predict, "If we can work on a certain amount of non-operatic repertoire with the orchestra and chorus to broaden their perspectives, if we can continue to develop and nurture some talented young singers . . . we could be in a position to offer very exciting performances even more consistently in the future."

Selected discography

Bach: *Cantata No. 202; Brandenberg Concerto Nos. 2-5,* Ravinia Festival Ensemble, RCA Gold Seal.
Bartok: *Concerto for Orchestra; Music for String Instruments,*

Percussion and Celesta, Chicago Symphony, Deutsche Grammophon (DG).

Beethoven: *Piano Concertos Nos. 1-5,* Chicago Symphony, Philips.

Brahms: *Piano Concerto No. 1,* Chicago Symphony, RCA.

Dvorak: *Symphony No. 7,* Chicago Symphony, RCA.

Haydn: *Creation,* Berlin Philharmonic, DG.

Mahler: *Symphony No. 5, Symphony No. 10, Adagio,* Philadelphia Orchestra, RCA.

Mendelssohn: *Symphonies: No. 3 in A Minor, Op. 56 (Scottish); No. 4 in A Major, Op. 90 (Italian),* Berlin Philharmonic, DG.

Mozart: *Cosi fan tutte, K. 588,* Vienna Philharmonic Orchestra and State Opera, DG.

Mozart: *The Magic Flute,* Vienna Philharmonic Orchestra and State Opera, RCA.

Puccini: *Tosca,* Philharmonia (London), Angel.

Ravel: *Daphnis et Chloe (complete ballet),* Berlin Philharmonic, DG.

Saint-Saens: *Cello Concerto No. 1;* Lalo: *Cello Concerto;* Bruch: *Kol Nidrei,* Chicago Symphony, DG.

Schoenberg: *Erwartung,* Metropolitan Opera, Philips Classics.

Schubert: *Symphony No. 9,* Chicago Symphony, DG.

Schuman: *Symphonies No. 2 and 3,* Berlin Philharmonic, DG.

Sibelius: *Violin Concerto;* Dvorak: *Violin Concerto,* Berlin Philharmonic, DG.

Strauss: *Ariadne auf Naxos,* Vienna Philharmonic Orchestra and State Opera, DG.

Tchaikovsky: *Evgeny Onegin,* Dresden State Orchestra and Chorus, DG.

Verdi: *Aida,* Metropolitan Opera, Sony Classical.

Verdi: *Otello,* National Philharmonic Orchestra (London), RCA.

Wagner: *Das Rheingold,* Metropolitan Opera, DG.

Wagner: *Die Walkurie,* Metropolitan Opera, DG.

Sources

Books

Annals of the Metropolitan Opera, edited by G. Fitzgerald and J. S. Uppman with an introduction by Levine, Metropolitan Opera Guild, 1990.

Chesterman, R., *Conductors in Conversation,* Robson, 1990.

Rubin, Stephen, *The New Met in Profile,* Macmillan, 1974.

Periodicals

Newsweek, September 30, 1991.

New York Post, June 4, 1971.

New York Times, January 17, 1982.

Opera News, December 9, 1972; September 1986; September 1990.

—*Jeanne M. Lesinski*

Patti LuPone

Singer, actress

Known equally well for her portrayal of Argentina's Eva Peron in *Evita* and her role as the mother of a mentally challenged teenager in the television series *Life Goes On,* singer and actress Patti LuPone has proven her versatility as a performer. Her resume includes work on Broadway, performances with the Royal Shakespeare Company, and appearances in films and on television. She has received recognition for her achievements in the form of a Tony—in addition to three other nominations for the award—a Drama Desk Award, and a Laurence Olivier Award, the British equivalent of the Tony.

Patti LuPone grew up in a musical family. An amateur pianist and opera buff, her mother, Angela LuPone, named her for her great aunt, the famous soprano Adelina Patti. The young LuPone took private lessons in voice, piano, drama, and dance. With her two brothers she formed a dance troupe and performed locally. Her brother Robert also sang and danced and would go on to win a Tony for his role in *A Chorus Line.* In high school Patti played tuba in the marching band and cello in the orchestra and sang in both the madrigal group and concert choir. As she explained in an interview with Linda Winer for *New York Newsday,* she decided at a very early age that she wanted to perform: "[When I was four] I did a tap number [in a show], looked down at the audience and said, 'Hey! They're all smiling at me! I can do whatever I want!' I was hooked . . . and [have] never looked back."

After high school LuPone applied for admittance to the opera program at the Juilliard School but was not accepted. Her brother Robert, who was at Juilliard studying dance, convinced her to audition for the newly formed drama program under the direction of famed actor and director John Houseman. In 1968 she was admitted into the first class, and in 1972 she was one of only 14 students out of 36 who graduated on time.

Houseman organized the graduates into a professional repertory troupe called the Juilliard Acting Company, later called the City Center Acting Company, then simply the Acting Company. LuPone was a member of the troupe for several years. In 1975 she appeared with the company in an adaptation of Eudora Welty's *Robber Bridegroom* and received a Tony nomination. After leaving the group in 1976, she performed primarily in musicals, including the 1976 Off-Broadway production of *The Baker's Wife,* by David Merrick, as well as the Broadway production of David Mamet's *Water Engine* and Studs Terkel's *Working,* both in 1978.

Born April 21, 1949, in Northport, Long Island, NY; daughter of Orlando Joseph and Angela Louise (maiden name, Patti) LuPone; married Matt Johnston, 1988; children: Joshua Luke (born 1990). *Education:* Juilliard School, bachelor of fine arts degree in drama, 1972.

Member of the Juilliard Acting Company (later known as City Center Acting Company, then the Acting Company), 1972-76. Singer and actress appearing in Off-Broadway productions, including *School for Scandal,* 1972, *The Woods,* 1972, *Next Time I'll Sing to You,* 1972, *Lower Depths,* 1972, *The Beggar's Opera,* 1973, and *The Baker's Wife,* 1976; in Broadway productions, including *Three Sisters,* 1973, *Robber Bridegroom,* 1975, *Working,* 1978, *Catchpenny Twist,* 1979, *Evita,* 1979-81, and *Anything Goes,* 1987; in motion pictures, including *King of the Gypsies,* 1978, *1941,* 1980, *Striking Back,* 1981, *Fighting Back,* 1982, *Cat's Eye,* 1985, *Witness,* 1985, *Wise Guys,* 1986, and *Driving Miss Daisy,* 1989; and on television shows, including *Life Goes On,* beginning in 1989.

Awards: Tony Award and Drama Desk Award, both 1980, both for *Evita;* Laurence Olivier Award, 1986, for *Les Miserables;* three Tony Award nominations.

Addresses: *Agent*—Gersh Agency Inc., 130 West 42nd Street, Suite 1804, New York, NY, 10036.

Chosen for Starring Role

In 1979 LuPone won the role that thrust her into the national spotlight: that of the Argentine first lady Eva Peron in *Evita,* by Andrew Lloyd Webber and Tim Rice. From the initial 200 women who auditioned for the role, 30 finalists were chosen and all were asked to sing the same two songs from the show. When LuPone's rendition of "Don't Cry for Me Argentina" brought tears to the eyes of the audience, the producer, Harold Prince, hired her.

Prince's decision surprised many, for such stars as Raquel Welch, Faye Dunaway, and Meryl Streep were said to have wanted the role. *People* announced, "Acting nobody Patti LuPone set her cap to be Evita and beat out Faye and Raquel." The show opened in the spring of 1979 in Los Angeles and San Francisco and hit Broadway in the fall. While the show received mixed reviews, critics praised LuPone's work. Walter Kerr commented in the *New York Times,* "Miss LuPone does sufficient justice to the score (almost everything is

sung); but little justice is done her [by the show]." In the spring of 1980 she won both a Tony and a Drama Desk Award for best featured actress.

After two years LuPone decided she had been Eva Peron for long enough; she needed a rest and new roles. But her fame seemed to work against her and finding good parts was difficult. As she maintained in a *New York Times* interview, playing in *Evita* had typecast her: "Casting directors forget what you did in the past. They think I'm blond and much older, so unless they need a blond fascist dictator, I won't get a call." However, parts did eventually come her way, and while pleased with her work, she later lamented the lack of public response. "I did some of my best work after *Evita* but it wasn't in the public eye, and it didn't command a lot of notice, therefore I was nothing," she informed David Sacks of the *New York Times Magazine.* Among her work from that period was a 1981 production of Shakespeare's *As You Like It* and singing roles in such revivals as the 1937 musical *The Cradle Will Rock,* by Marc Blitzstein, in 1983 and Lionel Bart's *Oliver!* in 1984. She also performed in a solo cabaret show that palyed at different New York supper clubs from 1980 to 1982 and met with disappointing reviews.

Royal Shakespeare Company Pioneer

In 1985 LuPone won the role of Fantine in *Les Miserables,* by Claude-Michel Schonberg. Although her character dies early in the play, her performance—and the Laurence Olivier Award for best actress she received—bounced her back into the spotlight. She rejected the offer to reprise the role on Broadway, however, and did not join the American cast production. She elaborated on her decision in an interview for the *New York Times Magazine:* "I'm very possessive about my theatrical memories. Two weeks after I opened at the Barbican in London, I knew I couldn't do it in New York. I was having a theatrical dream come true. I was with the Royal Shakespeare Company, the only American who has ever played a principal part, a fantastic part. . . . The issue was: I am a part of the English company."

In 1987, director Jerry Zaks invited LuPone to audition for his revival of the 1934 Cole Porter musical *Anything Goes.* "I was struck by the fact that she was very upfront," Zaks commented to the *New York Times Magazine*'s David Sacks. "She had vitality, a sense of humor, and a willingness to try things." After the show opened in October of that year, critics agreed with his choice. As William A. Henry III declared in *Time:* "If Porter really were to lend approval, it would be chiefly for Patti LuPone. As nightclub belter Reno Sweeney, she rivals the role's originator, Ethel Merman, in volume and clarity of voice, and far outdoes her in intelligence and heart."

Moved Into Television Roles

After leaving the cast of *Anything Goes* LuPone moved to Los Angeles to pursue television work "because there is so little work in New York now, and an actor has to go where the work is," she disclosed to a correspondent for the *New York Times.* In the fall of 1989 she joined the series *Life Goes On,* portraying the mother in a family that includes a teenage boy with Down Syndrome. Her character, a Broadway singer who gave up the stage to raise a family, still performs for some private and public occasions, giving LuPone occasional singing opportunities.

Patti LuPone is, as writer David Sacks noted in the *New York Times Magazine,* "a born performer, extroverted, impetuous. And mischievous—you sense in her a wayward enthusiasm that can hardly be contained." But she is uncomfortable with the trappings of fame and success. She recounted to Sacks in the same article, "During *Evita* I was constantly harassed—by my dance captain, my wardrobe mistress, and everyone else—to dress up. I was a star. There is an illusion you're expected to present. But I don't feel easy with that, because I don't think it's my responsibility to [be what I am not.]" She did admit in an interview for *Harper's Bazaar,* however, that fame has some advantages: "It does get you seated at the best restaurants."

While she is certainly successful in television, she may eventually go back to the musical stage. "I'll be able to retire from the theater," she proclaimed in *Harper's Bazaar,* "when I can finally sing in a Steven Sondheim musical that is directed by Harold Prince. That is my ultimate dream."

Selected discography

With others

Evita, MCA, 1979.
Les Miserables, First Night Records, 1985.
Anything Goes, RCA, 1988.

Sources

Harper's Bazaar, April 1982.
New York Newsday, October 18, 1987.
New York Times, March 2, 1979; September 26, 1979; October 7, 1979; June 8, 1980; June 23, 1980; February 28, 1980; March 3, 1980; October 27, 1985; October 20, 1987; October 22, 1987; January 19, 1992.
New York Times Magazine, January 24, 1988.
People, August 6, 1979; September 11, 1989.
Time, October 21, 1985; November 2, 1987; October 16, 1989; December 3, 1990.

—Robin Armstrong

Miriam Makeba

Singer, activist

South African singer and political activist Miriam Makeba is chief among those who have proclaimed the experiences of black South Africans. Throughout a career spanning more than three decades, she has established herself as a powerful voice in the fight against apartheid—the South African practice of institutional political, economic, and social oppression along racial lines. Often referred to as "Mother Africa" and "The Empress of African Song," Makeba is credited with bringing the rhythmic and spiritual sounds of Africa to the West. Her music is a soulful mix of jazz, blues, and traditional African folk songs shaded with potent political overtones. Using music as a primary forum for her social concerns, the singer has become a lasting symbol in the fight for racial equality and has come to represent the pain of all South Africans living in exile.

Makeba's first encounter with the severity of government rule in her native land came when she was just two and a half weeks old: Following her mother's arrest for the illegal sale of home-brewed beer, the infant served a six-month jail term with her. Makeba's formative years were equally difficult; as a teenager she performed backbreaking domestic work for white families and endured physical abuse from her first husband. She found solace and a sense of community in music and religion. Singing first in a choir, Makeba soon showcased her talents with local bands, achieving success on the regional club circuit.

Career Received Boost From Belafonte

Makeba captured international attention with her role in the film *Come Back, Africa,* a controversial anti-apartheid statement released in 1959. Following the film's debut at the Venice Film Festival, Makeba traveled to London, where she met respected American entertainer and social activist Harry Belafonte. Impressed by her unique and profound renderings of African folk songs, he served as her mentor and promoter in the United States, arranging performances for her in New York City clubs and a guest spot on *The Steve Allen Show.* This exposure brought Makeba worldwide acclaim and launched a cross-cultural music career of uncommon proportions.

The 1960s proved an especially tumultuous decade for Makeba. Her outspoken opposition to the repressive political climate in South Africa set the stage for harsh government retaliation. Makeba's call for an end to apartheid became increasingly powerful, and her recordings were subsequently banned in South Africa. More than three decades of exile began for the singer in 1960, when, seeking to return to her native land for her mother's funeral, her passport was invalidated by the

For the Record. . .

Born Zensi Miriam Makeba, March 4, 1932, in Prospect (near Johannesburg), South Africa; immigrated to United States, 1959; daughter of a Xhosa teacher and a Swazi domestic worker; married Sonny Pilay (a singer), 1959 (divorced, 1959); married Hugh Masekela (a musician), 1964 (divorced, 1966); married Stokely Carmichael (a civil rights activist), 1968 (divorced, 1978); married fifth husband, Bageot Bah (an airline executive); children: (first marriage) Bongi (daughter; deceased). *Education:* Attended Kimerton Training Institute, Pretoria, South Africa.

Domestic worker in Johannesburg, South Africa; vocalist; toured South Africa, Rhodesia (now Zimbabwe), and the Belgian Congo (now Zaire) with the Black Mountain Brothers, 1954-57; performed throughout Africa, the U.S., England, France, Denmark, and Italy, 1957—; recording artist; performed with singer Paul Simon's *Graceland* tour of Africa, 1987, and the U.S., 1988. Appeared in film *Come Back, Africa,* 1959. Former United Nations delegate from Guinea, West Africa.

Member: ASCAP (American Society of Composers, Authors, and Publishers).

Awards: Grammy Award for best folk recording, 1965, for *An Evening With Belafonte/Makeba;* Dag Hammarskjold Peace Prize, 1986.

Addresses: *Record company*—Polydor Records, Worldwide Plaza, 825 8th Ave., New York, NY 10019.

South African government. Makeba also endured turmoil in her personal life. Between 1959 and 1966 she suffered two failed marriages, one to singer Sonny Pilay and another to trumpeter Hugh Masekela. In the early 1960s she faced a serious threat to her health, battling cervical cancer through radical surgery.

Perhaps the biggest blow to Makeba's career, however, came with her 1968 marriage to American civil rights activist Stokely Carmichael. A self-avowed revolutionary, Carmichael took a militant "Black Power" stance that was often perceived as divisive and threatening to the fabric of American society. Having long used song as a vehicle to raise social and political awareness, Makeba was stunned by the devastating effect of her marriage on her career; her relationship with Carmichael effectively eliminated her arena for social expression in the West. In her autobiography *Makeba: My Story,* she recalled her suddenly unwelcome status in the United States: "My concerts are being canceled left and right. I

learn that people are afraid that my shows will finance radical activities. I can only shake my head. What does Stokely have to do with my singing?" When her record label, Reprise, refused to honor her contract in the States, Makeba moved with Carmichael to Guinea, West Africa.

Personal Tragedy

Although Makeba's marriage to Carmichael ended in 1978, she remained in Guinea for several years. She continued performing in Europe and parts of Africa, promoting freedom, unity, and social change. During the singer's time in Guinea, though, heartbreaking misfortune again touched her life. Her youngest grandson became fatally ill, and her only daughter, Bongi, died after delivering a stillborn child. Yet, through all of her trials, Makeba has derived consolation from her music and her undying faith in God.

In the spring of 1987 Makeba joined American folk-rock legend Paul Simon's phenomenal *Graceland* tour in the newly independent black nation of Zimbabwe. An unprecedented display of multicultural music and racial unity, the concert focused attention on the injustice of imperial racist policies in South Africa and displayed the talents of generations of South African musicians. Following the success and exposure afforded her by the *Graceland* tour, Makeba recorded her first American release in two decades, a tribal collection titled *Sangoma,* which means diviner-healer. Featuring African chants that the singer learned in her youth from her mother, the solo album cast a new light on the soulful, spiritual sounds of her native land. Makeba's follow-up album—the 1989 Polydor debut *Welela*—blended traditional songs with popular compositions.

Three Decades of Exile Ended

In a *Chicago Tribune* interview, Makeba summarized her thoughts on life in exile: "I have love, but I also have suffering. I am a South African. I left part of me there. I belong there." In June of 1990 Makeba was finally allowed to go home; she visited Johannesburg for the first time in 31 years. The following year Polydor released *Eyes on Tomorrow,* an upbeat protest album recorded in a Johannesburg studio. Featuring pioneering jazz trumpeter Dizzy Gillespie, rhythm and blues singer Nina Simone, and Hugh Masekela, *Eyes on Tomorrow* is generally considered a more commercial mix of pop, blues, and jazz than Makeba's previous efforts.

A spokesperson for civil rights throughout the world,

Makeba continues to stand as the embodiment of the black South African experience. As *New York Times* contributor Robert Farris Thompson put it: "She is a symbol of the emergence of Afro-Atlantic art and a voice for her people. Her life in multiple cultural and political settings—and her rich musical career, drawing on traditional and contemporary sources—have resonance for us all."

Selected writings

The World of African Song, edited by Jonas Gwangwa and E. John Miller, Jr., Time Books, 1971.

(With James Hall) *Makeba: My Story* (autobiography), New American Library, 1987.

Selected discography

An Evening with Belafonte/Makeba, RCA, 1965.

"Pata Pata" (single), 1967.

Sangoma, Warner Bros., 1988.

Welela, Polydor, 1989.

Eyes on Tomorrow, Polydor, 1991.

Africa, reissued, Novus, 1991.

Miriam Makeba Sings, RCA.

The World of Miriam Makeba, RCA.

Back of the Moon, Kapp.

Miriam Makeba in Concert, Reprise.

Sources

Books

Makeba, Miriam, and James Hall, *Makeba: My Story,* New American Library, 1987.

Periodicals

Africa Report, January 1977.

Chicago Tribune, March 20, 1988.

Ebony, April 1963; July 1968.

Ms., May 1988.

Nation, March 12, 1988.

New York Times, February 28, 1960; February 15, 1987; January 27, 1988; January 31, 1988; March 8, 1988; March 13, 1988; June 11, 1990.

Playboy, October 1991.

Rolling Stone, July 2, 1987.

Time, February 1, 1960.

Times Literary Supplement, March 11, 1988.

Tribune Books (Chicago), January 24, 1988.

Washington Post, April 19, 1988.

—*Barbara Carlisle Bigelow*

The Manhattan Transfer

Pop-jazz quartet

The Manhattan Transfer sings everything from 1940s swing to 1990s rap, with rock, bebop, and doo-wop in between—all in four-part harmony. When they started out, their intention was to perform music that no one else was doing. They wanted to explore the roots of America's pop-music heritage, not for nostalgia, but to create new sounds and provide fresh insight into older songs by reworking them in their jazz-oriented style. "The whole key," explained group founder Tim Hauser in Irwin Stambler's *Encyclopedia of Pop, Rock and Soul,* "was to sing four-part harmony. Nobody was doing it then, and nobody is doing it now. When you do four-part harmony, you get into jazz." They got into jazz and have become, as *Los Angeles Times* reviewer and jazz expert Leonard Feather described them, "without peer as a vocal jazz quartet."

The name of the group was taken from a John Dos Passos novel about New York City in the 1920s and was first used in the late 1960s by a previous incarnation of the Manhattan Transfer. The first Manhattan Transfer—Hauser, Gene Pistilli, Pat Rosalia, Erin Dickens, and

Marty Nelson—combined elements of rhythm and blues and country into what has been called a good-time, jug-band style. They recorded one album, *Junkin',* for Capitol Records in 1971. But Hauser left that year, and the group broke up in 1972.

The Manhattan Transfer that followed lists their official formation date as October 1, 1972, but group members had actually met the previous March. After he left the first Manhattan Transfer, Hauser drove a cab to make ends meet. One of his fares was a waitress named Laurel Masse. As the two talked, they discovered their mutual musical interests. Masse, also a singer, was familiar with Hauser's first group. Hauser, who was making demo tapes and trying to get back into the music business, invited her to join him. He met Janis Siegal a few weeks later at a party, where she was singing in a trio backing country-singer Diane David-son. Siegal also knew of the first Manhattan Transfer,

loved their harmonies, and agreed to join Hauser in his new venture.

Rounded Out the Quartet

Deciding to put a new Manhattan Transfer together, the trio needed a fourth member. They found Alan Paul working on Broadway in *Grease.* They rehearsed every day for six months, perfecting not only their singing, but creating a complete stage show. "We were going to perform," said Siegal in *Down Beat.* "We weren't going to be introspective on stage. We were going to give out. We were going to dress up." Their act was complemented by costumes, choreography, and acting. In 1973 they began performing in New York City cabarets. The following year they performed at a club called Reno Sweeney's—and knew they had arrived. Said Paul in an interview with *Down Beat:* "I started realizing it even before we got the record deal, when we were playing Reno Sweeney's and there were lines of people outside. You could feel the energy building. When we moved uptown to the Cafe Carlyle, and [rock stars] Mick Jagger and David Bowie came to see us, that's when I knew there's something going on."

By the end of 1974, the Manhattan Transfer was moving quickly. They signed with Atlantic Records and began recording their first album. The LP *Manhattan Transfer* was released in April of 1975. That spring the quartet toured Chicago, San Francisco, and Los Angeles. In Los Angeles, they played two weeks at the famed Roxy and appeared on the *Mary Tyler Moore Television Special.* Back in New York, CBS gave them their own television show: a four-week summer replacement series. Television gave them exposure, but perhaps the wrong kind. "To a lot of people it was like selling out," said Hauser in *Down Beat.* "In retrospect, I feel that those TV shows . . . kind of spoiled our underground image and gave a slick commercial feel to the act, which hurt us in the States."

A Smash in Europe

Meanwhile, though, their popularity soared in Europe. The *Manhattan Transfer* single "Tuxedo Junction" was a hit, and their 1975 European tour received overwhelming ovations. In Germany, they appeared on the television show *Star Parade* and won a German Grammy for best new group. In 1977, "Chanson D'Amour," from their second album, *Coming Out,* became a hit in France and England. They went on the road again, playing MIDEM, the music business convention in Cannes, France, where they performed for recording executives from all over the world. With their third album, *Pastiche,* the group's standing in the U.S. began to improve. The next release, *Extensions,* solidified their popularity with American audiences and won them their first Grammy, for Siegal's arrangement of the song "Birdland."

During these early years the Manhattan Transfer experienced internal problems and change. Relations with management became strained because the group disapproved of their continual supper-club bookings, which were financially successful but artistically unsatisfying. Financial disputes even led the group to court. In 1976 the quartet acquired new management that helped turn their fortunes around. Then, in 1979, Laurel Masse left the group. Finding a replacement was cause for anxiety. Said Hauser in *Down Beat:* "We didn't want 50 million aspiring singers calling us. We wanted somebody who could blend with our sound, who could cut it as a soloist, and someone we could get along with. Up until the seventh lady there were women who had one or two of these elements, but not all three. And then Cheryl [Bentyne] walked in. She sang 'Candy' and it was the *sound.*"

Solid Backgrounds

As a teenager, Cheryl Bentyne sang with her father's swing band; she was part of Seattle's New Deal Rhythm Band in her early twenties. After moving to Los Angeles, she sang locally until joining the Manhattan Transfer. Like Bentyne, the rest of the Manhattan Transfer had had previous pop-music experience. Hauser was in the rock group the Criterions in the 1950s and a member of the folk outfit the Troubadours Three during the following decade; Siegal, who started singing professionally at 12, recorded with the Young Generation before forming the country trio Laurel Canyon in the early 1970s; Paul had a history on Broadway, from performances in *Oliver* as a child to *Grease* in the early 1970s, with nightclub gigs in the interim. Hauser, Siegal, and Bentyne all have active solo careers in addition to their work with the group.

From the outset, the Manhattan Transfer demonstrated that they could handle a variety of musical styles. Their first three records focused on early rhythm and blues, rock, and swing but also featured newer, original works by group members and other contemporary musicians. With their fourth album, *Extensions,* the group moved into the area of jazz fusion and the technique of vocalese. Vocalese, in which vocals are added to instrumental jazz pieces—the voices imitating the sounds of the instruments—was popularized in the 1950s by the group Lambert, Hendricks and Ross. To help them perfect their technique, the Manhattan Transfer enlist-

ed the aid of Jon Hendricks. He wrote the words to Siegal's arrangement of the old Weather Report tune "Birdland" and taught the quartet how to blare and wail like trumpets and saxophones. In 1980 "Birdland" won Bentyne, Hauser, Paul, and Siegal their first two Grammy awards—and the respect of music critics who began to take them seriously as jazz artists.

Bridged the Jazz/Pop Gap

Mecca for Moderns again featured the hallmarks of Hendricks, on the cuts "(The Word of) Confirmation" and "Until I Met You" (originally titled "Corner Pocket"). But the Transfer also recorded songs in a contemporary pop style. "We always wanted to bridge the gaps [between jazz and pop]," said Siegal in *Down Beat.* In addition to the Hendricks collaborations, *Mecca* included "Boy From New York City," the group's first tune to hit *Billboard's* Top 10 pop chart. *Bodies and Souls,* their next venture, was their one attempt at a pure pop album. Making it for commercial reasons, they thought it would sell. The results were unexpected: *Bodies and*

"The whole key was to sing four-part harmony."
—Tim Hauser

Souls made the Top Twenty on jazz charts, but failed financially.

The Transfer's 1985 release, *Vocalese,* on the other hand, was pure jazz. Once again the group worked with Jon Hendricks. Hendricks, who wrote all the lyrics for the album, took a year off from his own group to collaborate with Hauser and company. The Transfer recruited other fine jazz musicians as well, including jazz and pop vocalist Bobby McFerrin, renowned pianist McCoy Tyner, and trumpet giant Dizzy Gillespie. Although initially Atlantic feared that an all-jazz album would fail, *Vocalese* triumphed financially as well as artistically, earning 12 Grammy nominations and three statuettes.

Off to Brazil

After *Vocalese* the quartet continued to explore new territory. For *Brasil,* they traveled to the Amazon Basin.

Fascinated with the tropical sounds they found there, the Transfer used the talents of top Brazilian musicians. Milton Nascimento, Ivan Lins, and Djavan all contributed songs; the group Uakti harmonized, and Djalma Correa provided percussion.

Hauser, Siegal, Paul, and Bentyne also continued to bridge the jazz/pop gap. With their 1991 release, *The Offbeat of Avenues,* they added the distinctive sounds of the 1990s to their trademark style. Many of the cuts on *Offbeat,* including the title track, feature a complex interplay of voices mixed with the smooth blend of harmony that characterizes the quartet's jazz sound. "Women in Love" even included a rap introduction. This album was further significant in representing a new creative direction for the group, Transfer members having written most of the material.

Perhaps unfairly, the Manhattan Transfer's versatility and flexibility have occasionally been something of a liability to them. They have received negative criticism from jazz purists for their pop work. In fact, some critics considered "Boy From New York City" a sellout; *People*'s Joanne Kaufman, for one, accused the Transfer of making "a bid for crossover success." But the group's diverse audience remains unfazed by their continuing stylist exploration. "Our audience is wild," said Cheryl Bentyne in an interview with *Down Beat*'s Michael Bourne. "They're very colorful, every age, shape, and size of person." This audience is also sizeable—the quartet's concerts, including a well-received 1992 acoustic jaunt—regularly sell out. Though the music press may have difficulty labeling their style, and radio stations may suffer distress over programming their music, category is markedly less important than quality to the Manhattan Transfer. They don't care what label a piece might have; they sing it "because," as Siegal pointed out in the *Encyclopedia of Pop, Rock & Soul,* "we like it! Because it's good music!"

Selected discography

On Atlantic Records, except as noted

The Manhattan Transfer, 1975.
Coming Out, 1976.
Pastiche, 1978.
Extensions (includes "Birdland"), 1979.
Mecca for Moderns, 1981.
Best of the Manhattan Transfer, 1981.
Bodies and Souls, 1983.
Bop Doo Wopp, 1985.
Vocalese, 1985.
Live, 1987.
Brasil, 1988.
The Offbeat of Avenues, Columbia, 1991.

Sources

Books

Stambler, Irwin, *Encyclopedia of Pop, Rock and Soul,* revised edition, St. Martin's, 1989.

Periodicals

Billboard, October 5, 1991.
Detroit Free Press, July 10, 1992.
Down Beat, March 1980; November 1985; April 1988; October 1987; October 1989; May 1990; April 1992.
Los Angeles Times, March 24, 1983; March 31, 1985; August 15, 1988.
Newsweek, December 30, 1974.
New York Times, April 6, 1980; July 7, 1980; September 18, 1981.
People, March 24, 1986; August 31, 1987; October 7, 1991.
Rolling Stone, June 26, 1980.

—*Robin Armstrong*

Curtis Mayfield

Singer, songwriter, guitarist, record company executive

In 1990, Curtis Mayfield was enjoying a comeback. His soul vocal group of the late 1950s and 1960s, the Impressions, had been nominated for a place in the Rock and Roll Hall of Fame, and a successful cover version of their 1961 hit "Gypsy Woman" had been recorded by the popular rock band Santana. *Take It to the Streets,* Mayfield's first album in more than five years, was released in early 1990, and he had toured the United States, Europe, and Japan to promote it. And Capitol Records was set to release the soundtrack to *The Return of Superfly,* a rap sampler featuring four original songs written and performed by Mayfield.

Then tragedy struck. On a windy summer night in August of 1990, Mayfield was getting set to start a concert at Wingate Field in Brooklyn. As he was plugging in his guitar, a gust of wind toppled a light tower near the stage, striking Mayfield in the head. The accident resulted in three broken vertebrae and quadriplegia. Remarkably keeping his spirits up, however, Mayfield began physical therapy in September of 1990 and made his first public appearance in February of 1991, when he donated $100,000 to establish the Curtis Mayfield Research Fund at the Miami Project to Cure Paralysis. Friends and family were reportedly hopeful that Mayfield's therapy would enable him to make at least a partial recovery.

Quit the Tenth Grade to Join Impressions

Born on June 3, 1942, Curtis Lee Mayfield grew up in a poor Chicago family that moved from neighborhood to neighborhood. By the time he was in high school his family had settled in the Cabrini-Green public housing projects on the city's north side. Mayfield's strongest early musical influence came from his membership in a local gospel group called the Northern Jubilee Gospel Singers, which included three cousins and acquaintance Jerry Butler. Mayfield told the *Detroit News* in 1974, "I was writing music when I was 10 or 11 years old." Mayfield's grandmother was a preacher in the Traveling Souls Spiritualist Church, and traces of church and gospel music are unmistakable in many of his compositions. Mayfield attended Chicago's Wells High School but left in the tenth grade to join what would become the Impressions.

The Impressions began performing in the mid-1950s as the Roosters, in Chattanooga, Tennessee, their line-up comprised of Fred Cash, Sam Gooden, Emanuel Thomas, and the brothers Richard and Arthur Brooks. Seeking to advance their musical careers, Gooden and the Brooks brothers went north to Chicago in 1957, settling in the Cabrini-Green projects. Jerry Butler was a senior in high school at the time, and he acted as a replacement for the Impressions vocalists who had stayed behind in Tennessee. According to Robert Pruter in *Chicago Soul,* Butler encouraged Mayfield to join the group, saying they needed someone "who could play an instrument and who could help us get our harmony together." By this time, Mayfield was writing gospel-influenced songs and had learned to play the guitar.

The group made some early recordings for the Bandera label and were then discovered by Eddie Thomas of Vee Jay Records, who became their manager and changed their name to the Impressions. The single "For Your Precious Love" was released on the company's subsidiary label, Falcon, and featured Jerry Butler's lead vocals. Its first issue sold over 900,000 copies. A Vee Jay executive signed the Impressions to a recording contract immediately after hearing the song, which he reportedly liked for its spiritual feel—a genuine departure from the doo-wop harmonies of the day.

First Stint as Lead Singer a Disappointment

Vee Jay promoted the group as "Jerry Butler and the Impressions" and developed Butler as a solo artist. After three singles, Butler left the group to go out on his own. Mayfield told Pruter, "When Jerry left . . . it allowed me to generate and pull out my own talents as a writer and a vocalist." Mayfield's soprano singing, however, contrasted sharply with Butler's baritone leads. The group released a few singles with Mayfield as leader and was then dropped by Vee Jay. From 1959 to 1961, the Impressions did not work as a group; Mayfield began writing songs and playing guitar for Butler in 1960.

By 1961 Mayfield had saved enough money—about a thousand dollars to regroup the Impressions and

take them to New York City to arrange a recording session. In July of that year they recorded "Gypsy Woman" for ABC-Paramount. Mayfield was only 18 when the group signed with ABC-Paramount. "Gypsy Woman" was the beginning of a seven-year string of rhythm and blues and pop hits—all composed by Mayfield. The Brooks brothers left the Impressions in 1962; the remaining members continued as a trio throughout the 1960s.

In 1963 the group recorded "It's All Right," which *Chicago Soul's* Pruter termed "the first single to define the classic style of the 1960s Impressions." Producer Jerry Pate "lifted the energy level considerably, adding blaring horns and a more forceful, percussive bottom," wrote Pruter. "It's All Right" was a crossover hit that went to Number Four on the pop charts and Number One on the rhythm and blues charts in the fall of 1963. The song featured "the lead switching off from among the three [group members] and the two others singing in harmony with the lead," elaborated Pruter. Though the song represented a new sound in rhythm and blues, critics have long noted that the feel of "It's All Right" sprung directly from Mayfield's gospel experience.

Impressions on Top

In 1964 the Impressions became a major act with a series of strong singles that included "I'm So Proud," "Keep On Pushing," and "Amen." By most accounts, Mayfield was profoundly motivated by the emergence of the civil rights movement. Civil rights leaders Martin Luther King, Jr., and Jesse Jackson adopted "Keep On Pushing" as an unofficial theme song for the movement. *Chicago Tribune* contributor Dan Kening wrote that Mayfield's "inspirational lyrics reflected a strong black consciousness while preaching the tenets of hard work, persistence, and faith as the key to achieving equality."

The group was at their peak in 1965 when they released "People Get Ready," a song featuring heavy gospel imagery and feeling. But by 1967 their hold on the market had begun to fade. Compounding this was the fact that in the late 1960s some relatively popular Impressions single releases were ill-received by black radio stations. As Pruter reported, "Surprisingly at that time, black radio had not kept pace with its black constituency and there was a lot of resistance by programmers over playing such 'overtly' political songs. The popularity of those songs had the effect of pushing black radio in the direction its listeners were going."

Founded Music Publishing Company at 21

In addition to composing, singing, and playing the guitar, Mayfield was also interested in setting up his own record label. In 1960, at the age of 21, he made the unprecedented move of establishing his own music publishing company, Curtom, while recording at Vee Jay. Mayfield began developing two labels in 1966, Mayfield and Windy C., but it was in 1968 that he founded his most successful label, also called Curtom. The budding entrepreneur took the Impressions away from ABC and also recorded and produced other acts. Mayfield's songwriting and producing abilities were a key factor in the label's success.

In August of 1970 Mayfield announced his departure from the Impressions. He began his solo career the following year, offering "a biting commentary of the American scene and impressions of oppressed people," according to a review in *Billboard*. A *New York Times* music critic said of his first solo album, *Curtis:* "Mayfield himself continues to be a kind of contemporary preacher-through-music. He sings in a breathlessly high, pure voice, breaking his phrases into speech-like patterns, his rhythms pushed by the urgency of his thoughts. . . . His message seems as important to him as his melody." Including songs of up to ten minutes, *Curtis* established Mayfield as an album rather than a singles artist.

Mayfield began a successful career writing soundtracks for films with the 1972 movie *Superfly.* The controversial film depicted the life of a drug dealer and was part of the then-popular genre of "blaxploitation" films. According to a *New York Times* review, "Mayfield's music is more specifically anti-drugs than the philosophical content of the movie, and it is also considerably more stylish in design and execution." Two Top Ten hit singles resulted from the soundtrack: "Freddie's Dead" and "Superfly."

Solidified Position as Solo Artist

Throughout the 1970s Mayfield continued to write soundtracks and solidify his reputation as a solo artist. His solo compositions featured a more intense style than was expressed in those he had written for the Impressions; instructive lyrics and social commentary were the norm. Bucking pervasive negative criticism, Pruter assessed Mayfield's 1970s output positively, writing, "Some of the very best black popular music of the 1970s came from Mayfield, who despite the many misses during the decade was one of the creative leaders in establishing a new contemporary style of rhythm and blues, one with a militant, harder edge."

Mayfield joined the Impressions in 1983 for a reunion tour. Original members Butler, Mayfield, Gooden, and Cash performed the 1960s hits of the Impressions along with Butler and Mayfield's more popular solo efforts. According to Robert Palmer of the *New York Times,* the performances "amounted to a capsule history of recent black popular music, from the slick doo-wop and grittier gospel-based vocal group styles of the 1950s to Mr. Butler's urbane pop-soul, Curtis Mayfield's soul message songs and later funk, and the styles the Impressions have tackled as a group."

Mayfield's influence on a new generation of performers is widely evident. His 1960s compositions for the Impressions have enjoyed numerous cover versions from a wide range of popular singers. Mayfield's characteristic falsetto and innovative guitar work—the latter a clear inspiration to guitar colossus Jimi Hendrix—helped set a new standard for contemporary music. And critics have pointed out that his anti-drug messages, most emphatically expressed in the songs for *Superfly,* are

---

"There's only been a couple of people I've met in the music business that to me are really heavy. Curtis is one of them."
—Ice-T

---

echoed in the films of the young black filmmakers who gained prominence in the late 1980s. Controversial rap singer and actor Ice-T, who lent vocals to "Superfly 1990," said in tribute to the artist, "There's only been a couple of people I've met [in the music business] that to me are really heavy. Curtis is one of them."

Selected discography

Singles; with the Impressions

(As Jerry Butler and the Impressions) "For Your Precious Love," Falcon, 1958.
"Gypsy Woman," ABC-Paramount, 1961.
"It's All Right," ABC-Paramount, 1963.
"I'm So Proud," ABC-Paramount, 1964.
"Keep On Pushing," ABC-Paramount, 1964.
"Amen," ABC-Paramount, 1964.
"People Get Ready," ABC-Paramount, 1965.

Albums; with the Impressions

The Impressions, ABC-Paramount, 1963.
The Never Ending Impressions, ABC-Paramount, 1964.
Keep On Pushing, ABC-Paramount, 1964.
People Get Ready, ABC-Paramount, 1965.
Ridin' High, ABC-Paramount, 1966.
The Fabulous Impressions, ABC-Paramount, 1967.
This Is My Country, Curtom, 1968.
Young Mods' Forgotten Story, Curtom, 1969.
Check Out Your Mind, Curtom, 1970.
The Vintage Years: Featuring Jerry Butler and Curtis Mayfield, Sire, 1976.

Albums; solo

Curtis, Curtom, 1970.
Curtis Live, Curtom, 1971.
Roots, Curtom, 1971.
Superfly (soundtrack; includes "Freddie's Dead"), Curtom, 1972.
Back to the World, Curtom, 1973.
Sweet Exorcist, Curtom, 1974.
Got to Find a Way, Curtom, 1974.
There's No Place Like America, Curtom, 1975.
Give Get Take and Have, Curtom, 1976.
Never Say You Can't Survive, Curtom, 1977.
Short Eyes (soundtrack), Curtom, 1977.
Do It All Night, Curtom, 1978.

Heartbeat, RSO/Curtom, 1978.
Something to Believe In, RSO/Curtom, 1979.
The Right Combination, RSO/Curtom, 1980.
Honesty, Boardwalk, 1982.
Take It to the Streets, Curtom, 1990.
The Return of Superfly (soundtrack; includes "Superfly 1990"), Capitol, 1990.

Sources

Books

Pruter, Robert, *Chicago Soul,* University of Illinois Press, 1991.

Periodicals

Billboard, August 29, 1970; February 6, 1971.
Chicago Tribune, September 2, 1990.
Detroit News, January 27, 1974.
Ebony, July 1973.
Guitar Player, August 1991.
Indianapolis Star, May 15, 1983.
Los Angeles Times, October 23, 1989; August 26, 1990.
Michigan Chronicle, June 19, 1976.
New York Times, December 6, 1970; May 6, 1983.

—*David Bianco*

MC
Lyte

Rap singer

In the early days of rap—the late 1970s and the first half of the 1980s—male rappers and deejays dominated the scene. Women rappers, wrote Dominique Di Prima in *Mother Jones,* were "the underground of the underground." Then, in the latter half of the decade, a wave of fierce, independent women took up microphones and turntables. Salt-n-Pepa, Roxanne Shante, Queen Latifah, Monie Love, and MC Lyte demonstrated clearly that women could not only rap as hard and as entertainingly as their male counterparts, but that they could achieve real commercial success in the burgeoning rap music industry. In addition, as David Thigpen wrote in *Time,* "Women have shown that rap can be far more significant and flexible than its critics have admitted. And that makes it all the more difficult to categorize, ghettoize or otherwise dismiss."

It would seem impossible to dismiss MC Lyte, who from her first single "I Cram to Understand U" to her 1991 smash album *Act Like You Know* has stood consistently at the front of the pack. Like some of her outspoken fellow women emcees, she has displayed an uncompromising attitude and a concern with social issues like safe sex and drugs. Yet MC Lyte is a storyteller— "one of rap's most proficient raconteurs," according to *Spin* critic Joan Morgan.

Recorded With Family Label

Born in the early 1970s in Queens, New York, Lana Moorer grew up in the East Flatbush neighborhood of Brooklyn. Her father started the record label First Priority in 1987, and her brothers performed and did production work for the label. Known as Milk and Gizmo of the rap unit Audio Two, Lyte's brothers went on to contribute to each of her three records.

With their assistance she recorded the single "I Cram to Understand U," and its reception raised expectations for her First Priority debut album, *Lyte as a Rock,* in 1988. "I Cram," about a boyfriend whose mysterious "other woman" turns out to be crack, announced the arrival of a major new rap artist. "Unlike the dozens of raps that are simply comic putdowns," wrote Peter Watrous in the *New York Times,* "Ms. Lyte's plaintive tone and her self-deprecating story add up to a complex emotional statement." Along with this celebrated tune, the title track, "10% Dis," and "Paper Thin" all became hits. "I Am Woman" quotes Helen Reddy's seventies hit song of the same name without irony, and adds "if you want a battle, I'm well prepared." The track "MC Lyte Likes Swingin'," produced by rap guru Prince Paul, begins with a typically confident assertion: "I may come on strong but that's what you like / You like a female MC who can handle the mike." Lyte remarked in a *Village Voice* interview that many female rappers choose to be sexy and sweet "when they could really be *smackin'* people with their rhymes."

Musically, Lyte's first album is relatively spare; its beats and samples are minimal and seem designed to emphasize Lyte's raps rather than function as songs. In 1989 she moved further in the direction of popular success with *Eyes on This.* The album, which *Rolling Stone* called a "slamming, street-smart" effort, yielded a number one rap single, "Cha Cha Cha," and two other top ten tracks, "Stop, Look, Listen" and "Cappucino." The single "I'm Not Having It," a safe-sex manifesto, was used in a widely-viewed TV commercial about AIDS. This song, as Michele Wallace remarked in *Ms.,* "comes down hard on the notion that women can't say no, and criticizes the shallowness of the male rap." Similarly, "Please Understand" addresses itself to unruly men. "I've never let a man dog me and I never will," Lyte told Deborah Gregory in an *Essence* profile. "It's just not gonna happen!"

Worked for Causes on Tour

In 1990 Lyte went on tour with rap superstars Heavy D. and Kool Moe Dee. "On stage," wrote Di Prima, "there's no getting around Lyte being rough and ready to get busy." *Vanity Fair*'s Kiki Mason wrote that Lyte "brings a gritty street presence to the stage, hurling her lyrics about drug abuse and difficult modern relationships at the audience." Her recognition grew by leaps and bounds: she became the first female rapper to perform on Arsenio Hall's talk show and at Carnegie Hall; the latter appearance was part of an AIDS benefit in 1990. In addition to playing concerts, Lyte toured schools and appeared at press conferences as part of Stop the Violence, an organization working to end violence in the black community.

As a leading woman of rap, Lyte is in an ideal position to communicate to a large audience her opinions on a variety of social issues. An ardent activist, she articulates her concerns about drug abuse, racism, and sexism through both her songs and her no-nonsense demeanor. For instance, *Mother Jones* quoted her response to male rappers calling women "bitches": "If you allow someone to call you a bitch and you answer . . . you're saying, It's okay to call me a bitch, and you can continue to call me that. So it's a matter of women taking a stand and telling them that they're not going for it." This "not going for it," she suggests, might include boycotting certain rap records to drive the message home. As far as the strong language in her own raps is concerned, Lyte sticks to her guns. "My mother keeps asking me why I have to swear in public," she told Mason. "But sometimes you need a shock so that people pay attention."

"The new female rappers are creating buoyant messages that transcend the inert boasting so common in male rap," Thigpen declared, echoing the sentiments of many critics who see positive role models in the new crop of women emcees. *Ebony*'s Renee Turner added that the "First Ladies of Rap" offer "a feminine view of urban reality." Lyte has indicated on more than one occasion that she is aware of her responsibility as one of these role models. Of "I Cram to Understand U," Lyte recalled to Di Prima, "It was just me putting myself in a situation that many other girls have been put in. I wanted to rap about it to show them that they're not the only ones going through this, and that, yes, it is possible for somebody to fall in love with someone and not know they're on drugs. . . . I put it in the first person to show the listeners that I can be whatever it is that I'm talking about."

Unlike previous waves of female pop stars, noted Gregory, Lyte is "not the least bit concerned with looking 'girly' or creating an image that's based on sex appeal." Wardrobe has long been a marker of her independence, but by 1990 her visibility as a performer led her to change her look from sweat pants to tailored outfits. She insisted in her interview with Di Prima, though, that she wasn't caving in to demands for a more "feminine" style: "That's not Lyte. When I get dressed up, it's because I'm pleasing myself, and I can afford to pay a designer."

Act Like You Know

In 1991 MC Lyte released her third album, *Act Like You Know.* She recruited a number of well-known rap producers—Mark the 45 King, Dee Jay Doc, Wolf & Epic—to assist her standbys Audio Two and King of

Chill. The sound on *Act Like You Know* is fuller than that of Lyte's previous releases, including a variety of R & B samples, heavy basslines, and funky beats. The first single, "When in Love," chronicles "the stupid things people do when they're in love," according to a quote from Lyte in an Atlantic press release. The lyrics provide some startling examples: "Like pickin' your lover's nose!" Lyte uses her storytelling skills to describe the perils of AIDS ("Eyes Are the Soul") and drunk driving ("Poor Georgie," the video of which fared well on MTV). In "Kamikaze" Lyte blasts rap that doesn't deal with real issues: "They try to keep me down because I talk to a beat / In other words I try to teach / But if I talk that Yang Yang s—t / Like You Can't Touch This / That s—t'll hit."

Writing for *Details,* Brantley Bardin declared that the album's "only real fault . . . is that with at least one message (if not six) per song, it verges on becoming the ultimate public service announcement." Lyte, however, stood by her messages, remarking in the *New York Times,* "I tried to pick topics and issues that hadn't been done to death by rappers. Then I tried to make it seem funny, to put the message in a palatable way." As she told Rhonda Baraka in *Tafrija,* being a rapper affords both the opportunity and the responsibility to make positive statements: "so that's your chance, whether it be an antidrug message or put a rubber on your willy, whatever the message is you can get it out. That's what I think is good about being in the entertainment business."

The ambitious multi-producer approach of *Act Like You Know* no doubt helped boost Lyte's sales, but it left critics divided. "If you consider yourself a rap aficionado, let alone an MC Lyte fan, skip the first side of *Act Like You Know,*" advised Morgan, who found the samples and arrangements of the album's first half overwrought. "It falls way off and lands squarely in pop-rap hell. . . . [Lyte's] voice has the eerie, anemic sound of a lost MC in a musical identity crisis." Even so, Morgan admitted, "She finds herself on the second side, thank God, and comes back kicking shit harder than ever over fat, simple drum beats and some seriously slamming samples." *People*'s Michael Small agreed that the album seemed like two uneven halves—the first "lush" and "curse-free" and the second featuring "simpler street beats" and "enough raunch and expletives to earn an R rating." Small asserted that "by trying to have it both ways, Lyte risks pleasing no one," although he conceded, "She's a great storyteller." Small's review concluded by admitting that teenagers might like the album, since the "confusing middle ground" they experience in their lives matches that of the record.

James Bernard, reviewing *Act Like You Know* for *Entertainment Weekly,* found that the album "finds MC Lyte softening her image without losing her edge," and that her stories of human desperation work because "rather than tossing around empty rhetoric, Lyte takes us face-to-face with these people, forcing us to look into their eyes." Ultimately Bernard awarded the album an "A-" and asserted that Lyte's voice, "with its lusty confidence, is the glue that holds this diverse collection together." *Sassy* raved that the "record hits you with crazy hard beats, and Lyte's rhymes talk about life from a distinctly girly perspective," while *Billboard* lauded *Act Like You Know* as "a toughtalking effort that takes no prisoners," calling Lyte's style "tough but caring and, above all, smart."

From Upstart to Stardom

In the course of a few years Lyte has grown from a teenaged upstart rapping on her dad's label to big-league star. She avoids the term "crossover" to describe her success; "Call it expansion," she urged Dream Hampton of *The Source.* Despite the glamour, though, she remains committed to spreading aware-

---

"Sometimes you need a shock so that people pay attention."

---

ness about social issues and—perhaps most of all—helping her fans see through the eyes of others. "I don't think it's my job" to be a cultural hero, she told Di Prima, but there is little doubt that women who follow Lyte's career have an example of a strong, independent woman artist. "Sure, I consider myself a role model for younger kids," she insisted in reply to Gregory, "but on the real tip—I'm just young and having fun." Despite shying away from important-sounding labels, Lyte appreciates the company of other women emcees. "Female rappers are coming out with something to say," she remarked to Turner. "And it is all beginning to open up, slowly but surely." When asked about her potential longevity, she told Baraka, "I think all that it is is knowing where you came from and not being phony."

A 1990 *Mother Jones* profile indicated that MC Lyte was "contemplating switching over to the business side of record making—not producing, but managing other acts. In the meantime she's started managing a few models and plans to add to her client list as soon as she moves out of rapping, which isn't quite yet." By the release of *Act Like You Know,* mentions of possible career changes dropped from Lyte's press coverage. Of course, given her accomplishments it would seem she could do anything she likes. And of course, as she noted in the same interview, "Nobody can force Lyte to do nothing I don't want to do."

Selected discography

On First Priority Records

Lyte as a Rock (includes "I Cram to Understand U," "Paper Thin," "10% Dis," "I Am Woman," and "MC Lyte Likes Swingin'"), 1988.

Eyes on This (includes "Cha Cha Cha," "Stop, Look, Listen," "Cappucino," and "I'm Not Having It,"), 1989.

Act Like You Know (includes "When in Love," "Eyes Are the Soul," "Poor Georgie," "Kamikaze," and "2 Young 4 What"), 1991.

Also contributor to video *Sisters in the Name of Rap*, PMV, 1992.

Sources

Art Forum, No. 17, 1992.
Billboard, September 21, 1991.

Details, September 1991.
Ebony, October 1991.
Entertainment Weekly, October 25, 1991.
Essence, August 1991.
Hits, January 13, 1992.
Mean Street, November 1991.
Mother Jones, September/October 1990.
Ms., December/January 1990-91.
New York Times, January 10, 1988; October 16, 1991.
People, January 27, 1992.
Rap Pages, April 1992.
Right On!, January 1992.
Rolling Stone, December 14, 1989; December 13, 1990.
Sassy, January 1992.
The Source, November 1991; December 1991.
Spin, October 1991.
Tafrija, December 1991.
Time, May 27, 1991.
Vanity Fair, July 1990.
Village Voice, January 19, 1988.
Yo!, April 1992.
ysb, November 1991.

Additional information for this profile was obtained from an Atlantic Records press release, 1991.

—*Simon Glickman*

Bette Midler

Singer, actress

In her early years she was known as "The Divine Miss M.," a campy, raucous vocalist at home in many forms of jazz, swing, and pop. Since then Bette Midler has become a respected film star and a spokesperson for research into acquired immune deficiency syndrome (AIDS), an illness that has killed more than 50 of her friends. For several years in the mid-1980s, Midler preferred starring in and producing movies to singing, but she has resurfaced as a pop music superstar with two Grammy-winning singles, "Wind Beneath My Wings" and "From a Distance."

In *Vanity Fair,* Joe Roth, the chairman of Twentieth Century-Fox, described Bette Midler as "one of the few superstars who connect *emotionally* with an audience as well as entertaining them—only a handful of people are capable of that." Few performers, especially women, sustain pop music careers into their middle years. Midler has managed the feat by virtue of her wide range of vocal stylings and her good rapport with fans of all ages. *Time* magazine contributor Richard Corliss called Midler "the most dynamic and poignant singer-actress of her time."

Midler was born in Honolulu, Hawaii, on December 1, 1945. Her father painted houses for the U.S. Navy. Named after the great screen actress Bette Davis, Midler grew up in rural Aiea, Hawaii, a lonely girl who found solace in old Hollywood musicals and the thought that she might become a performer some day. She recalled in *Time:* "I'd sing *Lullaby of Broadway* at the top of my lungs in the tin shower—it had really good reverb. People used to gather outside to call up requests or yell that I was lousy."

Midler's parents did not see eye to eye about their daughter's ambitions. Fred Midler was a strict disciplinarian who felt that stage work was for loose women. He never saw Midler in a live performance, even after she became famous. Midler's mother, on the other hand, encouraged all of her daughters to take music and dancing lessons. "My mother was all for my starting on this journey and going full-speed ahead," Midler remarked in *Time.*

After graduating from high school—where she was class president—Midler attended the University of Hawaii for a year. She also took a variety of part-time jobs, including sorting pineapple slices at a food processing plant. In 1965 she earned a place as an extra on the set of the film *Hawaii.* When the production company moved back to Hollywood to complete the movie, she went along. In Los Angeles she found work with United Artists as an extra, saving her wages to finance a trip to New York City.

Broadway and the Baths

After some months of odd jobs and small parts in Catskill Mountains productions, Midler auditioned for the Broadway play *Fiddler on the Roof*. She earned a chorus role in the New York company in 1966, but quickly graduated to the major part of Tzeitel, the eldest daughter. She stayed with *Fiddler on the Roof* for the next three years, augmenting her Broadway work with singing stints in clubs, including the famous Improvisation.

Midler used her club dates to experiment with different musical styles. She seemed most successful as a torch singer, but she noticed that the audiences liked to hear jokes between numbers. Slowly she developed the style that would become her trademark—strong vocals mixed with bawdy humor and a campy stage presence. She left the cast of *Fiddler on the Roof* in 1969 for an entirely new challenge.

One of Midler's acting teachers suggested that she apply to sing at the Continental Baths, a public bath

house catering to gay men. She was hired at $50 per night, and there she and her pianist-arranger Barry Manilow honed an outrageous and entertaining show that pulled musical numbers from every decade between 1930 and 1970. In her autobiography *A View From a Broad*, Midler recalled of the bathhouse: "I was able to take chances on that stage that I could never have taken anywhere else. The more outrageous I was, the more [the patrons] liked it. It loosened me up."

Billing herself as "The Divine Miss M.—Flash with class and sleaze with ease," Midler began to attract attention outside the gay community. By 1971 she had signed with an ambitious manager who promoted her to television talk shows and bigger stage revues. Almost a decade before the emergence of pop icon Madonna, Midler dared to flirt, make bawdy jokes, and dress flamboyantly in her act. By 1972 she had released an album and was singing in Las Vegas and at the Lincoln Center.

One of Midler's first big hits was an Andrews Sisters song, "Boogie Woogie Bugle Boy." *New Republic* correspondent Richard Poirier commented that the entertainer "has the vocal resources to sing in the style of any woman vocalist of the past 30 years. . . . Midler doesn't imitate or parody a specific singer through an entire song, however. Rather, like a person truly haunted, Midler in the phrasing of a song will suddenly veer off from one coloration into another. It sometimes happens with an air of true discovery. As with most great jazz singers, she therefore never does a song exactly the same way twice. The avenue of experimentation is always left open."

Career Ups and Downs

Her success as a singer assured, Midler moved on into film. Her first movie was *The Rose*, a serious work about a self-destructive rock star. The film was a success, earning Midler an Academy Award nomination for her acting skill and a Grammy Award for best vocal performance by a female for the title song. Flush with success, Midler felt invincible. Then her career took a nosedive. A concert film, *Divine Madness*, did not perform as expected at the box office. Worse, Midler's next movie, *Jinxed*, earned her a reputation for temperamental behavior that took years to live down. Her live appearances lacked the zest of earlier years, and she entered a prolonged depression. "I couldn't face the world," she admitted in *Time*. "I was drinking to excess—I was miserable."

Midler's 1984 marriage to businessperson and performance artist Martin von Haselberg helped her to regain her equilibrium. Around the same time she signed a contract with Touchstone Films, an adult-oriented division of Walt Disney Studios. Through Touchstone Midler starred in several well-received comedy films, including *Down and Out in Beverly Hills, Ruthless People,* and *Outrageous Fortune.* Together these movies earned more than $60 million and revived Midler's flagging career.

Midler has not lacked film roles since then. She has starred in such vehicles as *Beaches, Big Business,* filmmaker Woody Allen's *Scenes From a Mall,* and a movie she produced herself, *For the Boys.* The latter film was that rarest of all types of modern motion pictures—a musical—with Midler appearing as a U.S.O. performer through three wars.

Pop Stardom

Midler might have given up recording entirely, given her busy schedule in the film industry. Instead she released a 1991 album, *Some People's Lives,* that contained the Grammy Award-winning "From a Distance." The song topped the charts during the Desert Storm hostilities, in which several nations, including the United States, intervened in a dispute between Iraq and Kuwait; the lyrics present a view of the world from space, noting how peaceful earth seems.

Singing is one way in which Midler can communicate her concern for AIDS victims. "In her early divine crassness, Midler shared with her audiences the lighthearted freedom she was discovering in herself as a moxie-mouthing soubrette," wrote Kevin Sessums in *Vanity Fair* in 1991. "Now forty-five, Midler . . . is heavier-hearted, and no longer endows her fans with a frivolous sense of hope, but instead instills in them a survivor's hard-won dignity." Midler commented in *Vanity Fair* that her recent resurgence in the pop music field came as a surprise to her. "It was not planned at all," she said. "Not for one second. If it disappeared tomorrow, I wouldn't be surprised, either."

Still, she confessed in the same profile, "I feel I have to create. I have to dig in the earth. I have to make something grow. I have to bake something. I have to write something. I have to sing something. I have to put something out. It's not a need to prove anything. It's just my way of life."

Selected writings

A View From a Broad, Simon & Schuster, 1980.
The Saga of Baby Divine, Crown, 1983.

Selected discography

The Divine Miss M., Atlantic, 1972.
Bette Midler, Atlantic, 1973.
Broken Blossom, Atlantic, 1977.
Live at Last, Atlantic, 1977.
Thighs and Whispers, Atlantic, 1979.
Songs for the New Depression, Atlantic, 1979.
Divine Madness, Atlantic, 1980.
No Frills, Atlantic, 1984.
Mud Will Be Flung Tonight (comedy), Atlantic, 1985.
Some People's Lives, Atlantic, 1991.
For the Boys (motion pictue soundtrack), Atlantic, 1992.

Sources

Books

Midler, Bette, *A View From a Broad,* Simon & Schuster, 1980.
Midler, Bette, *The Saga of Baby Divine,* Crown, 1983.

Periodicals

New Republic, August 2, 1975.
Newsweek, May 22, 1972; June 30, 1986; January 26, 1987.
New York Times, December 3, 1972; December 29, 1972; January 14, 1973.
People, November 14, 1983; February 3, 1986.
Time, March 2, 1987.
Vanity Fair, December 1991.

—*Anne Janette Johnson*

Eric Nagler

Family entertainer

A popular family entertainer with roots in the folk tradition, Eric Nagler has established a reputation as a versatile performer whose infectious sense of play has attracted a cult-like following. Nagler devotees come to his concerts expecting not only to be entertained, but to join in the entertainment. Armed with an arsenal of ready-made music makers—including spoons, cans, combs, and keys—parents and children alike provide able accompaniment as Nagler jams on everything from the bleach-bottle banjo to the sewerphone—a whimsical, homemade instrument made of plumbing pipes and a washing machine agitator. "The novelty of the instruments captures people's imagination," he said in an interview with Michael Schulman in *Bravo,* "but their real purpose onstage is to help people feel that music-making is accessible. If somebody like me can get up and have fun with some plumbing pipe or a pair of spoons, they feel they can go home and have fun doing it too."

Nagler's down-home approach to music making has translated well to other media. With five records, three books, and two videos to his credit, Nagler debuted his award-winning television show *Eric's World* in 1991. The program became a frequent guest in family rooms throughout Canada.

Eric Nagler's love for music making and affinity for improvisation have their roots in the folk music revival of the 1950s and 1960s. Born into an intellectual Jewish family in Brooklyn, New York, Nagler rejected the cerebral music he was encouraged to play and gravitated toward bluegrass. "With bluegrass music," he explained to Schulman, "I could escape from my head and express something I couldn't express any other way." Eventually becoming a master of more than a dozen instruments, he learned to play the banjo at the age of 14, practicing with his contemporaries in the back of a Greenwich Village sandal shop in New York City. Nagler further honed his technique in Washington Square, where musicians gathered from throughout the city on Sunday afternoons, watching, listening to, and playing with "anybody and everybody in folk music, including Bob Dylan before he made it big," according to Schulman. In an effort to expand his repertoire, Nagler flirted with fiddle music for years, playing it first on the banjo and then on the guitar and mandolin. It wasn't until he was 30 years old, though, that he gathered the courage to get a fiddle "and start playing those tunes the way they were meant to be played."

Opened Toronto Folklore Center

In 1966 Nagler married Martha Beers, a member of the highly acclaimed folk group the Beers Family. Founded by Martha's father, Bob Beers, the Beers Family was known for its faithful renditions of Irish and Scottish ballads on traditional instruments. When Bob Beers died in an automobile accident in 1972, Martha and Eric Nagler vowed to continue the family tradition and recorded the albums *The Gentleness in Living* and *A Right and Proper Dwelling*—inspired by their log cabin in Canada's Ottawa Valley.

The Naglers moved to Toronto, Ontario, in 1968 to protest the war in Vietnam. While in Canada Eric pursued a graduate degree in clinical psychology at the Ontario Institute for Studies in Education and became involved in Toronto's folk music scene. He abandoned his doctoral studies a year later to open the Toronto Folklore Center, a gathering place for musicians modeled after a similar one in New York City.

It was also in Canada that Nagler found his calling. In the mid-1970s, as folk music began to lose its popular appeal, he joined those musicians who had discovered a largely untapped audience—children. After working as a studio musician, specializing in traditional and

homemade instruments, Nagler began to appear regularly with the popular Canadian children's performers Sharon, Lois and Bram in their concerts and on their recordings. By the time he had become a standard feature on their television program, the *Elephant Show,* Nagler had carved out a unique niche in what had become a burgeoning industry.

Instruments From Everyday Objects

In 1978 Nagler was given the opportunity to incorporate a playful sideline into his work when his friend Rick Avery asked him to take over the *Home Made Music* program. Featuring do-it-yourself instruments that Nagler had taught Avery to make, the *Home Made Music* show toured Ontario schools and libraries under the direction of Avery and his partner, Judy Greenhill. When Nagler embraced the program, he found that it allowed him both the opportunity to explore his fascination with homemade instruments and to develop his public performance technique.

Nagler's interest in simple instruments made from everyday objects was inspired by Bob Beers, who delighted in folk toys assembled from natural materials. When Nagler discovered that a plumbing pipe made as good a whistle as a willow branch, a host of whimsical instruments was born. Some were reincarnations of traditional music makers, such as the spoons; some were sheer invention, like the gazernowich, made from a broomstick, a door spring, bells, and a paint can; and some were adaptations of existing fare. The sewerphone, for example, was derived from the eclectic group Reverend Ken and the Lost Followers's sinker phone, a contraption, played tongue-in-cheek, that literally incorporated the kitchen sink.

The original purpose of these instruments, Nagler explained in an interview with *Contemporary Musicians* (*CM*), was to "hook" the audience. People were captivated by their outrageousness. Eventually, that purpose became secondary. An instrument that anybody could play was ideal as a vehicle through which an audience could make music together.

Host of *Eric's World*

Fostering togetherness by making music with his audience is one of Eric Nagler's main goals. Working with families while touring with the *Home Made Music* program gave Nagler an enormous respect for children. Children, he told *CM,* have a lot to offer adults. The product of a rhythmic, churning environment, they are "born to bop." And, as youngsters, they "listen with their whole bodies," and their sense of rhythm is complete. Nagler's appreciation for his young audiences caused him to redefine his role as that of a family, rather than children's, entertainer. Acting as a catalyst, he encourages children to use music to express themselves freely and parents to find "the child within."

Nagler discovered in the early 1990s, however, that a career in children's entertainment is not without its pitfalls. Charged with sexually assaulting a juvenile girl, he was exonerated at an early stage in the case after the results of a polygraph test and psychological exams prompted the prosecution to withdraw its accusations. Nagler commented on the ill effects of the charges in the *Toronto Star:* "My whole world turned upside-down. And my career just stopped—stopped dead in the water." Though some of his concerts were canceled or postponed during the ordeal, Nagler received the support of numerous loyal fans, and his television show continued to be a favorite on Canada's Family Channel and the United States's Nickelodeon.

As a family entertainer, Nagler has toured extensively, performing at children's festivals and in concert halls throughout North America. He has released a number of recordings, which have been well received by critics and audiences, on the Elephant Records, Oak Street Music, and Rounder Records labels. His first album, 1982's *Fiddle up a Tune,* won the American Library Association Award for Excellence and both *Come on In* of 1985 and *Improvise With Eric Nagler* of 1989 received prestigious Canadian Juno Award nominations for best children's album of the year. An established television personality and author of instructional books, Nagler appears frequently on *Sesame Street* and *Mr. Dress-Up* as well as on the *Elephant Show* and his own series, *Eric's World,* which was described by Hurst as "a hugely popular and critically acclaimed children's sitcom." Nagler summed up his impetus for pursuing a career in family entertainment for Hurst: "[Children are] so integrated, they interact, they're . . . whole people and, as an audience, far more exciting than adults who just sit there."

Selected writings

Eric Nagler Makes Music, McGraw-Hill Ryerson, 1989.
Eric Nagler's Groaners, Golden Books, 1990.
Eric Nagler's Joke Book, Golden Books, 1990.

Selected discography

The Gentleness in Living, Swallowtail Records, 1973.
A Right and Proper Dwelling, Philo Records, 1977.
Fiddle up a Tune, Elephant Records, 1982.
Come on In, Elephant Records, 1985.
Improvise With Eric Nagler, Oak Street Music (Canada), Rounder Records (U.S.), 1989.

Also released video *Making Music With Eric,* Golden Books, 1988.

Sources

Books

Baggelaar, Kristin, and Donald Milton, *Folk Music: More Than a Song,* Thomas Y. Crowell Company, 1976.

Periodicals

Ann Arbor News, December 13, 1991.
Bravo, July/August 1989.
Detroit Free Press, January 19, 1990; July 19, 1991.
National Geographic World, November 1989.
Toronto Star, January 26, 1992.
Variety, June 21, 1989; January 7, 1991.

Additional information for this profile was obtained from a December 14, 1991, interview with Eric Nagler.

—Nina Goldstein

Olivia Newton-John

Singer

Known for her clear, gentle voice, Olivia Newton-John has achieved stardom in the areas of pop, middle-of-the-road, and country music. Several movie and television roles in both singing and non-singing parts contribute to her list of accomplishments. In the early 1970s Newton-John, with her appealing looks and voice, became a superstar almost overnight. While critics knocked her music for being superficial and overly sentimental, the number of her fans and record sales grew rapidly. A decade after she first realized success, Newton-John dropped out of the spotlight to raise a family and promote more of her personal social causes, which include environmentalism and recycling.

Although she is widely thought to be Australian, Newton-John was actually born in Cambridge, England, where she was raised until the age of five. After moving to Australia her mother insisted that she keep her British passport, which was to come in handy later. As a teenager, Newton-John won an Australian talent contest that, as its prize, sent her to England. While there, she and another female performer from Australia, Pat Carroll, formed a singing duo and achieved a reasonable amount of success. The couple disbanded, though, when Carroll's visa ran out and she had to return to Australia. With her British passport Newton-John was able to continue with her career in England, now as a solo performer.

While in England Newton-John pursued a series of odd singing jobs, including joining a curious group called Tomorrow (some sources say Toomorrow), which was supposed to be England's answer to the successful U.S. pop group The Monkees. She appeared with Tomorrow in a science-fiction film, an endeavor she would like to overlook. Returning a little more to the mainstream, Newton-John began appearing on British singer Cliff Richard's television series, which helped her promote her first single, a cover of Bob Dylan's "If Not for You." A few more singles brought her acclaim in Great Britain, but it was not until the 1973 release of *Let Me Be There* that Newton-John became popular in the United States.

Achieved Fame in Country Music

The title single for *Let Me Be There* went on to win the singer a Grammy Award for best country female performance. Although she had originally positioned herself as a folk performer, Newton-John's uncomplicated style crossed over into the country music category as well. The performer also received two Grammys for her work on the 1975 release "I Honestly Love You." By this time, Newton-John had moved to Los Angeles, Califor-

For the Record. . .

B orn September 26, 1948, in Cambridge, England; daughter of Bryn (a university president) and Irene (Born) Newton-John; married Matt Lattanzi (an actor), 1984; children: Chloe. *Education:* Quit school at the age of 16 to sing professionally in England.

Singer with Pat Carroll and Cliff Richard in England; member of pop group Tomorrow (some sources say Toomorrow); recorded hit singles, including "If Not for You" and "Take Me Home Country Roads," early 1970s; moved to United States and recorded several successful albums; toured United States and other countries; actress and singer in films *Grease,* 1978, *Xanadu,* 1980, and *Two of a Kind,* 1983; actress in television film *A Mom for Christmas,* NBC, 1991. Owner of boutiques named "Koala Blue" (shops went bankrupt, 1991).

Awards: Grammy awards, 1971, for "Banks of the Ohio," 1973, best country vocalist, for "Let Me Be There," and 1974, record of the year and best pop vocal performance, both for "I Honestly Love You"; Country Music Association Award, 1973, for best country female vocal performance, and 1976, for best female singer; eight American Music awards; named officer of the Order of the British Empire.

Addresses: *Home*—Malibu, CA. *Management*—The Bill Sammeth Organization, 9200 Sunset Blvd., Ste. 1001, Los Angeles, CA 90069.

nia, and was busy touring and performing in Las Vegas, Nevada. Her albums were consistently going gold and platinum.

While fans perpetuated her stardom, critics were less enthusiastic. Artistically, Newton-John was considered superficial, vacuous, and lacking in musical integrity. Some claimed, as Chris Stoehr summarized in the *Detroit Free Press,* that "her music crosses over into several audiences because it has no style of its own." In that same article, Newton-John defended herself by asking, "Why do people like certain things? I don't know. Neither do the critics, that's for sure. It was not instant, you know, my success. . . . I was just a performer the audience found pleasant. And after all, the audience's opinion is the only one that counts, isn't it?"

Launched Film Career

In 1977, at one of singer Helen Reddy's parties, New-

ton-John was "discovered" by movie producer Allan Carr. The producer was pondering whom to cast in his upcoming film, *Grease,* and was struck by Newton-John's beauty. It is said that he practically begged her to take the female lead, which she did for a bargain $125,000. A little apprehensive, the performer began preparing for a role she reportedly hoped would make her the Doris Day of the era. Playing Sandy opposite actor John Travolta gave her newfound fame and visibility. The popular movie was accompanied by a successful soundtrack, which launched Newton-John and Travolta's duet single "You're the One That I Want"; the song landed a number one position on the charts.

In the film, Newton-John's character changes from a timid ingenue to a temptress who ultimately outgreases Travolta's bad boy role. In Newton-John's professional life, it could be said that this same sort of transformation was taking place. Allegedly no longer content to be a sweet, gentle-voiced crooner, Newton-John began to pump up her act. In 1978 she released the provocative recording *Totally Hot,* followed by the equally sexy *Physical* in 1981. *Physical* contributed three hit singles to the U.S. charts. Newton-John then went on a successful tour where she danced in tight-fitting workout gear. The artist also worked with friend and former co-star Travolta to tone her body into muscular perfection. The switch from innocent to racy occurred, Newton-John admitted in the *Detroit Free Press,* because "you change over the years; you grow and change. I hope that I wouldn't be the same at 33 that I was at 23. I didn't go out and take lessons in being something else; I've just grown."

Career Slowed

Newton-John's career toned down rather quickly from the frenzied peak of the early 1980s. She starred in a film with Travolta in 1983 called *Two of a Kind,* which faded from view without much notice. After that the singer seemed to be in a kind of semi-retirement. She married longtime companion Matt Lattanzi in 1984, and the couple had a daughter, Chloe. In 1988 Newton-John released another album, *The Rumour,* but mostly the actress was attending to her family and charitable concerns. "It sounds kind of boring to say I've been at home," Newton-John told *People* about her whereabouts from 1983 to 1991, "But that's the truth."

The singer came out of her virtual seclusion to star in a made-for-television-film, *A Mom for Christmas.* In the movie, she plays a mannequin who becomes real in order to take care of a girl without a mother. In 1989 she recorded an album of soothing songs for infants called *Warm and Tender* after realizing that she could find no music with which to comfort her young daughter. And in 1992 Newton-John released *Back to Basics: The Essential Collection 1971-92*, which includes four new tunes. That same year she announced that she had been diagnosed with an early and treatable form of breast cancer and reportedly put new musical projects on hold.

Though basically estranged from the limelight, Newton-John has increasingly turned to environmental projects as well as undertakings such as designing a 10,000-square-foot beach house in Malibu, California. She is unclear as to whether she will return to a life of singing stardom. Enjoying family life, Newton-John admitted in *People* that "all I need to hear is 'Good night, Mommy, I love you,' and there's no question everything is worth it."

Selected discography

Let Me Be There, MCA, 1973.
If You Love Me, Let Me Know, MCA, 1974.
Long Live Love, MCA, 1974.
First Impressions, MCA, 1974.
Have You Never Been Mellow, MCA, 1975.
Clearly Love, MCA, 1975.
Come On Over, MCA, 1976.
Don't Stop Believin', MCA, 1976.
Making a Good Thing Better, MCA, 1977.
Olivia Newton-John's Greatest Hits, EMI, 1977.

Grease Soundtrack, RSO, 1978.
Totally Hot, MCA, 1978.
Xanadu Soundtrack, MCA, 1980.
Physical, EMI, 1981.
Greatest Hits, EMI, 1982.
The Rumour, 1988.
Warm and Tender, Geffen, 1989.
Back to Basics: The Essential Collection 1971-92, Geffen, 1992.

Sources

Books

Pareles, Jon, and Patricia Romanowski, editors, *The Rolling Stone Encyclopedia of Rock and Roll,* Rolling Stone Press/ Summit Books, 1983.

Periodicals

Detroit Free Press, May 17, 1979; August 22, 1982; July 15, 1992.
Fortune, May 22, 1989.
High Fidelity, July 1989.
New York, December 4, 1989.
New York Daily News, May 1, 1977.
Parade Magazine, July 1, 1979; December 4, 1988.
People, February 24, 1975; July 31, 1978; December 24, 1990; August 19, 1991; June 22, 1992.
Redbook, November 1990.

—*Nancy Rampson*

Nirvana

Rock band

Three Seattle musicians who play what has become known as "grunge" rock seemed an unlikely bet for acceptance into the rock and roll establishment. Decidedly punkish in their musical style—albeit at a slower pace than was the hallmark of punk rock—strident in their lyrics, and unapologetic of their calculated-to-offend offstage personalities, the group nonetheless went from the "underground" status of their initial release, *Bleach,* to mega-stardom with their first major-label effort, *Nevermind,* within the space of a few years. The latter, featuring Kurt Cobain on guitar and vocals, Chris Novoselic on bass, and David Grohl on drums, jumped to the Number One spot on the *Billboard* rock chart and was cited in many music critics' Top Ten lists just months after its release.

Cobain and Novoselic grew up near Seattle, in Aberdeen, Washington, a secluded logging town 70 miles southwest of Seattle known largely for its overcast climate. Cobain's youth was often chaotic—he lived in a trailer park with his cocktail waitress mother after the breakup of his parents' marriage. Before his parents

For the Record. . .

Members include **Kurt Cobain** (grew up in Aberdeen, WA; son of Wendy O'Connor [a cocktail waitress]; married Courtney Love [a singer], February 24, 1992; children: Frances Bean), guitar and vocals, **Dave Grohl** (from Washington, DC), drums, and **Chris Novoselic** (from Aberdeen; wife's name, Shelli), bass. Cobain and Novoselic attended the Grays Harbor Institute of Northwest Crafts.

Group formed by Cobain and Novoselic, 1987; Grohl joined after succession of several drummers; played in clubs in Olympia, Tacoma, and Seattle, WA; signed with Sub Pop Records, 1988, released *Bleach,* 1989; toured Europe as opening act, 1989; signed with DGC record company, 1990, released *Nevermind,* 1991; toured the U.S., 1991.

Awards: Triple platinum award, for *Nevermind.*

Addresses: *Record company*—DGC, 9130 Sunset Blvd., Los Angeles, CA 90069.

split up, Cobain's mother recounted in *Rolling Stone,* he "got up every day with such joy that there was another day to be had. When we'd go downtown to the stores, he would sing to people." After the divorce, though, Cobain's personality underwent a transformation. "I think he was ashamed," his mother continued, "and he became very inward—he just held everything."

Until the age of nine, Cobain listened mostly to the Beatles. Then his father introduced him to heavier fare—Led Zeppelin, Kiss, and Black Sabbath. He started playing drums and hanging around with an Aberdeen group called the Melvins. Melvins leader Buzz Osborne took Cobain to a Black Flag concert, where he got his first taste of hard-core punk. Cobain was awed; he began to experiment with the guitar and tried to form a band. "I learned one Cars song and AC/DC's 'Back in Black,'" he told *Elle.* "And after that I just started writing my own. I didn't feel it was important to learn other songs because I knew I wanted to start a band." After repeatedly failing to get a group together, Osborne suggested that Cobain hook up with Chris Novoselic, a tall, shy Aberdeen kid two years older than Cobain.

Cobain and Novoselic Bound by Punk

According to Nirvana's record company press biography, Cobain and Novoselic had met at the Grays Harbor Institute of Northwest Crafts, where they were apparently "gluing seashells and driftwood on burlap"

and making mobiles of macaroni. Like Cobain, Novoselic had moved around a lot as a kid—they felt they were both misfits in a way. They further shared an appreciation for the hard-core music that was generally shunned by their heavy metal-loving peers. A tape of the San Francisco punk band Flipper cemented their commitment to the genre. "It made me realize there was something more cerebral to listen to than stupid cock rock," Novoselic told *Elle.* Exhibiting total rebellion against what they saw as the red-necked, macho establishment of their hometown, they spray painted the phrases "God is Gay," "Abort Jesus," and "Homosexual sex rules," on cars and bank buildings. For one offense Cobain was arrested and fined.

Cobain's mother kicked him out of the house after he quit high school. Homeless, he slept on friends' couches and even briefly found lodging under a bridge. By 1987, however, he and Novoselic were beginning to gain a reputation as Nirvana and were a hit at parties at Evergreen State College in Olympia.

With the help of Melvins drummer Dale Crover, the trio began to record, finishing ten songs in one afternoon taping session. The resulting demo was submitted to Sub Pop, Seattle's then-underground label, the directors of which signed them to a record contract right away. In 1988, after changing drummers, the band recorded *Bleach* in six days for $606.17. The album moved slowly at first, but eventually sold 35,000 copies between its debut and the release of the band's second effort, which caused a surge of *Bleach* sales.

Caught in Bidding War

After *Bleach,* Nirvana began looking for yet another drummer, this time settling, in the fall of 1990, on Dave Grohl of the Washington, D.C., band Scream. This lineup returned to the studio to find that the Nirvana sound had improved significantly. When Sub Pop sought a distributor for the upcoming second album, a bidding war ensued among record labels interested in buying Nirvana out of their Sub Pop contract. The group eventually signed to DGC, home of giants Guns 'n' Roses and Cher, for $287,000. Rumors persisted, however, that the label had shelled out up to $750,000 to obtain the trio. Cobain commented in *Spin* that those reports were "journalism through hearsay," adding that "the numbers kept getting bigger so that a lot of people believed that we were signed for a million dollars."

The group had mixed feelings about signing to a major label; they feared they would be labeled "sellouts" for trading their underground status for the promise of big money. But the opportunity to get their music heard by a larger audience—and thus spread their message to the mainstream—mitigated these concerns. Nirvana released *Nevermind* in the spring of 1991; the record took three weeks to record and earned the trio $135,000. Producer Butch Vig instinctively felt that the unintelligible, but mesmerizing, cut "Smells like Teen Spirit" would be a hit, even before it was completed in the studio. "It was awesome sounding," he told *Rolling Stone*. "I was pacing around the room, trying not to jump up and down in ecstasy."

Nevermind a Phenomena

Vig's prophecy came true: The *Nevermind* single "Smells Like Teen Spirit" soared to Number One after only a few months of airplay. The accompanying video, featuring a somewhat sinister high school pep rally—Cobain has said the song is about teenage apathy—complete with tattooed cheerleaders, a bald custodian, writhing fans, and pointedly unkempt band members, received heavy rotation on MTV. "Smells" earned perhaps the ultimate tribute when it was lampooned by rock parodist "Weird Al" Yankovic, whose own video was entitled "Smells Like Nirvana." And yet the most distinguishing aspect of *Nevermind* may have been that, as *New York Times* contributor Karen Schoemer pointed out, "Nirvana didn't cater to the mainstream; it played the game on its own terms. . . . What's unusual about [the album] is that it caters to neither a mainstream audience nor the indie rock fans who supported the group's debut album. . . ." Calling the release "one of the best alternative rock albums produced by an American band in recent years," Schoemer continued, "*Nevermind* is accessible but not tame. It translates the energy and abandon of college rock in clear, certain terms."

In performance, Nirvana pays homage to angry punks past—dating as far back as the mid-1960s guitar destruction of then-"mod" Pete Townshend, leader of Britain's the Who—by smashing their equipment onstage; Cobain has estimated that he's probably destroyed around 300 guitars. This behavior seems to please Nirvana's legions of fans, who throng to their shows in anticipation of such antics.

Despite Nirvana's rapid climb to the top, Cobain and company have tried to keep a balanced attitude. They rejected a limousine ride to their *Saturday Night Live* performance because they didn't want to be treated like stars. Cobain has of late refrained from drugs and the standard rock-star revelry, partially in deference to a recurring and painful stomach ailment. When questioned about the band's success, Cobain revealed in *Elle* "Well, it's a fine thing and a flattering thing, but it doesn't matter. We could be dropped in two years and go back to putting out records ourselves and it wouldn't matter to us, because success is not what we were looking for. . . . We just want people to be able to get the records."

Selected discography

Blew (EP), Sub Pop, 1989.
Bleach, Sub Pop, 1989.
Nevermind, DGC, 1991.

Sources

Elle, April 1992.
Guitar Player, February 1992.
Newsweek, January 27, 1992.
New York Times, January 8, 1992; January 13, 1992; January 26, 1992.
People, December 23, 1991.
Pulse!, March 1992.
Rolling Stone, November 28, 1991; February 20, 1992.
Spin, January 1992.

Additional information for this profile was obtained from a David Geffen Company press biography, 1991.

—*Nancy Rampson*

The Osborne Brothers

Bluegrass band

During the mid- to late-1960s, at a time when bluegrass purists insisted on traditional instruments and vocal arrangements, the Osborne Brothers were bucking the trend. Considered one of the first "progressive" bluegrass bands, the Osbornes have tried to broaden the appeal of bluegrass by adding country instruments and electrifying their guitars and mandolins. The results caused a furor, but since that time the pioneering efforts of Bob and Sonny Osborne have been acknowledged by a new generation of more tolerant—and more experimental—bluegrass musicians.

"The emergence of the band called the Osborne Brothers was to have an effect on bluegrass music that was as profound as the one Elvis [Presley] had on Nashville. And to some, almost as devastating," wrote Bob Artis in *Bluegrass.* The Kentucky-born brothers were simply trying to find an audience, trying to reach beyond the small folk market in order to tap the more lucrative vein of country fans. Some of their recordings feature drums, piano, and steel guitar—instruments that are more often used in country music—and for two decades they have been regulars on the Grand Ole Opry, a radio and television program showcasing country acts. Nevertheless, Bob Osborne's tenor vocals and the use of banjo, fiddle, and mandolin have assured the Brothers' status as bluegrass musicians. Two of their biggest hits, "Ruby" and "Rocky Top," rank among the most popular bluegrass singles ever released.

Country-Born but City-Bred

Both of the Osborne brothers were born in the Kentucky mountains during the Great Depression—Bob in 1931 and Sonny in 1937. Life was difficult for the Osborne family during the 1930s, and shortly after World War II they joined the great number of Appalachian Americans migrating to Midwestern manufacturing centers. Artis noted, "Just as the English and Scotch-Irish brought their culture and music to the New World, people like the Osbornes brought the music and culture of the mountains to the industrial North. The Blue Ridge and the Great Smokies were the initial breeding grounds of bluegrass, but the rolling hills and smoky cities of the central Midwest became the primary places of its growth and development in the 1950s."

In the case of the Osborne family, the point of destination was Dayton, Ohio. There Bob and Sonny grew up listening to the Grand Ole Opry on far-off WSM Radio in Nashville. Bob became an Ernest Tubb fan and taught himself to play the electric guitar his father had bought for him. Later in the 1940s, Bob became fascinated by a new form of music, also popularized by the Grand Ole

Opry—bluegrass, then in its early stages. Both Bob and Sonny gravitated to the sounds of Bill Monroe, Lester Flatt, and Earl Scruggs, imitating the early bluegrass masters in both singing and picking.

Bob Osborne was only 16 when he began playing in groups. By 1949 he had his own band, which already showed the dual influences of country and bluegrass. He made his radio debut on WPFB in Middletown, Ohio. The following year he began working with banjoist Larry Richardson at WHIS in Bluefield, West Virginia. Osborne and Richardson both joined the Lonesome Pine Fiddlers in 1950 and recorded several singles with the group on the Cozy label. In those days Bob Osborne played guitar and sang tenor vocals.

Osbornes United

In 1951 Bob Osborne and another member of the Lonesome Pine Fiddlers, Jimmy Martin, formed their own duo. They recorded a few numbers on the King label and travelled through the South performing live concerts in small venues. What might have been one of the best bluegrass duos in history was broken up by the Korean War. Bob Osborne was drafted and sent to serve in the war zone. He was wounded at Panmunjom when mortar fragments penetrated his helmet.

In the meantime Sonny Osborne had taken up the banjo and learned to pick in the Earl Scruggs style. In 1952, at the tender age of 14, he left Ohio for a stint with Bill Monroe's Blue Grass Boys, one of the biggest acts on the Grand Ole Opry. Sonny spent only a few months with Monroe, but the experience helped him to establish a more professional approach to the music business. By the time Bob returned from the service, his younger brother was ready to work full-time in music.

The Osborne Brothers were signed by Gateway Records in 1953. Their debut as a duo—with Bob now playing the mandolin and Sonny on banjo—came on radio station WROL in Knoxville, Tennessee, the same year. By 1954 they could be heard on WJR in Detroit. Jimmy Martin joined them there briefly, and the trio cut some singles for RCA. The future seemed secure for the fledgling group, but after a period of performing for the *Jamboree* on station WWVA in Wheeling, West Virginia, offers of work were scarce. The Osborne brothers returned to Dayton, where they worked as cab drivers and played music on weekends in southern Ohio bars and honky tonks.

Merged Bluegrass and Country

The late 1950s were a difficult time for many country and bluegrass acts, as rock and roll moved into center stage. Only sheer determination and the willingness to experiment saved the Osbornes from a lifetime of cab driving in Dayton. In 1956 they tried again at WWVA, this time with sideman Red Allen. A freewheeling vocal tour de force called "Ruby" won them a contract with MGM Records. Subsequent songs incorporated drums and steel guitars, but they also provided bluegrass with a lasting innovation—the tenor lead. As Artis put it in *Bluegrass,* "The high voice sang the melody instead of the harmony, and the arrangement spotlighted the beautiful, incredibly high voice of Bob Osborne. The result was a . . . polished sound that literally rewrote the book on bluegrass singing."

Bluegrass has the Osbornes to thank for yet another innovation. In 1959 the band played a live concert at Antioch College in Ohio. After a slow start with rock- and country-oriented songs, the brothers launched into an avalanche of more traditional bluegrass. The young crowd went wild, and a phenomenon was born. The Osbornes are acknowledged as the first bluegrass band to bring that musical form to a college audience. Festivals devoted solely to bluegrass music were only a small step away.

As the 1960s progressed, the Osborne Brothers found a mainstream country audience and toured widely. They became regulars on the Grand Ole Opry and even became the first bluegrass act to perform at Harrah's club in Lake Tahoe. Throughout the period, the two brothers were trying for a major country hit, so they made free use of country instruments and stylings. This alienated the growing cadre of bluegrass fans—and even some former Osborne Brothers sidemen—but it did allow them to place such songs as "Rocky Top" and "Georgia Pinewoods" on the country charts.

Many of the best-known bluegrass songs are instrumentals. If the genre has an anthem, however, it is "Rocky Top," the Osbornes' rowdy hymn to an independent, clean, and wild life in the mountains. Few bluegrass bands have overlooked "Rocky Top" since the Osbornes first recorded it in 1969, and many of the more recent versions of the song sound far more traditional than its debut.

When the duo decided to electrify their bluegrass instruments in the late 1960s, many purists completely renounced them. But the enhanced sound actually allowed the brothers to move back toward more traditional bluegrass, which they have played ever since. Their experiments with electrification—done simply to compete with louder country bands—encouraged younger performers who wanted to fuse bluegrass with jazz and rock.

In *Bluegrass,* Artis concluded that the Osborne Brothers "have been providing bluegrass with a much-needed thrust for . . . years, bringing about changes that even the most fanatic loyalist must see as necessary in the evolution of a music style that was founded on change. . . . If bluegrass music is alive and well . . . it is due in no small part to the two courageous young men from Hyden, Kentucky."

Selected discography

Singles

"Muleskinner Blues," Gateway.
"Jesse James," Gateway.
"Walking Cane," Gateway.
"20/20 Vision," RCA.
"Ruby," MGM.
"Once More," MGM.
"Rocky Top," Decca.

Albums

Once More, Vol. 1, Sugar Hill, 1986.
Once More, Vol. 2: Favorite Memories, Sugar Hill, 1987.
Singing, Shouting Praises, Sugar Hill, 1988.
Hillbilly Fever, CMH, 1991.
Best of the Osborne Brothers, MCA.
Bluegrass Collection, CMH.
Bluegrass Concerto, CMH.
Bluegrass Instrumentals, MGM.
Bluegrass Spectacular, RCA.
Bobby and His Mandolin, CMH.
(Contributors) *Early Bluegrass,* RCA.
Early Recordings of the Osborne Brothers, Gateway.
(With Mac Wiseman) *The Essential Bluegrass,* CMH.
Favorite Hymns, MCA.
From Rocky Top to Muddy Bottom, CMH.
Greatest Bluegrass Hits, Vol. 1, CMH.
Kentucky Calling Me, CMH.
Modern Sounds of Bluegrass Music, Decca.
#1, CMH.
Osborne Brothers, MCA.
Pickin' Grass and Singin' Country, MCA.
Ru-bee, MCA.
Some Things I Want to Sing About, Sugar Hill.
The Osborne Brothers and Red Allen, Rounder.
Up This Hill and Down, Decca.
Voices in Bluegrass, Decca.
Yesterday, Today and the Osborne Brothers, MCA.

Sources

Books

Artis, Bob, *Bluegrass,* Hawthorn, 1975.
The Illustrated Encyclopedia of Country Music, Harmony, 1977.
Kochman, Marilyn, editor, *The Big Book of Bluegrass,* Morrow, 1984.
Malone, Bill C., *Country Music U.S.A., Revised Edition,* University of Texas Press, 1985.
Sandberg, Larry, and Dick Weissman, *The Folk Music Sourcebook,* Knopf, 1976.
Shestack, Melvin, *The Country Music Encyclopedia,* Crowell, 1974.
Stambler, Irwin, and Grelun Landon, *The Encyclopedia of Folk, Country, and Western Music,* St. Martin's, 1969.

Periodicals

Country Music, September/October 1988; March/April 1990.
Stereo Review, June 1986.

—*Anne Janette Johnson*

Edith Piaf

Singer, actress

"**A** thousand years from now," wrote Monique Lange in *Piaf,* her biography of French songstress Edith Piaf, "Piaf's voice will still be heard, and each time we hear it we will wonder anew at its strength, its violence, its lyrical magic." Edith Piaf's rise from street urchin to concert-hall chanteuse was more romantic than any novel. Her end in drug and alcohol dependency was sadder than any melodrama. Her voice expressed the agony of millions, and millions followed her love affairs and her divorces, knew her songs, and revelled in the triumphant comebacks she made time and again. She was adored everywhere, but she never stopped searching for love.

Edith Giovanna Gassion was born on December 19, 1915, into a less-than-glamorous life in a working-class neighborhood of Paris. Her father, Louis, was an itinerant acrobat who traveled from town to town, performing at streetside for tips. Edith's mother, Anetta—who was many years her husband's junior—worked at a carnival, sang on the street, and later sang in cafes.

Edith's childhood was spent either on the road with her parents or shuttling between relatives. When she was still quite young, her father was drafted to fight in World War I. The poverty-stricken Anetta found it too difficult to care for a child on her own and abandoned Edith, leaving the youngster with her mother. Edith's existence with her grandmother was not a happy one: she was rarely fed, washed even less often, and was given wine to put her to sleep whenever she cried.

Lived With Madame Grandmother

Edith's father was appalled at the condition in which he found his daughter when he returned home on leave from the army. He took her to stay with his mother, who ran a whorehouse in Normandy. Life for the young Piaf in a brothel was better than one might expect. The ladies doted on Edith, and she was better fed than she had been thus far in her life. Unfortunately this arrangement did not last. When a local priest suggested that a brothel was not the best place to raise a child, Edith's father took her on the road.

Edith toured through France and Belgium with her father, collecting money proffered by passersby while he performed his tricks. Sometimes he told her to play upon the sympathies of women and ask them to be her mother. Other times he sent her out to sing; even as a child she had the kind of voice that could draw a crowd.

When she was 15 Edith left her father and, with her friend Mamone, began making her own way on the streets of Paris. To support themselves Edith would sing and Mamone would collect money. Sometimes they made enough for a room; other times they spent their earnings in a saloon and slept in parks or alleyways.

It was during this period that Edith met Louis Dupont. He and Edith began living together, and in February of 1933 they had a daughter, Cecille. In an effort to assert his dominance, Dupont forced Edith to stop singing. They each took low-paying jobs—which Edith was rarely able to keep—and spent the rest of their time in a cramped apartment in a Paris slum. Edith could not tolerate the loss of freedom for long. She eventually returned to her former life on the streets, taking Cecille with her. Sadly, the child died of meningitis before reaching her second birthday.

"Piaf" Took Flight

Not long after Cecille's death, yet another Louis came into Edith's life. In her autobiography, *The Wheel of Fortune,* Edith described her first meeting with Louis Leplee: "I was pale and unkempt. I had no stockings and my coat was out at the elbows and hung down to my ankles. I was singing a song by Jean Lenoir. . . . When I had finished my song . . . a man approached

me. . . . He came straight to the point: 'Are you crazy? You are ruining your voice.'" Leplee, the owner of Gurney's—a very popular Paris night spot at the time—knew talent when he heard it, even if it was ill-dressed and dirty. He offered Edith a job and gave her the name "La Mome Piaf" ("Kid Sparrow"). Within a week, the four-foot, ten-inch Piaf was appearing on stage in her trademark black attire. Within a few months she made her first recording, "L'Etranger" ("The Stranger") on Polydor Records.

Piaf's meteoric rise came to an abrupt halt six months later. On April 7, 1936, Louis Leplee was found murdered in his Paris apartment. Piaf was stricken by the news. The press went wild, splashing her picture all over the tabloids and calling her a suspect. Paris audiences grew so hostile that Piaf was forced to leave the city. She subsequently performed in the Paris suburbs, in Nice, and in Belgium.

When the scandal had died down and Piaf was able to return to Paris, in 1937, she began an important association with songwriter Raymond Asso. It was Asso, along with Marguerite Monnot, who wrote Piaf's first hit, "Mon Legionnaire" ("My Legionaire"). This song, like so many others she sang, told the story of a woman abandoned.

Asso became much more than a songwriter to Piaf. For three years he guided her career, teaching her how to be a star, and was her lover. In Margaret Crosland's *Piaf,* Asso stressed, "I trained her, I taught her everything, gestures, inflection, how to dress." Piaf, for her part, though she owed much to Asso, took a new lover when the French Army called him in August of 1939.

The War Years

Oddly, the years during the war were some of the best of Piaf's career. The cafes and theaters remained open during the German occupation of France, and she continued to sing. It was also during this time that her career expanded to include more roles on the stage and screen. In 1940 she appeared in Jean Cocteau's play *Le Bel indifferent,* and she had a role in Georges Lacombe's 1941 film *Montmartre-sur-Seine,* for which she also wrote several songs.

But while Piaf advanced her career, she also knew her role as a French citizen and did her part to help the war effort. She was a savior to the French prisoners of war at Stallag III, whom she entertained on two different occasions. After the first performance, she asked the Germans if she could have pictures taken with the prisoners for their families in France. When she returned to the camp for her second performance, she brought forged identity papers, which allowed many prisoners to escape.

After the war Piaf set out to make herself an international star. Her 1946 release of "La Vie en Rose" became a major American hit. She arrived in New York City in 1947 to begin a series of American engagements. The petite Piaf, with her simple black dress and songs of struggle and abandonment, was not the sexy, sophisticated Frenchwoman many Americans expected, and she initially met with little success. It was not until a performance at the Versailles—one of the most elegant supper clubs in New York—and several glowing reviews that Edith Piaf became the toast of Manhattan and later Hollywood society.

Love and Decline

While in New York, Piaf began an affair with Marcel Cerdan, the French boxer and newly crowned middleweight champion. Like all of her romances, the union was a torrid one. As a boxer, Cerdan traveled extensively, though Piaf wanted him to be with her. He was in the Azores when Piaf phoned and persuaded him to fly back to New York. Tragically, the plane on which he was returning crashed, killing everyone on board. Of Cerdan's death, in October of 1949, Piaf biographer Monique Lange declared, "It marked the beginning of her decline, of the period when she fell completely apart."

Throughout the 1950s Piaf appeared in films and had continued success as a performer and recording artist. But these successes were interspersed with periods of illness, drug use, and mental instability. In September of 1952 she married the singer Jacques Pills—an arrangement that soon ended in divorce. In the late 1950s a series of car accidents pushed her further into a dependence on morphine and other painkillers. In *Piaf*, Lange reported, "At the end of her life, when she was practically incapable of even getting up on stage, she had to have an injection in order to sing."

Despite rumors that she had died, by the late 1950s Piaf's career was once again on the upswing. Her 1959 recording "Milord" was one of her biggest hits, as was "Non je ne regrette," released in 1960. On December 29, 1960, she made a triumphant appearance at Paris's Olympia Theater, proving she still retained the adulation of France. She followed up these achievements by going on tour.

Unfortunately Piaf's renewed success did not last. Though she fell in love with and married the young French singer Theo Sarapo, her health was still declining. She died on October 10, 1963, leaving the world feeling the loss of its "La Mome Piaf."

Selected discography

At the Paris Olympia, EMI, 1990.
The Voice of the Sparrow: The Very Best of Edith Piaf, Capitol, 1991.
At Carnegie Hall, Capitol.
The Best of Edith Piaf, Capitol.
The Best of Edith Piaf, Volume 2, Capitol.
L'Integrale (Complete Recordings) 1936-1945, Polydor.
Master Series, Polydor.
Piaf, Capitol.
Piaf: Her Complete Recordings, 1946-1963, Angel.

Sources

Crosland, Margaret, *Piaf*, G.P. Putnam's Sons, 1985.
Lange, Monique, *Piaf*, Seaver Books, 1981.
Piaf, Edith, *The Wheel of Fortune*, Chilton Books, 1965.

—*Jordan Wankoff*

Jean-Luc Ponty

Violinist, composer

Jean-Luc Ponty has built a substantial reputation as a versatile jazz violinist who is equally at home in many musical genres: swing, bop, modal jazz, free jazz, and jazz-rock. The native of France has toured throughout the world and recorded dozens of records. Making a significant departure from his typical synthesizer-generated fusion fare in 1991, Ponty released an album of African music that was largely improvised in the studio. *Musician* called the widely acclaimed *Tchokola* "one of the most bumptious, upbeat cross-cultural collaborations to date."

Ponty's work, represented on many albums, is characterized by scored or improvised melodies over hard rhythmic bass patterns, combinations of electronic timbres, and violin virtuosity—electric or acoustic. Among the musician's instruments are two Barcus-Berry violins, which, though they are painted blue and sport various electronic pick-up devices, are made of wood and can be played acoustically. In addition, Ponty plays the violectra—a baritone violin with strings tuned one octave lower than those of a standard violin—and a Zeta violin, which is made of wood with a crystal pick-up.

The son of a provincial French music teacher, Ponty was given a violin at the age of three. Two years later he began serious violin and piano studies and was trained in the classical repertoire on these instruments. By the time he was 13, Ponty had decided to make music his career and quit school to devote his time entirely to music. Entering the prestigious Conservatoire National Superieur de Musique in Paris two years later, he excelled in his studies and won the 1960 Premier Prix for violin.

Discovered Jazz

During his conservatory years Ponty also discovered jazz. He listened to such musicians as Kenny Clarke, Bud Powell, and Dexter Gordon at Parisian nightclubs. As a diversion from his intense violin studies, Ponty took up the clarinet, and at age 17 he learned that a Parisian jazz band needed a clarinetist. Though he auditioned and was given the opportunity to learn the rudiments of jazz, classical music was still his main interest. Ponty eventually turned to the violin as a jazz instrument because that was the instrument at which he was most technically proficient. He has also expressed that he did not have the patience to learn other instruments more commonly used in jazz ensembles.

After completing his studies at the conservatory, Ponty joined the Concerts Lamoureux Symphony Orchestra in Paris and performed with local jazz groups in his spare time. Jazz won out over classical music, and in 1963 Ponty quit the symphony to begin a full-time career in jazz. He frequently performed in Parisian nightclubs, and after playing at the Antibes jazz festival—then the only major jazz festival in Europe—his career blossomed. Ponty was subsequently booked throughout Europe and offered a recording contract.

Ponty's entree into the world of American jazz came in 1967 when he attended a masterclass at the Monterey, California, Jazz Festival and came to the attention of the American public and recording industry. Before returning to France, Ponty performed in nightclubs and recorded three albums with the George Duke Trio.

By 1970 Ponty had formed his own jazz band, the Jean-Luc Ponty Experience, an ensemble that emphasized improvisation. But the classically trained Ponty was uncomfortable with the lack of structure in the jazz genre, and the musicians scattered only two years after the group's inception. The innovative Frank Zappa soon discovered Ponty and asked him to join his band, the Mothers of Invention. Although Ponty played four tours with the group and worked with other musicians as well, including rock and roll legend Elton John, he had not yet found his niche.

Formed Fusion Ensembles

Still searching for that elusive place in the jazz world, Ponty moved to Los Angeles, California, in 1983. He was composing and arranging his own music—with the hope of forming a band—when he was asked to join John McLaughlin's Mahavishnu Orchestra. Ponty was a member of this group, which performed pieces that were fusions of jazz and Eastern (mostly Indian) music, for two years before legal and personal disputes ended his association. But before the break-up Ponty was featured as a soloist on such albums as *Apocalypse* and *Visions of the Emerald Beyond*.

Ponty finally formed his own band, which, while the members varied from year to year, was made up of an electric guitarist, an electric bassist, a percussionist, and a keyboardist. The featured soloist on electric violin, Ponty composed and arranged his groups' repertoire and founded his own production company, JLP Productions. Early in his solo career Ponty frequently performed at jazz festivals, but he eventually turned to promotional tours, playing to packed houses in the United States and averaging six months a year on the road. Many of the violinist's albums have been popular by jazz music standards, particularly *Imaginary Voyage, Enigmatic Ocean,* and *A Taste for Passion,* and they have sold in the millions.

In 1980 Ponty dispersed his band, declaring that he needed a vacation. But within two years he had organized another ensemble and composed, arranged, and recorded *Mystical Adventures.* Featuring a less aggressive violin sound, the album was praised for more successfully utilizing the capabilities of the electronic synthesizer.

Embraced World Beat

Ponty's career has taken many varied turns. Following the release of *The Gift of Time* album in 1987, Ponty made a major tour of North America, South America, and Europe. He has also appeared as a classical performer with such ensembles as the New Japan Philharmonic, the Montreal Symphony, and the Toronto

Symphony, among others. His 1989 LP *Storytelling* also reflects Ponty's background in classical music; it is the first time in many years that he performed on acoustic violin.

Returning to Paris, France, Ponty jumped on the world beat bandwagon and joined a group of African musicians to record *Tchokola*. John Diliberto noted in *Down Beat* that "instead of writing African-derived music, Ponty decided to play the music itself, using compositions and forms from Senegal, Mali, Cameroon, and finding a way to fit in with his violin." Though the classically trained musician confessed to Diliberto, "some of [the] rhythms [on the album] were the most difficult I had to deal with in my life," *Tchokola* was heralded by Tom Cheney in *Musician* as "a graceful, sensitive and rootsy foray into world musicianship." Ponty, ever-willing to experiment, once told Zan Stewart of the *Los Angeles Times*, "Because I don't reject the past, my changes in style have not been zigzags. I just wanted to keep this feeling of fresh adventure in my work and not be stuck in styles, whether it's jazz or rock or anything else."

Selected discography

Sunday Walk, MPS, 1967.
Electric Connection, Pacific Jazz, 1968.
Jean-Luc Ponty: Experience, Pacific Jazz, 1969.
(With Frank Zappa and the Mothers of Invention) *King Kong*, Pacific Jazz, 1970.
Astrorama, Far East, 1972.
Open Strings, MPS, 1972.
Live in Montreux, Inner City, 1972.
(With Stephane Grappelli) *Ponty/Grappelli,* America, 1973.
(With Mahavishnu Orchestra) *Apocalypse*, Columbia, 1974.
Upon the Wings of Music, Atlantic, 1975.
(With Mahavishnu Orchestra) *Visions of the Emerald Beyond*, Columbia, 1975.
(With Grappelli, Stuff Smith, and Svend Asmussen) *Violin Summit*, MPS, 1975.
Imaginary Voyage, Blue Note, 1976.
Aurora, Atlantic, 1976.
Sonata Erotica, Inner City, 1976.
(With Grappelli) *Jean-Luc Ponty/Stephane Grappelli*, Inner City 1976.

Jazz 60's, Vol. 2, Pacific Jazz, 1976.
Enigmatic Ocean, Atlantic, 1977.
(With George Duke) *Cantaloupe Island*, Blue Note, 1977.
Cosmic Messenger, Atlantic, 1978.
Live, Atlantic, 1979.
A Taste for Passion, Atlantic, 1979.
Civilized Evil, Atlantic, 1980.
Mystical Adventures, Atlantic, 1982.
Individual Choice, Atlantic, 1983.
Open Mind, Atlantic, 1984.
Fables, Atlantic, 1985.
The Gift of Time, Columbia, 1987.
Storytelling, Columbia, 1989.
Tchokola, Epic, 1991.
(With Tracey Ullman) *Puss in Boots,* Rhino, 1992.

Also contributed to other albums by Frank Zappa and the Mothers of Invention, including *Overnite Sensation,* Rykodisc, and *Hot Rats,* and to Elton John's *Honky Chateau,* 1972.

Sources

Books

Berendt, Joachim, *The Jazz Book: From New Orleans to Rock and Free Jazz,* translated by Dan Morgenstern, Barbara Bredigkeit, and Helmut Bredigkeit, Lawrence Hill & Co., 1975.
Coryell, Julie, and Laura Friedman, *Jazz-Rock Fusion: The People, the Music,* Dell, 1978.

Periodicals

Boston Herald, November 5, 1987.
Detroit Free Press, September 27, 1991.
Down Beat, September 1991.
Los Angeles Times, January 5, 1986.
Musician, September 1991; November 1991.
New York Tribune, September 14, 1989.
The Oregonian, February 5, 1988.
Pittsburgh Post-Gazette, September 22, 1986.
Pittsburgh Press, November 2, 1987; December 2, 1989.
Sun-Times (Chicago), November 21, 1989.

—Jeanne M. Lesinski

The Pretenders

Rock band

As a woman breaking into rock, Pretenders founder and lead singer Chrissie Hynde offered a much-needed upset to the genre's domination by men. Even as she deplored her perceived lack of commercial "beauty," she was able to use this ostensible deficiency to her advantage—thus establishing herself as a serious songwriter and musician. She told Fred Schruers in a 1981 *Rolling Stone* story, "They're not looking at me like I'm some sex symbol or girl with huge tits bouncing around the stage. . . . And this thing [her guitar], this isn't an extension or a phallic symbol." Hynde has also insisted on being uncompromisingly straightforward in her music. *Newsweek* contributor Jim Miller noted her attack on the sexism prevalent in rock lyrics: [Her songs] are memorable not only for the skilled way in which Hynde reworks stock riffs, but also for the matter-of-fact, unsentimental manner in which sex is described from the viewpoint of a woman with appetites and a will of her own. Her best lyrics, at once tender and tough, are a bracing change from rock's stock erotic fare, which often features a macho stud laying waste to the enemy."

For the Record. . .

Members include **Martin Chambers** (born September 4, 1951, in Hereford, England), drums; **Peter Farndon** (born in 1953 in Hereford; drowned as a result of heroin intoxication, April 14, 1983; replaced by **Malcolm Foster** [born January 13, 1956, in Hereford]), bass; **James Honeyman-Scott** (born October 27, 1957, in Hereford; died of cocaine-induced heart failure, June 16, 1982; replaced by **Robbie McIntosh**, 1982), lead guitar, vocals, keyboards; **Chrissie Hynde** (born Christine Ellen Hynde, September 7, 1951, in Akron, OH; daughter of Bud [a telephone company employee], and Dee [a secretary] Hynde; married Jim Kerr (a singer), c. 1984 (divorced, 1990); children: (with Ray Davies [a singer and songwriter]), Natalie, (with Kerr) Yasmin; attended Kent State University, late 1960s to early 1970s), vocals, guitar.

Hynde worked for London rock tabloid *New Music Express;* Honeyman-Scott worked in a music shop; Chambers was a driving instructor; group formed in London, c. 1978; released single "Stop Your Sobbing" and album *Pretenders,* 1979; signed with Sire Records c. 1980; toured the U.S., 1980.

Awards: Gold record for *Pretenders;* platinum record for *Learning to Crawl.*

Addresses: *Record company*—Sire Records, 75 Rockefeller Plaza, New York, NY 10019.

Like other pivotal figures in popular music, Hynde did not initially fit neatly into the contemporary music scene, or for that matter, into her own band; while the rest of the original Pretenders were English—the band is known generally as an English one—Hynde was born in Akron, Ohio. Her upbringing took place against a typical blue-collar, Midwestern backdrop. Hynde's father, Bud, worked for Ohio Bell; her mother, Dee, worked part-time as a secretary. At an early age, Hynde adopted rock musicians as her idols—proto-punk Iggy Pop, guitarists Jeff Beck and Jimi Hendrix, English rock pioneers the Kinks, and Brian Jones of the early Rolling Stones; her desire to be in a rock band spawned a fantasy world that became Hynde's refuge from what she viewed as the static nature of life in Ohio.

An Unlikely Frontwoman

Despite her early devotion, however, Hynde had to fight her way slowly into the real music world. While male friends were playing in garage bands in Akron and Cleveland, Hynde had to teach herself to sing and play rhythm guitar without the feedback of a band or audience. She wrote songs as a teenager but had no forum for testing them. Shyness further limited her; she retreated to a closet whenever she wanted to sing, even after everyone left the house. Hynde had only one opportunity to play with a band in the U.S.—and that was only for one night, when she performed with a local band, Sat. Sun. Mat., whose Mark Mothersbaugh eventually went on to fame with the zany new-wave band Devo.

After a few years spent studying art at Kent State University in Ohio—during which she witnessed the fatal shooting of four student anti-war protesters during the infamous National Guard incident of 1970—Hynde left school to try her hand in the Cleveland rock circuit, where for several years she also held a series of odd jobs. Learning of the lively English music scene from the London rock tabloid *New Music Express,* Hynde decided to seek her fortune in London. She put the $1,000 she had saved as an investment in her future toward the move. Though the relocation was a gamble, she told Schruers, "I would rather have my head blown off than sit . . . in Akron, Ohio, and watch television or go to the mall." Most of her early years in London were so lean that she once viewed petty theft as an option. But Hynde did hold some jobs during that time. Writing for *New Music Express* connected her with several English musicians and producers; she also worked for a while in a small clothing store with Malcolm McLaren, who would figure prominently in the late 1970s punk-rock movement.

Between 1973 and 1978, however, Hynde's determination to become part of a rock band met with only near misses. Despite invitations to various gigs, during which her peers recognized her as a strong musician and songwriter, none of the men forming bands would accept Hynde as a full-fledged member. After one failed attempt to start a band with guitarist Mick Jones, she reconnected with McLaren, who invited her to join his latest effort, Masters of the Backside. Hynde was a member of that group long enough to rehearse with them, but not long enough to enjoy their success as the noted punk band the Damned. Jones returned to the picture briefly, asking Hynde to play on tour with his new band, the Clash; but the temporary membership proved frustrating as Hynde was again dropped before the band caught on.

Teamed With Bassist Farndon

In Dave Hill, who had recently formed Read Records, Hynde recognized an opportunity to put together her own band. Hill offered himself as her manager in 1978 and urged her to take her time in recruiting the musicians she needed to record a demo tape. First Hynde heard about a bassist, Peter Farndon, through a friend. Farndon had been in Sidney, Australia, playing with the Bushwackers, a folk-rock outfit. Back in his hometown of Hereford, he was in the market for a new band himself; with Hynde, he found both the first real musical break of his life and, for a while, a romantic relationship. Farndon described his first impression of Hynde to Kurt Loder of *Rolling Stone:* "I walked into the pub and there was this American with a big mouth across the other side of the bar. . . . As soon as we got down to her rehearsal room, which was the scummiest basement I'd ever been in in my life, the first thing we played was 'Groove Me,' by King Floyd. . . . I'll never forget it: we go in, we do a soul number, we do a country and western number, and then we did 'The Phone Call,' which is like the heaviest . . . punk-rocker you could do in 5/4 time. Impressed? I was *very* impressed."

Farndon brought in an exceptional lead guitarist, James Honeyman-Scott, who would later be described by *Rolling Stone's* James Henke as "the guitarist whose lyrical playing formed the bedrock of the group's sound." With Irish drummer Jerry Mcleduff, Hynde, Farndon, and Honeyman-Scott put together a demo featuring a number of cuts that would become Pretenders classics: "Precious," "The Wait," and "Stop Your Sobbing." Singer/songwriter Nick Lowe, one of Hynde's *New Music Express* connections, agreed to produce a single of "Stop Your Sobbing" backed with "The Wait." Hynde's years of dedication finally began to pay off in January of 1979 when Lowe released the first Pretenders single; "Stop Your Sobbing," a cover version of a Kink's tune, was an instant success in the United Kingdom.

Solidified Lineup

Before cutting the single, however, the band had found a drummer who could produce exactly the sound they were seeking. Martin Chambers beat the skins so much harder than the average drummer, even in rock, that he had a drum kit "specially built to withstand his onslaughts," reported *Rolling Stone's* Loder. Chambers and Honeyman-Scott had departed their hometown of Hereford some years earlier with a band called Cheeks. Although Cheeks lasted for three years, the band never cut an album, which left the drummer and guitarist without any real musical credits. Honeyman-Scott had been working in a music shop when bassist Farndon contacted him; Chambers was a driving instructor when Farndon and Honeyman-Scott asked him to audition.

The singles released after "Stop Your Sobbing" were received with mounting acclaim. In 1980, "Kid," "Talk of the Town," and "Brass in Pocket" all reached bestseller status in the U.K. "Brass in Pocket" even claimed the Number One spot on British charts. These scraps of recognition ultimately melded into a sure foundation with the early 1980 release of the first Pretenders album. Titled simply *Pretenders,* the record's cover pictured Hynde, Farndon, Honeyman-Scott, and Chambers clad in leather jackets—mostly unsmiling. The cover and music exemplified the unforgiving attitude that the Pretenders' blend of British punk and American

---

"I would rather have my head blown off than sit in Akron, Ohio, and watch television or go to the mall."
—Chrissie Hynde

---

rock brought to the music scene of the early 1980s. Chris Thomas, who replaced Nick Lowe as the band's producer, graced the album with the same production values that had helped create the sound of famed British bands the Sex Pistols and Roxy Music. In the U.K., the album instantly shot to Number One.

Warm Reception From U.S. Audiences

The band's reputation grew more gradually in the U.S. than in the U.K., but no less steadily. Once Sire Records won the American rights to *Pretenders* and released it in the U.S., the album's success led to a gold record and a promotional concert tour. Mikal Gilmore of *Rolling Stone* explained the band's appeal: "The Pretenders' chief strength onstage, as on record, was their rhythmic ingenuity. . . . Hynde, [Honeyman-]Scott and bassist Pete Farndon wove a taut meshwork of staggered, propulsive rhythms that drummer Martin Chambers would spike with sinewy snare-and-tom bursts. In effect, it was a reversal of rhythmic standards, with the drums, instead of guitar, dictating fierce melodic lines."

Critics and fans received the group's debut album with considerable excitement, promoting it to the Number Nine position on U.S. charts. *Pretenders* was later described, when placed at Number 20 of *Rolling Stone's* "Top 100 Albums of the Decade," as "more diverse than the machine-gun rhythms of punk, because the three Britons were accomplished musicians and Hynde had grown up on a diet of AM radio." American fans immediately hailed the Pretenders as the embodiment of a no-holds-barred rebellion that they craved. Of their reception at a Los Angeles-area concert, Gilmore concluded, "The point, I gather, was to herald these Anglo-American New Wavers as something like preordained, conquering pop heroes, and in a way, that's just what they were."

Backstage, the tone of the tour was rebellious as well. Bandmembers drank heavily while reaping the benefits of their burgeoning fortunes. Both Honeyman-Scott and Farndon were able to freely indulge their heroin addictions. Hynde became notorious for kicking out the windows of a police car after being arrested for disorderly conduct. Although the pace of the road took its toll—Chambers eventually collapsed from exhaustion—no one took a break after the tour. Instead, the Pretenders returned to London to immediately begin recording material for their next album.

Tensions Mount

1981 saw two more successful albums and more touring. *Pretenders II* and *Extended Play* cemented the band's reputation for skill and hard work. The tenor of the 1981 tour was markedly different from that of its predecessor, however. Chambers and Hynde, in particular, began to "settle down." The music was hard-hitting as ever, but the lifestyle behind it was changing. Chambers had married a woman who worked for Sire, and Hynde had met Ray Davies of the Kinks—one of her childhood idols—in a New York City nightclub. The meeting led to a committed relationship and, in 1983, to the birth of Hynde's first child, Natalie. Even with the mellowing of Chambers and Hynde, though, the tour presaged difficulties to come. When Chambers cut his hand opening a window sash (Hynde later admitted that a rare fit of temper inspired the drummer to punch a lamp), the injury was so bad that he couldn't play for a number of weeks. The band decided to postpone the tour rather than replace Chambers. Meanwhile, Farndon and Honeyman-Scott continued the excesses afforded them by their newfound wealth and fame. The former especially moved farther and farther away from the rest of the band, his heroin addiction increasingly affecting his playing. He became irritable and easily angered, behavior that seemed to intensify when Hynde turned her affections toward Davies.

Whatever the source of his demeanor, Farndon finally became so irascible that Honeyman-Scott refused to work with him; although the lead guitarist was also using heroin, he managed to maintain his professionalism. When the band returned to London after the 1981 tour, Hynde made the difficult decision to fire Farndon. Since the remaining trio again wished to begin recording material for their next album right away, Honeyman-Scott suggested his friend Robbie McIntosh as a replacement for Farndon. But the Pretenders were devastated when—the very next day—Honeyman-Scott died of cocaine-induced heart failure. The group that had come to life as a powerhouse of diligence, pumping out tours, hit singles, and albums at a remarkable pace, took a three-year break between the release of their second album and their third.

Tragedy struck again in 1983; on April 14, Pete Farndon drowned in a bathtub, the result of heroin intoxication. Though his death dealt a severe blow to his former bandmates, the work of preparing a new album was already underway. Chambers and Hynde had put together a temporary band for some early summer recording sessions in 1982. The resulting single was a good omen; "Back on the Chain Gang," backed with "My City was Gone," became the Pretenders' first hit single in the U.S., where it broke the Top Five.

Group Picked Up the Pieces

Robbie McIntosh had come in as the Pretenders' first permanent replacement member—on lead guitar—late in the summer of 1982. He brought in Malcolm Foster for an audition on bass. Forgoing the frantic pace, but with the old Pretenders dedication intact, the band had a strong album ready for release in 1984. *Learning to Crawl* debuted to critical acclaim in both the U.S. and the U.K., going platinum in the former, despite the inevitable reservations about the absence of Farndon and Honeyman-Scott. Various attempts to analyze the album in terms of the profound emotions surrounding the birth of Hynde's daughter and the trauma of Farndon and Honeyman-Scott's deaths led the Pretenders frontwoman to remark in *Rolling Stone,* "[It's] just a collection of ten measly songs. It's not a real important deal. I hate this sort of romantic or sentimental take people have on it—you know, the *tragic demise,* the *reawakening.* It wasn't like that at all."

Hynde, however, was no longer the defiant punk she had been. After her breakup with Davies, she met and married Jim Kerr, lead singer of Simple Minds. Hynde's second daughter, Yasmin, was born in April of 1985. Her activities during the hiatus between the release of *Learning to Crawl* and its follow-up, *Get Close,* cemented Hynde's growing reputation as a spokesperson for liberal political causes and as a musician who demanded quality.

Solitary Core of the Pretenders

For *Get Close,* both Chambers and Foster stepped aside as Hynde brought in a variety of session musicians to work on tracks for the album. Jimmy Iovine and Bob Clearmountain replaced longtime producer Thomas. The record emphasized keyboards, and L. Shankar's Indian violin even emerged on one song. *Get Close,* however, was ultimately panned. Critics seemed to feel the release lacked the power of the Pretenders' first two albums and failed to demonstrate the consistency of *Learning to Crawl.* Others argued that the album's format attempted to cover too large a variety of musical styles, and that the production experimented with too many musical effects, detracting from Hynde's vocals. Nonetheless, the first single, "Don't Get Me Wrong," enjoyed Top Ten status.

High Fidelity contributor Ken Richardson reported in 1988 that Hynde had put together "an all-new Pretenders band." Even McIntosh had vanished from this line-up, which would produce the album *Packed!* in 1990. As evidenced by their reviews of *Packed!,* critics had finally accepted that the original Pretenders—and their sound—would never be duplicated. And as it became clear that *Packed!* was more impressive, track after track, than *Get Close*—though certainly more mainstream than the group's earliest work—critics and fans alike seemed to realized that Chrissie Hynde had, in fact, become the Pretenders. Richardson characterized the duality of the band's sound thus: "The Pretenders were two different bands: purveyors of top 40 hits and, on their first two LPs, creators of potent new wave, grounded in punk energy."

Selected discography

On Sire Records

Pretenders (includes "Stop Your Sobbing" and "Brass in Pocket"), 1980.
Extended Play, 1981.
Pretenders II, 1981.
Learning to Crawl (includes "Back in the Chain Gang" and "My City Was Gone"), 1984.
Get Close (includes "Don't Get Me Wrong"), 1987.
The Singles, 1988.
Packed!, 1990.

Sources

High Fidelity, September 1988.
Musician, March 1984.
Newsweek, April 2, 1984.
People, March 23, 1987.
Rolling Stone, May 29, 1980; June 12, 1980; November 26, 1981; April 26, 1984; April 10, 1986; November 16, 1989.

—Ondine E. Le Blanc

Queensrÿche

Heavy metal band

Combining social consciousness and non-sexist lyrics with high-energy and guitar-oriented music, Queensrÿche has become known as an intellectual heavy metal band. Seattle youths Chris DeGarmo, Eddie Jackson, Scott Rockenfield, Geoff Tate, and Michael Wilton formed Queensrÿche as teenagers in 1983 with a definite agenda in mind: turning their strong passion for playing music into an original heavy metal band. Since then the group has pursued their musical dreams with as much passion as their playing. After spending years as opening acts for other bands, Queensrÿche released their ambitious 1988 concept album *Operation: Mindcrime,* which won critical and popular acclaim and was compared to the Who's *Tommy* and Pink Floyd's *The Wall.* Queensrÿche went on to headline their own concerts, bringing their progressive heavy metal music to sold-out audiences.

Queensrÿche started when DeGarmo and Wilton united with the intention of creating an original band. Many hours of jam sessions went into developing a unique brand of guitar playing. Wilton had briefly attended the

Cornish Institute of Allied Arts in Seattle, Washington, studying music theory, among other subjects. "I can attribute a lot of the obscure [musical] things that I do to some of the things that I learned at that college, like how to play . . . all these really different, weird African tribal rhythms and everything," Wilton told Steve Peters in *Guitar Player.* "It made me see things in a different light. I don't know if it actually makes me play any better, but knowledge never hurts. It helps for musicians to accept different forms of music and see the values in them."

Wilton and DeGarmo were meticulous about putting the band together. Both were serious about music, and they wanted the other members to have the same commitment. "We were looking for people who shared the same sort of passion, who were willing to stick it out to get there," DeGarmo proclaimed to Daina Darzin in *Spin.* The other members chosen were vocalist Tate, bassist Jackson, and drummer Rockenfield. The band has kept these original members throughout it's career.

Opening Act

Beginning in the early 1980s, the hard-working band began to see some success and performed as opening acts for more established groups like Iron Maiden, AC/DC, and Def Leppard. The work was difficult and, inevitably, frustrating. "Basically, you're just trying to not get things thrown at you," Tate was reported as saying in *Spin.* Tate also felt that their message was not connecting with the hyped-up fans. "It's difficult when your lyrics are going over people's heads, when the audience is going, 'What are these guys talking about?'"

Around the time of Queensrÿche's album *Rage for Order,* the band decided to try a new strategy: market a visual image. It was a decided departure for the no frills rock and rollers. Creating a gothic vampire image achieved using layers of lacquered hairspray and thick makeup, the band took to the stage. Tate admitted in *Spin* that "we failed miserably." In addition, their record failed to sell.

For a while it seemed that Queensrÿche would be forever assigned to the job of opening act. They had played for some of the biggest names in the heavy metal world, but they seemed to be relegated to the role of bridesmaid. That changed in 1988 with the release of their album *Operation: Mindcrime.* Peters, writing in *Guitar Player,* called the record "a chilling tale of brainwashing with distinct Orwellian overtones." Built as an "aural film" about a political assassin, with references to government scandal and lying that made reference to behavior in President Ronald Reagan's administration, the album fell into the favor of fans, going gold within four days of its release. Critics likewise paid attention, calling the band progressive and dubbing them the "thinking man's metal band."

While some might have considered this description to have a negative impact on the heavy metal circle—where superficiality and glitz often reign supreme—Queensrÿche was generally pleased with the label. "We don't try to ram messages down people's throats," DeGarmo explained in *Guitar Player.* "We just bring up things we're interested in and hope that people will think about it a little bit. We're just trying to promote some thinking." Wilton concurred in the same article, saying that "we try to write music that reflects the information we're absorbing at that point in our lives. We're like human sponges: That's why some songs have social impact."

Launched to Headlining Status

A well-played video for the single "Eyes of a Stranger" and an opportunity to host MTV's heavy metal showcase, the "Headbanger's Ball," also increased the visibility and popularity of the quintet. "Silent Lucidity," a ballad, became a top-ten single. Record label EMI's vice president of marketing Robert Smith commented in *Billboard* that with *Operation: Mindcrime* "Queensrÿche has lifted itself from opening-act status to a powerful headliner role."

The band found it difficult to come up with an album to follow the success of *Operation: Mindcrime.* "We do cided that everybody was trying to do sequels, in the movie business as well as the music business," Wilton commented in *Guitar Player.* "That probably would have been the easy way out, but we decided to do something completely different. . . . We didn't want to be labelled a concept band."

The next album proved definitively that Queensrÿche was not a concept band and at the same time put them over the commercial edge. *Empire,* released in 1990, was a more personal look at the world. The title track examined the problems of gang crime in Seattle. "It's about how tough it is for kids to find something to do with their lives when they're tempted with all the big bucks they can make selling drugs," Tate explained in *Spin.* "Resistance" mourned the excessive cancer rate around the former Hanford nuclear plant in the state of Washington. And the story of a homeless woman was sung on "Della Brown." *Empire* was a resounding success, going double platinum. Following its release, the band took their first headline tour of American arenas in 1991, playing to virtually sold-out crowds.

Diversity the Key

Though Queensrÿche has a distinctive sound, they change themes and techniques with every album. Asked if this created any stress on their band, DeGarmo replied in *Guitar Player:* "The band's open-mindedness has allowed for diversity among albums. . . . We're trying to paint an atmosphere with each song, and I always try to get different sounds out of a guitar." In fact, this ability to change their themes and sounds has accounted for much of the group's popularity; Wilton feels that it is what distinguished them from other bands in their field. "We've put ourselves in more of a universal category," he related in *Guitar Player.* "I don't consider us a heavy metal band; we're more adventurous. We tend to experiment. . . . We're not afraid to do that for the sake of keeping an image, because I don't think we really have an image. Our music is the image, and we feel we need to keep the music fresh and interesting."

Grateful for their success, Queensrÿche is happy that they didn't have to alter their approach, or "sell out," to achieve prominence. "We're fortunate that just being patient and persistent has finally paid off," DeGarmo told *Guitar Player.* "We're also happy that we've stuck to our method of madness. We haven't had to alter the game plan too radically to get there."

Selected discography

Queensrÿche (EP), 1983.
The Warning, EMI, 1984.
Rage for Order, EMI, 1986.
Operation: Mindcrime, EMI, 1988.
Empire, EMI, 1990.
Operation: LIVEcrime, EMI, 1991.

Sources

Billboard, August 16, 1986; June 10, 1989.
Guitar Player, November 1991.
Melody Maker, November 17, 1984.
Spin, June 1991.

—Nancy Rampson

Raffi

Singer, songwriter, musician, environmentalist

Singer Raffi Cavoukian, who bills himself as Raffi, is renowned for single-handedly revolutionizing the children's entertainment business. Since he first began performing for children in 1974, his name has become a household word in homes throughout North America; his songs are enjoyed by millions of children and adults alike, who throng to his concerts and buy his records to the tune of more than seven million albums. After more than a dozen years of building his career as a children's entertainer, Raffi has become a self-styled "eco-troubadour," working with adults to promote environmental causes.

Born in Cairo, Egypt, in 1948, Raffi is the son of an internationally acclaimed portrait photographer. His first musical memory is of his father playing the accordion and singing at family gatherings. When Raffi was ten years old, the family immigrated to Canada, where he grew up wanting to be a history teacher. As a child, he enjoyed listening to such singers as Bob Dylan, Pete Seeger, and Joni Mitchell. Raffi taught himself to play the guitar while in high school, and he attended the University of Toronto for several years before dropping out to work full time as a musician. Aspiring to a career as a folksinger, he played in coffeehouses and clubs in Toronto, where he gained a small but enthusiastic following.

In 1974 Raffi's mother-in-law asked him to perform at the day-care center she ran. His wife, Debi Pike, a kindergarten teacher, taught him a few songs, and he enjoyed himself entertaining the children. More offers for children's performances came. Realizing that he had much to learn about an audience of young listeners, mostly two to eight years old, he and Pike avidly read books on child development and psychology. Pike collaborated with Raffi on songs, and they also drew on the resources of their teacher friends Bert and Bonnie Simpson.

Recorded First Children's Album

Raffi's first record, *Singable Songs for the Very Young,* came about at the suggestion of his mother-in-law. Raffi borrowed four thousand dollars from a bank and rented a basement recording studio. Six months later the record was finished, and the singer distributed it himself. For several years he tried to sing to both adult and child audiences. In 1977 he released two records, *More Singable Songs for the Very Young* and *Love Light*, the latter a record for adults. Yet Raffi found himself increasingly more comfortable in front of the younger listeners. "I had put a lot of time and energy into my adult career, and I didn't want to give it up," he recalled to *Courier-Journal* writer Ira Simmons, "but

For the Record. . .

Born Raffi Cavoukian, July 8, 1948, in Cairo, Egypt; son of a portrait photographer; immigrated to Canada, 1959; married Debi Pike (a teacher). *Education:* Attended University of Toronto.

Folksinger in Toronto, Ontario; children's entertainer, 1974-89; "eco-troubadour," 1990—. Contributed voice characterization to animated film *FernGully,* Twentieth Century Fox, 1992.

Awards: Order of Canada, 1983; Grammy Award nomination for best recording for children, 1987; Parents' Choice Award, *Parents' Choice* magazine.

Addresses: *Home*—Vancouver, British Columbia, Canada. *Office*—c/o Troubadour Records Ltd., 1075 Cambie St., Vancouver, British Columbia, Canada M2M 3W3. *Publicist*—Sharon Weisz, W3 Public Relations, 8380 Melrose Ave., Suite 105, Los Angeles, CA, 90069.

Debi and others around me helped me see that making music for children was in and of itself valuable work. I came to see children for the people they were, and that enabled me to let my adult career go." By 1978 he was devoting all his energy to making music for children.

With largely word-of-mouth advertising, the popularity of Raffi's music grew steadily. His songs became favorites of schoolteachers and day-care workers, and in 1983 he was awarded the Order of Canada, that country's highest civilian award, for his work with children. Once Raffi granted A&M distribution rights in 1984, record sales soared. More than a million copies of *Singable Songs for the Very Young* have been sold, and it remains the strongest selling of his nine albums. By the end of the 1980s Raffi was performing to sell-out crowds on tours throughout North America and being called the "Bruce Springsteen of the younger set."

Secrets of Success

Raffi's fans appreciate him for his nonthreatening appearance, pleasant voice, and infectious enthusiasm. In addition, he respects his audience. He is praised for not condescending, and he sings about what interests young children: for example, peanut butter and jelly sandwiches, the zoo, and teddy bears. His music reflects a wide range of styles, including folk, reggae, ragtime, gospel, jazz, country, and calypso, and is spiced with humor. He mixes old favorites with original compositions and is not afraid to sing an occasional song in Spanish or French. While some songs are obviously silly and others allow children to get up and dance in the aisles or their living rooms, all of Raffi's tunes are upbeat. "I don't want to sing sad songs for the kids," he told Simmons. "I don't think it's fair to burden children with more anxieties than they already have." Many parents admire Raffi's songs because they present solid values, but the singer does not try to educate his listeners. "I don't see myself as an educator," he told *Providence Journal* writer Mike Boehm, "so I don't write with a view to impart lessons. I don't see that as my mission at all, and I'm not sure songs that try to do those things end up being good pieces of music. I'm interested in making good music."

Many agree that good music not only requires creativity but quality performers and equipment. Critics laud Raffi's Rise and Shine Band as being made up of true professionals—bassist Dennis Pendrith, drummer Bucky Berger, keyboardist Nancy Walker, and guitarist Mitch Lewis; in addition, their sound system is said to be state of the art. Raffi has refused to work in halls that seat more than three thousand and would not allow his concerts to be priced above $8.50 despite the overwhelming demand for seats. That a concert lasts only 50 minutes considerably reflects the attention span of his young listeners. Early in his career Raffi would meet with fans in the lobby after the concert, but he had to discontinue the practice when listeners would line up for several hours to have a chance to meet him.

Raffi has refused to make commercial endorsements. While he has turned down many lucrative offers to promote various products, he has approved the "Songs to Read" series of richly illustrated picture books based on some of his most well known songs; Raffi hopes that children's familiarity with the song lyrics will act as a bridge toward recognizing the printed word. Raffi has made two videotapes, which he tried to make as interactive as possible, and he is often dismayed by the use some parents make of them—as baby-sitters. "Television isn't a friend of children," the singer told the *Wall Street Journal*'s Alan Freeman. "Children need to play. They need to interact with other people. That's how they find out about the world around them."

Changed Direction

In the fall of 1988 Raffi decided to take a year off from giving concerts and interviews to think about future projects. "After ten years of touring I feel the time is right to make time for the private person," the singer told Martia Kohn in the *Denver Post.* When he returned to the concert stage, it was quickly evident what had been on his mind during the hiatus—the environment. The self-styled "eco-troubadour" would devote his time to promoting environmental causes, not performing specifically for children.

When he signed a new record distribution contract in 1990, Raffi stipulated that he would only release an album if the CD (compact disc) longbox or other excessive packaging were eliminated. MCA rose to the challenge, and some other musicians have followed his example. The album, released in September of 1990, was *Evergreen Everblue,* a collection of songs about ecology and environmental issues for a much older audience than that of most of his pervious work. "For fourteen years I have made music that blends my love for children and the earth. But the earth is dying and may not be able to provide for us much longer," he wrote in the *Evergreen Everblue* newsletter. "The critical urgency of the global environment crisis has led me to create something new. *Evergreen Everblue* is an ecology album for those of us old enough to understand the dangers and initiate change." His activities include leading workshops on the role of artists in mobilizing society to action, singing songs from his latest album at rallies, and appearing on talk shows to promote various environmental protection efforts. Raffi believes that the fate of the earth rests on the commitment of all to protecting the environment. In the words of the "eco-troubadour," "Evergreen, Everblue / As it was in the beginning, / We've got to see it through, / Evergreen, Everblue . . . / At this point in time / It's up to me—its up to you."

Selected writings

Published by Crown

The Raffi Singable Songbook, 1987.
The Second Raffi Songbook, 1987.
Down by the Bay, 1987.
Shake My Sillies Out, 1987.
One Light, One Sun, 1988.
The Wheels on the Bus, 1988.
The Raffi Everything Grows Songbook, 1989.
Tingalayo, 1989.
Five Little Ducks, 1989.
Everything Grows, 1989.

Raffi in Concert With the Rise and Shine Band, 1989.
Baby Beluga, 1990.

Selected discography

On Troubadour Records

Singable Songs for the Very Young, 1976.
More Singable Songs, 1977.
The Corner Grocery Store, 1979.
Baby Beluga, 1980.
Rise and Shine, 1982.
Raffi's Christmas Album, 1983.
One Light, One Sun, 1985.
Everything Grows, distributed by A&M, 1987.
Raffi in Concert With the Rise and Shine Band, 1989.
Evergreen, Everblue: An Ecology Album for the 90's, distributed by MCA Records, 1990.

Other

Also released videocassettes *A Young Children's Concert With Raffi,* 1985, and *Raffi and the Rise and Shine Band,* A&M, 1988.

Sources

Boston Herald, April 21, 1988.
Colorado Rocky Mountain News, March 16, 1988.
Courier-Journal (Louisville, KY), November 1, 1987.
Denver Post, January 19, 1986; October 9, 1988.
Evergreen Everblue (newsletter) Issue 1, 3, 1990.
Herald News (Passaic, NJ), October 28, 1986.
Madison Capital Times, April 7, 1986.
Minneapolis Tribune, November 29, 1985.
New York Daily News, September 25, 1988.
Parents' Magazine, November 1989.
Philadelphia Inquirer, November 9, 1987.
Providence Journal, November 27, 1987.
Sacramento Bee, December 16, 1985.
San Diego Union, February 22, 1986.
Virginian-Pilot (Norfolk), November 4, 1987.
Wall Street Journal, June 29, 1987.
Washington Post, November 8, 1987.

—*Jeanne M. Lesinski*

Steve Reich

Composer

Like Philip Glass, John Adams, and Terry Riley, Steve Reich belongs to a group of composers known as "minimalists," who write music based largely on patterns of repetition. Minimalism came into prominence when many American composers tired of what they considered the over-rigorous, emotionally bankrupt style of music that was held up as an example when they were students. As a descriptive label, "minimalism" can be ineffectual—since each minimalist composer has his own distinct voice—but the movement has become a prominent and important musical style.

Reich was born in New York City in 1936, and grew up playing the piano. But in his early teens his interest switched to percussion. In 1982 he told a *Newsweek* reporter: "I had heard [jazz alto saxophonist] Charlie Parker and was suddenly off on this great music. Around then, I also heard the Brandenburg concertos [by Baroque composer J. S. Bach] and [Igor Stravinsky's 1913 ballet] *The Rite of Spring* for the first time, and that made an indelible impression on me." As a result, he began studying percussion when he was 14 with Roland Kohloff, the principal timpanist of the New York Philharmonic.

When Reich entered Cornell University in 1953, it was as a philosophy major. While at Cornell he was introduced to many types of music by the musicologist William Austin, and by the time he graduated with a degree in philosophy in 1957, Reich had decided to become a composer. For the next six years he studied composition privately, first with Hall Overton in New York City and then at New York City's Juilliard School of Music with Vincent Persichetti and William Bergsma; he later attended Mills College in California, where he studied with Darius Milhaud and Luciano Berio and received a master's degree in composition in 1963.

Began Recording and Experimenting

It's Gonna Rain and *Come Out* are among Reich's first pieces and were composed in 1965 for electronic tape, with the same recorded material played on two tape recorders but slightly out of synchronization. Reich then began to experiment with this process, which became known as "phasing," in works for acoustic instruments, such as *Piano Phase* and *Violin Phase,* both written in 1967. The purpose of phasing was to create a musical process: "I do not mean the process of composition," Reich said in his book *Writings About Music,* "but rather pieces of music that are, literally, processes. . . . I want to be able to hear the process happening throughout the sounding music. . . . What

Born October 3, 1936, in New York, NY; son of Leonard Reich (an attorney) and Joyce Carroll (a singer and lyricist); married Beryl Korot (a video artist and professional weaver); children: Ezra; (previous marriage) another son. *Education:* Cornell University, B.A., 1957; private composition study with Hall Overton in New York City, 1957-58, with Vincent Persichetti and William Bergsma at Juilliard School of Music, 1958-61, and with Darius Milhaud and Luciano Berio at Mills College, where he received an M.A., 1963. Studied African drumming at Institute for African Studies at the University of Ghana, summer, 1970, and Balinese Gamelan Semar Pegulingan and Gamelan Gambang in Seattle, WA, summer, 1973, and Berkeley, CA, summer, 1974. Studied Hebrew cantillation in New York City and Jerusalem, Israel.

Composer. New School for Social Research, New York City, member of composition faculty, 1969-71. Founder, 1966, and director of Steve Reich and Musicians. Author of *Writings About Music,* Press of the Nova Scotia College of Art and Design, 1974.

Awards: National Endowment for the Arts grants, 1974 and 1976; Rockefeller Foundation grants, 1975, 1979, and 1981; Guggenheim fellowship, 1978; Koussevitzky Foundation award, 1981.

Addresses: *Home*—New York City. *Manager*—Lynn Garon Management, 1199 Park Ave., New York, NY 10028.

I'm interested in is a compositional process and a sounding music that are one and the same thing."

The composer founded the group Steve Reich and Musicians in 1966 for the purpose of performing his music, which called for various combinations of instrumentalists and vocalists. The group, which started out with three performers but has included as many as 40, began touring internationally, and Reich's music became increasingly prominent in new music concerts around the world.

In 1970 Reich, who had always been interested in non-Western music, went to the University of Ghana in Africa to study African drumming. Reviewers have noted that as a result, his music exhibited more richness and complexity, qualities said to be present in 1971's *Drumming*. The 90 minute composition was Reich's first widely known work, boosting him into fame

in the United States and Europe. It remains one of his most popular pieces. Reich also studied the music of the gamelan, or Indonesian percussion orchestra, in the early 1970s, and his musical style continued to develop in pieces such as *Music for Mallet Instruments, Voices and Organ* (1973), *Music for 18 Musicians* (1976), and *Octet* (1979).

Drew Inspiration From the Bible

In 1981 Reich composed a work for orchestra and voices, *Tehillim,* the first of his pieces with a written text: the 19th Psalm from the Hebrew Bible ("Tehillim" is Hebrew for "psalms" or "praises"). Reich had studied Hebrew cantillation, which is the art of the cantor—a synagogue official who sings or chants liturgical music and leads the congregation in prayer—and had rediscovered his Jewish roots during this period. *Tehillim* is considered one of Reich's most extraordinary works, and its performance in 1982 by the New York Philharmonic is often credited for bringing minimalist music into the established orchestral repertoire.

Reich's next major piece, *The Desert Music,* was written in 1983 for chorus and orchestra, with a text by American poet William Carlos Williams. It was considered a milestone work because it incorporated many of Reich's earlier techniques while being distinctly new. As K. Robert Schwartz wrote of *Desert Music* in *Musical America,* "Reich has miraculously remained faithful to his original aesthetic: steady pulse, tonal center, clarity of process, and repetition all remain essential facets of *The Desert Music.* Despite its tremendous advances in orchestral technique, in expressive range, in harmonic and melodic language, and in text setting, *The Desert Music* still possesses a satisfying integrity with Reich's larger body of work. Linked together by pulsing chordal cycles reminiscent of *Music for 18 Musicians,* partaking of the rhythmic construction first introduced in *Drumming* and the densely layered canons typical of *Tehillim, The Desert Music* retains organic ties with Reich's past while introducing new avenues for the future."

Different Trains

In the late 1980s Reich returned to composing for smaller performing forces. The culmination of his work during the decade was *Different Trains,* which uses five prerecorded voice tracks: Virginia, the woman who took care of Reich when he was a child; Lawrence Davis, a former Pullman porter; and the voices of three concentration camp survivors. The voice tracks are synchronized with train whistles and up to four record ed string quartets. Reich thought of *Different Trains* as a way to come to terms with his Jewish heritage and his identity. In an article in the *New York Times* he said, "I did this piece because, as a Jew, had I lived in Europe, I would not be here. It tries to present as faithfully as possible the era in which I survived, and in which [many European Jews] perished. . . . I hope that *The Desert Music* will have a future, but I don't know that I was born to do that kind of work for the rest of my life. Whereas I feel that I was born to do *Different Trains,* and that if I hadn't done it, no one else would have."

Reich is often considered the most thoughtful and interesting of the minimalists, and his music, in combination with that of colleagues Glass and Adams, has opened the doors for a new listening audience. In a *Musical America* article Reich said, "When American music was basically aping European serial music [in the fifties and early sixties], the audience was very limited. As American music has again become as natural an utterance for us as it was for [American composer Aaron] Copland in the thirties, then we're in a situation where normalcy has been regained. And the audience is reacting to that reality."

Selected discography

Come Out (composed in 1965)/*Piano Phase* (composed c. 1967)/*It's Gonna Rain* (composed in 1965)/*Clapping Music,* Elektra/Nonesuch.

Drumming (composed in 1971)/*Six Pianos*/*Music for Mallet Instruments, Voices and Organ* (composed in 1973), Deutsche Grammophon.
Variations for Winds, Strings and Keyboards, Philips.
Music for 18 Musicians (composed in 1976), ECM.
Tehillim (composed in 1981), ECM.
The Desert Music (composed in 1983), Nonesuch.
Different Trains (composed in the late 1980s), Elektra/Nonesuch.

Sources

Books

The New Grove Dictionary of American Music, edited by H. Wiley Hitchcock and Stanley Sadie, Macmillan, 1986.
Reich, Steve, *Writings About Music,* Press of the Nova Scotia College of Art and Design, 1974.

Periodicals

Grammophone, June 1991.
High Fidelity/Musical America, January 1986.
Musical America, January 1990.
Newsweek, March 29, 1982.
New York Times, November 8, 1987; May 28, 1989.

—*Joyce Harrison*

Paul Robeson

Singer, actor, activist

Paul Robeson—singer, actor, civil rights activist, law school graduate, athlete, scholar, author—was perhaps the best known and most widely respected black American of the 1930s and 1940s. Robeson was also a staunch supporter of the Soviet Union, and a man, later in his life, widely vilified and censored for his frankness and unyielding views on issues to which public opinion ran contrary. As a young man, Robeson was virile, charismatic, eloquent, and powerful. He learned to speak more than 20 languages in order to break down the barriers of race and ignorance throughout the world, and yet, as Sterling Stuckey pointed out in the *New York Times Book Review,* for the last 25 years of his life his was "a great whisper and a greater silence in black America."

Born in Princeton, New Jersey, in 1898, Robeson was spared most of the daily brutalities suffered by African Americans around the turn of the century. But his family was not totally free from hardship. Robeson's mother died from a stove-fire accident when he was six. His father, a runaway slave who became a pastor, was removed from an early ministerial position. Nonetheless, from his father Robeson learned diligence and an "unshakable dignity and courage in spite of the press of racism and poverty." These characteristics, Stuckey noted, defined Robeson's approach in his beliefs and actions throughout his life.

Racist Incident Soured Law Career

Having excelled in both scholastics and athletics as a youth, Robeson received a scholarship to Rutgers College (now University), where he was elected to Phi Beta Kappa in his junior year and chosen valedictorian in his senior. He earned varsity letters in four sports and was named Rutgers' first All-American in football. Fueled by his class prophecy to be "the leader of the colored race in America," Robeson went on to earn a law degree from Columbia University, supporting himself by playing professional football on the weekends. After graduation he obtained a position with a New York law firm only to have his career halted, as was recalled in Martin Baulm Duberman's *Paul Robeson,* when a stenographer refused to take down a memo, saying, "I never take dictation from a nigger." Sensing this episode as indicative of the climate of the law, Robeson left the bar.

While in law school, Robeson had married fellow Columbia student Eslanda Cardozo Goode, who encouraged him to act in amateur theatrical productions. Convinced by his wife and friends to return to the theater after his departure from law, Robeson joined the Provincetown Players, a group associated with playwright Eugene O'Neill. Two productions in which he starred, *The Emperor Jones* and *All God's Chillun Got Wings,* brought Robeson critical acclaim. Contemporary drama critic George Jean Nathan, quoted by *Newsweek*'s Hubert Saal, called Robeson "thoroughly eloquent, impressive, and convincing."

Thus Robeson continued on the stage, winning applause from critics and audiences, gaining an international reputation for his performances on the London stage, and eventually extending his acting repertoire to include films. His stage presence was undeniable, and with the musical *Show Boat* and Shakespeare's *Othello,* Robeson's reputation grew even larger. In *Show Boat* he sang the immensely popular "Ol' Man River," displaying a powerful, warm, soothing voice. Robeson, realizing his acting range was limited both by the

choice of roles available to him as a black performer and by his own acting abilities, turned to singing full time as an outlet for his creative energies and growing social convictions.

Found a Moral Cause in Song

Robeson had been giving solo vocal performances since 1925, but it wasn't until he traveled to Britain that his singing became for him a moral cause. Robeson related years later in his autobiography, *Here I Stand,* that in England he "learned that the essential character of a nation is determined not by the upper classes, but by the common people, and that the common people of all nations are truly brothers in the great family of mankind." Consequently, he began singing spirituals and work songs to audiences of common citizens and learning the languages and folk songs of other cultures, for "they, too, were close to my heart and expressed the same soulful quality that I knew in Negro music." Nathan Irvin Huggins, writing in the *Nation,* defined this pivotal moment: "[Robeson] found the finest expression of his talent. His genuine awe of and love for the common people and their music flourished throughout his life and became his emotional and spiritual center."

Continued travels throughout Europe in the 1930s brought Robeson in contact with members of politically left-leaning organizations, including socialists and African nationalists. Singing to, and moving among, the disadvantaged, the underprivileged, the working classes, Robeson began viewing "himself and his art as serving the struggle for racial justice for nonwhites and economic justice for workers of the world," Huggins noted.

Went to the Soviet Union

A critical journey at that time, one that changed the course of his life, was to the Soviet Union. *Paul Robeson* author Duberman depicted Robeson's time there: "Nights at the theater and opera, long walks with [film director Sergei] Eisenstein, gala banquets, private screenings, trips to hospitals, children's centers, factories . . . all in the context of a warm embrace." Robeson was ecstatic with this new-found society, concluding, according to *New York Times Book Review* contributor John Patrick Diggins, "that the country was entirely free of racial prejudice and that Afro-American spiritual music resonated to Russian folk traditions. 'Here, for the first time in my life . . . I walk in full human dignity.'" Diggins went on to assert that Robeson's "attraction to Communism seemed at first more anthropological than ideological, more of a desire to discover old, lost cultures than to impose new political systems. . . . Robeson convinced himself that American blacks as descendants of slaves had a common culture with Russian workers as descendants of serfs."

Regardless of his ostensibly simple desire to believe in a cultural genealogy, Robeson soon become a vocal advocate of communism and other left-wing causes. He returned to the United States in the late 1930s, *Newsweek's* Saal observed, becoming "a vigorous opponent of racism, picketing the White House, refusing to sing before segregated audiences, starting a crusade against lynching, and urging Congress to outlaw racial bars in baseball."

Would Not Denounce Communism

After World War II, when relations between the United States and the Soviet Union froze into the Cold War, many former advocates of communism backed away from it. When the crimes of Soviet leader Josef Stalin became public—forced famine, genocide, political purges—still more advocates left the ranks of communism. Robeson, however, was not among them. *National Review* contributor Joseph Sobran explained why: "It didn't matter: he believed in the idea, regardless of how it might be abused. In 1946 the former All-American explained his loyalty to an investigating committee: 'The coach tells you what to do and you do it.' It was incidental that the coach was Stalin." Robeson could not publicly decry the Soviet Union even after he, most probably, learned of Stalin's atrocities because "the cause, to his mind," *Nation* contributor Huggins theorized, "was much larger than the Soviet Union, and he would do nothing to sustain the feeding frenzy of the American right."

Robeson's popularity soon plummeted in response to his increasing rhetoric. After he urged black youths not to fight if the United States went to war against the Soviet Union, a riot prevented his appearing at a concert in Peekskill, New York. But his desire was never to leave the United States, just to change, as he believed, the racist attitude of its people. In his autobiography Robeson recounted how during the infamous McCarthy hearings, when questioned by a Congressional committee about why he didn't stay in the Soviet Union, he replied, "Because my father was a slave, and my people died to build this country, and I am going to stay right here and have a part of it just like you. And no fascist-minded people will drive me from it. Is that clear?"

In 1950 the U.S. Department of State revoked Robeson's passport, ensuring that he would remain in the United

States. "He was black-listed by concert managers—his income, which had been $104,000 in 1947, fell to $2,000—and he was removed from the list of All-Americans," Saal noted in *Newsweek.* America's highest prize, its honor, was removed from him. His career died.

Pariah Status

Robeson's passport was restored in 1958 after a Supreme Court ruling on a similar case, but it was of little consequence. By then he had become a nonentity. When Robeson's autobiography was published that year, leading literary journals, including the *New York Times* and the *New York Herald-Tribune* refused to review it. Robeson traveled again to the Soviet Union, but his health began to fail. He tried twice to commit suicide. "Pariah status was utterly alien to the gregarious Robeson. He became depressed at the loss of contact with audiences and friends, and suffered a series of breakdowns that left him withdrawn and dependent on psychotropic drugs," Dennis Drabble ex-

---

"The common people of all nations are truly brothers in the great family of mankind."

---

plained in *Smithsonian.* Slowly deteriorating and virtually unheard from in the 1960s and 1970s, Robeson died after suffering a stroke in 1976.

During his life Paul Robeson inspired thousands with his voice—raised in speech and song. But because of his singular support for communism and Stalin, because his life in retrospect became "a pathetic tale of talent sacrificed, loyalty misplaced, and idealism betrayed," according to Jim Miller in *Newsweek,* Robeson disappeared in sadness and loneliness. His life, full of desire and achievement, passion and conviction, "the story of a man who did so much to break down the barriers of a racist society, only to be brought down by the controversies sparked by his own radical politics," *New York Times Book Review* contributor Diggins pronounced, "is at once an American triumph and an American tragedy."

Selected writings

Here I Stand, Othello Associates, 1950, Deacon, 1971.

(Contributor) *Paul Robeson: The Great Forerunner*, Freedomways, 1971, Dodd, 1985.

Paul Robeson: Tributes, Selected Writings, edited by Roberta Yancy Dent, The Archives, 1976.

Paul Robeson Speaks: Writings, Speeches, Interviews, 1918-1974, edited by Philip S. Foner, Brunner, 1978.

Columnist for *People's Voice*, 1940s; editor and columnist for *Freedom*, c. 1951-55. Contributor to periodicals.

Selected discography

American Balladeer—Golden Classics, Volume 1, Collectables.

Man & His Beliefs—Golden Classics, Volume 2, Collectables.

Historic Paul Robeson—Golden Classics, Volume 3, Collectables.

Collector's Paul Robeson, Monitor.

Essential Paul Robeson, Vanguard.

Favorite Songs, Volume 1, Monitor.

Favorite Songs, Volume 2, Monitor.

Live at Carnegie Hall, Vanguard.

Paul Robeson, Pearl.

Paul Robeson Sings "Ol' Man River" & Other Favorites, Angel.

The Odyssey of Paul Robeson, reissue, Omega/Vanguard Classics, 1992.

Sources

Books

Duberman, Martin Baulm, *Paul Robeson*, Knopf, 1988.
Robeson, Paul, *Here I Stand*, Beacon, 1971.

Periodicals

American Heritage, April 1989.
Commentary, May 1989.
Nation, February 7, 1976; March 20, 1989.
National Review, May 19, 1989.
New Leader, February 20, 1989.
Newsweek, February 2, 1976; February 13, 1989.
New York Review of Books, April 27, 1989.
New York Times Book Review, October 21, 1973; February 12, 1989.
Smithsonian, October 1989.
Time, February 2, 1976; March 13, 1989.
Times Literary Supplement, September 5, 1958.

—Rob Nagel

Nile Rodgers

Guitarist, producer

Nile Rodgers is best known as the lead guitarist and coleader, along with bassist Bernard Edwards, of Chic, one of the most successful disco groups of the late 1970s. Rodgers, who considers himself first and foremost a jazz guitarist, has also released three recordings under his own name; but Rodgers's talents extend into other creative realms. In 1986 Ted Fox wrote in his book *In the Groove* that Rodgers "may be the hottest producer on the pop music scene today." Though Rodgers started out as a guitarist and remains in demand as a session musician, he is firmly entrenched in other aspects of the music industry and has significantly expanded the creative horizons of the dance music form.

A native of New York City, Rodgers grew up in a musical family. His father had played percussion for Sam Cooke and Harry Belafonte, and an uncle taught the teenaged Nile the art of orchestration. At age 16, Rodgers talked his way into a band on the strength of his then-nonexistent ability to play the guitar. "Then I was so embarrassed about not being able to play that I got very, very serious about it," he recalled to Gene Santoro of *Down Beat*.

Rodgers's devotion to the guitar coincided with the expansion of that instrument's potentialities in the rock music scene of the late 1960s. Moving rapidly through folk guitar styles, Rodgers came into contact with the music of such pioneers of the electric guitar as Steve Miller and Jimmy Page and has cited Jimi Hendrix as a major influence. "I still have every record, still know every song of his," Rodgers told Santoro. Continuing explorations led him to the formal study of jazz and classical guitar.

Weaned at the Apollo

Professional success first came with acceptance into the house band of Harlem's legendary Apollo Theater. Rodgers backed such notables as Aretha Franklin and Nancy Wilson and soon began to rise through the ranks of New York City's session musicians. The repetitive but somehow irresistible guitar riffs he contributed to Betty Wright's 1972 hit, "Clean Up Woman," showcased Rodgers's quintessential guitar style, soon to become Chic's trademark.

Rodgers had been introduced to Bernard Edwards in 1970, and the two were active in various nightclub ensembles. The duo, along with drummer Tony Thompson, attempted to land a recording contract with jazz-rock fusion material of a type extremely popular in the mid-1970s, but found that as an African-American band their efforts were blocked. "The labels weren't

Born September 19, 1952, in New York, NY.

Member of house band, Apollo Theater, New York City, early 1970s; session and nightclub musician, New York City, c. 1971-77; coleader of group Chic, 1977-83; producer of recordings by numerous artists, 1979—; released solo recordings, mid-1980s; formed group Outloud, 1987; coleader of reunited Chic, 1992—.

Selected awards: Named number one pop singles producer, *Billboard,* 1985; named top singles producer, *Music Week,* 1985; Grammy Award for guitarist Jeff Beck's record *Flash,* 1986.

Addresses: *Record company*—Warner Bros. Records, 75 Rockefeller Plaza, New York, NY 10019. *Management*—Borman Entertainment, 9220 Sunset Blvd., Ste. 320, Los Angeles, CA 90060.

interested in a black fusion band. Unless you had a [reputation] in the industry by playing with a Miles Davis or Chick Corea, you couldn't break through," Rodgers told Nelson George in *Musician.*

Influenced Development of Disco

The popularity of lush, mechanical dance music, or disco, was on the rise when Rodgers and Edwards next set out to land a record deal. Atlantic Records released "Dance, Dance, Dance" as Chic's debut single in 1977. Uncomplicated, yet imaginative and varied in a supremely entertaining way, the track synthesized several elements of Rodgers's long apprenticeship and set the tone for hundreds of forthcoming disco records. As Nelson George assessed, the record was "a wonderfully calculated piece of disco marketing. It had funky hand claps and slinky guitar riffs to galvanize black dancers, while its swirling strings and campy cheer of 'Yowsah, Yowsah, Yowsah,' recalling the dance marathons of yore, captured the gay audience." "Dance, Dance, Dance" reached the Number Six position on *Billboard's* pop charts in 1977.

The follow-up Chic single, "Everybody Dance," also cracked the pop Top 40 and entered the rhythm and blues Top 15, establishing the band as a major presence on the disco scene. Then, in 1978, Rodgers and Edwards unveiled "Le Freak" to an assemblage of Atlantic Records department heads. Leaner and more economical than "Dance, Dance, Dance," the record

juxtaposed explosive chants of "Freak out! Le freak, c'est chic!" with spare, intense dialogue between Rodgers's guitar and Edwards's bass. The Atlantic executives were mystified, Rodgers recalled in an interview with *Musician* contributor Baird: "By the time the song was finished playing, everybody had left, because they couldn't figure out what to say to us." But the duo's judgment was vindicated when the single sold 8 million copies. "Le Freak" remains the best selling single in the history of the Warner Bros. conglomerate and propelled the second Chic album, "C'est Chic," to platinum status.

A later album, *Risque,* also went platinum in 1979, spawning the monster hit "Good Times," the foundation for several early compositions in the emerging rap music style. Other successful singles followed, held together by Rodgers's hypnotic guitar, always prominent in the mix. But things began to turn sour for Chic around 1980. Later Chic albums sold poorly, creative tensions flared between Rodgers and Edwards, and the two parted ways in 1983. The biggest factor was simply that the disco phenomenon had run its course. Another cause was Rodgers's and Edwards's desire to infuse the dance medium with greater lyric seriousness. "I remember walking into a store and a girl saying to me, 'I don't understand why you stopped writing songs about dancing and making love,'" Rodgers recounted to *Musician's* Baird.

Hot Pop Producer

Rodgers soon found himself in great demand as a solo producer. He, in partnership with Edwards, had already supervised Sister Sledge's anthemic "We Are Family" and one of Diana Ross's most successful solo LPs, 1980's *Diana.* Although Rodgers admitted to Fox that he believes in electronic musical technology "to the highest order," his productions have varied widely according to the musical styles and personalities of the artists he has supervised, including Jeff Beck, Duran Duran, Al Jarreau, Mick Jagger, and Stevie Ray Vaughan. Rodgers's metronome-like guitar style proved perfect for the dance-rock of the 1980s. In 1983 he helped transform David Bowie into a contemporary dance-rocker on *Let's Dance;* more significant still was his production of Madonna's *Like a Virgin* in 1984, to which Rodgers contributed a spare but punchy backdrop. Both albums went multiplatinum.

Rodgers recorded two solo albums over the course of the 1980s and briefly formed a group known as Outloud, which released a self-titled album in 1987. Each of the three works was a complex dance-music production, often united by some overarching lyrical theme. All the recordings failed commercially, but attracted critical attention; Chuck Eddy of the *Village Voice* called the LPs "conceptual coups like Chic never pulled off."

Chic Reunited

Chic's 1992 reunion came about as a result of a birthday party for Rodgers that Edwards attended. Along with late-night TV musicians Paul Shaffer and Anton Fig, they performed "Le Freak" and "Good Times" and were rewarded with wild applause. A new album, *Chicism,* took a year to record and went through several creative transformations, as Rodgers and Edwards largely discarded the rap-and-sample techniques of early 1990s dance music in favor of the classic Chic style. The decision may have been a wise one in view of the backward-looking mania for disco that was gaining strength in early 1992.

Looking back on the origins of the sound that characterized Chic's best records, Rodgers credited the complex guitar and bass interplay with the group's attempt to cover intricate pop arrangements within a small group context. His own importance in creating the multilayered texture for which disco's best productions are remembered—strings and a heavy bass line enlivened by hand claps and complex guitar syncopations—cannot be understated. Nile Rodgers's contributions seem likely to continue influencing pop music's mainstream.

Selected discography

With Chic

Chic (includes "Dance, Dance, Dance" and "Everybody Dance"), Atlantic, 1977.
C'est Chic (includes "Le Freak"), Atlantic, 1978.
Risque (includes "Good Times"), Atlantic, 1979.
Real People, Atlantic, 1980.
Take It Off, Atlantic, 1981.
Soup for One (motion picture soundtrack), Atlantic, 1982.
Tongue in Chic, Atlantic, 1982.
Believer, Atlantic, 1983.

Chicism, Warner Bros., 1992.
Dance, Dance, Dance: The Best of Chic, Atlantic, 1992.

Solo albums

Adventures in the Land of the Good Groove, Mirage, 1983.
B-Movie Matinee, Warner Bros., 1985.
(With Outloud) *Out Loud,* Warner Bros., 1987.

Producer

Sister Sledge, *We Are Family,* Cotillion, 1979.
Diana Ross, *Diana,* Motown, 1980.
Debbie Harry, *Koo Koo,* 1981.
David Bowie, *Let's Dance,* EMI America, 1983.
Madonna, *Like a Virgin,* Sire, 1984.
Jeff Beck, *Flash,* CBS, 1985.
The Power Station, *The Power Station,* Capitol, 1985.
Thompson Twins, *Here's to Future Days,* 1985.
Duran Duran, *Notorious,* Capitol, 1986.
Grace Jones, *Inside Story,* 1986.
The B-52's, *Cosmic Thing,* Reprise, 1989.
Vaughan Brothers, *Family Style,* CBS, 1990.

Also producer of singles and albums by numerous other recording artists, including Al Jarreau's "Moonlighting," Hall & Oates's "Adult Education," Steve Winwood's "Higher Love," and David Bowie's "Real Cool World" from the motion picture soundtrack *Cool World,* Warner Bros., 1992.

Sources

Books

Fox, Ted, *In the Groove,* St. Martin's, 1986.

Periodicals

Billboard, July 14, 1990.
Down Beat, September 1985.
Musician, November 1980; April 1992.
Rolling Stone, March 19, 1992.
Village Voice, December 29, 1987.

—*James M. Manheim*

Rush

Rock band

The Canadian power trio Rush attracted a large international following in the mid-1970s with their eclectic brew of metal, progressive rock, and fantasy-oriented lyrics. Since then the group has kept up with the times, gradually developing a more pop-oriented sound, but their career approach has remained more or less the same: bypass the critics and Top Forty radio and sell records by touring constantly. In the wake of their enormous success—a 1991 *Maclean's* profile revealed that the trio had been ''a multimillion-dollar entity for 15 years''—Rush has earned grudging respect from some of their harshest critics. Perhaps more notably, though, the once unfashionable fusion they pioneered in the 1970s has emerged as an influence on many cutting edge rock acts of the late 1980s and early 1990s, including Faith No More, Jane's Addiction, and Fishbone. What critics of the 1980s derided as ''dinosaur rock'' gained a new relevance in the 1990s, causing many fans, musicians, and critics to reassess Rush's work.

Rush's success has allowed them to take a more

Members include **Geddy Lee** (born Geddy Weinrib, July 29, 1953, in Toronto, Ontario, Canada), vocals, bass, keyboards; **Alex Lifeson** (born August 27, 1953, in Surnie, British Columbia, Canada), guitar; and **Neil Peart** (born September 12, 1952, in Hamilton, Ontario; replaced **John Rutsey**, 1974), drums.

Group formed in Toronto, Ontario, Canada, 1968; recording and performing artists, 1968—. Released independent debut LP, *Rush,* 1974; released first Mercury album, *Fly By Night,* 1975.

Addresses: *Manager*—Ray Danniels, SRO Management, Inc., 189 Carlton St., Toronto, Ontario, Canada M5A 2K7. *Record company*—Atlantic Records, 75 Rockefeller Plaza, New York, NY 10019.

loyal core of followers and managed to make new converts with each tour and record.

Lee and Lifeson's Bar Band

The Rush enterprise began in the late 1960s. Lee and Lifeson met in high school in Ontario, Canada. Influenced by the heavy psychedelic rock of Cream and Jimi Hendrix, the guitarist and bassist began playing together; by 1968 they had formed a group with Lifeson's friend John Rutsey on drums. The group struggled on the club scene until a major legislative development—the lowering of the legal drinking age to 18 in Canada—increased their schedule threefold. Soon they were playing gigs throughout the week, and were not constrained to dances that required them to play oldies. After several years and numerous frustrated attempts to generate record company interest, they elected to make their own album. Their debut LP, *Rush,* appeared on the Moon Records label in 1974, sold surprisingly well in the United States—thanks in part to substantial airplay on a Cleveland, Ohio, radio station—and led Mercury Records to sign them. Soon the group had booked a U.S. tour. At that point, however, a falling out led to Rutsey's departure.

Desperate, Lee and Lifeson auditioned and hired drummer Neil Peart; soon the trio achieved "international band" status by playing in such exotic places as Florida and Pennsylvania. For the first several years their touring schedule would be incredibly rigorous. As Lee explained to *Rolling Stone*'s David Fricke, "The strategy was, 'There's a gig. We'll go play it.'" Ray Danniels, who managed the band from its inception, elaborated: "It was the drive-till-you-die philosophy." Peart's drumming had given breadth and complexity to the group's sound, and his lyrics were ambitious and unusual, as witnessed by fantasy excursions like "By Tor and the Snow Dog."

relaxed approach to their careers; all three live quiet, domestic lives. As bassist-singer Geddy Lee remarked in *Maclean's,* "it's a darn good job and we do very well. But now, I'm not afraid to say no to Rush. My family's extremely important to me." This mellowed perspective has also permitted Lee, guitarist Alex Lifeson, and drummer-lyricist Neil Peart to demonstrate that their reputation for taking themselves too seriously has been exaggerated. "People have always accused us of being deadly serious, but we all can look back at our albums and see the jokes," Lee insisted in an interview with *Musician*'s J. D. Considine, though he admitted this perspective came with time. "It's funny, when you're younger you seem to have this intentional furrowed brow when you're writing your music. It's like, 'This is serious music!' God knows what serious music is, but when you're a little bit older, you seem to have a lighter hand."

Lightness of touch would probably not have been the attribute that leapt to the minds of Rush fans or critics of the 1970s who attempted to describe the trio. The group's early albums featured science fiction opuses and songs based on the work of ultra-individualist writer Ayn Rand, all set to music jammed with complex time changes, extended solos, and bombastic riffing. Lee's voice, which *Rolling Stone*'s Michael Azerrad called "a shrill screech," has had many detractors over the years. With 1980's *Permanent Waves,* however, the band turned a corner; the album contained their first radio hit—appropriately titled "The Spirit of Radio"—and drew their first respectful press. Though reviews were mixed over the next decade, the group retained a

In 1975 Rush released *Fly by Night,* the first LP with their permanent lineup. But neither *Fly by Night* nor the subsequent release *Caress of Steel* sold impressively. According to Fricke, these two records "bear the scars of the group's naivete." Rush wasn't succeeding, at least by rock business standards. "Then we realized how stupid we were," Lee remembered. "Because of all these people putting pressure on us, we were looking at ourselves through their eyes. From then on, we knew exactly what our direction was going to be, and were determined to have success strictly on our own terms."

Spokesmen of "Prog" Rock

1976's elaborate concept album *2112,* according to John Swenson of *Rolling Stone,* "marked the band's evolution into spokesmen for a lost generation of Seventies rockers influenced by groups as disparate as the Who, Cream, Procol Harum and King Crimson." Featuring songs like "Temples of Syrinx," *2112* grabbed a whole new audience, as did the subsequent Rush tour, which included the group's first appearances in the United Kingdom. *Melody Maker's* Steve Gett reported that Rush, "for a relatively unknown band, went down tremendously." Chris Welch, writing for the same publication, noted that the trio "surprised a lot of people by selling out and getting a standing ovation at their gigs— not bad for a band virtually unknown here until recently." 1976 also saw the release of a double live record, *All the World's a Stage.*

The following year the band came out with *A Farewell to Kings,* which *Melody Maker's* Michael Oldfie called "Rush's best yet." Oldfie was particularly enraptured by "Cygnus X-1;" he summarized the song as "the story of a doomed journey through the universe to the Black Hole of the title." This was only "Book One" of a continuing story, however: "for those of us waiting to get to Cygnus X-1, the next album can't come soon enough," the reviewer continued.

The sequel to *A Farewell to Kings* arrived in 1978. *Hemispheres,* which took longer than the band had anticipated to complete, featured a title track that was meant, according to *Rolling Stone's* Michael Bloom, to complete "Cygnus X-1," although "the musical and thematic references are only tangential." Bloom approved of much of the record's musical content—especially the instrumental "La Villa Strangiato," but had reservations about Peart's lyrics and Lee's "often unnecessarily strident" voice.

"Spirit of Radio" First Hit Single

Rush's real breakthrough came in 1980 with *Permanent Waves.* Fricke claimed that "Rush demonstrate a maturity that even their detractors may have to admire," and expressed particular admiration for the single "The Spirit of Radio;" his review concluded with the contention that "this band is among the very best in its genre." Soon *Rolling Stone* ran a feature about the group's new access to FM radio—thanks to "The Spirit of Radio." The band members owned that the new album reflected a more earthbound set of concerns; ironically, the single and another *Permanent Waves* track—"Natural Science" —were critical of the industry that had given the band the cold shoulder in the past. According to

Swenson, the two songs "carve up the record industry as a pack of charlatans."

Peart admitted that the tone of *Permanent Waves* was "a bit angry," summarizing its message as "Stop bullshitting." Years later he told Bob Mack in *Spin* that he still considered "Radio"—a song that mixed reggae, pop, and metal in a radical new way—"a valid musical gumbo" designed "to represent what radio should be." Swenson observed that "The Spirit of Radio" in all likelihood had "gotten more airplay than Rush's entire catalog put together, and it's brought them a whole new audience." The album made the Top Five.

The band's critical popularity, such as it was, didn't last long. Gett, reviewing 1981's *Moving Pictures* for *Melody Maker,* called the LP "self-indulgent. . . . The album may be technically superb but it really doesn't generate much excitement." He concluded that "A lot of fans will feel betrayed." Rather than presenting more radio-friendly material, the band had put together longer,

> *"People have always accused us of being deadly serious, but we all can look back at our albums and see the jokes."*
> —Geddy Lee

more difficult music at a time when critics were hoping for greater simplicity. But, as Fricke had noted, "critics don't count at all" in Rush's genre. As Lifeson explained to Brian Karrigan in *Melody Maker,* "the media isn't something that we tend to worry about in the band any more. It's more of a management or record company thing." 1981 also saw the release of a double live album, *Exit. . .Stage Left,* that sold tremendously.

In and Out of Favor in the '80s

But Rush's albums always had a substantial audience, whether reviews were favorable or not. Harrigan called *Signals* of 1983 Rush's "major breakthrough," observing that "the album was packed with diverse musical strands and had such an aura of celebration about it that it suggested the band themselves had found a great release and allowed everything they had to come through." Harrigan reported that British concert audiences "greeted Rush in complete awe." By 1984, with its new release, *Grace Under Pressure,* Rush was—

according to Derek Oliver of *Melody Maker*—"one of the world's most popular rock bands."

Rush's new sound was influenced by British new wave pop from the likes of U2, Simple Minds, the Police, and Ultravox. Oliver was struck by *Grace Under Pressure*'s "accessibility," while acknowledging that it was "seen by many as Rush's most adventurous album to date." And like numerous other interviewers, Oliver commented on how "immensely likeable" he found Geddy Lee.

The following year Rush released *Power Windows*, which *Rolling Stone*'s Fricke praised as a record that "may well be the missing link between [English progressive-rockers] Yes and [seminal English punk band] The Sex Pistols." The reviewer referred to the LP's single "The Big Money" as "the best of Rush's Cool Wave experiments to date"; he commented that on *Power Windows*, as on *Grace Under Pressure*, the band "tightened up their sidelong suites and rhythmic abstractions into balled-up song fists, art-rock blasts of angular, slashing guitar, spatial keyboards [played by Lee] and hyperpercussion, all resolved with forthright melodic sense."

End to "Obsession"

1987 saw the release of *Hold Your Fire*, which contained the single "Time Stand Still," featuring singer Aimee Mann of the group 'Til Tuesday on backing vocals. According to a *Maclean's* reporter, after the tour for this album the three members of Rush returned to Canada sick and virtually estranged from their families. At that point, according to Lee, he, Lifeson, and Peart "discovered that we didn't have to be obsessed about Rush 24 hours a day." They arranged to spend more time doing other things; Lee would get ten days off with his family for every three weeks of touring, while Lifeson and Peart devoted themselves to athletic pursuits.

Hold Your Fire—along with *Power Windows*—provided the material for 1989's double live set *A Show of Hands*. Azerrad panned the record as a sterile, bombastic marathon, observing that "the music has the emotional emptiness of bad jazz fusion." By this time *Melody Maker* had fallen out of love with Rush's sound; Mick Mercer's acidic review of *A Show of Hands* revealed the group's lowered status with the publication: "The removal of Rush from society," Mercer fantasized, "as with the gradication of tuberculosis, was greeted with the establishment of internationally agreed public holidays." Though the album was rather unpopular with other critics as well, a *People* reviewer spoke highly of the 1989 *Show of Hands* videocassette: "Even those who don't usually enjoy Rush may find this 14-song concert video by the Canadian power-pop trio to their liking."

A New Respectability

Rush earned some accolades for their 1989 studio album *Presto*, released by their new label, Atlantic. *Stereo Review* called the record "proof that progressive rock is alive and well and in capable hands." The LP included the single "Show Don't Tell," the message of which was so popular with some American schoolteachers that the video for the song was actually shown in their classrooms. David Hiltbrand remarked in *People* that the band's "rock formalism has never been better realized," though he had less admiration for "the cartoonishly high pitch and overwrought intensity" of Lee's voice.

Another Atlantic album, *Chronicles*, was released in 1990, and by 1991 Rush had a new hit album on their hands, *Roll the Bones*. The latter LP entered the *Billboard* album chart at Number Three, and if it didn't please everyone—Craig Tomashoff of *People* called it "audible proof that dinosaurs still roam the earth"—it sold faster than any previous Rush album. In addition, the single "Dreamline" was for a time the most requested song on U.S. rock stations, and the concert tour that supported the album was a smash in a dry concert season. The admiration expressed for Rush by a variety of groundbreaking alternative bands of the early 1990s—and the trio's clear influence even on many bands that did not mention them—gave Rush a new respectability in the music world.

From their days as a teenaged blues-metal act to their international fame as progressive rock's longest lasting big act, Rush have stuck to their vision; critical attitudes have changed, but the trio's commitment to themselves and their audience have paid off handsomely. As Lee remarked in a *Guitar Player* interview, "It's such a satisfying musical situation that, whenever push comes to shove, we always count our blessings. It's something you appreciate more the older you get."

Selected discography

Rush, Moon Records, 1974.

On Mercury Records

Fly by Night (includes "By-Tor and the Snow Dog"), 1975.
Caress of Steel, 1975.
2112 (includes "Temples of Syrinx"), 1976.

All the World's a Stage, 1976.
A Farewell to Kings (includes "Cygnus X-1"), 1977.
Hemispheres (includes "La Villa Strangiato"), 1978.
Permanent Waves (includes "The Spirit of Radio" and "Natural Science"), 1980.
Moving Pictures, 1981.
Exit. . .Stage Left, 1981.
Signals, 1983.
Grace Under Pressure, 1984.
Power Windows (includes "The Big Money"), 1985.
Hold Your Fire (includes "Time Stand Still"), 1987.
A Show of Hands, 1989.

On Atlantic Records

Presto (includes "Show Don't Tell"), 1989.
Chronicles, 1990.
Roll the Bones (includes "Dreamline"), 1991.

Sources

Guitar Player, September 1991.
Maclean's, September 30, 1991.
Melody Maker, July 23, 1977; November 5, 1977; May 12, 1979; February 28, 1981; November 7, 1981; May 28, 1983; May 5, 1984; January 28, 1989.
Musician, April 1990.
People, April 24, 1989; January 22, 1990; November 18, 1991.
Rolling Stone, March 22, 1979; May 1, 1980; June 26, 1980; May 28, 1981; January 30, 1986; April 20, 1989.
Spin, March 1992.
Stereo Review, April 1990.

—*Simon Glickman*

Sam and Dave

Soul duo

When Sam Moore and Dave Prater were inducted into the Rock and Roll Hall of Fame in 1992, it was largely in recognition of their hard-driving soul hits of the 1960s. Songs like "You Don't Know Like I Know," "Hold On, I'm Comin'," "Soul Man," and "I Thank You" made the duo one of the most popular soul acts of the era. Sam and Dave were part of the Memphis Sound, which revolved around the Stax and Volt family of record labels and included soul stars such as Otis Redding and Wilson Pickett, songwriters like Isaac Hayes, and songs that featured backup musicians like Booker T and the MGs and the Memphis Horns. It was through their energetic stage show that Sam and Dave earned their nickname Double Dynamite.

Born in Miami, Sam Moore sang with a gospel group that toured Florida before turning to soul music. His mother was a teacher, his father a deacon, and his grandfather a Baptist preacher. According to Gerri Hirshey's *Nowhere to Run,* Moore was approached by the manager of the famous gospel group the Soul Stirrers to replace Sam Cooke, who had left the group to start his own soul and pop career. Moore was reportedly ready to leave Miami and tour with the Soul Stirrers, but he changed his mind after attending a Jackie Wilson show and decided he wanted to sing like Jackie Wilson.

Moore met Dave Prater while working the King of Hearts Club in Miami. Prater was a laborer's son from Ocilla, Georgia. He went to Miami in 1957 to get a job singing, but he was working as a short-order cook and baker's assistant to make ends meet. One night in 1961, Prater joined Moore on stage during a segment of Moore's act that involved audience participation. The two singers seemed to click, and the Sam and Dave duo was born.

Moore recalled in *Melody Maker,* "We didn't really have a recording contract in those days. Some of the records we made were distributed around Florida. . . . Then we had a contract with Roulette, but they didn't do anything. They weren't really in the soul bag, they were more into jazz and pop." Moore and Prater met Atlantic Records producer Jerry Wexler while they were recording for Roulette. Wexler was interested in them and finally signed the duo in 1964. He immediately sent them to Memphis to record on the Atlantic subsidiary, Stax Records. "We recorded in Memphis because Jerry wanted that sound. It wouldn't have been any good for us to record in New York, because we wanted a new sound . . . what eventually became the Memphis Sound," Moore told *Melody Maker.*

For the Record. . .

D uo comprised of **Samuel David Moore** (born October 12, 1935, in Miami, FL), and **David Prater** (born May 9, 1937, in Ocilla, GA; died from injuries sustained in a car accident, 1988).

Formed as duo in Miami in 1961, playing various club dates; signed recording contract with Roulette in the early 1960s; signed to Stax Records by Atlantic Records producer Jerry Wexler, 1964; toured extensively and scored big hits in late 1960s with songs like "Hold On! I'm a Comin'" and "Soul Man"; duo dissolved in the early 1970s, except for a few occasional engagements; interest in the group rekindled by the Blues Brothers' rendition of "Soul Man," 1980; Prater found another "Sam" and performed with him as Sam and Dave, beginning in 1981; Moore began performing solo following Prater's death in 1988 and appeared in the film *Tapeheads,* Pacific Arts, 1989.

Awards: Inducted into the Rock and Roll Hall of Fame, 1992.

Addresses: *Agent*—Sam and Dave's Legendary Sam Moore, c/o Hallmark Entertainment, Inc., 8033 Sunset Blvd., #1000, Los Angeles, CA 90046.

Leaders of the Memphis Sound

At Stax, Sam and Dave were assigned to the songwriting-production team of Isaac Hayes and David Porter. The two singers were already "like Siamese twins when they came to us. They were incredibly tight," recalled Memphis musician and producer Steve Cropper in *Nowhere to Run.*

Moore told *Melody Maker,* "The sound that we wanted didn't just happen. We worked at it, sometimes we'd be in the studio at four and five in the morning. . . . We had to get something new. And that's what Hayes and Porter did. Those fellas came up with an original sound for Sam and Dave." Rock historian Charlie Gillett noted the gospel roots of Sam and Dave's sound in his book *The Sound of the City,* writing, "The use of two voices answering each other in a rapid dialogue at times, echoing each other's phrases at others, and singing harmony in the choruses was a standard device of real—that is, church-based—gospel singing. . . . With Stax, Sam and Dave made records that surpassed the excitement of earlier duo performances because they were answering not only each other but the encouraging riffs of the band."

The year 1966 began with Sam and Dave's first chart hit on Stax, "You Don't Know Like I Know." While it only reached the bottom of *Billboard*'s Top 100 pop charts, it was a solid rhythm and blues hit, peaking at Number Seven and staying on the R & B charts for 14 weeks. The song was followed by "Hold On, I'm Comin'," the duo's first song to hit it big. As Moore related in *Melody Maker,* "'You Don't Know Like I Know' got us known, but it was 'Hold On, I'm Comin'' that really exploded." The song became a Number One R & B hit.

The duo released two more top ten rhythm and blues hits in 1966, "Said I Wasn't Gonna Tell Nobody" and "You Got Me Hummin'." They started 1967 off with the soulful ballad "When Something Is Wrong With My Baby," which went to Number Two on the R & B charts. In the spring of 1967 they went on tour as part of the Stax/Volt Revue. Starting off with seven nights at New York's Apollo Theater, the five-week tour featured Otis Redding as the headliner and Sam and Dave as the number two act. The tour concluded in England and Europe, where Sam and Dave would return later in the year on the strength of their biggest hit, "Soul Man."

"Soul Man" Topped the Charts

"Soul Man" was released in the fall of 1967. It had sold a million copies within five weeks, while Sam and Dave were in Europe on the final leg of their Sweet Soul Tour. The song was a Number Two pop hit for three weeks on *Billboard*'s charts and stayed at Number One on the R & B charts for seven weeks. On the Sweet Soul Tour, Sam and Dave were accompanied by a full orchestra and soul singers Arthur Conley and Percy Sledge.

The duo followed up their hugely successful "Soul Man" in early 1968 with "I Thank You," another top ten hit on both the R & B and pop charts. According to Peter Guralnick in his book *Sweet Soul Music,* "Sam and Dave were becoming the hottest stage act in the country. . . . They combined the frenzied activity of James Brown and the vocal dynamism of Wilson Pickett with the rough gospel harmonies." For the next couple of years, the Sam and Dave Revue gave concerts and toured college campuses in a large bus that carried their 35-piece assemblage. According to *Time* magazine, their college tour in the fall of 1968 grossed approximately $1.5 million.

The Breakup

Moore's personal differences with Prater stemmed from a 1968 incident in which Prater shot his own wife in a domestic dispute. Moore recalled in *Nowhere to Run,* "I told him I'd work and travel with him, but that I would never speak or look at him." As a result, Moore and Prater would usually arrive separately for their shows. After 1969 Prater showed up unpredictably and was even absent from some performances of the Sam and Dave Revue. Author Gerri Hirshey noted that they were never again interviewed together.

No doubt their personal differences were exacerbated by Moore's heroin addiction. As Moore told Hirshey in *Nowhere to Run,* "Word got out [that] Sam and Dave [were] bad news. We were reduced to playing toilets. I'd lie, I'd miss shows. I'd find guys in my dressing room who'd heard about my habit. And they were always there with more." It was not until 1981, some six months after Moore and Prater's final performance together, that Moore was able to kick his habit by enrolling in a special program.

Interest in Sam and Dave was rekindled in the late 1970s by the Blues Brothers' rendition of "Soul Man." Comedians John Belushi and Dan Ackroyd first performed the song as part of their routine on the television show *Saturday Night Live,* then later in the 1980 film *The Blues Brothers.* By 1981, Prater had found another "Sam" and was performing with him as Sam and Dave. Sam Moore filed a lawsuit contending that Prater had no rights to the name "Sam and Dave." In 1985 a federal judge in Los Angeles enjoined Atlantic Records from selling an album and single under the name Sam and Dave that featured Dave Prater and Sam Daniels, the unauthorized replacement for the original Sam.

Dave Prater was killed in an automobile accident in 1988. In the years following Prater's death, Moore began a solo tour as "Sam and Dave's Legendary Sam Moore." In 1992, a retrospective LP, *Soul Men,* was released by Rhino/Atlantic.

Selected discography

Singles

"I Need Love," Roulette, 1964.

"No More Pain," Roulette, 1964.
"It Feels So Nice," Roulette, 1965.
"You Don't Know Like I Know," Stax, 1966.
"Hold On, I'm Comin'," Stax, 1966.
"When Something Is Wrong With My Baby," Stax, 1967.
"Soul Man," Stax, 1967.
"I Thank You," Stax, 1968.
"Soul Sister, Brown Sugar," Atlantic, 1968.
"Born Again," Atlantic, 1969.

Albums

Sam and Dave, Roulette, 1966.
Hold On, I'm Comin', Stax, 1966.
Double Dynamite, Stax, 1966.
Soul Man, Stax, 1967.
I Thank You, Atlantic, 1968, reissued, Rhino/Atlantic, 1992.
Best of Sam and Dave, Atlantic, 1969.
Back Atcha, United Artists, 1975.
Soul Men, Rhino/Atlantic, 1992.

Sources

Books

Gillett, Charlie, *The Sound of the City: The Rise of Rock 'n' Roll,* Dell, 1972.
Guralnick, Peter, *Sweet Soul Music,* Harper & Row, 1986.
Hirshey, Gerri, *Nowhere to Run: The Story of Soul Music,* Times Books, 1984.
Joel Whitburn's Top Pop Singles, 1955-1990, Record Research, 1991.
Joel Whitburn's Top R & B Singles, 1942-1988, Record Research, 1988.

Periodicals

Billboard, December 28, 1968; July 18, 1970; August 31, 1985.
Melody Maker, July 26, 1969; January 31, 1970; March 24, 1973.
New York Times, December 16, 1968.
Rolling Stone, February 6, 1992.
Time, October 25, 1968.

—David Bianco

Artie Shaw

Clarinetist, bandleader, composer, writer

Artie Shaw had everything at the height of his career. One of the most popular and lauded musicians of the late 1930s and 1940s, he formed successful bands almost at will, earned up to an estimated $30,000 a week, and married some of the most desirable women in America. Yet he disbanded groups soon after he formed them, scorned the money he earned, and divorced eight wives—some within a few months after marriage. At the age of 44, he simply walked away from his greatest accomplishment, confirming what author George Bernard Shaw is credited as having said, "There are two tragedies in life. One is not to get your heart's desire. The other is to get it." Gunther Schuller noted in his book *The Swing Era: The Development of Jazz, 1930-1945* that to begin to solve the mystery of Artie Shaw one must answer "how the rather mediocre clarinet player that Shaw was" early in his career could become within ten years "one of the two or three most outstanding clarinetists in all of jazz—some would say *the* greatest of them all."

The desire that precipitated this transformation developed in Shaw's childhood. When he was seven years old, his family moved from his birthplace, New York City, to New Haven, Connecticut, where, for the first time, Shaw—née Arthur Arshawsky—was reviled for being Jewish. Already a sensitive child, he withdrew further. "I had an enormous need to *belong,* to have some feeling of roots, to become part of a community, all out of a terrible sense of insecurity coupled with an inordinate desire to prove myself worthy," Shaw recounted years later in his autobiography, *The Trouble With Cinderella: An Outline of Identity.*

Shaw subsequently reasoned that money, success, and fame would fulfill his yearnings and felt he could achieve these as a musician—first as a saxophonist, then as a clarinetist. He quit school and did nothing but play his instrument. "I went at it daily for as much as six or seven hours," Shaw wrote in his autobiography, "and then quit only because my teeth ached and the inside of my lower lip was ragged and cut from the constant pressure of the mouthpiece and reed." He was only 14 years old.

Fervid Dedication to Craft

Shaw learned that any great artist's latent talent is brought to the fore by desire and dedication to his craft. For a person to create something he "must be prepared to spend his life at it—if he wants to do it well, or even as well as he can. This is a matter of self-dedication," he reasoned in *The Trouble With Cinderella.* And so for the next ten years Shaw did just that: he practiced, learned from local musicians, sat in with local bands, became a studio musician, went on tour with larger bands, played with theater orchestras, learned to arrange music, and began composing. In 1936 Shaw formed the first of many bands he would subsequently lead.

By 1938 Shaw had "developed a real ability to spin long, elegant, vibrant, seamless lines, almost as if he [were] trying to capture on his clarinet what a violin, without the need to breathe, could do so naturally and effectively," Schuller claimed. *Down Beat*'s Howard Mandel, critiquing recordings from that period, declared, "In Shaw's lips and hands the clarinet bent as pliantly as a blade of grass, it thrilled him to make glissandi, fast or sad melodies, and wonderful virtuosic turns."

Popular Success Unwanted

No one "could have convinced me of the misery I was heading for in my pursuit of the same old $ucce$$-Fame-Happiness-Cinderella constellation," Shaw wrote in his autobiography. As his artistic playing began to change and mature, so did his artistic vision. "Shaw was, in his best years, an uncompromising searcher for the lofty and the expressive, for real musical substance, not only in his own playing but in the styles and concepts of his bands," Schuller observed. But society's definition of musical success differed; in the field of popular entertainment Shaw was trying to create art.

The incredible popularity of the 1939 recording "Begin the Beguine," an old Cole Porter song, thrust Shaw and his band into the disparaging limelight. To his chagrin, this and other recordings, including "Frenesi," "Summit Ridge Drive," and "Star Dust," became successful for what he saw as the wrong reasons. He was creating music to which he wanted people to listen, not jitterbug. Years later, he told John S. Wilson of the *New York Times,* "If they want to dance, it's their business. My business is to play music that is very, very hearable. Mozart wrote dance music but nobody dances to it. It's a matter of training an audience."

Shaw was never able to control his listeners. "From that general period until 1954, Shaw sifted in and out of music like a reprise," Robert Lewis Taylor noted in the *New Yorker.* "He worked up a number of fine bands, but scuttled them quickly when they grew popular; he felt crushed by success and was angered by adulation." Shaw even suffered several nervous breakdowns and retreated from the music business many times only to return with new groups and new combinations: small ensembles, large groups, a jazz group surrounded by a symphonic ensemble of strings, woodwinds, and his famous Gramercy Five harpsichord. But nothing worked to his satisfaction. "The fact that Shaw had at least eight different bands between 1936 and 1955 . . . is symptomatic of both his searching and his confusion, and ultimately of his inability to find what he was looking for," Schuller contended in *The Swing Era.*

Walked Away at His Peak

Shaw quit playing his clarinet in 1954 and left the music business. He cited countless reasons for his sudden departure: the insensitivity and ignorance he encountered in the popular music business; the stifling effect of the public's continued demand for his past hit recordings; creative stagnation; and his desire to pursue other interests such as creative writing. But these justifications, Christopher Porterfield noted in *Time,* have hidden to dissuade "the conviction, still held by many fans, critics, and fellow musicians, that a gift like Shaw's is something you just don't abandon." Shaw returned in 1983—during a resurgent interest in big bands—to help reorganize a band under his name, but did not perform himself, rendering it inconsequential.

In his musical career and other endeavors, Shaw sought goals and truths—some real and some imagined. But the drive that propelled him toward those ideals also pushed them out of his reach. "The closer an artist gets to perfection," he explained to *People*'s Richard Lemon, "the further up his idea of perfection is, so he's chasing a receding horizon." Schuller concluded that this personal sense of unattainable achievement should not have dimmed Shaw's place among us: "That Shaw was able in his *finest* accomplishments to sweep us along in his searching and discoveries and at one point—1939—represent the best the Swing Era had to offer, we can hold forever in highest esteem." But Shaw, a man who walked away from music when his tone was "crystalline, his lines distinctively long and sinuous, full of witty, sometimes startling interjections and exuberant flurries," Porterfield commented, leaves a lasting impression that is forever muddied, stained by the mystery of "the richness of what was, the wistfulness of what might have been."

Selected writings

The Trouble With Cinderella: An Outline of Identity (autobiography), Farrar, Straus, and Young, 1952.
I Love You, I Hate You, Drop Dead! Three Variations on a Theme (novellas), Fleet, 1965.
The Best of Intentions: And Other Stories, John Daniel, 1989.

Selected compositions

Composer of "Interlude in B flat," 1936; "Free for All," 1937; "Any Old Time," 1938; "Nightmare," 1938; "Moonray," 1939; "Back Bay Shuffle," 1939; "Summit Ridge Drive," 1940; and "Concerto for Clarinet," 1940.

Selected discography

Singles

"Begin the Beguine," Bluebird, 1938.

"Any Old Time," Bluebird, 1938.
"Nightmare," Bluebird, 1938.
"Traffic Jam," Bluebird, 1939.
"Frenesi," Victor, 1940.
"Summit Ridge Drive," Victor, 1940.
"Star Dust," Victor, 1940.
"The Blues," Victor, 1940.
"Concerto for Clarinet," Victor, 1940.
"Moon Glow," Victor, 1941.
"Evensong," Victor, 1942.
"Suite No. 8," Victor, 1942.
"September Song," Victor, 1945.
"Little Jazz," Victor, 1945.

Reissues and compilations

Artie Shaw: A Legacy, Book of the Month Club.
(With Mel Tormé and the Mel-Tones) *Artie Shaw & His Orchestra, Vols. 1-2*, Musicraft.
The Best of Artie Shaw, MCA.
The Complete Artie Shaw, Vols. 1-7, RCA/Bluebird.
The Complete Gramercy Five Sessions, RCA/Bluebird.
Free for All, Portrait Masters.
The Last Recordings, Musicmasters, 1992.
Personal Best, Bluebird/RCA, 1992.
The Uncollected Artie Shaw, Vols. 1-5, Hindsight.

Sources

Books

Schuller, Gunther, *The Swing Era: The Development of Jazz, 1930-1945*, Oxford University Press, 1989.
Shaw, Artie, *The Trouble With Cinderella: An Outline of Identity*, Farrar, Straus, and Young, 1952.

Periodicals

Down Beat, November 1980; April 1985; February 1986.
High Fidelity, November 1984.
Newsweek, January 2, 1984.
New Yorker, May 19, 1962.
New York Times, August 16, 1985.
New York Times Book Review, April 18, 1965.
People, June 1, 1981; October 29, 1984.
Publishers Weekly, August 4, 1989.
Stereo Review, June 1981; October 1982.
Time, May 18, 1992.

—*Rob Nagel*

Siouxsie and the Banshees

Rock band

Siouxsie and the Banshees began their career as fans of the Sex Pistols but eventually evolved into arguably the only original British punk rock act to survive into the 1990s, outlasting the Sex Pistols and even the punk movement itself. Indeed, the band has become highly popular, as evidenced by their lofty positions on the British pop charts, in spite of—perhaps even because of—their uneven output and brooding, abrasive style.

Led by punk's original princess, Siouxsie Sioux, who was born Susan Dallion in Chislehurst, England, the Banshees got their less-than-organized start in London in 1976. Part of a clique of Sex Pistols fans known as the Bromley Contingent, Siouxsie and her original lineup—bassist Steven Severin, guitarist Marco Pirroni, and future Sex Pistol Sid Vicious on drums—first took the stage at London's 100 Club Punk Festival on September 20, 1976. They played a tortured, rambling version of "The Lord's Prayer"—until they became bored. "We weren't musicians," Siouxsie admitted, as quoted by Jon Savage in his book *England's Dreaming*.

"There was a vacant space in the [100 Club] show, and I volunteered, 'We've got a band.' We hadn't. So the next day we rehearsed with Sid on drums. Billy Idol said yes at the time but vanished. *The Cry of the Banshees* had been on television a couple of nights before and we thought banshee was a great word."

Visually, the band began as a contrasting political statement: Siouxsie with her swastika arm band and dominatrix look, backed by three pretty-boy musicians. Though she eventually shied away from punk's nihilistic politics and safety-pin-pierced skin, Siouxsie avidly embraced punk's ethos. Punk cleared the air of what many saw as rock's gaudy commercialism and lazy superstars. The genre—often described as anti-entertainment—offered women the opportunity to fully participate in the creation of the music and involved a new aesthetic that would completely reform rock's standards. "One of the songs we did was 'She Loves You' by the Beatles and 'Young Love' by the Bay City Rollers," Siouxsie told Savage. "It was just taking the piss out of all the things we hated. What would you like to throw in for a shock tactic? What can we mutilate and destroy?"

Siouxsie recalled the band's early punk days in the *Detroit Free Press:* "The beginning was living for the moment rather than predicting or reminiscing. At the same time, we had a certain arrogance [about] not signing record deals, because of [the record companies'] limited idea of how long something like this would last. So even then, there seemed to be a notion that we wanted to last awhile." Despite their resistance, in 1977 the group released a gloomy single, "Hong Kong Garden," before signing with Polydor and releasing *The Scream* in 1978.

Full of icy wails and macabre imagery, the album, which included a sardonic version of the Beatles single "Helter Skelter," was released in England and reached only a limited audience in the United States. *The Scream* also marked the beginning of what was to become the band's continually changing lineup. Vicious departed for dark martyrdom with the Sex Pistols and was replaced by Kenny Morris. John McKay took over for Pirroni, who joined the group Adam and the Ants. Bassist Severin remained and would, along with Siouxsie, see the band into the 1990s. It was not until 1988 that the Banshees's personnel remained static for two consecutive tours and albums.

In June of 1978, Siouxsie and the Banshees had the distinction of being featured in *The Punk Rock Movie,* a series of 8mm clips shot at London's famed Roxy club by guerilla filmmaker Don Letts. Other participants in the film included the Sex Pistols, the Clash, the Slits, X Ray Spex, and Johnny Thunders.

Compared to 1979's mournful *Join Hands* LP, *The Scream* seemed absolutely sunny. Yet *Join Hands* established many of the characteristics that would typify the Banshees' sound: Siouxsie's atonal singing riding over manic percussion beds and eerie, dense guitar arrangements. *Join Hands* also hinted at a break with punk's savage aim; Siouxsie appeared to owe as much to artist and singer Yoko Ono's art-music permutations as she did to the punk group the Clash. Two days into a British tour to support the album, McKay and Morris abruptly quit. Percussionist Budgie joined the group on drums, while Robert Smith of the Cure filled the guitar void and completed the tour.

Toured the U.S.

Siouxsie and the Banshees entered the 1980s with the release of *Kaleidoscope,* a recording that continued to demonstrate increased nuance and subtlety; melody and arrangement crept into the songs in place of an angry wall of noise. Since the group was again lacking a guitarist, Steve Jones, a graduate of the Sex Pistols, and former Magazine guitarist John McGeoch were called in to share the duty on the album. McGeoch decided to stay with the band and for the first time, Siouxsie and the Banshees toured the United States.

With a somewhat secure lineup, the Banshees continued to move away from the stark aspects of punk without abandoning its egalitarian ideals. In 1981 the group released *Juju*. Called "strong and satisfying" in *The Trouser Press Record Guide,* the album featured increasingly powerful and complex arrangements, anchored by Siouxsie's improving vocals and apocalyptic poetry.

By the latter part of 1981, alternative music—literally an alternative to mainstream rock and commercial radio programming—was taking hold in America. Assisted by the loose, grass-roots network of college radio stations, many new bands representing the rebellious nature of punk began successfully touring in the United States. Siouxsie Sioux became as highly regarded for her forbidding fashion presentation as she was for her music. The "look," initiated largely by Siouxsie and still present at alternative concerts well into the 1990s, was characterized by dark eyeliner, jet-black hair cut in a Cleopatra-like bob, a ghostly pallor, and the requisite black clothing.

In 1982 the group signed with Geffen Records and released *A Kiss in the Dreamhouse,* an LP more experimental and less pop than *Juju*. Guitarist McGeoch fell ill early in the promotional tour for the album and was replaced by Robert Smith, who once again came to the rescue by rounding out the band.

Siouxsie, together with Budgie—with whom she was romantically involved and would later marry—formed the group the Creatures. This endeavor was to serve as an artistic point of departure from the Banshees. They released a five-song, voice-and-percussion EP, followed by two other LPs—*Feast* in 1983 and *Boomerang* six years later.

Hyaena Heralded Band's New Sound

A live Banshees LP, *Nocturne,* recorded with Smith on guitar during two nights at the Royal Albert Hall, was released in 1983. Though Smith's band, the Cure, was about to reach international success, he remained with the Banshees for the recording of *Hyaena,* released in 1984. *Hyaena* served as the hallmark of the "new" Siouxsie and the Banshees sound: an eerie blend of industrial rhythms and symphonic arrangements made the music more accessible. Another Beatles cover, "Dear Prudence," showcased Siouxsie's lucid singing and growing affection for psychedelia. The departing Smith was then replaced by former Clock DVA guitarist John Carruthers.

The mid-1980s were Siouxsie's self-described "dark period," during which she feared being written off by fans and critics alike. Prompting these fears were a broken kneecap, suffered in a 1985 show, and her decision to move away from her signature style, which was being imitated around the world. As she explained in the *Detroit Free Press,* "People were even calling it the Siouxsie look, which really scared me. When they're selling it in shops and models start to look like you, that's when it's time for a change. I think the changes are more compulsive than planned, but I think it's vital to be able to continue and not turn into something you don't want to be."

1986 and 1987 were relatively quiet years for Siouxsie and her Banshees; *Tinderbox,* a warm LP that featured the hit "Cities in Dust" appeared, followed by *Through the Looking Glass,* an eclectic anthology of other artists' songs. In late 1987 a fourth Banshee, multi-instrumentalist Martin McCarrick, was added to the group to

---

"Performing was just taking the piss out of all the things we hated. What would you like to throw in for a shock tactic? What can we mutilate and destroy?"
—Siouxsie Sioux

---

play keyboards. Jon Klein from Specimen also joined the group to replace yet another exiting guitarist, Carruthers.

Sales Increased in Late '80s

Peepshow was released in 1988 and featured high-tech dance grooves and alarming lyrics. Though it was wicked cabaret to many critics, *Peepshow* became the Banshees' then-best-selling record. Two years later, longtime producer Mike Hedges was replaced by Stephen Hague for the recording of *Superstition*. Hague had had great success in creating pop accessibility for such alternative acts as the Pet Shop Boys, New Order, and Pere Ubu.

Superstition, released in 1991, was perhaps the band's most cohesive work to date. The success of the alternative radio hit single "Kiss Them for Me" eventually swelled into a mainstream breakthrough, aided by

Siouxsie and the Banshees' featured spot on the summer 1991 Lollapalooza concert tour. Showcasing other out-of-the-mainstream acts like Jane's Addiction, Nine Inch Nails, and Ice-T, the underground tour was the summer's only consistently successful concert draw.

Siouxsie and the Banshees have shown remarkable adaptability over the years, overcoming personnel changes that would have spelled the end of most bands. Musically, their sound evolved enough from its original punk roots to appeal not only to fans of that genre but also to alternative and even pop aficionados.

Selected discography

The Scream, Polydor, 1978.
Join Hands, Polydor, 1979.
Kaleidoscope, PVC, 1980.
Juju, PVC, 1981.
Once Upon a Time—The Singles, PVC, 1981.
A Kiss in the Dreamhouse, Polydor, 1982.
Nocturne, Geffen, 1983.
Hyaena, Geffen, 1984.
Cities in Dust (EP), Geffen, 1985.
Tinderbox, Geffen, 1986.
Through the Looking Glass, Geffen, 1987.
Peepshow, Geffen, 1988.
The Peel Sessions, Strange Fruit, 1991.
Superstition, Geffen, 1991.

Contributed single "Cities in Dust" to *Out of Bounds* (film soundtrack), 1986, and "Face to Face" to *Batman Returns* (film soundtrack), Warner Bros., 1992.

Sources

Books

Rock of Ages: The Rolling Stone History of Rock and Roll, edited by Ken Tucker, Summit Books, 1986.
The Rolling Stone Encyclopedia of Rock and Roll, edited by Jon Pareles and Patricia Romanowski, Rolling Stone Press/Summit Books, 1983.
The Rolling Stone Rock Almanac, Collier Books, 1983.
Savage, Jon, *England's Dreaming,* St. Martin's Press, 1991.
The Trouser Press Record Guide, Fourth Edition, edited by Ira Robbins, Collier Books, 1991.

Periodicals

Chatelaine, February 1989.
Detroit Free Press, December 6, 1991.
Library Bulletin, September 1991.
New Musical Express, September 24, 1988.
People, June 9, 1986; April 27, 1987.
Stereo Review, April 1986; January 1989.
Variety, June 18, 1986; October 26, 1988.

Additional information for this profile was obtained from a Warner Bros. press release, 1992, and a Geffen Records press release, 1991.

—Stewart Francke

Stephen Sondheim

Composer, lyricist

"If you told me to write a love song tonight," Broadway composer and lyricist Stephen Sondheim told Samuel G. Freedman in the *New York Times Magazine,* "I'd have a lot of trouble. But if you tell me to write a love song about a girl with a red dress who goes into a bar and is on her fifth martini and is falling off her chair, that's a lot easier and it makes me free to say anything I want." Redefining the concept of American musicals, the composer is known for peopling his productions with complex characters, including murderous barbers, lascivious fairy-tale figures, and presidential assassins. While Sondheim has garnered numerous prestigious honors throughout his career, his works are sometimes considered controversial for their serious subject matter and have often elicited mixed response from reviewers. A writer for *Opera News,* though, stated that "the richest, most complex voice in American music history . . . does not serve up happy endings. [Sondheim] makes you think and feel and quite often, admit unpleasant truths. His songs are at once simple and multi-textured, easily grasped and elusive; the deeper you mine, the richer the lode."

Born March 22, 1930, in New York City, Sondheim grew up in the affluent atmosphere of Central Park West in Manhattan. His father was a dress manufacturer, and his mother was the firm's fashion designer and an interior decorator. Although Sondheim played piano at four years old, his interest in theater began five years later when his father took him to a production of the Broadway musical *Very Warm for May* in 1939. "The curtain went up and revealed a piano. A butler took a duster and brushed it up, tinkling the keys," Sondheim divulged to William A. Henry III in *Time.* "I thought that was thrilling." The event was one of the happier moments in Sondheim's childhood before his parent's divorce. After his mother won custody of Sondheim, she denied the boy any contact with his father. "She would have members of her family follow me to see if I met him in secret," Sondheim disclosed later in *Time.* "She would telephone his apartment to see if I answered, then hang up. I was a substitute for him, and she took out all her anger and craziness on me. . . . It was not a great relationship."

Friends With the Hammersteins

A few years after his parents divorced, Sondheim found a close friend in a boy his age named Jamie Hammerstein. Jamie's father was lyricist Oscar Hammerstein II, who wrote the songs for *Very Warm for May* as well as for many other Broadway hits, including *South Pacific* and *Oklahoma!* invited to the Hammerstein's family farm in Doyleston, Pennsylvania, when he was 12 years old.

Born Stephen Joshua Sondheim, March 22, 1930, in New York, NY; son of Herbert Sondheim (a dress manufacturer) and Janet Sondheim Leshin (a fashion designer and interior decorator; maiden name, Fox). *Education:* Williams College, B.A. (magna cum laude), 1950; graduate study in music composition and theory with Milton Babbitt for two years; studied privately with Oscar Hammerstein II.

Lyricist and composer of American musicals, including *West Side Story,* 1957, *Gypsy,* 1959, *A Funny Thing Happened on the Way to the Forum,* 1962, *Anyone Can Whistle,* 1964, *Do I Hear a Waltz?,* 1965, *Company,* 1970, *Follies,* 1971, *A Little Night Music* (includes "Send in the Clowns"), 1973, *Pacific Overtures,* 1976, *Sweeney Todd, the Demon Barber of Fleet Street,* 1979, *Merrily We Roll Along,* 1981, *Sunday in the Park With George,* 1984, *Into the Woods* (includes "No One Is Alone"), 1989, and *Assassins,* 1991. Lyricist and composer for Leonard Bernstein's Broadway production *Candide,* 1973, and for music for television and movies, including *Evening Primrose,* 1966, *Reds,* 1981, and *Dick Tracy,* 1990. Contributed to Barbra Streisand's LP *Broadway Album,* 1985.

Awards: Numerous citations, including Grammy awards, Tony awards, and New York Drama Critics awards for best musical; Pulitzer Prize, 1985, for *Sunday in the Park With George.*

Addresses: *Home*—246 East 49th St., New York, NY 10017. *Office*—c/o Flora Roberts, 65 East 55th St., New York, NY 10022.

Sondheim remained for the summer. He found a family substitute in the Hammersteins when his mother, who had bought a house in Doyleston that autumn, commuted to her job in Manhattan. Jamie Hammerstein told *Time* that "by Christmas, Stephen was more a Hammerstein than a Sondheim." Surrogate father to the adolescent Sondheim, Oscar Hammerstein was also his musical mentor in the years that followed. After he wrote a musical entitled *By George* at boarding school, the 15-year-old Sondheim requested the elder Hammerstein's opinion. "I was never allowed to be self-indulgent, because I was brought up by a taskmaster from an early age," Sondheim related to Freedman. "The first influence I had was a highly professional, highly rule-conscious man. He didn't say obey the rules, he just pointed them out." Sondheim revealed in *Time* that Hammerstein told him his novice musical was "the worst thing I have ever read—but I didn't say it was untalented."

One of the most successful American lyricists, Hammerstein influenced Sondheim's musical development over the intervening years until the young man graduated from Williams College. In 1950 Sondheim won the Hutchinson Prize, which enabled him to study structure and theory with avant-garde composer Milton Babbitt. During his fellowship with Babbitt, Sondheim told Freedman, he discovered his former and present mentor "represented two different fields. One was theater, the other music. What I was learning from Milton was basic grammar—sophisticated grammar, but grammar. It was a language, whereas what I learned from Oscar was what to do with language." Sondheim sought a career in show business after finishing his education. Off to a slow start, he went on audition after audition, and one stage show he wrote was called off upon the producer's death. At one point in his early career, Sondheim found himself in Hollywood writing scripts for the television situation comedy *Topper.* The turning point in his career came when he was offered the opportunity to write the lyrics for the musical *West Side Story* in 1957.

Established Reputation with Dance Musical

Considered one of the masterpieces of the American theater, *West Side Story* established Sondheim as a prominent Broadway lyricist at the age of twenty-seven. He followed the successful show with *Gypsy* in 1959. Calling *Gypsy* "the most perfectly achieved dance musical" in the *New York Times Magazine,* Frank Rich postulated that Sondheim "made his reputation with the dance musical." While 1962 marked the success of the burlesque comedy *A Funny Thing Happened on the Way to the Forum,* Sondheim was composer and lyricist for plays with varying degrees of acceptance over the next decades. His movement away from the traditional musical format of snappy tunes and happy endings toward a darker design offended critical sensibilities. "While praising Sondheim's brilliance," wrote Steven Holden in *Atlantic,* "theater critics have routinely complained that his work is cold and decadent and called his music tuneless." Offbeat and experimental productions such as *Anyone Can Whistle* (1964), *Do I Hear a Waltz?* (1965), *Company* (1970), *Follies* (1971), *A Little Night Music* (1973), *Pacific Overtures* (1976), the operatic *Sweeney Todd, the Demon Barber of Fleet Street* (1979), and *Merrily We Roll Along* (1981) brought Sondheim an intellectual cult following.

Extended Musical Limits

"The world has finally caught up with Stephen Sondheim. After 20 years of wary regard as, variously, the savior of the American musical, a heartless antimelodist or a closet opera composer, Sondheim—who is all the above and much more—is currently on a roll on the New York musical scene," wrote Allan Rich in *Newsweek* with the appearance of Sondheim's 1984 musical *Sunday in the Park With George.* A lyricist and composer who has been known to find inspiration in unlikely sources, Sondheim based *Sunday in the Park With George* on pointillist art. Portraying painter George Seurat and the characters from Seurat's neo-impressionist work *A Sunday Afternoon on the Island of La Grande Jatte,* the unusual musical was a commercial success as well as a prize winner. A writer for *Time* reported: "From his big-time debut in 1957 as the lyricist of *West Side Story* to his 1985 Pulitzer Prize for *Sunday in the Park With George* . . . , Sondheim . . . has steadily pushed toward—or beyond—the limits of what the score, the narrative, the very premise of a musical can be."

"A new show by Stephen Sondheim is still the most exciting event in the American theater," wrote Jack Kroll in *Newsweek* in 1987 with the advent of Sondheim's musical *Into the Woods.* Sondheim found the impetus for *Into the Woods* from child psychoanalyst Bruno Bettelheim's discussion of fairy tales in *The Uses of Enchantment.* Reviewers were divided in their opinion of the show, but advance ticket sales netting $2.3 million illustrated that Sondheim had found his audience. One of the songs, "No One Is Alone," entered the ranks of standard Sondheim ballads. Throughout his career Sondheim has battled unfavorable comparisons with his mentor Hammerstein in many reviews. *Into the Woods* was an exception. Ash De Lorenzo noted in *Vogue* that "the score of *Into the Woods* accomplishes what the score of *Oklahoma!* and *Carousel* did: it makes the whole piece come together. A circle has been completed."

Assassins

Sondheim followed *Into the Woods* with the musical *Assassins.* Reviewing the play in 1991, a writer for *Newsweek* cited the Sondheim collage of persons, including John Wilkes Booth, Lee Harvey Oswald, and "Squeaky" Fromme, who murdered, or attempted to murder, U.S. presidents, "the most audacious, far out and grotesque work of his career." A reviewer for *Time* reported that "even fans of [Sondheim's] audible wit and nonpareil invention wondered how such a show could be put together. The work . . . amply, at times brilliantly, demonstrates how. The question that lingers is why." Robert Sandla in *Theatre Crafts* offered the challenge of the project as explanation for why Sondheim would produce the play. "Put aside, for a moment, the queasiness you might feel when you learn that presidential assassins are the subject of a brand new musical. . . . And consider, instead, the purely technical imperatives confronted by the designers of *Assassins.*"

Dubbed "Broadway's brightest hope," Sondheim "may yet become the giant he saw his teacher [Hammerstein] to be—one who leaves our theater profoundly and permanently changed," *New York Times Magazine* reviewer Frank Rich prophesied in 1984. The subject of a book by Craig Zadan titled *Sondheim & Company,* which delves more into the composer's career accomplishments than his life story, Sondheim is required

---

"I was never allowed to be self-indulgent, because I was brought up by a taskmaster from an early age."

---

reading in musical theater history. Not always praised but generally acknowledged for expanding the limits of the American musical, Sondheim alternately irritates and moves his audiences with songs and subject matter. "Of course," Kroll proposed, "Sondheim would write a musical about amoebas, or aardvarks."

Selected writings

Topper (television script), NBC, 1953.
Stephen Sondheim's Crossword Puzzles, Harper, 1980.

Also author of other television scripts and screenplays. Contributor to books on theater and theatrical biographies, including Oscar Hammerstein's biography *Getting to Know Him,* Random House, 1977. Contributor of crossword puzzles to *New York* magazine.

Selected discography

West Side Story, Columbia, 1957.
Gypsy, Columbia, 1959.
A Funny Thing Happened on the Way to the Forum, Capitol, 1962.
Anyone Can Whistle, Columbia, 1964.

Do I Hear a Waltz?, Columbia, 1965.

Company, Columbia, 1970.

Follies, Capitol, 1971.

A Little Night Music (includes "Send in the Clowns"), Columbia, 1973.

Sondheim: A Musical Tribute, 1973.

Pacific Overtures, RCA, 1976.

Side by Side by Sondheim, RCA, 1977.

Sweeney Todd, the Demon Barber of Fleet Street, RCA, 1977.

Merrily We Roll Along, RCA, 1981.

Sunday in the Park With George, RCA, 1984.

Into the Woods, RCA, 1987.

Assasins, RCA, 1988.

Sources

Books

Zadan, Craig, *Sondheim & Company*, 2nd edition, Harper, 1986.

Periodicals

Atlantic, December 1984.

Library Journal, December 1986.

Newsweek, October 29, 1984; November, 16, 1987; February 4, 1991; June 22, 1992.

New York, December, 8, 1986; August 20, 1990.

New Yorker, July 2, 1990.

New York Times Magazine, April 1, 1984; October 21, 1984.

Opera News, November 1985.

People, February 17, 1986; March 17, 1986; October 1, 1990.

Psychology Today, January/February 1989.

Stereo Review, October 1982; October 1985.

Theatre Crafts, March 1991.

Time, June 16, 1986; November 16, 1987; December 7, 1987; September 25, 1989; February 4, 1991.

U.S. News & World Report, February 1, 1988.

Vogue, February 1988.

—Marjorie Burgess

Spinal Tap

Rock band

When American comedian-actors Michael McKean, Christopher Guest, and Harry Shearer first donned long-haired wigs and flamboyant costumes to portray the mythical British heavy metal band Spinal Tap, they were putting over what they thought was a pretty amusing parody of rock and roll excess. But when they collaborated with director Rob Reiner on the film *This is Spinal Tap*—an improvisatory comedy with a documentary style—they unwittingly made an enormous contribution to the folklore of popular music. *Stereo Review*'s Steve Simels spoke for many when he called *This is Spinal Tap* "possibly the funniest movie ever made about rock-and-roll."

The film's humor derived chiefly from its creators' clear understanding of and affection for the world of rock; the songs and situations depicted in the film became standard points of reference for musicians and fans. A soundtrack album featured the three heavy metal posers playing and singing the songs from the film. In fact, the popularity of the non-existent band was such that McKean, Guest, and Shearer—as vocalist and rhythm

Members include **Derek Smalls** (Harry Shearer: born December 23, 1943, in Los Angeles, CA; divorced; B.A. in political science, University of California, Los Angeles, 1964, graduate study at Harvard University, 1964-65), bass; **David St. Hubbins** (Michael McKean: born October 17, c. 1948, in New York, NY; married, has a son named Colin Russell; attended New York University, studied theater at the Carnegie Institute of Technology), guitar and vocals; and **Nigel Tufnel** (Christopher Guest: born February 5, 1948, in New York, NY; son of Peter Haden-Guest [member of British Parliament]; married Jamie Lee Curtis [an actress], has a daughter; attended Bard College and New York University), lead guitar.

Other members have included **Pete "James" Bond** (died of spontaneous combustion, 1976), drums; **John "Stumpy" Pepys** (died in a gardening accident), drums; **Eric "Stumpy Joe" Childs** (died of a melanin overdose), drums; **Mick Shrimpton** (died of spontaneous combustion, 1984), drums; **Joe "Mama" Besser** (joined band, 1984; presumed dead), drums; **Viv Savage** (died of purported swamp gas poisoning), keyboards; and **Richard Shrimpton** (joined group, early 1990s), drums.

Group started by St. Hubbins and Tufnel, early 1960s; released debut single "(Listen to the) Flower People," 1967; appeared on television broadcast *The TV Show*, ABC-TV, 1978; appeared in film *This Is Spinal Tap*, Embassy, 1984; released *This is Spinal Tap* soundtrack, Polydor, 1984, and reunion album *Break Like the Wind*, MCA, 1992.

Addresses: *Record company*—MCA Records, 70 Universal City Plaza, 3rd floor, Universal City, CA 91608.

guitarist David St. Hubbins, lead guitarist Nigel Tufnel, and bassist Derek Smalls, respectively—toured, did interviews and, in 1992, released a second Spinal Tap album, *Break Like the Wind.* By then the whole music world was in on the joke: A bevy of real-life rock stars appeared on the 1992 release, and journalists delighted in retracing the imaginary history of "Tap."

Real Rock Foundation

Guest and McKean had dabbled in rock in the 1960s. The two met in a poetry class at New York University and were soon sharing an apartment and writing songs together. In 1970 McKean moved to Los Angeles, where he worked with Shearer in the comedy group The Credibility Gap. Six years later McKean landed the role of Lenny Kosnowski on the hit television series *Laverne and Shirley.* He would later fill Lenny's shoes on a 1950s-style rock album by an assemblage called Lenny and the Squigtones that debuted on the show.

By the time McKean had gotten a foothold in America's consciousness as half of the duo Lenny and Squiqqy, Guest had become a successful comedy writer, having won an Emmy Award for his work on *The Lily Tomlin Special.* While working for the noted humor magazine *National Lampoon,* Guest had utilized his guitar skills in composing rock parodies. In 1974, according to *Rolling Stone,* Guest came up with the character of Nigel Tufnel after overhearing a conversation between a spaced-out musician and his manager. Shearer named his creation, bass player Derek Smalls, after an imaginary actor cited in the liner notes of a 1973 record by British art-metal rockers Jethro Tull, a band that Spinal Tap would later parody in its medieval epic "Stonehenge."

It wasn't until 1978, though, that Spinal Tap came together as a band. Guest, McKean, Shearer, and director Rob Reiner were working on *The TV Show,* an ABC-TV comedy special; for one sketch Spinal Tap performed a song called "Rock and Roll Nightmare." The three musician-comics and their director liked the rock parody so much that they cast about for funding to make a feature-length Spinal Tap movie. After a number of missteps, they managed to get the film made. Soon the fictional history of Spinal Tap, as chronicled in the film and in later interviews, would become rock and roll legend.

Rock and Roll Creation

The heavy metal bombast of the group's mature sound, the members of Spinal Tap revealed in the film *This Is Spinal Tap,* was preceded by a number of early styles. St. Hubbins and Tufnel, friends from an early age— according to Tap mythology—played together in rootsy early-1960s "skiffle" groups in the fabricated London district of Squatney. The trio worked with a succession of drummers throughout Spinal Tap's career, all of whom died mysteriously. Their early singles, like "Gimme Some Money," share the gritty, rhythm-and-blues-inflected sound of British Invasion groups like the Animals and the early Rolling Stones. 1967's "(Listen to the) Flower People," featured on the alleged album *Spinal Tap Sings "(Listen to the) Flower People" and Other Favorites,* is a hippie anthem highlighted by a vintage late-1960s Tufnel solo in the style of the Indian sitar. The group's follow-up record, *We Are All Flower People,* described by Peter Occhiogrosso of *Entertain-*

ment Weekly as "pure red ink," indicated that a change of style was inevitable.

In the early 1970s Tap apparently metamorphosed into the metal titans the world would come to love—or at least tolerate. The titles of the band's releases during the first years of the decade suggest their content: *Nerve Damage, Blood to Let, Intravenus de Milo.* The latter avowedly went platinum when record retailers actually returned a million copies. With 1973's *Brainhammer,* Occhiogrosso opined, "The band [hit] its lumbering stride," resembling nothing so much as "a brontosaurus in fight trim." 1975 saw *The Sun Never Sweats*—the title cut of which includes the metaphysical lyric "We may be gods/Or just big marionettes"—and the triple-live *Jap Habit,* which reportedly remained in the Number 112 position on the *Billboard* album chart for 82 of its 84 weeks on the chart. Tap next dabbled in glitter-rock with *Bent For the Rent,* a disastrous experiment featuring the non-hit single "When a Man Looks Like a Woman."

It was during this period that Tap gained its well-deserved reputation as "The Loudest Band in England," thanks in large part to the blistering lead guitar of Nigel Tufnel. Wolf Marshall of *Guitar World* noted that Tufnel's playing "has earned him an eternal place in the pantheon of rock guitar legends" and that his solos "have delighted millions and caused thousands of guitarists to set themselves ablaze." As the often confused but virtuosic axeman confided to Marty DiBergi—onscreen director of *This is Spinal Tap,* played by actual film director Reiner—he in fact acquired special amplifiers with volume knobs that went to a setting of eleven, rather than the customary ten. This, he explained, gave him the chance to go beyond the limit. When asked why he didn't just make the ten setting louder, Tufnel was stumped. "But this goes to eleven," he insisted.

Stairway to Heaven

In 1976 drummer Peter "James" Bond spontaneously combusted onstage, giving rise to a fatal tradition: each subsequent Tap skins-pounder has been inadvertently offered up in sacrifice to the gods of metal—each death more gruesome than the last. The founding members of Spinal Tap recounted some of this grim history for Nesbitt Birely of *Pulse!* Their sorry tale revealed that John "Stumpy" Pepys died in "a bizarre gardening accident," Eric "Stumpy Joe" Childs overdosed on melanin, authored by Webster's as "a dark brown or black animal or plant pigment"—and Mick Shrimpton, like Bond, burst into flame at his drumkit. Joe "Mama" Besser, Shrimpton's replacement for Tap's

1984 Japan tour, met a more uncertain fate. "We assume he's dead," St. Hubbins told Teisco Del Rey of *Guitar World.* "He was not a well man," explained Smalls. "He had a jazz background."

Viv Savage, Tap's keyboardist, met his maker while visiting Shrimpton's grave. "It was like swamp gas," Smalls informed Del Rey. It turned out that Savage—unbeknownst to his bandmates—had played drums before taking up the keyboards. Tufnel, St. Hubbins, and Smalls agree that these deaths are part of a curse. They told *Pulse!*'s Birely of an encounter with heavy metal band Megadeth's drummer. "The drummer said, 'Let me give you a pair of my sticks,'" St. Hubbins recalled, as Tufnel and Smalls recoiled in horror. "I don't want to be in this group called Spinal Tap and *touch* a drumstick," he responded.

Descent Into Obscurity

During the late 1970s Tap was less prolific than they had been—due to a strict injunction by their label, the

---

"It's a fine line between clever and stupid."
—David St. Hubbins
—This Is Spinal Tap

---

obscure Polymer Records, to "stay the hell out of the studio." In 1980 the band released *Shark Sandwich,* dubbed "Heavy Metal heaven" by *Entertainment Weekly* contributor Occhiogrosso, despite its misfired publicity campaign: The promotional "sandwiches" were largely crushed or lost in the mail. In *This is Spinal Tap,* director DiBergi reads the members a terse review of *Shark Sandwich:* "shit sandwich." 1982 saw the release of *Smell the Glove;* sales of the album suffered due in part to its nondescript cover. The group's original cover concept—a decidedly sexist image involving a woman on all fours—was suppressed at the last minute and replaced with a plain, albeit somewhat shiny, black sleeve. The group was baffled and annoyed by the label's decision to pull the cover, particularly Tufnel, who had trouble differentiating between the words "sexy" and "sexist."

In the group's opinion, *This is Spinal Tap,* essentially a tour film that chronicled the group's descent into obscurity in the early 1980s, was a betrayal. DiBergi's "warts and all" approach (St. Hubbins called it "all warts"—created the impression, as the singer guitarist complained to *Pulse!* contributor Birely, that the group was "sort of second-rate. A great big joke." This perception no doubt derived from the portrayal of such tour glitches as the malfunctioning "pod" stage prop that traps Smalls during the sci-fi production number "Rock and Roll Creation" and the too-small monolith for the Druid setpiece "Stonehenge." Nonetheless, the 1984 soundtrack album remains one of two available Spinal Tap records, and though Occhiogrosso noted that it was "more of a greatest hits package than a bold step forward," it includes a generous sampling of important Tap songs: "Gimme Some Money," "(Listen to the) Flower People," "Rock and Roll Creation," "Stonehenge," "Sex Farm," "Hell Hole," "Tonight I'm Gonna Rock You Tonight" and that bass-heavy celebration of the derriere, "Big Bottom."

Tapped Out

The film ended with footage of Spinal Tap's Japan tour, which culminated in the explosion of drummer Mick Shrimpton. Subsequently the band fell apart; they worked on various solo projects and settled into what seemed to be post-Tap existence. St. Hubbins saw the London premiere of his rock musical *Saucy Jack,* based on the life of 19th-century serial killer Jack the Ripper; it was a colossal flop.

Tufnel was inexplicably drafted into the Swiss army, though he has not been forthcoming about the details; he also worked on various solo projects. In the proud tradition of musician endorsements, Tufnel appeared in an ad for a limited series of Marshall amplifiers, the volume knobs of which exceeded even his legendary eleven. The ad copy read "It goes to twenty—that's nine louder, innit?" Most intriguingly, the guitar ace spent some time recording "world" music in Micronesia, he told *Spin*—on the dubious-sounding Pei-Pei islands.

Smalls toured northern England with some Spinal Tap tribute bands and also joined the Christian speedmetal outfit Lambsblood. St. Hubbins eventually settled in Pomona, California, with his wife, Janine Pettibone, whose disastrous attempts to manage Spinal Tap with the help of astrological charts had prompted Tufnel to quit the group at one point. Basking in domestic bliss in Pomona, St. Hubbins coached a local soccer team and produced local bands. Spinal Tap, it appeared, was a distant and strange-smelling memory.

Funeral Resurrected Band

St. Hubbins, Tufnel, and Smalls ran into one another at the funeral of former Tap manager Ian Faith, the hard-drinking, cricket bat-wielding father figure whose iron hand had shepherded the group through much of *This is Spinal Tap.* Faith had—according to the band—sold off the rights to the group's back catalog without telling them. "He took everything personally," bass player Smalls declared in *Guitar World,* "including our royalties." (With a shocking July, 1992, interview, *Spy* magazine revealed that Faith was, in fact, alive and had faked his death in order to spare Tap a messy investigation of their finances). In any event, at the funeral the three decided to get together and jam for old times' sake; in St. Hubbins's words, "it was great." They published an ad for a new drummer—"Drummer died. Need new one. Must have no immediate family."—and several rock notables applied, including Fleetwood Mac founder Mick Fleetwood, who showed up at the audition in a flame-retardant suit. Ultimately, though, Tap settled on Richard Shrimpton, former drummer Mick's younger and more talented brother.

The group decided to record a reunion album, and MCA Records established a new label, Dead Faith Records—named to celebrate the departure of the aforementioned embezzling ex-manager—just for Tap. As St. Hubbins confided to *Rolling Stone* while the group was in the studio, "The concept for the new album is sales." Tufnel added, "What we're saying with this album is, 'We're back. Come back with us. Join us, won't you, in a consumer sense.'"

Dusted off for *Wind*

By this time Spinal Tap had become so cool, so synonymous with the glamour, grime, and brain damage of rock, that big-name performers rushed to associate themselves with the new album. A variety of hot producers—among them Danny Kortchmar, Steve Lukather, and T-Bone Burnett—worked behind the scenes, while guest artists like rock diva Cher and guitar heroes Jeff Beck, Joe Satriani, and Slash of Guns 'N' Roses lent their talents to various tracks. The result was 1992's *Break Like the Wind,* an assemblage of new songs and re-mixed old ones. Thus, like the *This Is Spinal Tap* soundtrack album, *Wind* is a mini-lesson in Spinal Tap history; it includes a 1961 demo recording of "All the Way Home," the first St. Hubbins-Tufnel collaboration, psychedelic-era gems like "Rainy Day Sun" and "Clam Caravan," and the brand new anthems "The Majesty of Rock" and "Bitch School." Of the latter song—the suggestive video of which appeared on MTV—the band insisted it was about dog training and therefore not offensive to women. *Entertainment Weekly's* Occhiogrosso was "ambivalent" about the highly commercial feel of the new album but gave it an "A" anyhow. *Rolling Stone* meanwhile, declared the record "clever criticism disguised as bathroom humor," admiring the band's status as "a joke that everyone is in on—unlike most metal, which some people think isn't funny."

Spinal Tap was back in the public eye and would soon begin another concert tour. Whether or not the road ahead promised more jammed pods, out-of-proportion sets, and exploding musicians only time would tell. But the members of the loudest band in the world were philosophical. "We're not about heavy rock or metal or hard rock or leather trousers," Smalls remarked to *Guitar World*'s Del Rey. "We're doing what we stand for. And one of the reasons we got back together was to make a stand for generic rock and roll. Good old generic rock and roll."

Selected discography

On Polymer Records (not available)

Spinal Tap Sings "(Listen to the) Flower People" and Other Favorites, 1967.
We Are All Flower People, 1968.
Nerve Damage, 1970.
Blood to Let, 1971.
Intravenus De Milo, 1972.
Brainhammer, 1973.
The Sun Never Sweats, 1975.

Jap Habit, 1975.
Bent for the Rent, 1977.
Shark Sandwich, 1980.
Smell the Glove, 1982.
Silent But Deadly.

Other

This is Spinal Tap (soundtrack), Polydor, 1984.
Break Like the Wind, Dead Faith/MCA, 1992.

Sources

Detroit Free Press, June 19, 1992.
Entertainment Weekly, April 17, 1992.
Guitar Player, October 1990.
Guitar World, April 1992.
Metro Times (Detroit), June 10, 1992.
People, July 30, 1984.
Pulse!, March 1992.
Rolling Stone, May 24, 1984; January 23, 1992; April 2, 1992.
Spin, May 1992.
Spy, July/August 1992
Stereo Review, June 1984.
This is Spinal Tap (film), Embassy, 1984.

Additional information for this profile was obtained from a February, 1992, MCA Records press release.

—Simon Glickman

The Statler Brothers

Country group

The Statler Brothers took an old form—the gospel quartet—modernized it, and charged into country music as a vocal group in the mid-1960s. Since then they have earned more awards than any other country act and have topped the readers polls in *Music City News* almost every single year. Despite the band's name, only two of the four members are brothers, and none of them are named Statler; one would be hard pressed to find any falseness or stagy contrivance about the men otherwise. As Ken Robinson put it in the *Fresno Bee*, the Statler Brothers—Harold and Don Reid, Jimmy Fortune, and Philip Balsley—"are kings of 'down-home,' having spent their lives in and around Staunton, Virginia. As such, their [work] succeeds in warming the heart and soul with sentimental paeans to true love and days gone by. . . . Beneath a surface of cornball humor and nostalgia lie thoughtful lyrics that point to our human travails and longings."

As vocal ensembles gained popularity in country music, groups like Alabama and the Kentucky Headhunters lured younger generations of fans. The Statler

Brothers paved the way for such acts, but they offer a more wholesome approach that appeals to fans of mainstream country music. Lead singer Don Reid admitted in the *Richmond News Leader:* "I guess we're just dull. . . . We try not to get involved in anything controversial. We entertain and keep it light. We leave the messages to Western Union."

Country Choir Boys

Every member of the Statler Brothers, past and present, hails from Virginia. Three of them—Harold and Don Reid and Phil Balsley—were born and raised in Staunton, a small town in the Shenandoah Valley. Their earliest experience with music was in a church choir in their hometown, so it was natural for them to gravitate to gospel music. By 1010 Harold Reid, Balsley, Joe McDorman, and Lew C. DeWitt from nearby Roanoke County formed a group called the Four Star Quartet. They sang primarily at gospel concerts and church gatherings in the Shenandoah Valley and eventually changed the name of their outfit to the Kingsmen.

McDorman left the group in the 1960s, and Harold's younger brother Don Reid joined. The Reid brothers have become the unofficial spokespersons for the act over the years, especially the wisecracking Harold. During the 1950s and early 1960s the group honed its talents to a professional level, with Don Reid at baritone, Phil Balsley in the second tenor range, Harold at bass, and DeWitt taking the high tenor. Their break in the business came when they decided to diverge from straight gospel and sing country songs in four-part harmony instead. From the beginning they performed songs they wrote themselves, including the immensely popular "Flowers on the Wall."

New Name, New Sound

The name Statler comes from a local brand of tissues the men found in a hotel room one night. Harold saw the name on the tissue box and recommended it as the moniker for their new country group. Don Reid commented in the *Los Angeles Times:* "We could just as easily be known as the Kleenex Brothers."

The Statlers popularity heightened when Johnny Cash caught their act in 1964 and engaged the foursome as an opener for his road show. The Statlers worked with Cash for nearly eight years, and during that time they became almost as well known as the Man in Black himself. Their first hit, "Flowers on the Wall," topped the country *and* the pop charts. Though they faced competition from the Beatles and the Supremes, the Statler Brothers won the 1965 Grammy Award for best pop song.

Numerous hits followed, including "Ruthless," "Bed of Roses," "I'll Go to My Grave Loving You," "Who Am I to Say?," "Elizabeth," "Do You Remember These?," "Too Much on My Heart," and "Class of '57." The latter song, a serious look at the lives of some small-town high school graduates, led acclaimed novelist Kurt Vonnegut to call the Statlers "America's poets." Despite Don Reid's assertion that the group would stay away from including political messages in their works, the Statlers also scored a hit with "More Than a Name on a Wall," a song about war veterans.

Voted vocal group of the year every year between 1972 and 1979 by the Country Music Association, the Statler Brothers earned the honor several times in the 1980s as well. Nowhere have the Statlers dominated more than in this polls, however. For more than two decades, the fan-voted *Music City News* awards have named the Statler Brothers vocal group of the year virtually every year.

Even the arrival of such groups as Alabama and Shenandoah have done little to erode the popularity of the Statlers, who have won more awards than any act in the entire history of country music.

Television Replaced Touring

It is wonder, then, that cable television's Nashville Network (TNN) has engaged the Statler Brothers to host a weekly television variety show. The easygoing, joke-strewn Statler style is perfectly suited for the television variety format. *The Statler Brothers Show* was the first variety show produced by TNN, and the musical foursome write and produce much of the material. They also choose the guests, who have included such classic performers as Jerry Lee Lewis and newcomers like Mark Chestnutt. Because cable stations are under less pressure to produce hit programming, it is likely that the Statlers will become a Saturday night staple on the Nashville Network.

Most country musicians relocate to Nashville even before they find success, but the Statler Brothers have never left Staunton, Virginia. They live there and run their business from a former elementary school that the Reids and their children attended. Several family members help arrange road trips and guide fans through an on-site museum. Harold Reid told the *Fresno Bee* that the musicians were "too green or too stubborn" to trade their roots for life on Music Row. "We just didn't want to leave home," he confessed. "We have family and friends here. We're closer to them by living here."

Charity Work

The Statler Brothers are also known for their charity work. Their benefit concert to aid cleanup efforts after Hurricane Hugo earned $200,000. They have also organized and starred in an annual Fourth of July gala in Staunton for almost a quarter of a century.

Richmond News Leader contributor Joe Edwards described the singers as "four family men with bedrock values appealing to the heartland with grassroots songs about love, nostalgia and growing up in small town USA." Stability is even evident in the quartet's membership. The group's only personnel change occurred when DeWitt had to retire in 1982 due to illness—he died in 1990—and was replaced by Jimmy Fortune.

Charlotte Observer correspondent Ken Garfield observed of the perennially popular quartet that aside from the stage name, "there is no more falsehood to find in a group that seemingly has been around longer than the steel guitar; that has turned simplicity into a country music art form; and that has struck a sweet-sounding chord over 25 years of concerts, albums, awards, and TV appearances." Garfield concluded:

"I guess we're just dull. We try not to get involved in anything controversial. We entertain and keep it light."
—Don Reid

"Let the world and country music change, say the Statler Brothers. They can live with it, just so long as they can keep the customers satisfied with a theme that hasn't varied since they rode out of Staunton."

Selected discography

On Mercury Records, except where noted

Flowers on the Wall, Columbia, 1966.
The Statler Brothers Sing the Big Hits, Columbia, 1967.
Pardners in Rhyme, 1985.
Four for the Show, 1986.
Radio Gospel Favorites, 1986.
Maple Street Memories, 1987.
The Statler Brothers Greatest Hits, Vol. 3 (includes previously unreleased songs), 1988.
Live and Sold Out, 1989.
All American Country, 1991.
Words and Music, PolyGram, 1992.
Bed of Roses.
Pictures of Moments to Remember.
Innerview.
Country Music Then and Now.
The Statler Brothers Sing Country Symphonies in E Major.
Alive at the Johnny Mack Brown High School.
Sons of the Motherland.
Best of the Statler Brothers.
Holy Bible: Old Testament.
Holy Bible: New Testament.
Holy Bible: New & Old Testament.
The World's Favorite Hymns.
Harold, Don, Phil and Lew.
The Country America Loves.
Best of the Statler Brothers, Volume II: Rides Again.
Atlanta Blue.
Carry Me Back.
Christmas Present.
Entertainers on and off Record.

The Legend Goes On.

The Originals.

Short Stories.

The Statler Brothers' Tenth Anniversary.

The Statler Brothers Today.

Music, Memories & You.

Best of the Statler Brothers, Vol. 1.

Best of the Statler Brothers, Vol. 2: Rides Again.

The Big Hits, Columbia.

Christmas Card.

Oh Happy Day, Columbia.

Today.

Sources

Books

The Illustrated Encyclopedia of Country Music, Harmony, 1977.

Shestack, Melvin, The Country Music Encyclopedia, Crowell, 1974.

Stambler, Irwin and Grelun Landon, The Encyclopedia of Folk, Country, and Western Music, St. Martin's, 1969.

Periodicals

Charlotte Observer, February 1, 1991.

Country Music, September/October 1991.

Fresno Bee, February 9, 1990; February 13, 1990.

Greensboro News & Record, February 22, 1991.

Los Angeles Times, August 16, 1990.

Richmond News Leader, February 18, 1989.

Richmond Times-Dispatch, May 24, 1990; July 3, 1991.

St. Louis Post-Dispatch, June 1, 1989.

Saturday Evening Post, September 1984.

—Anne Janette Johnson

Sly Stone

Singer, songwriter, producer

With his groundbreaking group Sly and the Family Stone, Sylvester Stewart—or Sly Stone, as he came to be called—pioneered the psychedelic funk sound that would electrify the Woodstock generation of the late 1960s and profoundly influence the direction taken by rhythm and blues and, in the subsequent decades, other black music forms from soul to disco to rap. While Stone's flamboyant persona, uplifting songs, and ethnically diverse band earned a massive following, political and personal difficulties hampered his career and eventually drove him out of the music scene. During the most intensely productive segment of his career, however, he was, according to pop music critic Dave Marsh, "one of the greatest musical adventurers rock has ever known."

Sylvester Stewart was born in Dallas, Texas, in March of 1944. He began his recording career early—at age four—as a vocalist on the gospel tune "On the Battlefield for My Lord." In the fifties his family moved to the San Francisco area. Stewart and his brother Freddie learned to play various instruments and made music under the name the Stewart Four. Stewart also played and sang with doo-wop groups. In high school he sang with a group called the Viscanes, appearing on their record "Yellow Moon." At age sixteen he made a solo record called "Long Time Away" which gained him some modest fame. As a student at Vallejo Junior College he learned music theory and composition, putting what he learned into practice at weekend performing gigs.

At a show in 1964 Stewart met Tom "Big Daddy" Donahue, a disc jockey from San Francisco. Donahue told him about a record label he had formed with another former DJ. Stewart agreed to join the new venture, Autumn Records, and after cutting a few records of his own began to develop his talents as a producer. Working with bands like the Beau Brummels and the Great Society—the latter's singer, Grace Slick, would later front the psychedelic supergroup Jefferson Airplane—Stewart honed the studio skills he would later put to considerable use with his own group. In 1966, though, he left Autumn Records and became a disc jockey at radio station KSOL in San Francisco. He soon gained notoriety as one of the more eccentric voices on radio, blending sound effects with public service announcements and mixing soul singles with rock and roll records by Bob Dylan and the Beatles. According to Irwin Stambler in the *Encyclopedia of Pop, Rock & Soul,* by the time Stewart moved over to Oakland's station KDIA "he was generally considered the top R & B commentator" in the area.

Born Sylvester Stewart, March 15, 1944, in Dallas, TX; married Kathy Silva, June 1974 (divorced, 1974); children: Sylvester Bubb Ali Stewart, Jr. *Education:* Attended Vallejo Junior College.

At age four sang on gospel record "On the Battlefield for My Lord"; cut first solo record, c. 1960; worked as record producer and disc jockey, 1964-66; signed with Epic Records and released first LP with Sly and the Family Stone, 1967; recording artist with Epic and Warner Bros., 1967-83.

Awards: Platinum award for single "If You Want Me to Stay."

Formed "Family"

At the same time, he was writing and playing with his own band, the Stoners. The group broke up in 1966, so Stewart and ex-Stoners trumpet player Cynthia Robinson formed a new ensemble. Stewart enlisted brother Freddie as guitarist and his sister Rosie to play piano. With the addition of saxophonist Jetty Martini, bassist Larry Graham and drummer Greg Errico (Martini's cousin), the Family Stone was born.

Stewart changed his name to Sly Stone, and the band soon attracted the attention of Columbia Records A&R executive David Kapralik. The group signed with Columbia, releasing its debut LP, *A Whole New Thing,* in 1967 on the Columbia subsidiary Epic Records. The album didn't fare particularly well—according to Timothy White's book *Rock Stars,* it "lacked the fizzy familial feel of their live shows"—but the group's single "Dance to the Music," released early in 1968, became a solid hit and provided the title for the group's next album. Charles Shaar Murray asserted in *Crosstown Traffic* that the song "changed the course of popular music. It was succeeded by a clutch of pop-soul crossover hits which somehow contrived to meld James Brown's funk with the Beatles' tuneful optimism, records as universally accessible as anything since early Motown."

In an essay included in *The Rolling Stone Illustrated History of Rock & Roll,* rock critic Dave Marsh noted that "Dance to the Music" exploded the formal categories of soul and R & B because the vocals and the instruments fought it out for space right on the disc." Sly Stone had created a rock band that played in the traditions and spirit of soul music. "Dance to the Music" was the harbinger of hits to come; it reached the Top Ten of both the pop and soul charts, followed by a string of other hits. "Everyday People"—a song from *Life!* that gave the group its first Number One hit and helped popularize the slogan "different strokes for different folks"—"Stand!" and "I Want to Take You Higher" all increased the visibility of Sly Stone and his band. *Stand!,* the album containing the latter two singles, appeared in 1969. It also included the influential non-hit "Don't Call Me Nigger, Whitey."

Revolutionary Thinking

The band, in its composition as much as its sound, crystallized much of the idealism and revolutionary thinking of the period. As Marsh observed, "Here was a band in which men and women, black and white, had not one fixed role but many fluid ones. The women played, the men sang; the blacks freaked out, the whites got funky; everyone did something unexpected, which was the only thing the listener could expect." A 1987 *Rolling Stone* piece devoted to "The Top 100" rock albums included *Stand!*—as well as two subsequent Sly and the Family Stone records. "On *Stand!* Stone's talent seems boundless," the magazine declared, calling the album's best songs "anthems you can dance to, soaring hymns of equality and self-determination set to a sweaty gutbucket beat." According to White, "*Stand!* . . . was the album-length masterwork that 'Everyday People' had presaged; in one fell stroke it gave black music a new inner complexion while revolutionizing every other rock rhythm section extant."

The year 1969 brought more hit songs, most notably "Hot Fun in the Summertime" and the phonetically titled "Thank You Falettinme Be Mice Elf Again" ("thank you for lettin' me be myself again"). Greil Marcus described Stone's peak in his book *Mystery Train:* "Sly was a winner. It seemed he had not only won the race, he had made up his own rules. Driving the finest cars, sporting the most sensational clothes, making the biggest deals and the best music, he was shaping the style and ambition of black teenagers all over the country." The group's moment of greatest visibility came in 1969 when they performed at the Woodstock festival, the gigantic concert in New York state that stood as the summit and symbol of the hippie generation. A supplement in *Rolling Stone* advertising the *Woodstock* movie noted, "Many of [Stone's] songs have social consciousness, yet they are able to appeal to both black and white, short-haired and long-haired people of all ages."

Sly and the Family Stone's rendition of "I Want to Take You Higher" looked for a brief time like the embodiment of a generation's dreams: black and white musicians bringing an activist throng to its feet with irresistible rock and roll music. Marsh claimed in a 1973 *Creem* review that Stone "was almost forced into the role of house nigger for the Woodstock Nation"—someone who, as Marsh later claimed, "could make race a safe issue"—but the audience's thunderous response and its flashing the peace sign at the word "higher," as per Stone's instructions, suggest that Stone's message and appeal were hardly apolitical. Murray's description of the Woodstock performance gives it a ritual cast: "There's Sly's happy family in their baddest threads doing that old-time boogaloo while their chief mocks and exorcises generations of racial terror, shoving his huge grinning black mug into young America's face, going 'BOOM-lakka-lakkalakka, BOOM-lakka-lakka-lakka. . .'"

Trouble

In 1970, riding on the wave of his hits, Stone began to cancel many of his shows and appear late for others. "According to his agent," reported *Rolling Stone,* "he canceled 26 of the 80 engagements scheduled for him in 1970." Some blamed the excesses of his lifestyle—Stone's regalia, onstage and off, was ostentatious to say the least and matched by his alleged fondness for drugs—for what the magazine called "the most erratic performance record since [drug-addicted actress-singer] Judy Garland." Kapralik, who had become the band's manager, created a split-personality narrative to explain the star's behavior to journalists and record executives: "OK, that's Sylvester Stewart, he's a poet," Kapralik told *Rolling Stone.* "And then there's Sly Stone, the street cat, the hustler, the pimp, the conniver, sly as a fox and cold as a stone. . . . That's the strutter, the street dude who walks up there with that charisma that holds an audience captive, right? 400,000 at Woodstock and 25,000 at Madison Square. He's irresponsible, opportunistic and unethical and he pimps our minds if we let him."

Of Stone's drug habit, Kapralik reasoned that factions in the black political community, especially the revolutionary group the Black Panthers, along with former band members and his family, were in a tug-of-war over the star: "That poor kid was torn apart. And when you are torn apart that means a lot of pain. And one of the clinical ways to ease the pain is cocaine." April of 1970 saw a near-riot at a Washington D.C. concert; also, a rumor that Stone had insulted black DJs brought about a short ban of his records from local soul stations. Meanwhile, to ease record company anxieties about new "product," a *Greatest Hits* album was released in 1970. This collection appeared in *Rolling Stone*'s Top 100 seventeen years later, and in 1981 rock critic Robert Christgau ranked it "among the greatest rock and roll LPs of all time." In August of 1970 Sly and the Family Stone appeared at the famed Isle of Wight music festival. As J. Green wrote in the festival issue of the *Evening Standard,* "Sometimes something emerges which breaks all the rules, shatters the accepted conventions, survives the hype and wins through. Sly and the Family Stone are such a band."

Courageous Honesty

More difficulties, more cancellations, and more accusations surfaced in 1971. *Rolling Stone* reported that by October Stone had "canceled 12 shows out of 40" and was "late for two shows." In November the band at last released a new album. *There's a Riot Goin' On* was unlikely to banish concerns about Stone and his group, however. "The record was no fun," wrote Marcus. "It was slow, hard to hear, and it didn't celebrate anything.

"There's Sylvester Stewart, he's a poet. And then there's Sly Stone, the street cat, the hustler, the pimp, the conniver, sly as a fox and cold as a stone."
—David Kapralik

It was not groovy. In fact, it was distinctly unpleasant, unnerving." Yet, as Marcus and other critics agreed, the record was a groundbreaking statement. "Maybe this is the new urban music," speculated Vince Aletti in *Rolling Stone.* "Gone is the energy and flash that exploded in Sly's early music. . . . There's no exhilaration left and no immediately clear message. Only an overwhelming feeling of exhaustion." However, Aletti conceded, the album showed Sly's inner state with courageous honesty, "at the same time holding a mirror up to all of us. . . . *There's a Riot Goin' On* is one of the most important f—king albums of the year." White, writing in *Rock Stars,* called the album "a broody, militant, savage indictment of all the decayed determinism of the 1960's," while Marsh opined that it "might be the only truly epic album of the 70's." Christgau's book awarded it an "A+" and assessed, "Despairing, courageous and very hard to take, this is one of those rare albums whose whole actually does exceed the sum of its parts."

Despite the political edge and apparent lethargy and

struggle of *There's a Riot Goin' On,* however, it went to Number One on the album chart and yielded three hit singles, "Family Affair," "(You Caught Me) Smilin'," and "Runnin' Away." It also featured a slowed-down and provocative rendition of "Thank You Falettinme Be Mice Elf Again," retitled "Thank You for Talkin' To Me Africa." Furthermore, according to Marsh and Marcus, Aletti's initial thought was correct: this was the new urban pop sound. A slew of politicized and skeptical if not downright pessimistic soul songs overtook the airwaves in the wake of *There's a Riot Goin' On.*

Faltered in '70s

Stone's inconsistencies continued to dominate press reports about him, and his frequent run-ins with police increased in 1972. Since the star "got busted five times in as many months last year," *Rolling Stone* announced in February of 1973, "we award him a bust of himself." The joke held little appeal for Stone's handlers; a long time had lapsed without a new album, and *Riot* raised doubts that the Sly Stone of old would ever take audiences "higher" again. "We've been recording, rescheduling, [and] regrouping . . . on everything we like to do, what we have to do, and things we wish we could do," Stone explained in an interview quoted in *Rock Stars.*

Stone was accurate when he said "regrouping," as the band went through several personnel changes in the early seventies. Graham left and was replaced by Rusty Allen; Andy Newmark replaced drummer Errico, and Stone recruited sax player Pat Rizzo. In August of 1973, *Rolling Stone* ran a profile featuring plenty of anecdotes about Stone's unreliability. "He's sort of like Mercury," a record company publicist admitted. "You think you've got your hands on him, but before you realize it he's slipped away." Stone reportedly felt that he didn't owe his fans anything for missed concerts: "I got nothing to pay back," he was quoted as saying in *Rolling Stone.*

Stone's fans would have to wait until October for *Fresh!* The new LP contained "If You Want Me to Stay," which went platinum, and one other hit, "Frisky." Marsh, reviewing the album for *Creem,* saw it as "Sly coming to terms with himself as rock star." He concluded that "there have been few albums as rich as this one released in 1973, if there have been any," and expected the record would yield hit songs "because Sly, however great the contradictions he feels may be, is a truly great rock singer in the first place." Vernon Gibbs, writing for *Crawdaddy,* agreed: "The music is quite worthy of the founder of progressive soul. It gives us plenty of ass-shaking rhythms for the present and reason for optimism about the future. . . . Make no

mistake about it, friends and neighbors, Sly is back and just as freshly chirping as ever."

Musical Output Dwindled

In June of 1974 Stone married his girlfriend, Kathy Silva. The ceremony took place before television cameras at New York City's Madison Square Garden just before a concert. By the end of the year they were divorced, with Silva seeking custody of the couple's one-year-old son, Sylvester Bubb Ali Stewart, Jr. That year Sly and the Family Stone released *Small Talk,* an album that sank without much fanfare. In December, Stone walked out on a Muscular Dystrophy benefit in Washington, D.C. More arrests and conflicts followed, and Stone's musical output dwindled.

In 1976 the band put out *Heard Ya Missed Me, Well I'm Back,* but the album was generally dismissed by critics as a half-hearted effort. Stambler reported that "for a time after 1976, [Stone] was essentially out of the music business." He signed with Warner Brothers after a couple of unproductive years and in 1979 released *Back on the Right Track* with many of his original band members. Epic, meanwhile, seized the opportunity to release a record containing several Sly and the Family Stone tracks rerecorded with disco instrumentation. Entitled *Ten Years Too Soon,* it repulsed many of Stone's fans and critics, who saw it as the most cynical business move imaginable by a record label. Epic also released *Anthology,* an updated greatest hits package, in 1981. That same year Stone made an appearance on *The Electric Spanking of War Babies,* an album by George Clinton's group Funkadelic.

In 1982 Sly and the Family Stone started a tour, but Stone's drug problems led him to check into a treatment program in Florida. He released a new album, *Ain't But the One Way,* in 1983; *Stereo Review*'s Joel Vance wrote approvingly that "it's clear at least that [Stone] very much wants to come back with this comeback album. He's sure got my vote." Stone made some concert appearances the next year with soul star Bobby Womack. The rest of the decade saw him make news only with new arrests and court appearances. *Jet* magazine reported the star's being jailed for parole violation in Florida in June of 1987; in December of 1989 he was reportedly held in Connecticut on a drug charge. These short announcements read like career obituaries, noting casually that "in the 1960's Stone's group, Sly and the Family Stone, had several hits, including 'I Want to Take You Higher.'" Anyone acquainted with the legacy of Stone's achievements would know how much more there was to the story.

Selected discography

A Whole New Thing, Epic, 1967.
Dance to the Music (includes "Dance to the Music"), Epic, 1968.
Life! (includes "Everyday People"), Epic, 1968.
Stand! (includes "Stand!," "I Want to Take You Higher," and "Don't Call Me Nigger, Whitey"), Epic, 1969.
Greatest Hits (includes "Hot Fun in the Summertime" and "Thank You Falettinme Be Mice Elf Again"), Epic, 1970.
There's a Riot Goin' On (includes "Family Affair," "[You Caught Me] Smilin'," "Runnin' Away," and "Thank You for Talkin' to Me Africa"), Epic, 1971.
Fresh! (includes "If You Want Me to Stay" and "Frisky"), Epic, 1973.
Small Talk, Epic, 1974.
Heard Ya Missed Me, Well I'm Back, Epic, 1976.
Back on the Right Track, Warner Bros., 1979.
Ten Years Too Soon, Epic, 1979.
Anthology, Epic, 1981.
Ain't But the One Way, Warner Bros., 1983.

With others

Woodstock (includes "I Want to Take You Higher"), Cotillion, 1970.
(With Funkadelic) *The Electric Spanking of War Babies,* Warner Bros., 1981.

Sources

Books

Christgau, Robert, *Christgau's Record Guide: Rock Albums of the Seventies,* Ticknor & Fields, 1981.
Marcus, Greil, *Mystery Train: Images of America in Rock 'n' Roll Music,* E. P. Dutton & Co., Inc., 1975.
Murray, Charles Shaar, *Crosstown Traffic: Jimi Hendrix and the Rock 'n' Roll Revolution,* St. Martin's Press, 1989.
The Rolling Stone Illustrated History of Rock & Roll, edited by Jim Miller, Random House/Rolling Stone Press, 1976.
Stambler, Irwin, *Encyclopedia of Pop, Rock & Soul,* revised edition, St. Martin's Press, 1989.
White, Timothy, *Rock Stars,* Stewart, Tabori & Chang, 1984.

Periodicals

Crawdaddy!, September 1968; October 1973.
Creem, September 1973.
Evening Standard, August 22, 1970.
Jet, July 2, 1984; November 11, 1986; June 22, 1987; December 4, 1989.
Rolling Stone, March 19, 1970; April 16, 1970; October 14, 1971; December 23, 1971; February 1, 1973; August 30, 1973; August 27, 1987.
Stereo Review, July 1983.

—*Simon Glickman*

The Texas Tornados

Country/rock group

Called the "Tex-Mex equivalent of the Traveling Wilburys and Grateful Dead" by Gary Graff of the *Detroit Free Press,* the Texas Tornados are Flaco Jimenez, Augie Meyers, Doug Sahm, and Freddy Fender. Each an accomplished solo artist in his own right, the four joined forces in 1989, creating a soulful mix of country, rhythm and blues, ballad singing, Texas rock and roll, and *conjunto*—a type of music that mixes Mexican Norteno with German and Czechoslovakian polkas and waltzes. As a *Pollstar* correspondent put it, "The Tornados are not country, they're not rock and roll. They've taken their sound straight from the sawdust-floored cantinas of South Texas and spiced it up a bit."

The Tornados made their first appearance in December of 1989. Though all had played together at various times, the band members did not actually perform as a group until Sahm brought them together for a gig in San Francisco. "Cameron Randle, at Refugee Management, sort of put the whole thing together, and got together with Warner Brothers," Sahm told the *Tulsa World.* "They were lookin' and we were bookin'."

Initially, not all were excited about giving up solo careers to join the group. "I was not very enthusiastic about being with any group at all," Fender admitted in the *Austin American-Statesman,* "but the only way I could get on a major label was with four people, so I said what the hell."

A Whirlwind of Praise

The Tornados' first record received critical acclaim—the *Houston Chronicle* called *Texas Tornados* "almost too good to be true . . . Jalapeno-laced, tequila-spiked cross-cultural border music the way you always imagined it could sound in your sun-baked dreams." The album also sold better than the band had expected. Sahm, for one, was ecstatic: "One week in *Billboard,* we were charted in rock, 21 in Latin and 29 with a bullet on the country album chart. . . . We're selling more country records than half those country artists with white hats."

The critical reception to the group's second effort, 1991's *Zone of Our Own,* was even better. *Country Music* called *Zone of Our Own* "a clear improvement from a group whose musical standards are beyond reproach." An *Austin American-Statesman* correspondent announced, "This second blow by the all-star, Tex-Mex aggregation is stronger than the first. . . . [It] underscores the crucial connections between the . . .

rock of Doug Sahm, the border (and border transcending) musics of Freddy Fender and Flaco Jimenez and the Tejano-flavored country of Augie Meyers."

Like their records, the Tornados' whirlwind live shows prompted ecstatic critical reactions. A *Houston Chronicle* reporter wrote, "The Texas Tornados nearly blew the roof off at Rockefeller's;" a *CMJ* writer observed, "The Texas Tornados reminded some hardened New Yorkers just what a kick live music can be;" and in the *Chicago Sun-Times* a reviewer summed up the opinion of many: "They delivered everything a fan might have hoped. . . . A killer show."

Pre-Tornados Days of Sahm and Meyers

All members of the Texas Tornados joke about their ages; at the group's inception, Sahm, at 48, was the only member under 50. "You've heard of [the pop group] New Kids on the Block?" Fender told *People* "Well, we're the old farts in the neighborhood." Each had come to the Texas Tornados after long careers in border music.

Doug Sahm burst on the national seen in 1965 as a member of the Sir Douglas Quintet, which released the hit "She's About a Mover." Sir Douglas was one of the most outlandish groups in rock history. Conceived by Sahm and producer Huey "Crazy Cajun" Meaux, the group wore Edwardian costumes and pretended to be part of the wave of British groups that were dominating the charts at the time. In reality all were from Texas and two were Mexican.

Sahm began his career at age 12. Known as "Little Doug," he was a steel guitar-playing prodigy who was invited to join the Grand Ole Opry at 13. Little Doug even sat on Hank Williams's knee at one of that singer's last public performances. Over the course of more than 40 pre-Tornados albums, Sahm proved himself equally at home assaying acid-drenched psychedelia, country, Gulf Coast blues, big band pop, and *conjunto.* In 1983 he reunited the Sir Douglas Quintet for a huge international hit, 1983's "Meet Me in Stockholm."

Augie Meyers' career has run parallel with Doug Sahm's since the 1950s. Meyers had begun playing guitar as therapy for polio, and later a black gospel pianist introduced him to the rudiments of the keyboard. When Sahm and his parents started going to Meyers's mother's grocery store in their mutual hometown of San Antonio, young Doug and Augie would talk about their respective bands. Later, when the Sir Douglas Quintet exploded, Meyers' Vox organ sound—described by some as "cheesy"—was an integral part of hits like "She's About a Mover" and "Mendocino."

Upon the Quintet's split, Meyers formed the Western Headband and showed a deft touch with the accordion and the bajo sexto, a Mexican gut-stringed guitar. Since then Meyers and Sahm have remained close, often touring and performing together.

Fender: "Mexican Elvis"

Like that of Doug Sahm, Freddy Fender's career has hinged on a few hits and a mass of talent. Born Baldemar Huerta in the Rio Grande Valley town of San Benito, Fender had his first hit, "Wasted Days and Wasted Nights," in 1959. Some called him the "Mexican Elvis," or "El Bebop Kid." He had the potential for a promising career, but his rise was cut short in the early 1960s, when police caught him with marijuana and sent him to jail for three years.

In the early 1970s the same Huey P. Meaux who turned out the Sir Douglas Quintet steered Fender into country music. The resulting hits included the bilingual smash "Before the Next Teardrop Falls" and a remake of "Wasted Days and Wasted Nights."

Fender released his last solo album in 1981 and spent much of the 1980s playing more mainstream country music." In 1988 Robert Redford cast him as the mayor in his film *The Milagro Beanfield War.* Before the formation of the Texas Tornados, Fender was playing solo gigs for what he called "peanuts."

Jimenez's Accordion Prowess

Of all the group's members, Flaco Jimenez has had the steadiest, if the least flashy, career. Born Leonardo Jimenez in 1939, he grew up in a musical household. His grandfather, Patricio Jimenez, was an accordion player. His father, Santiago Jimenez, Sr., was one of the inventors of *conjunto.* In the mid-1950s Flaco had his first hit, "Hasta La Vista," which he followed with a long string of Spanish-language hits based on the rancheras, polkas, and boleros of his native San Antonio.

In 1973, Sahm called Jimenez to play on *Doug Sahm and Band,* a rowdy, loose album that featured rock legend Bob Dylan and New Orleans pianist Dr. John. In 1974 Jimenez appeared in Les Blank's groundbreaking documentary *Chulas Fronteras.* As his reputation grew beyond the Mexican and Mexican-American communities, Jimenez began collaborating with more mainstream artists. He played on Ry Cooder's soundtrack to the film *The Boarder* and on albums by Cooder, Peter Rowan, Dwight Yoakam, and, of course, Doug Sahm. His own album, *Ay Te Dejo en San Antonio,* won a Grammy Award in 1986. When not playing with the Texas Tornados, Jimenez brings his Hohner Corona diatonic accordion from San Antonio's El West Side to the capitals of Europe and even Japan.

Tornados Took Shape

Coming together in 1989 after years in the music business as solo performers was a venture that elicited mixed emotions in the members of the Texas Tornados. Fender, for example, told the *Detroit Free Press*'s Graff, "If we were kids, it would be different. But we're grown men, and the older you get, the more you value your independence." Nevertheless, the Texas Tornados materialized "thanks to mutual respect and interest in each other's music," according to Graff.

While all four Tornados enjoy playing in the group, none has completely given up on his solo career. Most see the band—which in mid-1992 had just completed their third album and were under contract to complete a fourth—as a springboard to renewed individual popularity. Sahm explained to Graff in 1992, "We've got to do our individual projects, but by doing those, we don't burn out on the main one, which *is* the Tornados." When asked if solo stardom was a hard dream to give up, Fender responded in the *Los Angeles Times,* "Is pork chops greasy? I guess we all want it."

Selected discography

Texas Tornados, Reprise, 1990.
Los Texas Tornados, Reprise, 1991.
Zone of Our Own, Reprise, 1991.

Sources

Austin American-Statesman, September 16, 1991; November 14, 1991.
CMJ, October 19, 1990.
Country Music, March/April 1991.
Detroit Free Press, June 19, 1992.
Entertainment Weekly, October 18, 1991.
Houston Chronicle March 14, 1991.
Los Angeles Times, August 16, 1990.
Metro Times (Detroit), June 10, 1992.
New York Times, September 30, 1990.
People, December 2, 1991.
Pollstar, August 27, 1990.
Sun-Times (Chicago), September 24, 1990.
Tulsa World, July 15, 1990.

—*Jordan Wankoff*

Pam Tillis

Singer, songwriter

For Pam Tillis, being the daughter of a famous country star has been a mixed blessing. Tillis's success as a singer-songwriter came after years of avoiding the sort of traditional country music popularized by her father, the stuttering Grand Ole Opry favorite Mel Tillis. The attractive young country star actually cut her teeth on pop, rock and roll, jazz, and even punk rock before settling into more mainstream country fare. As Jack Hurst noted in the *Chicago Tribune,* however, Pam, "a fixture on Nashville's progressive end for more than a decade, suddenly appears to have found her father's ladder to stardom."

The breakthrough for Tillis was *Put Yourself in My Place,* her first release for Arista Records. She wrote or co-wrote seven of ten songs on the album and earned her first Top Ten country hit with the winsome "Don't Tell Me What To Do." Both the album and the single reveal a new commitment to country music by an artist who all but shunned the genre in her earlier years. *Philadelphia Inquirer* reviewer Dan DeLuca lauded Tillis for her move to the country mainstream, concluding: "Add Pam Tillis to the growing list of savvy young country-music women who write 'em and sing 'em their own way."

Like many children of entertainers, Pam Tillis had an erratic childhood. The oldest of the Tillis children, she was born in Plant City, Florida, shortly before her father began to pursue a singing career. She was very young when the family moved to Nashville with little more than the clothes on their backs, but her father slowly made his way in the country music field and then hit superstardom in the late 1960s. Pam began studying piano at age eight and received her first guitar at eleven. Though she liked country music, she was also influenced by many other styles. "I like it all," she told a *Chicago Tribune* reporter, "rockabilly, honky-tonk, Celtic folk—and you can't go any further back than that."

Joined Rock Band

What she did not like—and still remembers painfully—were the occasions when her father would drag her onto the stage at the Grand Ole Opry. "I hated it," she recalled in *People.* "It was an ego-bruiser. I just couldn't stand getting up there and having all that [creativity] in me and having to go through *his* material. And I felt I was, like, on display: 'Here, he's got offspring!'"

Tillis was 15 when her parents divorced. Her personal rebellion took the form of an interest in hard rock and punk music. A brief stay at the University of Tennessee ended when she joined a rock band and began to perform. The band was not terribly successful, however, and by 1976 she found herself back in Nashville,

Born July 24, 1957, in Plant City, FL; daughter of Mel Tillis (a country singer-songwriter); married Rick Mason (a painter), c. 1978 (divorced); married Bob DiPiero (a songwriter), February 14, 1991; children: (first marriage) Ben.

Singer and songwriter, 1975—. Made first stage appearance with father, Mel Tillis, at age 8; wrote songs for father's music publishing company, 1976-77; member of a jazz band in San Francisco, 1977-78; signed with Warner Bros., Nashville, c. 1982; moved to Arista Records, Nashville, 1990; had first Number One song, "Don't Tell Me What To Do," 1991; staff writer for Tree Publishing.

Awards: Nominated for a Horizon Award, Country Music Association (CMA), 1991.

Addresses: *Record company*—Arista Records, 1 Music Circle, Nashville, TN 37203. *Other*—P.O. Box 25304, Nashville, TN 37202.

writing songs for her father's music publishing company. The following year she moved to San Francisco, where she worked in a jazz band.

Tillis related in *People* that throughout her youth her father pressed her to record country music, promising to find her a producer and an agent. She could not accept his help on his terms, though. "My daddy doesn't necessarily understand the kind of music I do," she said. "He always had me singing little-girl songs, and I'd be crushed, and then he'd get mad at me." Becoming part of the punk scene of San Francisco, Tillis married a painter and had a son. The marriage soon ended, and she drifted back to Nashville, determined to make music in her own style.

Signed With Arista Records

In 1983 Tillis signed a contract with Warner Bros. and released her first album, *Above and Beyond the Doll of Cutie.* The work was a departure from standard Nashville fare, to say the least. One critic compared it to the recordings of Pat Benatar and other hard-rocking female vocalists. Tillis noted in *People* that her career choices were strongly influenced by her father's fame. "I think I subconsciously chose pop and R & B, everything but country, because I didn't like competing on *his* turf," she said. For his part, Mel Tillis reacted

to his daughter's choice of material with equal parts of indifference and mild criticism.

Warner Bros. released Tillis after her first album sold moderately but did not yield any hits. She continued to write songs, this time for Tree Publishing, and she was pleasantly surprised when the executives from Arista Records offered her another opportunity to record. Her 1990 contract with Arista was tendered after producer Tim Dubois heard her sing at the famed Bluebird Cafe.

Late in 1990 Tillis released *Put Yourself in My Place,* a more traditional work that features a number of songs she wrote herself; the LP's first Number One hit was "Don't Tell Me What to Do," a song *Country Music's* Rich Kienzle described as having "a strong lyric, one that Pam more than does justice." Tillis remarked in the *Chicago Tribune* that she switched to so-called "pure country" in reaction to audience demand. "Being a musician, my personal taste is to the . . . left," she said. "But getting out there and playing for people—I've been doing shows even without a record, playing all over—you just get a feel for what people want to hear. I don't think it's a thing of the album pandering or catering. People are calling it 'new traditional' or 'solid country,' but there are things I'm bringing to the table vocally that I picked up from other styles. I just think it's an honest arrival at a point."

Demonstrated Versatility

Put Yourself in My Place was well received by critics and country audiences alike. Songs such as the autobiographical "Melancholy Child," the hit "Don't Tell Me What to Do," and "I've Already Fallen"—a ballad Tillis co-wrote with her husband, Bob DiPiero—demonstrate the versatility the singer achieved after years of experimenting with various musical styles. Kienzle called the album "a quirky but likable effort with a distinctive edge that . . . tips its hat to contemporary, country-rock and traditional sounds, combining the best of them all." Praising the album in *Entertainment Weekly,* Alanna Nash found that "Tillis shows here how well she can craft smart and sassy country material—everything from bluegrass to Celtic to country-pop—and also sell it with a commanding, big-voiced presence."

Needless to say, Tillis's father is happy that she has returned to the country fold. Pam expresses little regret for the route she has taken to stardom—she still maintains that she has learned from all of her experiences, good and bad, and that she is ready to embrace success on her own terms. Hurst contended that the multi-talented Tillis "is following in [her father's] footsteps by becoming one of Nashville's finer songwriters. . . .

[Her work] also makes clear that she is one of the town's more adept singers." The critic concluded: "Having grown up in the midst of 'traditional' Nashville, [Pam] now shows not only that she has the talent to perform her father's style of music but also that she can do it with stunning emotional authenticity."

Selected discography

Above and Beyond the Doll of Cutie, Warner Bros., 1983.
Put Yourself in My Place (includes "Don't Tell Me What to Do," "Melancholy Child," and "Maybe It Was Memphis"), Arista, 1991.
Homeward Looking Angel, Arista, 1992.

Sources

Chicago Tribune, November 29, 1990; January 24, 1991.
Country America, June 1991; June 1992.
Country Music, May/June 1991; May/June 1992.
Entertainment Weekly, March 15, 1991.
People, November 14, 1983; May 27, 1991.
Pulse!, February 1991.

Additional information for this profile was obtained from Arista Records press material, 1991.

—*Anne Janette Johnson*

A Tribe Called Quest

Rap group

Three high-school friends from New York City—Q-Tip, Phife, and Ali—comprise the progressive, quick-witted, hip-hop group known as A Tribe Called Quest. The trio are some of the founding members of, and brightest stars among, the Native Tongues, an informal collective of New York-based rappers that includes De La Soul, the Jungle Brothers, Black Sheep, Monie Love, and Queen Latifah. A Tribe Called Quest's second album, *The Low End Theory,* demonstrated the group's popularity in February of 1992 by ringing up gold sales, while at the same time illustrating the Tribe's outstanding creativity.

Q-Tip, Phife, Ali, and Jarobi—who would remain a full-fledged member of the group only until 1991—were classmates at New York City's Murry Bergtraum High School for Business Careers. In 1988 they met the members of De La Soul at a Fourth of July concert. From this holiday congregation was born the Native Tongues. A Tribe Called Quest helped form the musicians' alliance to preserve the essence of hip-hop, maintain rap's sharp edge, and to avoid trite commercialization of the

For the Record. . .

Members include **Ali** (born Ali Shaheed Muhammed in 1970, in Brooklyn, NY), **Phife** (born Malik Taylor, April 10, 1970, in Brooklyn), and **Q-Tip** (born Jonathan Davis, November 20, 1970, in New York, NY). Previous lineup included **Jarobi,** who left the band in 1991.

Group formed in 1988; all members attended the Murry Bergtraum vocational school in New York City; signed with Jive Records; released *People's Instinctive Travels and the Paths of Rhythm,* 1990. Appeared on *Late Night With David Letterman,* NBC-TV, 1992.

Awards: Gold record for *The Low End Theory.*

Addresses: *Record company*—Jive Records, 137-139 West 25th Street, New York, NY 10001.

genre. The performers of the Native Tongues are not linked in a formal business sense but perform guest raps on each others' albums and hail each other with affection in their liner notes.

A Tribe Called Quest began their recording career by releasing the single "Description of a Fool" in July of 1989, followed by the memorable "I Left my Wallet in El Segundo" in January of 1990. When offers started pouring in from major record labels across the country, A Tribe Called Quest chose to sign with the distinctly hip-hop-oriented Jive Records, figuring correctly that this label best represented their sound. Q-Tip—also known as the Abstract—the group's lead rapper and chief rhyme crafter, "rhymes like the sound is coming directly out of his throat," according to *Source* contributor Chris Wilder. Ali serves as the trio's DJ, and Phife, who also goes by Phife Dawg, generally plays the backup role of straight-man to Q-Tip. The group's earliest releases championed a hip-hop sound true to the music's roots. Said a *Source* reviewer of their unique style, as evidenced on their second release, "Instead of just throwing a beat over a loop, the Tribe combine distinct pieces of music, program their own beats, and transform their samples into a sound that is truly their own."

Jazzy Loops

On their debut album, *People's Instinctive Travels and the Paths of Rhythm,* A Tribe Called Quest forged a new path in rap by fusing jazz with the pop structure of hip-hop. *Art Forum* characterized the release by its "jazzy loops, laid-back rapping style, and offbeat rhymes." Q-

Tip, a self-proclaimed abstract poet, told *Rap Express* contributor Michael A. Gonzales, "My father was the one who turned me on to both jazz and poetry. When everyone was looking on old records for beats to rap over, I just pulled out all these jazz albums. . . . I can play electric bass by ear, but I wanna play an upright bass and form a jazz quartet and play small clubs. . . . Like the Duke Ellington records my father used to spin. That's the stuff I wanna play." The Tribe's first album was such a bold innovation that other groups quickly began to pilfer their uncommon jazz-rap style.

After the release of *Instinctive Travels,* Q-Tip contributed his talent for rhyme to Deee-Lite's platinum-selling single "Groove Is in the Heart" and lent a hand to Lenny Kravitz and Sean Lennon's "Give Peace A Chance" single. The Tribe as a group contributed cameo raps to the Jungle Brothers album *Straight Out of the Jungle* and to De La Soul's single "Buddy." In fact, most of the band's material for their first album was written in 1985 and 1986 when they initially began to make rap appearances on the albums of fellow musicians. While in the studio working on their second album, A Tribe Called Quest chalked up an acoustic appearance on MTV's *Unplugged,* performing with rap heavyweights LL Cool J, MC Lyte, and De La Soul.

Second Album Stressed Rap Basics

The follow-up to *People's Instinctive Travels and the Paths of Rhythm* was dubbed *The Low End Theory.* The phrase "low end theory" refers to the visceral, bottom-heavy bass sounds and drum beats at the core of the band's music. Explained Q-Tip in *The Source,* "the music is low and when you hear it loud you feel it." Ali elaborated, remarking, "It's lower than anything—you can't hear it on any Walkman speakers, you need a good system to hear it. That's how deep the frequencies are." Though still heavily influenced by jazz, *The Low End Theory* is less avant-garde than the Tribe's previous effort; as is suggested in the title, the record provides a more street-oriented sound, offering a simpler, more gut-level hip-hop style than did *Instinctive Travels.* And though the marked "positivity" of the first record found a place on the second, *Low End* featured several songs that signaled the group's growing distaste for the music industry.

On that topic Q-Tip has been particularly vocal. Aside from what he and other rappers view as standard record company practice of creating images of rap stars that are sometimes not really representative of the actual artist and a tendency to condescend to the artist, the leader of the Tribe is especially alarmed at the lack of artist control of the business end of rap and the growing exploitation of the genre by whites. At an emotional 1991 New Music Seminar panel discussion in New York City, speaker Q-Tip ventured: "There's [record company people] who live in Connecticut, got a fat house. They probably sit back and listen to Fleetwood Mac and shit. Then they'll sign someone like Vanilla Ice. Why don't they go to Brooklyn or out to Queens and find some kid on the street? He knows what he likes!" Tip went on, admonishing, "We gotta wake up and realize what [record company recruiters are] doing. They're trying to destroy hip-hop the same way they destroyed rock & roll."

Low End Boasts Numerous Highlights

On *The Low End Theory*, Phife significantly emerged from behind Q-Tip's shadow, with vocals a bit quicker and higher-pitched than Tip's, most notably on the cuts "Butter" and "Buggin' Out." Asserted *The Source*, "Those who questioned Phife's microphone techniques on the first album will swallow those doubts as he practically steals the show on this one. Phife provides a more straight-up b-boy approach to complement Tip's mellow vibes." *Source* contributor Wilder reflected along the same lines, musing, "Maybe Phife's very noticeably improved lyrical skills . . . are what make this album a follow-up that does not disappoint." Also not disappointing was the single "Scenario," an infectious duet with the group Leaders of the New School, the video of which received quite a bit of exposure on MTV. Another video, for the single "Check the Rhime," featured erstwhile Tribe member Jarobi and drew praise from Wilder, who called it "as creative on screen as Quest is on the mixing board, with crazy abstract visual effects done tastefully."

Another distinguishing characteristic of *The Low End Theory* is the presence of legendary jazz bassist and former Miles Davis Quintet member Ron Carter, who agreed to contribute his skills to the release even though he had never heard of the group before they obtained his home phone number, called him up, and implored him to work with them. Carter agreed to listen to their music, and after doing so, quickly assented to join forces with the Tribe.

Major Exposure

The Low End Theory was much lauded by critics; *The Source* gave it their highest rating, establishing the record as "a hip-hop classic." After the release went gold, Q-Tip and posse performed live on television's *Late Night With David Letterman*. And in July of 1992, various media reported that Q-Tip would star with dance diva Janet Jackson in *Poetic Justice*, filmmaker John Singleton's follow-up to his controversial and enormously popular *Boyz N the Hood*.

A Tribe Called Quest has won accolades for their use of complex musical structures and the fresh collage of sonic information they have produced. They call themselves A Tribe Called Quest because they are committed to braving new paths, guided purely by their passion for music. Of that dedication Phife said in *Art Forum*, "It's not always raking in money and being on MTV. You go through your share of ups and downs and you've got to really love the music. That's why I always tell kids, if it's in your blood and soul 100 per cent, THEN GO FOR IT." Along with this drive, the Tribe have met with success through their crusade to bring hip-hop back to the gut-thumping, thought-provoking "low end"—far removed from the diluting effects of commercialism and elaborate theatrical antics—while at the same time infusing the genre with the exuberance and sophistication of jazz. In so doing, A Tribe Called Quest has expanded the envelope of rap. Said mixmaster Ali in *The Source* of the group's evolution, "There's so many sides to us and so many personalities that we could go all kinds of ways and different directions."

Selected discography

People's Instinctive Travels and the Paths of Rhythm, Jive, 1990.
The Low End Theory, Jive, 1991.

Also contributed to Jungle Brothers LP *Straight Out of the Jungle*, De La Soul single "Buddy," and soundtrack to *Boomerang*, Paramount, 1992. Q-Tip appeared on the Deee-Lite single "Groove Is in the Heart," from the album *World Clique*, 1991, and contributed to Lenny Kravitz and Sean Lennon's single "Give Peace A Chance," 1991.

Sources

Art Forum, Number 17, 1992.
Billboard, October 26, 1991.
Entertainment Weekly, December 6, 1991.
Michigan Daily (University of Michigan), September 24, 1991.
Playboy, January 1992.
Pulse!, December 1991.
Rap Express, January 1992.
Right On, April 1992.
Source, November 1991; January 1992.
Spin, July 1992.
Streetsound, February 1992.

—*B. Kimberly Taylor*

Van Halen

Rock band

Van Halen exploded onto the national rock scene in 1977 with a distinctively heavy sound, a wise-cracking, over-the-top lead singer, and a guitar player whose fiery, innovative solos would earn accolades from music critics and some of his most famous colleagues. Though the band changed singers after achieving their first Number One hit, Van Halen has remained one of the biggest attractions in rock, its combination of heavy metal energy and pop songcraft almost single-handedly preparing Top Forty radio for the bevy of crossover metal acts that followed them.

At the heart of this high-profile show business enterprise is Edward—known popularly as Eddie and, to his wife, Ed—Van Halen, a shy, near-reclusive musical inventor who tinkers with his guitar day and night. "It's the free-flowing energy and imagination of Edward's playing that captures the music's spirit," commented *Musician's* J. D. Considine, who called the guitarist's solos "flashy, unpredictable and totally idiomatic, adhering to a logic that seems to apply solely to electric guitar." That sound, along with the thunderous bottom

Members include **Michael Anthony** (born June 20, 1955, in Chicago, IL), bass and vocals; **Sammy Hagar** (born c. 1949 in Monterey, CA; replaced **David Lee Roth** [born October 10, 1955, in Bloomington, IN], 1985), vocals and guitar; **Alex Van Halen** (born May 8, 1955, in Nijmegen, the Netherlands), drums; and **Edward Van Halen** (born January 26, 1957, in Nijmegen; married Valerie Bertinelli [an actress], 1981; children: Wolfgang), guitar and vocals. Alex and Edward are the sons of Jan (a musician) and Eugenia Van Halen.

Group formed c. 1974; performed gigs in Sunset Strip clubs, Los Angeles, CA, 1974-75; signed with Warner Bros. Records and released first album, *Van Halen,* 1978.

Awards: Named top album rock artist by *Billboard,* 1991; favorite heavy metal/hard rock album, American Music Awards, 1991, Grammy Award, 1992, and double platinum record, 1992, all for *For Unlawful Carnal Knowledge.*

Addresses: *Publicist*—Solters/Roskin/Friedman, Inc., 5455 Wilshire Blvd., Los Angeles, CA 90036. *Record company*—Warner Bros., 3300 Warner Blvd., Burbank, CA 91505.

end provided by bassist Michael Anthony and drummer Alex Van Halen—Eddie's older brother—have kept the band at the top of the metal heap despite the departure of theatrical frontman David Lee Roth in 1985 and subsequent arrival of veteran singer-guitarist Sammy Hagar. Though Van Halen's 1991 album, *For Unlawful Carnal Knowledge,* received mixed reviews, it shot to Number One on the U.S. charts, and the group's tour to support the album bucked a national trend of dismally low ticket sales.

From Ivory to Metal

The Van Halen brothers were born in the Netherlands in the 1950s. Their father, Jan, a professional clarinetist and saxophonist, fought with the Dutch Resistance against the Nazis. He met his wife, Eugenia, in Indonesia. Jan Van Halen encouraged his sons to be musicians, but didn't approve of rock and roll. Both boys took classical piano lessons. When Eddie was eight and Alex about ten, the family moved to the United States, settling in California. There the brothers discovered rock music. "I got a paper route so I could pay for my $41.25 St. George drum kit," Eddie told Considine,

"and while I was out throwing the papers, my brother was playing my drums. He got better, so I said, 'Okay, you can keep the damn drums.'" The younger Van Halen picked up the guitar at age 12, thus beginning a long and passionate love affair with the instrument.

Neither of the brothers fared particularly well in school, but they persisted in their musical pursuits, eventually forming a band together, which they called Mammoth. The brothers played various instruments—at one time Eddie played piano and Alex wielded saxophone. Eddie sang, and after going through a number of bass players, he and Alex recruited Michael Anthony. "Then I got sick of singing," Eddie remembered, "and we got Dave [Roth] in the band." Roth had been singing in a group called the Red Ball Jets and owned a public address system. The quartet that would become Van Halen coalesced throughout 1974 and 1975, playing Los Angeles hard rock clubs like Gazzarri's on the famed Sunset Strip.

"Van Halen" Classier Than "Rat Salade"

Eddie wanted to call the group Rat Salade, but Roth felt Van Halen sounded classier. They soon generated a large local following and were signed by Warner Bros. Records; in 1978 they released their debut LP, *Van Halen.* It took the rock world by storm. Eddie's lightning-fast solos—characterized by screaming tremolo-bar effects and his patented fingertapping technique—signaled a new era in hard-rock guitar. Roth's flamboyant vocals, trademark shriek, and quirky humor gave the group personality. The first single, a remake of the Kinks' 1964 hit "You Really Got Me," was a substantial hit.

Reviews of the first LP, however, like those of many subsequent Van Halen albums, were mixed. *Melody Maker* called *Van Halen* "an outstanding and thoroughly recommended (but only to the converted) debut," and correspondent Steve Gett referred to it as "unquestionably one of the greatest heavy-rock releases of our time." Meanwhile, Charles M. Young—reviewing the record for *Rolling Stone*—noted that "Van Halen's secret is not doing anything original while having the hormones to do it better." But critics were never terribly relevant to the band's career. Metal fans adored them, making a hero of Eddie and cheering Roth's cock-of-the-walk theatrics. Their 1979 sophomore effort, *Van Halen II,* sold tremendously and yielded the hit "Dance the Night Away," a rock anthem that crossed a memorable pop hook with Eddie's singular riffing. Despite its popularity, Timothy White dismissed the album in *Rolling Stone,* referring to the group's "stilted instrumental blarings" and chiding Roth for his wolf-whistling improvisations. *Melody Maker*'s Gett, on the other hand, called *Van Halen II* "a more constructive and better balanced HM [heavy metal] package than one might at first have expected."

Groupies and Rubble

Soon Van Halen was touring the world, playing to large crowds and sparking considerable gossip about their backstage activities. Stories detailing the band's demands of M&Ms candies—with the brown ones removed—became legendary in music circles. Alex earned the reputation of a notorious womanizer. Eddie, the perpetually shy one, married actress Valerie Bertinelli; the two flouted expectations by remaining together throughout the band's spectacular ascent, though 1990 reports of the guitarist's alleged problems with drugs and alcohol also hinted at tension in the marriage. Roth's peculiar charisma alternately confused and amused interviewers. "To call him vain would be an understatement," wrote Gett in a 1979 profile. "Narcissistic would be more appropriate."

In the same article, Roth, nonetheless, perhaps best described the band's appeal: "It's energy, man, it's youth—that's what everybody's about, at least in some way, no matter how many five-syllable words you may know. A part of you is 15 years old, and that's where Van Halen comes in." Roth's worldview made many die-hard rockers look tame by comparison. He told *Musician*'s Young, "You make a few good friends, you burn a trail across the world, leaving a permanent shadow of groupies and rubble as never before in the history of rock 'n' roll, and one day, it's Miller Time."

Van Halen's third record, *Women and Children First,* delivered the hard rock goods on "Everybody Wants Some!" and "The Cradle Will Rock. . ." *Rolling Stone*'s David Fricke commented, "Megalomania of this kind is an acquired taste, yet the haste with which *Women and Children First* bullied its way into the Top Ten suggests that there's a little Van Halen in everybody." Fricke also praised Eddie's playing, noting that the guitarist "harnesses feedback almost as well as [sixties guitar innovator] Jimi Hendrix did and displays smarts plus speed in his solos."

Eddie a Guitar Hero

Other musicians were even more emphatic about Eddie Van Halen's gifts: "That incredible virtuosity combined with that beautiful grin allows me to forgive him for letting David Lee Roth stand in front of him," Pete Townshend, leader of the famed British rock band The Who, remarked in *Rolling Stone;* groundbreaking guitarist-composer Frank Zappa thanked Eddie "for reinventing the guitar"; in *Musician,* Andy Summers of the pop/new wave trio the Police called him "a natural virtuoso," adding, "What impresses me is his passion, his spirit and his musicality. Really, I think he is the greatest rock guitarist since Hendrix." For all the comparisons to Hendrix, Eddie revealed in *Musician* that his guitar hero was actually England's Eric Clapton, guitarist for the Yardbirds, Cream, Derek and the Dominoes, and later, an accomplished solo artist. In the early days, Eddie would play Cream records at a slow speed to learn every single note of every solo.

Van Halen followed up *Women and Children First* with 1981's *Fair Warning,* which included the upbeat single "So This Is Love." Of the band's customary recording process, Alex explained to *Melody Maker* contributor Gett, "We take all the stage gear into a big room and play. [Producer] Ted Templeman just sits there and controls the dials behind a two-way mirror. We play, he sits there and puts it on the album." The band favored

---

"I tell ya, to boil the whole thing down, it's just a whole lot of fun. I've never had so much fun in my life."
—Eddie Van Halen

---

this live approach for its time-efficiency—they were often in a hurry to get back on the road—and for the spontaneous feel of the result. In any case, *Fair Warning,* which *Melody Maker* lauded as "a masterblast of American metal," was a more laborious affair: Eddie told *Guitar Player* that it "took longer than any album we've ever done." Thus they favored a faster, more simple approach to their next LP, *Diver Down.* Recorded in 12 days, the album contained a number of cover tunes, including a hit version of Roy Orbison's "Pretty Woman" and another Kinks song, "Where Have All the Good Times Gone?" Jan Van Halen sat in with his sons on one track, leading them on a foray into swing; *Diver Down* also contained some acoustic blues. *Melody Maker* didn't like it much: "The worst yet?" asked a reviewer rhetorically—answering, "Probably." Even so, the faithful rushed to buy it.

Crossover Success

In 1982 Eddie recorded a guitar solo for Michael Jackson's "Beat It," one of several huge hits from Jackson's enormously popular album *Thriller*. On the strength of the solo alone, Jackson reached a corner of the rock market that had previously eluded him. Despite the immense revenues generated by the song, Eddie accepted no payment for his work on it. As in many other instances, he was playing for the fun of it. The publicity, however didn't hurt the band. *1984,* released that year, featured "Jump," Van Halen's first Number One hit. With a simple synthesizer hook, played by Eddie, the song—which Roth had vetoed two years before—brought the group to Top Forty radio and almost by itself created "Lite Metal." The album contained a number of other hits with popular videos, notably the raunchy "Hot For Teacher." *Rolling Stone* would eventually include *1984* in its Top 100 Albums of the Eighties, mostly because of "Jump."

Despite this breakthrough to mainstream success, Roth left Van Halen the following year. Eddie told *Musician's* Considine that Roth was trying to get a film made and that the band was "basically in the twilight zone, not knowing whether Dave wanted to do a record or not." Eventually Eddie, Alex, and Mike let the singer go. The "musical tension" that critics had admired in the band had at last, reportedly, turned into outright animosity. Roth went on to a successful solo career. After weighing the options, Eddie invited former Montrose member Sammy Hagar to try out for the spot vacated by Roth. Hagar remarked, "It was magic. Boom. Overnight. Instantly. Automatically." Perhaps no one was as pleased as Eddie. "When we walked out of that studio," explained the guitarist, standing on a chair to demonstrate, "Pretend the chair ain't there." The old tension turned into a new camaraderie; Van Halen was having fun again. "This is the real Van Halen," Eddie proclaimed. Of the new addition Considine remarked, "Sammy has plenty of range and can scream like a banshee, but his sound is always under control. To a certain extent, it's the vocal equivalent of Eddie's guitar sound, combining a cutting edge with an underlying warmth. Best of all, Sammy's melodic instincts are so in sync with Edward's that the songs move forward like a sonic juggernaut."

Fans Didn't Miss Roth

The reaction of metal fans to Roth's departure could be measured in part by the results of *Hit Parader's* 1986 "Man of the Year" readers' poll. Roth came in first, and Eddie in fourth; they would both retain the loyalty of Van Halen fans. The first post-Roth Van Halen record, *5150,* was another monster hit. Taking its title from police code for an escaped mental patient—a label so beloved by self-proclaimed oddball Eddie that he used it for the name of his home recording studio—*5150* boasted the radio-friendly single "Why Can't This Be Love?" Critics missed Roth's eccentricity; Roy Traskin's *Musician* review was typical in its declaration that "Van Hagar is just another rock 'n' roll band, boasting one brilliant musician [Eddie] and one boring frontman." *Melody Maker* pragmatically concluded, "Van Halen used to be flash and sleazy. Now they're just flash. For the most part the songs are just as good and, anyway, all of their albums have been flawed. So don't worry about it." *5150* went to Number One three weeks after its release, and Van Halen continued to sell out huge arenas.

The next album, *OU812,* was released in 1988 and went to Number One in two weeks. The group fared brilliantly on that year's "Van Halen's Monsters of Rock" tour. In 1991, to even greater fanfare, Van Halen released *For Unlawful Carnal Knowledge,* which earned them a bevy of awards. *Billboard* deemed the group top album rock artist, and *For Unlawful Carnal Knowledge* received the favorite heavy metal/hard rock album nod at the American Music Awards. In 1992, Van Halen nabbed its first Grammy award. Hagar was honored as 1992's outstanding vocalist at the San Francisco Bay Area Music Awards. And the album's sales were phenomenal—it went double platinum; *For Unlawful Carnal Knowledge* was credited by many retailers as the single impetus for bringing rock fans back into record stores after a long slump. Similarly, the group's barnstorming 1991 concert tour was one of a very few that flourished in that recessionary season. Critics were harder to please than fans, of course; *Rolling Stone's* John Milward complained that with the addition of Hagar "the band has substituted an increasingly dense sound for a distinct personality." But *For Unlawful Carnal Knowledge* yielded a clutch of hits, including "Top of the World," the hard-rocking "Poundcake," and the melodic "Right Now"—the innovative video of which made it to *Entertainment Weekly* critic Jim Mullen's "Hot Sheet."

And the top of the world is where Van Halen has remained—after more than a decade of touring and recording. A generation of young guitarists has attempted to match Eddie Van Halen's innovative style, though he averred in a *Guitar Player* interview, "I don't like people doing things exactly like me." In 1991 Eddie unveiled an Ernie Ball-Music Man guitar he'd had designed to his specifications, only agreeing to put his name on it after a rigorous development process. He dismissed persistent questions about a solo album by declaring that with Van Halen he could do anything he wanted. "I tell ya, to boil the whole thing down," he told *Musician's* Considine, "it's just a whole lot of fun. I've never had so much fun in my life."

Selected discography

On Warner Bros. Records

Van Halen (includes "You Really Got Me"), 1978.
Van Halen II (includes "Dance the Night Away"), 1979.
Women and Children First (includes "Everybody Wants Some!" and "The Cradle Will Rock. . ."), 1980.
Fair Warning (includes "So This Is Love"), 1981.
Diver Down (includes "Pretty Woman" and "Where Have All the Good Times Gone?"), 1982.
1984 (includes "Jump" and "Hot for Teacher"), 1984.
5150 (includes "Why Can't This Be Love?"), 1986.
OU812, 1988.

Sources

For Unlawful Carnal Knowledge (includes "Poundcake," "Right Now" and "Top of the World"), 1991.

AB, August 12, 1991.
Entertainment Weekly, February 21, 1992; May 1, 1992.
Guitar Player, December 1982; October 1987; May 1991; January 1992.
Hit Parader, Spring 1987.
Melody Maker, June 3, 1978; October 21, 1978; April 14, 1979; June 2, 1979; June 28, 1980; May 30, 1981; May 8, 1982; February 4, 1984; April 5, 1986.
Musician, September 1982; March 1984; June 1984; February 1986; June 1986; February 1987.
Rolling Stone, May 4, 1978; July 12, 1979; June 26, 1980; June 21, 1984; November 16, 1989; August 22, 1991.
Village Voice, July 22, 1981.

—*Simon Glickman*

The
Weavers

Folk group

"Folk singing in the U.S. didn't really begin with the Weavers, of course," a *Newsweek* correspondent wrote in 1963, "It just seems that way sometimes." As early as the late 1940s, the Weavers set the stage for the so-called "folk revival" of the 1960s, topping the record charts with their versions of "Goodnight Irene," "Tzena, Tzena," and a host of other hits. According to David Dunaway in his book *How Can I Keep From Singing: Pete Seeger,* when poet Carl Sandburg heard them, he wrote: "The Weavers are out of the grass roots of America. I salute them. . . . When I hear America singing, the Weavers are there." They created a strong and essential link between the music of the first part of the twentieth century and the music of the 1990s; few folk performers and audiences exist who do not consider the Weavers a major influence on their musical lives.

Prior to World War II Pete Seeger and Lee Hays had been part of another folk group, the Almanac Singers, but the ensemble broke up at the outset of the war. Seeger helped found People's Song, Inc., which pub-

For the Record. . .

Members included **Ronnie Gilbert** (vocals), born c. 1927 in New York, NY; daughter of factory workers; married Marty Weg (divorced); received master's degree in clinical psychology; **Lee Hays** (vocals), born in 1914 in Little Rock, AR; died from diabetes, August 26, 1981, in Croton-on-Hudson, NY; son of William (a minister) and Ellen (a court reporter) Reinhardt; attended the College of the Ozarks; **Fred Hellerman** (guitar, vocals), born May 13, 1927, in New York, NY; graduated from Brooklyn College; **Pete Seeger** (banjo, guitar, vocals), born May 3, 1919, in Patterson, NY; son of Charles (a conductor, musicologist, and educator) and Constance (a violinist and teacher; maiden name, de Clyer) Edson; married Toshi Aline Ohta, July 20, 1943; children: Daniel Adams, Mike Salter, Virginia; attended Harvard University, 1936-38. Seeger was replaced in 1958 by **Erik Darling** (banjo, vocals), born September 25, 1933, in Baltimore, MD. Darling was replaced in 1962 by **Frank Hamilton** (banjo, vocals), who was replaced c. 1963 by **Bernie Krause** (vocals).

Group formed in 1948 in New York City; began to receive critical attention while playing at New York's Village Vanguard, 1949-50; signed by Decca Records, 1950; performed at clubs, on radio, and on television; blacklisted by the House Un-American Activities Committee (HUAC) and FBI as possible communists, 1952; Carnegie Hall reunion concert, 1955; performed under blacklist, 1955-63; disbanded 1963; reunited for Carnegie Hall concert, 1980, which was the subject of documentary *Wasn't That a Time*.

lished bulletins combining a song sheet and a folk music newsletter. Hanging around People's Songs were a number of folk singers, including Hays, Fred Hellerman, and Ronnie Gilbert; in 1948 they formed a quartet. At the time, Hellerman was reading Gerhart Hauptmann's play *The Weavers*—about a European peasant revolt—and suggested this as their name. Given the number of folk songs about weavers, the name fit well. The title also described the way their strange combination of voices—an alto, two baritones, and as Seeger called himself, a "split tenor"—worked together. According to Gene Marine of *Rolling Stone,* they worked out arrangements "so that the voices crossed and recrossed continually—giving a different and singularly appropriate meaning to the group's name."

Amassed Huge Repertoire

The Weavers' first step was to gather songs—not difficult with Seeger's incredible mental repertoire. They borrowed songs from their friends and from around the world. Seeger and Hays wrote "Tomorrow Is a Highway" and "If I Had a Hammer"; Hays contributed "Kisses Sweeter Than Wine," "Lonesome Traveler," and "Wasn't That a Time," which he composed with help from poet Walter Lowenfels.

On Thanksgiving of 1948 the Weavers debuted at Irving Hall in New York City and then played wherever and whenever they could. The following summer, however, an event almost discouraged them enough to call it quits. Performing at an outdoor concert in Peekskill, New York, along with scholar, actor, and singer Paul Robeson, they met with violence from local right wing groups and police. According to Dunaway, the performers and the audience were attacked with rocks and nightsticks, injured by the broken glass of smashed car windows, and assailed with such verbal taunts as "'Go home you white niggers,' 'Kikes,' and 'Go on Back to Russia.'"

The Weavers were not going to let the events at Peekskill discourage them. Dunaway wrote that Seeger felt a duty "to reach out to the faces behind the rocks at Peekskill." At the end of 1949, a few months after the attack, the group signed a contract to play at New York City's Village Vanguard. They received little attention at first, but before long, folklorist Alan Lomax brought Carl Sandburg in to hear them, and with Sandburg's comments, the press started to take notice. The Village Vanguard stint lasted six months, and as Marine noted, "suddenly it was as if everyone in Manhattan simultaneously discovered folk music."

The Weavers next step toward the mainstream came when they signed with Decca Records. They recorded "Tzena, Tzena," an Israeli folk song, and Huddie "Leadbelly" Ledbetter's "Goodnight Irene." Both sides of the single were virtually instant hits. *Time* magazine announced, "Last week a group of four high-spirited folksters known as the Weavers succeeded in shouting, twanging and crooning folk singing out of its cloistered corner into the commercial big time." The correspondent wasn't exaggerating: the record sold two million copies—"Goodnight Irene" and "Tzena, Tzena" remained at Numbers One and Two, respectively, on the charts for months. The group followed this success with more hits, including "Wreck of the John B.," "The Roving Kind," "So Long," "Lonesome Traveler," "Old Smoky," "Wide Missouri," and "Wimoweh." "If you know any of these songs today," Marine wrote, "it's almost certainly because of the Weavers."

The Weavers' concerts became as popular as their recordings. They appeared on television and in chic night clubs—strange places for folksingers who might be more accustomed to union rallies. The songs for which they were becoming famous were not particularly political, and they rarely performed any protest and union-organizing songs at nightclubs. Although some folk artists were able to ride on the coattails of the Weavers' popularity, others disparaged the Weavers for being too commercial. Whether out of jealousy or true indignation, they attacked the Weavers for "violating either the purity of the music or the political principles underlying it," noted Marine.

Targeted by Right-Wing Groups

Not political enough for some on the liberal left, the Weavers' connections to radical left wing groups and progressive causes made them far too political for those on the conservative right. Marine suggested that they were apparently trying to "subvert America by singing American folk songs." The events at Peekskill were only a taste of what was to come. As the Weavers' fame grew, so did anticommunist sentiment, spurred by the House Un-American Activities Committee (HUAC)—a council of the House of Representatives initiated in 1938 for the express purpose of ferreting out alleged communist sympathizers. The HUAC, a vicious harrier of suspected enemies of the United States, along with the FBI, was determined to destroy the American Left, and for a time they virtually succeeded.

The first attempts of the HUAC and the FBI to target the Weavers failed. Yet before long, as "information" was supplied to sponsors and club owners, jobs for the musicians began disappearing, and their scheduled appearances were canceled. The bomb came in 1952 when Harvey Matusow, a supposed communist informer, testified before the HUAC that Seeger, Gilbert, and Hellerman were members of the Communist Party. Matusow later recanted and, according to Dunaway, admitted to "perjury and conspiring with the U.S. attorneys to give false testimony." But for a time, the Weavers were blacklisted. Decca stopped recording them and by 1953 had deleted their old records from the label's catalogue. They were essentially banned from radio or television. As Willens wrote, Hays used to say, "We had to take a sabbatical, and it turned into a mondical and a tuesdical."

Seeger was able to continue performing occasionally, especially on college campuses. Gilbert started a family, Hellerman worked as a guitarist, accompanist, and composer, and Hays wrote mysteries. Accusations continued to dog Seeger and Hays in particular, and in 1955 the two were required to testify before Congress. Both appeared but refused to answer accusations, or to "name names." Seeger was cited for contempt of Congress, indicted, tried, and convicted. After several

years with a possible jail term hanging over his head, his conviction was reversed in 1962.

In spite of its power, the blacklist was not the complete tragedy for the Weavers that it had been for many others. In 1955, their former manager, Harold Leventhal, organized a reunion concert at Carnegie Hall, and they sold out two shows. Although still blacklisted, a small record company, Vanguard, agreed to sell the recording of the concert, and the album revived their populari-

---

"The Weavers are out of the grass roots of America. When I hear America singing, the Weavers are there."
—Carl Sandburg

---

ty. Gilbert later related in *The Progressive* that "None of us was terribly happy playing in the high class saloons and all that anyway. Sometimes it was fun, but most of the time that wasn't what turned us on." They seemed to take it in stride, especially Hays, who is known for his witticisms on the subject. At their reunion concert in 1980 he quipped that "If it wasn't for the honor, I'd just as soon not have been blacklisted."

Circumvented Blacklist

In the eyes of most of the recording and broadcasting industries, though, the Weavers simply did not exist. Seeger dropped out of the group in 1958. His departure was the result of a number of factors, but the spark was a conflict over whether or not to record a jingle for a cigarette commercial. Hays saw it as a way to break through the blacklist, but Seeger hated the idea of doing a commercial, especially one for cigarettes. Seeger was outvoted; he agreed to record the jingle, then resigned. Later, Seeger told Willens that the commercial may have been the impetus of his departure, but he had also been busy with his family, his solo work, and his teaching. Additional work with the Weavers was too burdensome. Ironically, the jingle never played on the air—the blacklist was stronger than they had thought.

Seeger was replaced by Erik Darling. Darling remained with the group until 1962, when he left to form the Rooftop Singers. Frank Hamilton took Darling's place and was subsequently succeeded by Bernie Krause.

At a 1963 Carnegie Hall concert, all of them, including Seeger, appeared on stage together.

By the early 1960s the Kingston Trio; Peter, Paul and Mary; Joan Baez; Bob Dylan; and other performers had made folk music popular again. Vanguard and Folkways reissued old Weavers recordings, and new groups recorded their songs, making some hits for the first time, including the Kingston Trio's version of "Where Have All the Flowers Gone" and Peter, Paul, and Mary's interpretation of "If I Had a Hammer." Despite new successes, much of the recording industry was skittish. In 1962 the Weavers were invited to perform on a televised *Dinner With the President,* but before long the blacklist cropped up again and they were immediately uninvited. Jumping on the folk music bandwagon, ABC launched a folk music show called *Hootenanny,* to which the Weavers were also not invited. Under pressure, ABC decided that the Weavers could perform if they signed a "loyalty oath." On principle, the group refused, and as a result, several other performers decided not to appear as well.

Reunion Demonstrated Continued Popularity

By this time, the Weavers' attentions were drifting in different directions. Bernie Krause, Seeger's third replacement, wasn't working out, and according to Willens, the group had their share of tensions. They officially disbanded after a December farewell concert at Chicago's orchestra hall. In November of 1980, the original members came together for another reunion at Carnegie Hall. A single newspaper advertisement instantly sold out two shows, and in *The Progressive* Nat Hentoff commented, "I had expected a kind of historical relic in the music of this reunion, but the collective and individual verve of these eclectic descendants of Tom Paine hasn't diminished—at least not on that night." *Wasn't That a Time,* a documentary of the concert and its preparations, was filmed and released shortly thereafter.

Hays, who had been fighting diabetes for some time, passed away several months after the concert. Gilbert, holding a masters degree in clinical psychology, maintained a practice while working on theater projects and a tour. Hellerman followed a career as a record producer, arranger, and recording musician, and worked in theater as well. Seeger continued performing, recording, and remained politically active.

Perhaps the Weavers' greatest gift was their ability to introduce so many people to the music they loved.

"Few groups have managed to cross over the line of commercialism without forfeiting artistic integrity and qualitative standards," wrote Kristin Baggelaar and Donald Milton in *Folk Music: More Than a Song.* "Throughout their career, the Weavers tried to maintain a balance between the purity of traditional material and the polish of professionalism, and they introduced to concert, cabaret, radio, and television audiences sophisticated yet genuine interpretations of the folk song." Their dedication to folk music survived a period of anticommunist sentiment, the blacklist, and time; in the process the Weavers influenced multiple generations of folk musicians and audiences, changing forever the nature of American folk song.

Selected discography

Singles

"Dig My Grave"/"Wasn't That a Time," Charter, 1949.
"The Hammer Song"/"Banks of Marble," Hootenanny, 1949.
"Around the World"/"Tzena, Tzena" (Hebrew), Decca, 1950.
"Tzena, Tzena" (English)/"Goodnight Irene," Decca, 1950.
"So Long"/"Lonesome Traveler," Decca, 1950.
"Wreck of the John B."/"The Roving Kind," Decca, 1950.
"On Top of Old Smoky"/"The Wide Missouri," Decca, 1951.
"When the Saints Go Marching In"/"Kisses Sweeter Than Wine," Decca 1951.
"Wimoweh"/"Old Paint," Decca, 1952.
"Hard Ain't It Hard"/"Run Home to Mama," Decca, 1952.
"Little Boxes"/"Where Have All the Flowers Gone," Columbia, 1963.
"Waist Deep in the Big Muddy"/"Down by the Riverside," Columbia, 1967.

Albums

The Weavers, Charter, 1949.
Folk Songs of America and Other Lands, Decca, 1951.
We Wish You a Merry Christmas, Decca, 1952.
The Weavers at Carnegie Hall, Vanguard, 1955.
The Weavers at Home, Vanguard, 1958.
The Weavers on Tour, Vanguard, 1958.
Best of the Weavers, Decca, 1959.
Folk Songs Around the World, Decca, 1959.
The Weavers at Carnegie Hall, Vanguard, 1960.
The Weavers at Carnegie Hall, Volume 2, Vanguard, 1960.
Traveling On, Vanguard, 1960.
Weavers Gold, Decca, 1962.
Almanac, Vanguard, 1962.
The Weavers Reunion at Carnegie Hall, Vanguard, 1963.
The Weavers Reunion at Carnegie Hall, Part 2, Vanguard, 1965.
The Weavers Songbag, Vanguard, 1967.

Sources

Books

Baggelaar, Kristin, and Donald Milton, *Folk Music: More Than a Song,* Thomas Y. Crowell Co., 1976.

Dunaway, David King, *How Can I Keep From Singing: Pete Seeger,* McGraw-Hill Book Co., 1981.

The Penguin Encyclopedia of Popular Music, edited by Donald Clarke, Viking, 1989.

Stambler, Irwin, and Grelun Landon, *The Encyclopedia of Folk, Country, and Western Music,* second edition, St. Martin's Press, 1983.

Willens, Doris, *Lonesome Traveler: The Life of Lee Hays,* W. W. Norton & Co., 1988.

Periodicals

Advertising Age, October 24, 1988.

Journal of American Folklore, October 1990.

Los Angeles Times, May 8, 1985.

Newsweek, May 13, 1963.

New York Times, February 8, 1952; December 1, 1980; June 19, 1981.

The Progressive, October 1981; June 1990.

Rolling Stone, April 13, 1972; October 15, 1981.

Time, September 25, 1950.

—*Megan Rubiner*

Dottie West

Singer, songwriter

Singer-songwriter Dottie West, a glamorous pillar of country music, first garnered widespread attention for her duet work with late country star Jim Reeves. After writing the hit "Is This Me?" for Reeves, she recorded "Love Is No Excuse" with him. In addition to duets with other artists, including Don Gibson and Kenny Rogers, West, who died in 1991, made a name for herself as a solo performer; she scored hits with "Here Comes My Baby" and "A Lesson in Leavin'" and became known for her trademark performance apparel, which usually consisted of high-heeled boots, tight jeans, and low-cut blouses. A regular feature of Nashville's Grand Ole Opry, she also turned her award-winning commercial jingle for Coca-Cola, "Country Sunshine," into a country chart-climber.

West was born Dorothy Marie Marsh on October 11, 1932, in McMinnville, Tennessee. Though she was the eldest of ten children and had to work hard in cotton and sugar cane fields to contribute to the family's finances, her parents also exposed her to country music, which she loved from an early age. West sang in the church choir, and her father taught her to play the guitar before he deserted the family when Dottie was 13. While managing to help her mother in a family-owned restaurant, West was also able to continue her music lessons and after graduating from high school, entered Tennessee Technological University with the goal of majoring in music.

Mixed With Country's Elite

At the university West studied many genres of music, but country remained her favorite. She met another country fan there among her fellow students—Bill West, who majored in engineering but enjoyed playing steel guitar as a hobby. The two began performing together at campus functions and married while still completing their mutual degrees. After both graduated, the couple moved to Cleveland, Ohio, where Bill West landed a job with an electronics firm. The Wests, however, still pursued their interest in playing country music and made appearances at local clubs. They were so successful in the region that they made regular appearances on the Cleveland television program *Landmark Jamboree*.

By 1959 Dottie West had attracted the attention of the small record label Starday, which signed her to a contract. Moving to Nashville, West and her husband were able to mix with famous or soon-to-be-famous country singers, including Willie Nelson, Roger Miller, and Patsy Cline. At get-togethers with these friends, West began learning to write songs. The first one she finished, "Is This Me?," caught the notice of Jim Reeves.

For the Record. . .

Born Dorothy Marie Marsh, October 11, 1932, in McMinnville, TN; died in an automobile accident, September 4, 1991; daughter of Hollis Marsh; married Bill West (an electronics engineer and musician), 1952 (divorced, 1969); married Byron Metcalf (a drummer), mid-1970s (divorced, 1980); married Alan Winters (a manager and sound engineer), c. 1983; children: Four from first marriage, including daughter Shelly and son Kerry. *Education:* Graduated from Tennessee Technological University during the 1950s.

Singer, songwriter, and guitarist. Performed with husband, Bill West, in the Cleveland, OH, area, during the late 1950s; appeared on local television show *Landmark Jamboree;* signed with Starday Records, 1959; featured artist on the Grand Ole Opry, c. 1964-91; commercial jingle writer and performer for Coca-Cola, beginning in 1970. Appeared on television shows, including *The Jimmy Dean Show, Country Music Hall, Faron Young Show,* and the *Tonight Show;* and in films, including *Second Fiddle to a Steel Guitar* and *There's a Still on the Hill.*

Selected awards: Writer's Award, Broadcast Music, Inc. (BMI), c. 1961, for "Is This Me?;" Grammy Award for best country vocal performance, 1964, for "Here Comes My Baby;" nominated for several Grammy Awards; Clio Award for best commercial of the year, c. 1973, for "Country Sunshine;" Country Music Association (CMA) awards for vocal duo of the year, 1978 and 1979, for recordings with Kenny Rogers.

Reeves not only recorded it but brought West to the attention of his label, RCA, which signed her to sing duets with Reeves and to record solo albums.

Around the same time, both West and her husband were hired as songwriters by Tree Publishing Company. Together they penned "Here Comes My Baby," a song that not only garnered West her first Grammy Award for vocal performance but was recorded by many other artists, including Perry Como. During the same period, she cut "Love Is No Excuse" with Reeves. But this lucrative vocal partnership came to an end when Reeves was killed in a plane crash in 1964.

Jingle Writer for Coca-Cola

West made a major duet pairing once when she recorded an album with Don Gibson in 1968. The title track

from the effort, *Rings of Gold,* reached Number One on country charts. Though Gibson did not wish to tour, West did, and the duo split after only one record. West continued to have success as a solo artist during the late 1960s with such songs as "Would You Hold It Against Me?," "What's Come Over My Baby," and "I'm a Country Girl." The last hit garnered West an offer to write a commercial based on it for Coca-Cola in 1970; the soft drink company liked the result so much that it signed her to a lifetime contract as a jingle writer.

In 1973 West provided Coca-Cola with another, even more successful ad featuring a song called "Country Sunshine." The immense popularity of the commercial prompted West to release the song as a single, and it became one of her biggest hits. The ad itself also netted West a prestigious Clio Award for commercial of the year; she was the first country artist ever to win that particular honor.

At about the same time, West's first marriage ended in divorce and she married her drummer Byron Metcalf, who was 11 years her junior. According to the *Washington Post,* West once commented, "Older men have been chasing around young girls for years, so it should be OK for women to be involved with younger guys." Her marriage to Metcalf ultimately dissolved because, West told Jim Albrecht of *Country Style,* of Metcalf's drinking problem. In the early 1980s, West wedded for the third time to another younger man, sound engineer Alan Winters. She told *People's* Dolly Carlisle: "We're a perfect match. He's very mature for his age, and I grew up to be a kid."

West and Rogers: A Popular Pairing

In 1976 West signed with the United Artists label. Her friend, country star Kenny Rogers, recorded on United Artists as well, and one evening in 1978 both he and West were scheduled for recording sessions. Rogers was early for his own and sat in on West's; he decided to sing with her on the cut "Every Time Two Fools Collide." Studio executives liked the results and persuaded the duo to cut an entire album together. Released in 1978, *Every Time Two Fools Collide* earned Rogers and West a Country Music Association (CMA) award for duo of the year. The following year brought them the same award, this time for the album *Classics.* In addition to "Every Time Two Fools Collide," Rogers and West had hit singles with "Anyone Who Isn't Me Tonight," "Til I Can Make It on My Own," and "All I Ever Need Is You."

During the 1980s, West continued to generate solo hits, most notably "A Lesson in Leavin'." Her popularity as a featured performer on the Grand Ole Opry endured as well. Also in that decade, West had the pleasure of watching her daughter Shelly West achieve country stardom with her hit "Jose Cuervo."

On September 4, 1991, West was killed in a car accident on her way to a performance at the Grand Ole Opry. Her car had broken down, and she was picked up by a businessman who lost control of his vehicle while driving 30 miles an hour over the posted speed limit. Frantic about getting to the Opry on time, she had urged him to speed. West, in fact, had always shown such determination throughout her singing career, and with her resolve, she helped clear the way for other women performers to become prominent in the country music industry. According to country great Tammy Wynette, as quoted in the *Chicago Tribune*, "[West] paved the way for so many of us." *Country Music*'s Rich Kienzle summed up West's significant musical accomplishments: "A master composer and vocalist, in the last three decades [of her life] she helped many new artists who had a major impact on where [country] music was headed. And in a nation where much of the population is aging, she proved glamour and style didn't end with youth."

Selected discography

Singles

"Here Comes My Baby," RCA, c. 1964.
(With Jim Reeves) "Love Is No Excuse," RCA, c. 1964.
"Would You Hold It Against Me?," RCA, 1966.
"Paper Mansions," RCA, 1967.
(With Don Gibson) "Rings of Gold," RCA, 1968.
"I'm a Country Girl," RCA, c. 1969.
"What's Come Over My Baby," RCA, c. 1969.
"Country Sunshine," RCA, 1973.
"When It's Just You and Me," United Artists, 1976.
(With Kenny Rogers) "Every Time Two Fools Collide," United Artists, 1978.
(With Rogers) "Anyone Who Isn't Me Tonight," United Artists, c. 1978.
(With Rogers) "Til I Can Make It on My Own," United Artists, c. 1979.

(With Rogers) "All I Ever Need Is You," United Artists, c. 1979.
"A Lesson in Leavin'," United Artists, 1980.
"You Pick Me Up," United Artists, c. 1980.
"Leavin's for Unbelievers," United Artists, c. 1981.
"Are You Happy, Baby?," United Artists, 1981.

Albums

Here Comes My Baby, RCA, 1965.
Dottie West Sings, RCA, 1966.
Suffer Time, RCA, 1966.
With All My Heart, RCA, 1967.
Sacred Ballads, RCA, 1967.
I'll Help You, RCA, 1967.
(With Don Gibson) *Rings of Gold*, RCA, 1968.
Country and West, RCA, 1970.
Legend in My Time, RCA, 1971.
Careless Hands, RCA, 1971.
Have You Heard, RCA, 1971.
I'm Only a Woman, RCA, 1972.
(With Kenny Rogers) *Every Time Two Fools Collide*, United Artists, 1978.
(With Rogers) *Classics*, United Artists, 1979.
Special Delivery, United Artists, 1979.
Wild West, United Artists, 1981.
Collector's Series, RCA, 1985.

Sources

Books

Stambler, Irwin, and Grelun Landon, *The Encyclopedia of Folk, Country, and Western Music*, St. Martin's, 1984.

Periodicals

Chicago Tribune, September 5, 1991.
Country Music, November/December 1991.
Los Angeles Times, September 5, 1991.
New York Times, September 5, 1991.
People, September 12, 1983.
Washington Post, September 5, 1991.

—Elizabeth Wenning

Yes

Rock band

The English band Yes were among the pioneers of what came to be known as "progressive rock" or "art rock." Their tightly orchestrated songs—usually outfitted with vaguely mystical lyrics—are noted for their dense harmonies, wild time signatures, and virtuosic soloing to produce what singer and co-founder Jon Anderson called "arranged excitement," though detractors have singled the band out as purveyors of pompous, overwrought soundscapes. From their formation in 1968, Yes have gone through numerous personnel changes and stylistic explorations, surviving over two decades of changing musical fashion; in 1991 they brought together most of their alumni for the collective effort *Union.*

Yes was the brainchild of two musicians: singer Jon Anderson and bassist Chris Squire. The two met in 1968 at London's Marquee Club, Anderson told *Rolling Stone*'s Steve Turner, and the singer figured Squire to be "a Simon and Garfunkel type." He was correct in assuming the bassist liked Simon and Garfunkel; in any case they found enough in common musically to begin

writing songs together. They found drummer Bill Bruford through an advertisement in *Melody Maker*—Bruford appeared in the add with his cheap drumkit, which he had painted to look like a more expensive brand—and enlisted guitarist Peter Banks and keyboardist Tony Kaye. The band began to work toward a new sound that would blend the intensity of rock with the formal grandeur of classical music and the stylistic and rhythmic adventurousness of jazz.

Early LPs Didn't Sell

The band made converts with their early live appearances and released their first LP, *Yes,* for Atlantic Records in 1969. In addition to their originals, *Yes* featured cover versions of songs by The Beatles and The Byrds. Lester Bangs, reviewing the album for *Rolling Stone,* declared Yes "a fine, developing group" and called the record "a pleasurable one," though "the excitement of true innovation is missing." Their sophomore effort, *Time and a Word,* released in 1970, included a souped-up rendition of folk star Richie Havens's "No Opportunity Necessary, No Experience Needed" that sported symphonic keyboards and a theme from a cowboy film. The record was engineered by Eddie Offord, whose consistent production work with Yes in ensuing years would make him virtually a band member.

Neither of these two albums, however, had much commercial impact; meanwhile, Banks had left the band, and Yes had to find a new guitarist. They hired Steve Howe, a classically trained musician whose style was heavily influenced by jazz players like Django Reinhardt and Wes Montgomery. With Howe's creative input, the group set to work on its next record. Released in 1971, *The Yes Album* marks the beginning of the signature sound that would bring them international fame in the seventies. In addition to epic tracks like "Starship Trooper," "Yours Is No Disgrace," "Perpetual Change," and "I've Seen All Good People," the LP sported a live solo acoustic piece by Howe entitled "The Clap," Anderson's story-song "A Venture," and several others. Anderson's lyrics, like the band's sound, took their most recognizable form beginning with this record. The world seemed ready for rock and roll with words like, "On a sailing ship to nowhere leaving anyplace/If the summer change to winter yours is no disgrace." *Rolling Stone*'s praise for the album was measured: reviewer John Koegel admired the band's new maturity and original material but lamented the lack of cover versions; even so, he wrote that the band "play[s] as though of one mind," singling out Squire's "creative bass work."

Enter Wakeman

Yes embarked on its first U.S. tour to support *The Yes Album,* but shortly thereafter keyboardist Tony Kaye left the band, joining Banks to form a new group called Flash. Yes sought out Rick Wakeman, formerly of the folk-rock band The Strawbs, to take Kaye's place. Wakeman, a classically trained pianist and rock session player who had already been deemed a new superstar by the British rock press, brought to Yes a flashy virtuosity that suited the band's increasingly challenging arrangements. The ensemble's next record, *Fragile,* would become one of the textbook examples of the "progressive rock" LP. Released in 1972, *Fragile* included the band's first hit single, "Roundabout," a few other group compositions, and a solo turn by each band member. Wakeman's solo track was an electronic rendition of a piece by composer Johannes Brahms. The record is noteworthy not only as the band's breakthrough hit but as the first of many Yes albums to feature cover art by graphic artist Roger Dean. Dean's fantasy landscapes and distinctive lettering would become the visual coefficients of the Yes sound for legions of fans worldwide.

Fragile was also the group's first hit with critics. Richard Cromelin's *Rolling Stone* review—though not an unqualified rave—suggested that Yes had cleared a big hurdle. Cromelin noted the "show-off syndrome" marring some of the songs but admired the record overall; he called "Roundabout"'s instrumental break "a tour-de-force, a complete knockout, and perhaps the most quietly devastating moment to appear on a record in recent memory." The 1972 follow-up album, *Close to the Edge,* broke even more new ground. With its title track taking up the entire first side—separated into "movements"—*Close to the Edge* gained a reputation over time as one of the band's finest works and perhaps the definitive "progressive rock" album. Containing three symphonic tunes—"Close to the Edge," "And You & I," and "Siberian Khatru"—the LP fulfills the genre's promise to provide a mental and emotional journey. The elaborate arrangements, critics and fans agreed, had never seemed so integrated before. Cromelin's review again chided the band somewhat for its signature faults and Anderson's "inaccessible" lyrics but noted that "Yes have formed a coherent musical language from the elements that have been kicked around by progressive rockers for ages."

Yes went on tour to support the two albums in 1972, but Bruford left the band before the tour began and was replaced by Plastic Ono Band alumnus Alan White. Highlights of the shows appeared on a three-record live set, 1973's *Yessongs,* and in a concert film with the same title. While on tour, Anderson was reading Paramahansa Yogananda's *Autobiography of a Yogi* and—inspired by a footnote—began to write songs with Howe that would form the group's next opus, the two-record *Tales From Topographic Oceans.* Released in 1973 and divided into four "movements," *Tales* tried the patience of critics and even alienated some fans. Gordon Fletcher began his *Rolling Stone* review by remarking bluntly that "this album is too long" and went on to complain about the band's "psychedelic noodling" and the "mechanical" feel of the music. "Composers Jon Anderson and Steve Howe no doubt understand the relationship between *Tales* and their personal search for Truth, Knowledge, Culture and Freedom," he added, "but they haven't clued in the rest of us." *Rolling Stone*'s 1975 review of the next Yes album, *Relayer,* reminded readers that *Tales* was "four sides of hope-

lessly dense complexity that left many observers recoiling in utter dismay and taxed even the group's most ardent supporters."

Relayer Went Gold Despite Critical Drubbing

Even Wakeman found *Tales* a bit too pompous to stomach and took a hiatus from the group. As *Pulse!* critic and avowed progressive rock fan Steve Hochman remarked, something too overblown for Wakeman had to be pretty overblown: "This is a man possessed of such refined taste and sense of proportion that he later staged his rock version of the Arthurian myths as an ice show!" Anderson and company hired Swiss-born keyboardist Patrick Moraz to take Wakeman's place. The group's next LP, *Relayer,* hit the stores late in 1974 and went gold, despite mostly negative reviews. *Relayer,* commented a writer for *Rolling Stone,* "may exhaust even the devoted. Singer Jon Anderson's words plumb

---

Yes's unmistakable fusion of cosmic lyrics, symphonic arrangements, and rock and roll theatrics has struck a resounding chord with listeners for well over two decades.

---

the depths of turgidity," while the record as a whole, despite some nice moments, "is an excessive, pretentious and ill-conceived album. The folly of Yes's extreme approach is becoming only too apparent." Reviewers for *Melody Maker* continued to favor the group, however, and commented approvingly of Moraz's contribution to the live sound in a 1976 concert review. Even *Rolling Stone* admitted as much: "The evening's surprise," commented Elliot Cahn, "was how much the five-man group sounded like Yes before the departure of Wakeman."

In 1975 Atlantic released *Yesterdays,* an anthology of tracks from the first two Yes albums and a ten-minute rendition of Paul Simon's "America" recorded in 1972 with Wakeman and Bruford. That year Yes won five awards in a *Melody Maker* readers' poll, indicating, along with their impressive concert turnouts, that critics and fans differed over the band's direction. The various band members had done some solo work, and started work on some new material; Moraz expressed dissatisfaction with the new songs. By 1977, Moraz had departed and Wakeman returned to Yes. A 1977 *Rolling Stone* article suggested that the veteran multi-keyboardist's return brought the group back to earth, quoting White as saying that "I feel a touch of lightheartedness now in the band. Rick brings that touch of humor back into the music." The group completed its next LP, *Going for the One,* for a fall release. *Rolling Stone*'s John Swenson wrote that with this record the band had overcome its "cosmic torpor." A writer for *Melody Maker* was more enthusiastic, labeling *Going for the One* a "triumphant return . . . a classic Yes album." The album features several hardrocking songs, including the title track, Squire's "Parallels," and "Awaken."

Non-Cosmic Hits

Anderson told *Melody Maker* that year that he was moving away from the "cosmic interplanetary thoughts" of his past songwriting, and promised that the following year the group would "put out a really hot album." In the studio in 1978, the band expressed excitement over its new material. "Rejoining the band was the best day's work I ever did," Wakeman confided to *Melody Maker*'s Chris Welch. Welch was similarly enthusiastic about the album when reviewing *Tormato* a few months later: "Anybody who has followed Yes from their inception will be delighted with this in some ways startling rebirth of their music." A writer for *Rolling Stone*, however, had little good to say about anything on *Tormato* but Squire's playing, deriding the album with tomato-related puns like "squishy," "overripe," and "rotten." Fans, however, showed enthusiasm over the album and its single "Don't Kill the Whale," which helped *Tormato* to become Yes's radio breakthrough in the U.S., going gold and ultimately platinum.

Despite this success, a new shakeup changed the Yes lineup. Squire, Howe, and White differed with Anderson about the new album's direction; Wakeman wanted to send his parts in on tape from his home in Switzerland. As a result, the singer and keyboardist drifted away from the project, leaving Squire and company to try to piece something together. An unlikely solution came in the form of Trevor Horn and Geoff Downes, known for their work as the new wave duo The Buggles. Horn and Downes had submitted a song to the band, were invited into the studio to help record it, and soon found they'd been recruited as members of the group. Many Yes fans were shocked at the news, but as Howe told *Melody Maker*'s Karl Dallas, the new lineup seemed "the logical next step." Horn took over vocals and Downes played keyboards, and the group put together a new Yes album, *Drama*. The lyrics and arrangements for songs like "Into the Lens," "Tempus Fugit," and

"Machine Messiah" were consistent with classic Yes stylings, but a writer for *Melody Maker* found *Drama* "mediocrity disguised as majesty." The band toured "in the round"—using a unique revolving stage—to support the LP.

After *Drama* the group was quiet for a while. In 1981 Atlantic released an anthology of live material called *Yesshows,* which Dallas found "a better album than *Drama* on the whole" and a more interesting variation on the recorded version of the songs than was offered by *Yessongs.* Steve Howe left the group to play with the pop supergroup Asia—a brainchild of Horn's and Downes's—so he wasn't available for the next project, 1985's *90125.* But that project took a while to assemble.

Return of Anderson

In 1982 Squire and White had hired South African guitarist Trevor Rabin, while Tony Kaye reclaimed the keyboard position. The new lineup was going to be called Cinema when it recorded the album, with Horn producing. The lead vocals weren't working out, however. As Squire told *Rolling Stone,* "I just threw this out one night—'Let's get Jon Anderson back'—and it sort of freaked everyone out." Anderson listened to the new material, and agreed to return as lead vocalist. His presence made everyone comfortable with calling the group Yes again. *90125* was Yes's first album on the Atco label (its title came from its catalog number).

The new sound was extremely streamlined, as best exemplified by the radio-smart single "Owner of a Lonely Heart," penned by Rabin. Thanks to the single, the album zoomed up to the U.S. top ten albums chart. Squire told *Rolling Stone* that this was "not really a reunion; it's more a reestablishing, I think." J. D. Considine, reviewing the LP for the magazine, lauded its "surprisingly spritely and poppish" sound, crediting Horn for skillfully orchestrating the band's "choirboy vocal harmonies." *Musician* noted that the new Yes's concerts were impressive as far as new material was concerned, "but the old songs sat there like a lump. Trevor Rabin isn't Steve Howe. Tony Kaye isn't Rick Wakeman or Patrick Moraz. . . . Having made a stunning rock comeback, Yes can afford to leave 'Starship Troopers' behind on its path toward new music."

By 1987 musical fashion had so changed that *Melody Maker* lumped its former darlings in with other "dinosaurs" of progressive rock: "More carefully informed observers of the genre might disagree, but if only for the sheer long-windedness of virtually everything they ever recorded, Yes deserve to be recognised as the definitive prog-rock band." Yes had left that image behind, however, and in 1987 released another slick pop album for Atco records, *Big Generator*, which a writer for *Guitar Player* called "a mixed offering, but in the balance a fine showcase for [Rabin's] wide-ranging talents."

Which Yes is Yes?

By 1989, new divisions caused new squabbles. *Rolling Stone* reported that Anderson, Bruford, Wakeman, and Howe were working on a new project but couldn't call themselves Yes because Squire, White, and Kaye owned the name. The foursome had signed to Arista, and the two record companies issued conflicting statements about which band was really Yes. *Anderson, Bruford, Wakeman, and Howe* was the name of the non-Yes LP released in 1989 by Arista. A *Stereo Review* writer gave the album a mixed review: "Singing about transcendence is not necessarily the same thing as getting there." *People* was less kind: "The toothless foursome flail around for almost an hour, trying to recapture some of their old glory. . . . The end result is tedious." *Rolling Stone*'s Jimmy Guterman ventured, "On *Anderson, Bruford, Wakeman, and Howe*, four musicians play their parts without coming into any contact, without establishing any common ground." Nonetheless, the album yielded a hit single, "Brother of Mine."

"Common ground" was exactly what the various members of Yes were about to find. Anderson was working on the new Anderson, Bruford, Wakeman, and Howe (ABWH) record when he ran into Rabin, who brought Anderson in to work on his solo project. Meanwhile, Squire, White, and Kaye had been working with Offord on a new Yes album, and asked Anderson to contribute some vocals. Squire was then persuaded to sing some parts for the ABWH record, and it became clear to everyone involved that a unifying project would be ideal.

After some negotiation, the new Yes came together for an album—1991's *Union*—and a tour. The group meant "union" in a literal sense, and so included Anderson, Howe, Rabin, Squire, Wakeman, Kaye, Bruford, and White. With two drummers, two keyboardists, and two guitarists, this new outfit struck progressive rock fans like Hochman as a wonderfully appropriate "monument to excess," but Arista—which got the new band as Atlantic combined Atco with another subsidiary— evidently found it just right. A press release gushed, "The unified Yes combines the best of classic Yes with the best of modern Yes," and quoted Anderson as saying, "It will be good for Yes to get under one banner and wave the Yes flag in the nineties."

Produced by Jonathan Elias, a longtime Yes fan, *Union* wasn't exactly the bona fide sensation that Arista hype suggested. *Rolling Stone* panned it as "an eclectic miscarriage that almost isn't worth laughing about." Such critical disapproval had accompanied some of the band's biggest successes, however; the band's apparent lack of enthusiasm was another matter. "It would be fair to say none of us are entirely happy in any way, fashion or form with the *Union* album," Wakeman told Parke Puterbaugh in a *Rolling Stone* profile. "However, having said that, there's a lot of really good songs—it shows in small areas what can happen, and it acts as a vehicle for this tour and the future." The single "Lift Me Up" garnered substantial rotation on Top 40 radio, and the group began its tour to sellout crowds. As if to put to rest any doubts about the ongoing appeal of Yes's older material, Atco—just prior to its merger with the EastWest label—assembled a four-CD boxed set of remastered Yes material entitled *Yesyears*. Reviewers may have sneered—"It isn't the package . . . that makes this box set seem excessive," wrote Considine, "It's the music"—but fans were delighted.

Whatever critics might say about Yes, the band's unmistakable fusion of cosmic lyrics, symphonic arrangements, and rock and roll theatrics has struck a resounding chord with listeners for well over two decades. And in spite of various lineup changes, bad reviews, and a measure of infighting, Yes have managed to maintain their unique union and place in rock history.

Selected discography

On Atlantic

Yes, 1969.
Time and a Word (includes "No Opportunity Necessary, No Experience Needed"), 1970.
The Yes Album (includes "Starship Trooper," "Yours Is No Disgrace," "Perpetual Change," "I've Seen All Good People," "The Clap," and "A Venture"), 1971.
Fragile (includes "Roundabout"), 1972.
Close to the Edge (includes "Close to the Edge," "And You & I," and "Siberian Khatru"), 1972.
Yessongs, 1973.
Tales From Topographic Oceans, 1973.
Relayer, 1974.
Yesterdays (includes "America"), 1975.
Going for the One (includes "Going for the One," "Parallels," and "Awaken"), 1977.
Tormato (includes "Don't Kill the Whale"), 1978.
Drama (includes "Into the Lens," "Tempus Fugit," and Machine Messiah"), 1980.

Yesshows, 1981.

On Atco

90125 (includes "Owner of a Lonely Heart"), 1985.
Big Generator, 1987.
Yesyears, 1991.

On Arista

Anderson, Wakeman, Bruford, and Howe (includes "Brother of Mine"), 1989.
Union (includes "Lift Me Up"), 1991.

Sources

Books

Stambler, Irwin, *Encyclopedia of Pop, Rock, and Soul,* St. Martin's Press, 1989.

Periodicals

Down Beat, May 23, 1974.

Guitar Player, January 1988.
Melody Maker, March 11, 1972; September 20, 1975; August 7, 1976; July 9, 1977; July 16, 1977; November 26, 1977; May 6, 1978; September 16, 1978; June 14, 1980; August 16, 1980; January 1, 1981; October 10, 1987.
Musician, August 1984.
People, July 24, 1989.
Pulse!, December 1991.
Rolling Stone, February 2, 1970; July 22, 1971; March 16, 1972; March 30, 1972; November 9, 1972; March 28, 1974; June 19, 1975; August 28, 1975; September 20, 1975; September 8, 1977; October 6, 1977; December/January, 1978-79; January 19, 1984; February 2, 1984; February 23, 1989; August 10, 1989; June 13, 1991; June 27, 1991; July 11, 1991; October 3, 1991.

Additional information for this profile was obtained from an Arista Records press release, 1991.

—Simon Glickman

Cumulative Indexes

Subject Index

Volume numbers appear in **bold**.

Cello
Gray, Walter
  See Kronos Quartet
Harrell, Lynn **3**
Jeanrenaud, Joan Dutcher
  See Kronos Quartet
Ma, Yo-Yo **2**

Children's Music
Harley, Bill **7**
Lehrer, Tom **7**
Nagler, Eric **8**
Raffi **8**
Sharon, Lois & Bram **6**

Christian Music
Grant, Amy **7**
King's X **7**
Patti, Sandi **7**
Petra **3**
Stryper **2**

Clarinet
Adams, John **8**
Dorsey, Jimmy
  See the Dorsey Brothers
Fountain, Pete **7**
Goodman, Benny **4**
Shaw, Artie **8**

Classical
Anderson, Marian **8**
Arrau, Claudio **1**
Bernstein, Leonard **2**
Boyd, Liona **7**
Bronfman, Yefim **6**
The Canadian Brass **4**
Chang, Sarah **7**
Clayderman, Richard **1**
Copland, Aaron **2**
Davis, Chip **4**
Fiedler, Arthur **6**
Galway, James **3**
Gingold, Josef **6**
Harrell, Lynn **3**
Horowitz, Vladimir **1**
Jarrett, Keith **1**
Kennedy, Nigel **8**
Kissin, Evgeny **6**
Kronos Quartet **5**
Levine, James **8**
Ma, Yo-Yo **2**
Marsalis, Wynton **6**
Midori **7**
Ott, David **2**
Parkening, Christopher **7**
Perlman, Itzhak **2**
Phillips, Harvey **3**
Rampal, Jean-Pierre **6**
Salerno-Sonnenberg, Nadja **3**
Schickele, Peter **5**
Segovia, Andres **6**
Stern, Isaac **7**
Takemitsu, Toru **6**
von Karajan, Herbert **1**
Wilson, Ransom **5**
Yamashita, Kazuhito **4**
Zukerman, Pinchas **4**

Composers
Adams, John **8**
Anka, Paul **2**
Atkins, Chet **5**
Bacharach, Burt **1**
Berlin, Irving **8**
Bernstein, Leonard **2**
Bley, Carla **8**
Brubeck, Dave **8**
Byrne, David **8**

Also see Talking Heads
Cage, John **8**
Clarke, Stanley **3**
Coleman, Ornette **5**
Cooder, Ry **2**
Cooney, Rory **6**
Copland, Aaron **2**
Davis, Chip **4**
Davis, Miles **1**
de Grassi, Alex **6**
Ellington, Duke **2**
Eno, Brian **8**
Enya **6**
Gillespie, Dizzy **6**
Glass, Philip **1**
Grusin, Dave **7**
Guaraldi, Vince **3**
Hamlisch, Marvin **1**
Hancock, Herbie **8**
Handy, W. C. **7**
Hartke, Stephen **5**
Hunter, Alberta **7**
Jarre, Jean-Michel **2**
Jarrett, Keith **1**
Jones, Quincy **2**
Jordan, Stanley **1**
Kitaro **1**
Lee, Peggy **8**
Lloyd Webber, Andrew **6**
Mancini, Henry **1**
Masekela, Hugh **7**
Metheny, Pat **2**
Monk, Meredith **1**
Monk, Thelonious **6**
Morton, Jelly Roll **7**
Nascimento, Milton **6**
Newman, Randy **4**
Ott, David **2**
Parker, Charlie **5**
Ponty, Jean-Luc **8**
Reich, Steve **8**
Reinhardt, Django **7**
Ritenour, Lee **7**
Rollins, Sonny **7**
Satriani, Joe **4**
Schickele, Peter **5**
Shaw, Artie **8**
Shorter, Wayne **5**
Solal, Martial **4**
Sondheim, Stephen **8**
Story, Liz **2**
Summers, Andy **3**
Sun Ra **5**
Takemitsu, Toru **6**
Talbot, John Michael **6**
Tyner, McCoy **7**
Washington, Grover Jr. **5**
Zimmerman, Udo **5**

Conductors
Bacharach, Burt **1**
Bernstein, Leonard **2**
Copland, Aaron **2**
Domingo, Placido **1**
Fiedler, Arthur **6**
Jarrett, Keith **1**
Levine, James **8**
Mancini, Henry **1**
Marriner, Neville **7**
Rampal, Jean-Pierre **6**
Schickele, Peter **5**
von Karajan, Herbert **1**
Zukerman, Pinchas **4**

Contemporary Dance Music
Abdul, Paula **3**
The B-52's **4**
The Bee Gees **3**
Brown, Bobby **4**

Brown, James **2**
Cherry, Neneh **4**
Clinton, George **7**
De La Soul **7**
Depeche Mode **5**
Eurythmics **6**
Exposé **4**
Fox, Samantha **3**
Gang of Four **8**
Hammer, M.C. **5**
Harry, Deborah **4**
Ice-T **7**
Idol, Billy **3**
Jackson, Janet **3**
Jackson, Michael **1**
James, Rick **2**
Madonna **4**
Pet Shop Boys **5**
Prince **1**
Queen Latifah **6**
Rodgers, Nile **8**
Salt-N-Pepa **6**
Simmons, Russell **7**
Technotronic **5**
The Village People **7**
Was (Not Was) **6**
Young M.C. **4**

Contemporary Instrumental/New Age
Ackerman, Will **3**
Clinton, George **7**
Collins, Bootsy **8**
Davis, Chip **4**
de Grassi, Alex **6**
Enya **6**
Hedges, Michael **3**
Jarre, Jean-Michel **2**
Kitaro **1**
Kronos Quartet **5**
Story, Liz **2**
Summers, Andy **3**

Cornet
Handy, W. C. **7**

Country
Acuff, Roy **2**
Alabama **1**
Anderson, John **5**
Asleep at the Wheel **5**
Atkins, Chet **5**
Auldridge, Mike **4**
Black, Clint **5**
Brooks, Garth **8**
Buffett, Jimmy **4**
The Byrds **8**
Campbell, Glen **2**
Carpenter, Mary-Chapin **6**
Carter, Carlene **8**
The Carter Family **3**
Cash, Johnny **1**
Cash, June Carter **6**
Cash, Rosanne **2**
Clark, Roy **1**
Cline, Patsy **5**
Coe, David Allan **4**
Cooder, Ry **2**
The Cowboy Junkies **4**
Crowe, J. D. **5**
Crowell, Rodney **8**
Daniels, Charlie **6**
Denver, John **1**
The Desert Rose Band **4**
Dickens, Little Jimmy **7**
Dylan, Bob **3**
Flatt, Lester **3**
Ford, Tennessee Ernie **3**

Gayle, Crystal **1**
Gill, Vince **7**
Gilley, Mickey **7**
Griffith, Nanci **3**
Haggard, Merle **2**
Hall, Tom T. **4**
Harris, Emmylou **4**
Hartford, John **1**
Hay, George D. **3**
Hiatt, John **8**
Highway 101 **4**
Jackson, Alan **7**
Jennings, Waylon **4**
Jones, George **4**
The Judds **2**
The Kentucky Headhunters **5**
Kristofferson, Kris **4**
Lang, K. D. **4**
Lee, Brenda **5**
Little Feat **4**
Loveless, Patty **5**
Lovett, Lyle **5**
Lynn, Loretta **2**
Lynne, Shelby **5**
Mandrell, Barbara **4**
Mattea, Kathy **5**
Miller, Roger **4**
Milsap, Ronnie **2**
Monroe, Bill **1**
Murray, Anne **4**
Nelson, Willie **1**
Newton-John, Olivia **8**
The Nitty Gritty Dirt Band **6**
The Oak Ridge Boys **7**
O'Connor, Mark **1**
Oslin, K. T. **3**
Owens, Buck **2**
Parsons, Gram **7**
    Also see the Byrds
Parton, Dolly **2**
Pearl, Minnie **3**
Pride, Charley **4**
Rabbitt, Eddie **5**
Raitt, Bonnie **3**
Rich, Charlie **3**
Rodgers, Jimmie **3**
Rogers, Kenny **1**
Scruggs, Earl **3**
Skaggs, Ricky **5**
The Statler Brothers **8**
Stevens, Ray **7**
Strait, George **5**
The Texas Tornados **8**
Tillis, Mel **7**
Tillis, Pam **8**
Tritt, Travis **7**
Tubb, Ernest **4**
Tucker, Tanya **3**
Twitty, Conway **6**
Van Shelton, Ricky **5**
Watson, Doc **2**
Wells, Kitty **6**
West, Dottie **8**
Whitley, Keith **7**
Williams, Don **4**
Williams, Hank, Jr. **1**
Williams, Hank, Sr. **4**
Wills, Bob **6**
Wynette, Tammy **2**
Yoakam, Dwight **1**
Young, Faron **7**

Dobro
Auldridge, Mike **4**
    Also see the Country Gentlemen
    Also see the Seldom Scene
Burch, Curtis
    See the New Grass Revival
Knopfler, Mark **3**

Drums
See **Percussion**

Dulcimer
Ritchie, Jean **4**

Fiddle
See **Violin**

Film Scores
Anka, Paul **2**
Bacharach, Burt **1**
Berlin, Irving **8**
Bernstein, Leonard **2**
Byrne, David **8**
    Also see Talking Heads
Cafferty, John
    See the Beaver Brown Band
Cliff, Jimmy **8**
Copland, Aaron **2**
Ellington, Duke **2**
Ferguson, Maynard **7**
Grusin, Dave **7**
Guaraldi, Vince **3**
Hamlisch, Marvin **1**
Hancock, Herbie **8**
Harrison, George **2**
Hedges, Michael **3**
Jones, Quincy **2**
Knopfler, Mark **3**
Lennon, John
    See the Beatles
Mancini, Henry **1**
Mayfield, Curtis **8**
McCartney, Paul
    See the Beatles
Metheny, Pat **2**
Nascimento, Milton **6**
Richie, Lionel **2**
Robertson, Robbie **2**
Rollins, Sonny **7**
Sager, Carole Bayer **5**
Schickele, Peter **5**
Taj Mahal **6**
Waits, Tom **1**
Williams, Paul **5**
Young, Neil **2**

Flute
Anderson, Ian
    See Jethro Tull
Galway, James **3**
Rampal, Jean-Pierre **6**
Wilson, Ransom **5**

Folk/Traditional
Arnaz, Desi **8**
Baez, Joan **1**
Belafonte, Harry **8**
Blades, Ruben **2**
Brady, Paul **8**
Bragg, Billy **7**
The Byrds **8**
The Carter Family **3**
Chapin, Harry **6**
Chapman, Tracy **4**
The Chieftains **7**
Childs, Toni **2**
Clegg, Johnny **8**
Cockburn, Bruce **8**
Cohen, Leonard **3**
Collins, Judy **4**
Crosby, David **3**
    Also see the Byrds
de Lucia, Paco **1**
Dr. John **7**
Dylan, Bob **3**
Elliot, Cass **5**
Enya **6**
Estefan, Gloria **1**

Galway, James **3**
The Gipsy Kings **8**
Griffith, Nanci **3**
Guthrie, Arlo **6**
Guthrie, Woodie **2**
Harding, John Wesley **6**
Hartford, John **1**
Iglesias, Julio **2**
Indigo Girls **3**
Kuti, Fela **7**
Ladysmith Black Mambazo **1**
Lavin, Christine **6**
Leadbelly **6**
Lightfoot, Gordon **3**
Los Lobos **2**
Makeba, Miriam **8**
Masekela, Hugh **7**
McLean, Don **7**
Mitchell, Joni **2**
Morrison, Van **3**
Nascimento, Milton **6**
N'Dour, Youssou **6**
Near, Holly **1**
Ochs, Phil **7**
O'Connor, Sinead **3**
Odetta **7**
Parsons, Gram **7**
    Also see the Byrds
Paxton, Tom **5**
Peter, Paul & Mary **4**
The Pogues **6**
Prine, John **7**
Redpath, Jean **1**
Ritchie, Jean, **4**
Rodgers, Jimmie **3**
Santana, Carlos **1**
Seeger, Pete **4**
    Also see the Weavers
Simon, Paul **1**
Snow, Pheobe **4**
Sweet Honey in the Rock **1**
Taj Mahal **6**
Thompson, Richard **7**
Vega, Suzanne **3**
Watson, Doc **2**
The Weavers **8**

French Horn
Ohanian, David
    See the Canadian Brass

Funk
Brown, James **2**
Clinton, George **7**
Collins, Bootsy **8**
Fishbone **7**
Gang of Four **8**
Jackson, Janet **3**
Mayfield, Curtis **8**
Parker, Maceo **7**
Prince **1**
The Red Hot Chili Peppers **7**

Fusion
Anderson, Ray **7**
Beck, Jeff **4**
Clarke, Stanley **3**
Coleman, Ornette **5**
Corea, Chick **6**
Davis, Miles **1**
Fishbone **7**
Hancock, Herbie **8**
Metheny, Pat **2**
O'Connor, Mark **1**
Ponty, Jean-Luc **8**
Reid, Vernon **2**
Ritenour, Lee **7**
Shorter, Wayne **5**
Summers, Andy **8**

Washington, Grover, Jr. **5**

Gospel
Anderson, Marian **8**
Brown, James **2**
The Carter Family **3**
Charles, Ray **1**
Cleveland, James **1**
Cooke, Sam **1**
Ford, Tennessee Ernie **3**
Franklin, Aretha **2**
Houston, Cissy **6**
Jackson, Mahalia **8**
Knight, Gladys **1**
Little Richard **1**
The Oak Ridge Boys **7**
Presley, Elvis **1**
Redding, Otis **5**
Take 6 **6**
Watson, Doc **2**
Williams, Deniece **1**
Womack, Bobby **5**

Guitar
Ackerman, Will **3**
Allman, Duane
    See the Allman Brothers
Atkins, Chet **5**
Baxter, Jeff
    See the Doobie Brothers
Beck, Jeff **4**
Belew, Adrian **5**
Berry, Chuck **1**
Betts, Dicky
    See the Allman Brothers
Boyd, Liona **7**
Buck, Peter
    See R.E.M.
Buckingham, Lindsey **8**
    Also see Fleetwood Mac
Campbell, Glen **2**
Clapton, Eric **1**
Clark, Roy **1**
Cockburn, Bruce **8**
Collins, Albert **4**
Cooder, Ry **2**
Cray, Robert **8**
Daniels, Charlie **6**
de Grassi, Alex **6**
de Lucia, Paco **1**
Dickens, Little Jimmy **7**
Diddley, Bo **3**
Earl, Ronnie **5**
    Also see Roomful of Blues
The Edge
    See U2
Flatt, Lester **3**
Frampton, Peter **3**
Frehley, Ace
    See Kiss
Garcia, Jerry **4**
George, Lowell
    See Little Feat
Gibbons, Billy
    See ZZ Top
Gilmour, David
    See Pink Floyd
Gill, Vince **7**
Green, Peter
    See Fleetwood Mac
Guy, Buddy **4**
Haley, Bill **6**
Harrison, George **2**
Healey, Jeff **4**
Hedges, Michael **3**
Hendrix, Jimi **2**
Hillman, Chris
    See the Desert Rose Band
    Also see the Byrds

Holly, Buddy **1**
Hooker, John Lee **1**
Howlin' Wolf **6**
James, Elmore **8**
Jardine, Al
    See the Beach Boys
Johnson, Robert **6**
Jones, Brian
    See the Rolling Stones
Jordan, Stanley **1**
Kantner, Paul
    See Jefferson Airplane
King, Albert **2**
King, B. B. **1**
Knopfler, Mark **3**
Leadbelly **6**
Lindley, David **2**
Marr, Johnny
    See the Smiths
May, Brian
    See Queen
Mayfield, Curtis **8**
McGuinn, Roger
    See the Byrds
Metheny, Pat **2**
Montgomery, Wes **3**
Nugent, Ted **2**
Owens, Buck **2**
Page, Jimmy **4**
    Also see Led Zeppelin
Parkening, Christopher **7**
Perry, Joe
    See Aerosmith
Prince **1**
Raitt, Bonnie **3**
Ray, Amy
    See Indigo Girls
Reid, Vernon **2**
    Also see Living Colour
Reinhardt, Django **7**
Richards, Keith
    See the Rolling Stones
Ritenour, Lee **7**
Robertson, Robbie **2**
Robillard, Duke **2**
Rodgers, Nile **8**
Santana, Carlos **1**
Saliers, Emily
    See Indigo Girls
Satriani, Joe **4**
Scofield, John **7**
Segovia, Andres **6**
Skaggs, Ricky **5**
Slash
    See Guns n' Roses
Springsteen, Bruce **6**
Stewart, Dave
    See Eurythmics
Stills, Stephen **5**
Summers, Andy **3**
Taylor, Mick
    See the Rolling Stones
Thompson, Richard **7**
Townshend, Pete **1**
Tubb, Ernest **4**
Vai, Steve **5**
Van Halen, Edward
    See Van Halen
Vaughan, Jimmie
    See the Fabulous Thunderbirds
Vaughan, Stevie Ray **1**
Walker, T-Bone **5**
Walsh, Joe **5**
    Also see the Eagles
Watson, Doc **2**
Weir, Bob
    See the Grateful Dead
Wilson, Nancy
    See Heart

Winter, Johnny **5**
Yamashita, Kazuhito **4**
Yarrow, Peter
    See Peter, Paul & Mary
Young, Angus
    See AC/DC
Young, Malcolm
    See AC/DC
Young, Neil **2**

Harmonica
Dylan, Bob **3**
Guthrie, Woodie **2**
Waters, Muddy **4**
Wilson, Kim
    See the Fabulous Thunderbirds

Heavy Metal
AC/DC **4**
Aerosmith **3**
Danzig **7**
Def Leppard **3**
Faith No More **7**
Fishbone **7**
Guns n' Roses **2**
King's X **7**
Led Zeppelin **1**
Metallica **7**
Mötley Crüe **1**
Nugent, Ted **2**
Osbourne, Ozzy **3**
Petra **3**
Queensrÿche **8**
Reid, Vernon **2**
    Also see Living Colour
Roth, David Lee **1**
    Also see Van Halen
Soundgarden **6**
Spinal Tap **8**
Stryper **2**
Whitesnake **5**

Humor
The Coasters **5**
Jones, Spike **5**
Lehrer, Tom **7**
Pearl, Minnie **3**
Russell, Mark **6**
Schickele, Peter **5**
Spinal Tap **8**
Stevens, Ray **7**
Yankovic, "Weird Al" **7**

Inventors
Paul, Les **2**

Jazz
Anderson, Ray **7**
Armstrong, Louis **4**
Bailey, Pearl **5**
Basie, Count **2**
Belle, Regina **6**
Berigan, Bunny **2**
Bley, Carla **8**
Blood, Sweat and Tears **7**
Brubeck, Dave **8**
Calloway, Cab **6**
The Canadian Brass **4**
Carter, Benny **3**
Carter, Betty **6**
Charles, Ray **1**
Clarke, Stanley **3**
Cole, Nat King **3**
Coleman, Ornette **5**
Coltrane, John **4**
Connick, Harry, Jr. **4**
Corea, Chick **6**
Davis, Miles **1**
DeJohnette, Jack **7**

Eckstine, Billy **1**
Ellington, Duke **2**
Ferguson, Maynard **7**
Fitzgerald, Ella **1**
Fleck, Bela **8**
    Also see the New Grass Revival
Fountain, Pete **7**
Galway, James **3**
Gillespie, Dizzy **6**
Goodman, Benny **4**
Guaraldi, Vince **3**
Hampton, Lionel **6**
Hancock, Herbie **8**
Hedges, Michael **3**
Hirt, Al **5**
Holiday, Billie **6**
Horn, Shirley **7**
Hunter, Alberta **7**
Jarreau, Al **1**
Jarrett, Keith **1**
Jones, Quincy **2**
Jordan, Stanley **1**
Kennedy, Nigel **8**
Kirk, Rahsaan Roland **6**
Kronos Quartet **5**
Lee, Peggy **8**
Mancini, Henry **1**
The Manhattan Transfer **8**
Marsalis, Wynton **6**
Masekela, Hugh **7**
McFerrin, Bobby **3**
Metheny, Pat **2**
Monk, Thelonious **6**
Montgomery, Wes **3**
Morton, Jelly Roll **7**
Nascimento, Milton **6**
Parker, Charlie **5**
Parker, Maceo **7**
Paul, Les **2**
Ponty, Jean-Luc **8**
Professor Longhair **6**
Rampal, Jean-Pierre **6**
Reid, Vernon **2**
    Also see Living Colour
Reinhardt, Django **7**
Roberts, Marcus **6**
Robillard, Duke **2**
Rollins, Sonny **7**
Sanborn, David **1**
Santana, Carlos **1**
Schuur, Diane **6**
Scofield, John **7**
Severinsen, Doc **1**
Shaw, Artie **8**
Shorter, Wayne **5**
Solal, Martial **4**
Summers, Andy **3**
Sun Ra **5**
Take 6 **6**
Torme, Mel **4**
Tyner, McCoy **7**
Vaughan, Sarah **2**
Waits, Tom **1**
Walker, T-Bone **5**
Washington, Dinah **5**
Washington, Grover, Jr. **5**

Keyboards, Electric
Corea, Chick **6**
Davis, Chip **4**
Emerson, Keith
    See Emerson, Lake & Palmer/Powell
Eno, Brian **8**
Hancock, Herbie **8**
Jackson, Joe **4**
Jarre, Jean-Michel **2**
Jones, Booker T. **8**
Kitaro **1**
Manzarek, Ray

See the Doors
McDonald, Michael
    See the Doobie Brothers
McVie, Christine
    See Fleetwood Mac
Pierson, Kate
    See the B-52's
Sun Ra **5**
Waller, Fats **7**
Wilson, Brian
    See the Beach Boys
Winwood, Steve **2**
Wonder, Stevie **2**

Liturgical Music
Cooney, Rory **6**
Talbot, John Michael **6**

Mandolin
Bush, Sam
    See the New Grass Revival
Duffey, John
    See the Seldom Scene
Hartford, John **1**
Lindley, David **2**
Monroe, Bill **1**
Rosas, Cesar
    See Los Lobos
Skaggs, Ricky **5**

Musicals
Allen, Debbie **8**
Andrews, Julie **4**
Bacharach, Burt **1**
Bailey, Pearl **5**
Berlin, Irving **8**
Buckley, Betty **1**
Burnett, Carol **6**
Carter, Nell **7**
Channing, Carol **6**
Chevalier, Maurice **6**
Crawford, Michael **4**
Crosby, Bing **6**
Curry, Tim **3**
Davis, Sammy, Jr. **4**
Garland, Judy **6**
Hamlisch, Marvin **1**
Lloyd Webber, Andrew **6**
LuPone, Patti **8**
Masekela, Hugh **7**
Moore, Melba **7**
Patinkin, Mandy **3**
Peters, Bernadette **7**
Robeson, Paul **8**
Sager, Carole Bayer **5**
Sondheim, Stephen **8**

Opera
Adams, John **8**
Anderson, Marian **8**
Battle, Kathleen **6**
Carreras, José **8**
Cotrubas, Ileana **1**
Domingo, Placido **1**
Norman, Jessye **7**
Pavarotti, Luciano **1**
Price, Leontyne **6**
Sills, Beverly **5**
Te Kanawa, Kiri **2**
von Karajan, Herbert **1**
Zimmerman, Udo **5**

Percussion
Bonham, John
    See Led Zeppelin
Collins, Phil **2**
    Also see Genesis
DeJohnette, Jack **7**
Densmore, John

See the Doors
Dunbar, Aynsley
    See Jefferson Starship
    See Whitesnake
Fleetwood, Mick
    See Fleetwood Mac
Hart, Mickey
    See the Grateful Dead
Henley, Don **3**
Jones, Kenny
    See The Who
Jones, Spike **5**
Kreutzman, Bill
    See the Grateful Dead
Mason, Nick
    See Pink Floyd
Moon, Keith
    See The Who
N'Dour, Youssou **6**
Palmer, Carl
    See Emerson, Lake & Palmer/Powell
Peart, Neil
    See Rush
Powell, Cozy
    See Emerson, Lake & Palmer/Powell
Sheila E. **3**
Starr, Ringo
    See the Beatles
Watts, Charlie
    See the Rolling Stones

Piano
Arrau, Claudio **1**
Bacharach, Burt **1**
Basie, Count **2**
Berlin, Irving **8**
Bley, Carla **8**
Bronfman, Yefim **6**
Brubeck, Dave **8**
Bush, Kate **4**
Charles, Ray **1**
Clayderman, Richard **1**
Cleveland, James **1**
Cole, Nat King **3**
Collins, Judy **4**
Collins, Phil **2**
    Also see Genesis
Connick, Harry, Jr. **4**
DeJohnette, Jack **7**
Domino, Fats **2**
Dr. John **7**
Ellington, Duke **2**
Feinstein, Michael **6**
Flack, Roberta **5**
Frey, Glenn **3**
Glass, Philip **1**
Grusin, Dave **7**
Guaraldi, Vince **3**
Hamlisch, Marvin **1**
Hancock, Herbie **8**
Horn, Shirley **7**
Hornsby, Bruce **3**
Horowitz, Vladimir **1**
Jackson, Joe **4**
Jarrett, Keith **1**
Joel, Billy **2**
John, Elton **3**
Kissin, Evgeny **6**
Levine, James **8**
Lewis, Jerry Lee **2**
Little Richard **1**
Manilow, Barry **2**
McDonald, Michael
    See the Doobie Brothers
McVie, Christine
    See Fleetwood Mac
Milsap, Ronnie **2**
Monk, Thelonious **6**
Morton, Jelly Roll **7**

Barrett, (Roger) Syd
　See Pink Floyd
Basie, Count **2**
Becker, Walter
　See Steely Dan
Belew, Adrian **5**
Benton, Brook **7**
Berlin, Irving **8**
Berry, Chuck **1**
Black, Clint **5**
Blades, Ruben **2**
Bono
　See U2
Brady, Paul **8**
Bragg, Billy **7**
Brickell, Edie **3**
Brooks, Garth **8**
Brown, Bobby **4**
Brown, James **2**
Browne, Jackson **3**
Buck, Peter **5**
　See R.E.M.
Buck, Robert
　See 10,000 Maniacs
Buckingham, Lindsey **8**
　Also see Fleetwood Mac
Buffett, Jimmy **4**
Bush, Kate **4**
Byrne, David **8**
　Also see Talking Heads
Calloway, Cab **6**
Carpenter, Mary-Chapin **6**
Carter, Carlene **8**
Cash, Johnny **1**
Cash, Rosanne **2**
Cetera, Peter
　See Chicago
Chapin, Harry **6**
Chapman, Tracy **4**
Charles, Ray **1**
Childs, Toni **2**
Clapton, Eric **1**
Cleveland, James **1**
Clinton, George **7**
Cockburn, Bruce **8**
Cohen, Leonard **3**
Cole, Nat King **3**
Collins, Albert **4**
Collins, Judy **4**
Collins, Phil **2**
Cooder, Ry **2**
Cooke, Sam **1**
Cooper, Alice **8**
Costello, Elvis **2**
Crenshaw, Marshall **5**
Croce, Jim **3**
Crofts, Dash
　See Seals & Crofts
Crosby, David **3**
　Also see the Byrds
Crowe, J. D. **5**
Crowell, Rodney **8**
Daniels, Charlie **6**
Davies, Ray **5**
Denver, John **1**
Diamond, Neil **1**
Diddley, Bo **3**
Difford, Chris
　See Squeeze
Dion **4**
Domino, Fats **2**
Doucet, Michael **8**
Dozier, Lamont
　See Holland-Dozier-Holland
Dylan, Bob **3**
The Edge
　See U2
Ellington, Duke **2**
Emerson, Keith

　See Emerson, Lake & Palmer/Powell
Etheridge, Melissa **4**
Everly, Don
　See the Everly Brothers
Everly, Phil
　See the Everly Brothers
Fagen, Don
　See Steely Dan
Ferry, Bryan **1**
Flack, Roberta **5**
Flatt, Lester **3**
Fogelberg, Dan **4**
Fogerty, John **2**
Frampton, Peter **3**
Frey, Glenn **3**
　Also see the Eagles
Gabriel, Peter **2**
Garcia, Jerry **4**
Gaye, Marvin **4**
George, Lowell
　See Little Feat
Gibb, Barry
　See the Bee Gees
Gibb, Maurice
　See the Bee Gees
Gibb, Robin
　See the Bee Gees
Gibbons, Billy
　See ZZ Top
Gibson, Debbie **1**
Gift, Roland **3**
Gill, Vince **7**
Gilley, Mickey **7**
Gilmour, David
　See Pink Floyd
Goodman, Benny **4**
Gordy, Berry, Jr. **6**
Grant, Amy **7**
Griffith, Nanci **3**
Guthrie, Arlo **6**
Guthrie, Woodie **2**
Guy, Buddy **4**
Haggard, Merle **2**
Hall, Daryl
　See Hall & Oates
Hall, Tom T. **4**
Hamlisch, Marvin **1**
Hammer, M.C. **5**
Harding, John Wesley **6**
Harley, Bill **7**
Harris, Emmylou **4**
Harrison, George **2**
　Also see the Beatles
Harry, Deborah **4**
Hartford, John **1**
Hawkins, Screamin' Jay **8**
Healey, Jeff **4**
Hedges, Michael **3**
Hendrix, Jimi **2**
Henley, Don **3**
　Also see the Eagles
Hiatt, John **8**
Hidalgo, David
　See Los Lobos
Hillman, Chris
　See the Desert Rose Band
　Also see the Byrds
Holland, Brian
　See Holland-Dozier-Holland
Holland, Eddie
　See Holland-Dozier-Holland
Holly, Buddy **1**
Hornsby, Bruce **3**
Hutchence, Michael
　See INXS
Hynde, Chrissie
　See the Pretenders
Ian, Janis **5**
Ice-T **7**

Idol, Billy **3**
Isaak, Chris **6**
Jackson, Alan **7**
Jackson, Joe **4**
Jackson, Michael **1**
Jagger, Mick **7**
　Also see the Rolling Stones
James, Rick **2**
Jarreau, Al **1**
Jennings, Waylon **4**
Jett, Joan **3**
Joel, Billy **2**
Johansen, David **7**
John, Elton **3**
Jones, Brian
　See the Rolling Stones
Jones, George **4**
Jones, Mick
　See The Clash
Jones, Quincy **2**
Jones, Rickie Lee **4**
Joplin, Janis **3**
Judd, Naomi
　See the Judds
Kane, Big Daddy **7**
Kantner, Paul
　See Jefferson Airplane
King, Albert **2**
King, B. B. **1**
King, Ben E. **7**
King, Carole **6**
Knopfler, Mark **3**
Kravitz, Lenny **5**
Kristofferson, Kris **4**
Lake, Greg
　See Emerson, Lake & Palmer/Powell
Lang, K. D. **4**
Lavin, Christine **6**
Lee, Peggy **8**
Lehrer, Tom **7**
Lennon, John
　See the Beatles
Lennon, Julian **2**
Lightfoot, Gordon **3**
Little Richard **1**
Llanas, Sammy
　See the BoDeans
L.L. Cool J **5**
Loggins, Kenny **3**
Loveless, Patty **5**
Lovett, Lyle **5**
Lowe, Nick **6**
Lynn, Loretta **2**
Lynne, Jeff **5**
Lynne, Shelby **5**
MacDonald, Barbara
　See Timbuk 3
MacDonald, Pat
　See Timbuk 3
Madonna **4**
Manilow, Barry **2**
Manzarek, Ray
　See the Doors
Marley, Bob **3**
Marley, Ziggy **3**
Marx, Richard **3**
Mattea, Kathy **5**
May, Brian
　See Queen
Mayfield, Curtis **8**
McCartney, Paul **4**
　Also see the Beatles
McGuinn, Roger
　See the Byrds
McLean, Don **7**
McDonald, Michael
　See the Doobie Brothers
McVie, Christine
　See Fleetwood Mac

Medley, Bill **3**
Mellencamp, John "Cougar" **2**
Merchant, Natalie
  See 10,000 Maniacs
Mercury, Freddie
  See Queen
Miller, Roger **4**
Miller, Steve **2**
Milsap, Ronnie **2**
Mitchell, Joni **2**
Morrison, Jim **3**
Morrison, Van **3**
Morton, Jelly Roll **7**
Nascimento, Milton **6**
Near, Holly **1**
Nelson, Rick **2**
Nelson, Willie **1**
Nesmith, Mike
  See the Monkees
Neville, Art
  See the Neville Brothers
Newman, Randy **4**
Newmann, Kurt
  See the BoDeans
Nicks, Stevie **2**
Nugent, Ted **2**
Oates, John
  See Hall & Oates
Ocasek, Ric **5**
Ocean, Billy **4**
Ochs, Phil **7**
O'Connor, Sinead **3**
Odetta **7**
Orbison, Roy **2**
Osbourne, Ozzy **3**
Oslin, K. T. **3**
Owens, Buck **2**
Page, Jimmy **4**
  Also see Led Zeppelin
Palmer, Robert **2**
Parsons, Gram **7**
  Also see the Byrds
Parton, Dolly **2**
Paul, Les **2**
Paxton, Tom **5**
Penn, Michael **4**
Perez, Louie
  See Los Lobos
Perry, Joe
  See Aerosmith
Pierson, Kate
  See the B-52's
Plant, Robert **2**
  Also see Led Zeppelin
Pop, Iggy **1**
Prince **1**
Prine, John **7**
Professor Longhair **6**
Rabbitt, Eddie **5**
Raitt, Bonnie **3**
Ray, Amy
  See Indigo Girls
Redding, Otis **5**
Reed, Lou **1**
  Also see the Velvet Underground
Reid, Vernon **2**
  Also see Living Colour
Rich, Charlie **3**
Richards, Keith
  See the Rolling Stones
Richie, Lionel **2**
Ritchie, Jean **4**
Robertson, Robbie **2**
Robillard, Duke **2**
Robinson, Smokey **1**
Rodgers, Jimmie **3**
Roth, David Lee **1**
  Also see Van Halen
Rotten, Johnny

See the Sex Pistols
Russell, Mark **6**
Rutherford, Mike
  See Genesis
Sade **2**
Sager, Carole Bayer **5**
Saliers, Emily
  See Indigo Girls
Satriani, Joe **4**
Schneider, Fred III
  See the B-52's
Scruggs, Earl **3**
Seals, Jim
  See Seals & Crofts
Sedaka, Neil **4**
Seeger, Pete **4**
  Also see the Weavers
Sheila E. **3**
Shocked, Michelle **4**
Siberry, Jane **6**
Simmons, Gene
  See Kiss
Simmons, Patrick
  See the Doobie Brothers
Simon, Carly **4**
Simon, Paul **1**
Skaggs, Ricky **5**
Slick, Grace
  See Jefferson Airplane
Smith, Patti **1**
Smith, Robert
  See The Cure
  Also see Siouxsie and the Banshees
Sondheim, Stephen **8**
Spector, Phil **4**
Springsteen, Bruce **6**
Stanley, Paul
  See Kiss
Stanley, Ralph **5**
Starr, Ringo
  See the Beatles
Stevens, Cat **3**
Stevens, Ray **7**
Stewart, Dave
  See Eurythmics
Stewart, Rod **2**
Stills, Stephen **5**
Sting **2**
Stipe, Michael
  See R.E.M.
Strait, George **5**
Streisand, Barbra **2**
Strickland, Keith
  See the B-52's
Strummer, Joe
  See The Clash
Summers, Andy **3**
Taj Mahal **6**
Taylor, James **2**
Thompson, Richard **7**
Tilbrook, Glenn
  See Squeeze
Tillis, Mel **7**
Tillis, Pam **8**
Timmins, Margo
  See the Cowboy Junkies
Timmins, Michael
  See the Cowboy Junkies
Tone-Lōc **3**
Torme, Mel **4**
Tosh, Peter **3**
Townshend, Pete **1**
  Also see The Who
Tritt, Travis **7**
Tubb, Ernest **4**
Twitty, Conway **6**
Tyler, Steve
  See Aerosmith
Vai, Steve **5**

Also see Whitesnake
Vandross, Luther **2**
Van Halen, Edward
  See Van Halen
Van Shelton, Ricky **5**
Vega, Suzanne **3**
Bono
  See U2
Waits, Tom **1**
Walker, T-Bone **5**
Waller, Fats **7**
Walsh, Joe **5**
  Also see the Eagles
Waters, Muddy **4**
Waters, Roger
  See Pink Floyd
Weir, Bob
  See the Grateful Dead
Welch, Bob
  See the Grateful Dead
West, Dottie **8**
Whitley, Keith **7**
Williams, Deniece **1**
Williams, Don **4**
Williams, Hank, Jr. **1**
Williams, Hank, Sr. **4**
Williams, Paul **5**
Wills, Bob **6**
Wilson, Brian
  See the Beach Boys
Wilson, Cindy
  See the B-52's
Wilson, Ricky
  See the B-52's
Winter, Johnny **5**
Winwood, Steve **2**
Womack, Bobby **5**
Wonder, Stevie **2**
Wynette, Tammy **2**
Yoakam, Dwight **1**
Young, Angus
  See AC/DC
Young, Neil **2**
Zappa, Frank **1**

Trombone
  Anderson, Ray **7**
  Dorsey, Tommy
    See the Dorsey Brothers
  Miller, Glenn **6**
  Watts, Eugene
    See the Canadian Brass

Trumpet
  Armstrong, Louis **4**
  Berigan, Bunny **2**
  Coleman, Ornette **5**
  Davis, Miles **1**
  Ferguson, Maynard **7**
  Gillespie, Dizzy **6**
  Hirt, Al **5**
  Jones, Quincy **2**
  Loughnane, Lee **3**
  Marsalis, Wynton **6**
  Masekela, Hugh **7**
  Mills, Fred
    See the Canadian Brass
  Romm, Ronald
    See the Canadian Brass
  Severinsen, Doc **1**

Tuba
  Daellenbach, Charles
    See the Canadian Brass
  Phillips, Harvey **3**

Vibraphone
  Hampton, Lionel **6**

Viola
Dutt, Hank
See Kronos Quartet
Jones, Michael
See Kronos Quartet
Killian, Tim
See Kronos Quartet
Zukerman, Pinchas **4**

Violin
Acuff, Roy **2**
Anderson, Laurie **1**
Bush, Sam
See the New Grass Revival

Chang, Sarah **7**
Coleman, Ornette **5**
Daniels, Charlie **6**
Doucet, Michael **8**
Gingold, Josef **6**
Gray, Ella
See Kronos Quartet
Harrington, David
See Kronos Quartet
Hartford, John **1**
Hidalgo, David
See Los Lobos
Kennedy, Nigel **8**
Lewis, Roy

See Kronos Quartet
Marriner, Neville **7**
Midori **7**
O'Connor, Mark **1**
Perlman, Itzhak **2**
Ponty, Jean-Luc **8**
Salerno-Sonnenberg, Nadja **3**
Shallenberger, James
See Kronos Quartet
Sherba, John
See Kronos Quartet
Skaggs, Ricky **5**
Stern, Isaac **7**
Wills, Bob **6**
Zukerman, Pinchas **4**

Musicians Index

Volume numbers appear in **bold**.

Hawkins, Screamin' Jay **8**
Hay, George D. **3**
Haynes, Warren
  See the Allman Brothers
Hays, Lee
  See the Weavers
Hayward, Richard
  See Little Feat
Headon, Topper
  See The Clash
Healey, Jeff **4**
Heart **1**
Hedges, Michael **3**
Hellerman, Fred
  See the Weavers
Helm, Levon
  See the Nitty Gritty Dirt Band
Hendrix, Jimi **2**
Henley, Don **3**
  Also see the Eagles
Herman's Hermits **5**
Herndon, Mark
  See Alabama
Hetfield, James
  See Metallica
Hewson, Paul
  See U2
Hiatt, John **8**
Hidalgo, David
  See Los Lobos
Highway 101 **4**
Hill, Dusty
  See ZZ Top
Hillman, Chris
  See the Desert Rose Band
    Also see the Byrds
Hirt, Al **5**
Hodo, David
  See the Village People
Hoffman, Guy
  See the BoDeans
Holiday, Billie **6**
Holland, Brian
  See Holland-Dozier-Holland
Holland-Dozier-Holland **5**
Holland, Eddie
  See Holland-Dozier-Holland
Holland, Julian "Jools"
  See Squeeze
Holly, Buddy **1**
Honeyman-Scott, James
  See the Pretenders
Hooker, John Lee **1**
Hopwood, Keith
  See Herman's Hermits
Horn, Shirley **7**
Horn, Trevor
  See Yes
Hornsby, Bruce **3**
Horovitz, Adam
  See the Beastie Boys
Horowitz, Vladimir **1**
Hossack, Michael
  See the Doobie Brothers
Houston, Cissy **6**
Houston, Whitney **8**
Howe, Steve
  See Yes
Howlin' Wolf **6**
Hubbard, Preston
  See the Fabulous Thunderbirds
  See Roomful of Blues
Hughes, Glenn
  See the Village People
Hughes, Leon
  See the Coasters
Hunt, Darryl
  See the Pogues
Hunter, Alberta **7**

Hunter, Shepherd "Ben"
  See Soundgarden
Hutchence, Michael
  See INXS
Hutton, Danny
  See Three Dog Night
Hyman, Jerry
  See Blood, Sweat and Tears
Hynde, Chrissie
  See the Pretenders
Ian, Janis **5**
Ibbotson, Jimmy
  See the Nitty Gritty Dirt Band
Ice Cube
  See N.W.A.
Ice-T **7**
Idol, Billy **3**
Iglesias, Julio **2**
Indigo Girls **3**
INXS **2**
Irons, Jack
  See the Red Hot Chili Peppers
Isaak, Chris **6**
The Isley Brothers **8**
Isley, Ernie
  See the Isley Brothers
Isley, Marvin
  See the Isley Brothers
Isley, O'Kelly, Jr.
  See the Isley Brothers
Isley, Ronald
  See the Isley Brothers
Isley, Rudolph
  See the Isley Brothers
The Jackson 5
  See the Jacksons
Jackson, Alan **7**
Jackson, Eddie
  See Queensrÿche
Jackson, Freddie **3**
Jackson, Jackie
  See the Jacksons
Jackson, Janet **3**
Jackson, Jermaine
  See the Jacksons
Jackson, Joe **4**
Jackson, Karen
  See the Supremes
Jackson, Mahalia **8**
Jackson, Marlon
  See the Jacksons
Jackson, Michael **1**
    Also see the Jacksons
Jackson, Randy
  See the Jacksons
Jackson, Tito
  See the Jacksons
The Jacksons **7**
Jagger, Mick **7**
    Also see the Rolling Stones
Jam Master Jay
  See Run-D.M.C.
James, Cheryl
  See Salt-N-Pepa
James, Doug
  See Roomful of Blues
James, Elmore **8**
James, Etta **6**
James, Rick **2**
Jane's Addiction **6**
Jardine, Al
  See the Beach Boys
Jarobi
  See A Tribe Called Quest
Jarre, Jean-Michel **2**
Jarreau, Al **1**
Jarrett, Keith **1**
Jasper, Chris
  See the Isley Brothers

Jay, Miles
  See the Village People
Jeanrenaud, Joan Dutcher
  See Kronos Quartet
Jefferson Airplane **5**
Jefferson Starship
  See Jefferson Airplane
Jennings, Waylon **4**
Jessie, Young
  See the Coasters
Jethro Tull **8**
Jett, Joan **3**
Jimenez, Flaco
  See the Texas Tornados
Jobson, Edwin
  See Jethro Tull
Joel, Billy **2**
Johansen, David **7**
Johanson, Jai Johanny
  See the Allman Brothers
John, Elton **3**
Johnson, Brian
  See AC/DC
Johnson, Courtney
  See the New Grass Revival
Johnson, Daryl
  See the Neville Brothers
Johnson, Robert **6**
Johnson, Shirley Childres
  See Sweet Honey in the Rock
Johnston, Bruce
  See the Beach Boys
Johnston, Tom
  See the Doobie Brothers
Jones, Booker T. **8**
Jones, Busta
  See Gang of Four
Jones, Brian
  See the Rolling Stones
Jones, Davy
  See the Monkees
Jones, George **4**
Jones, John Paul
  See Led Zeppelin
Jones, Kendall
  See Fishbone
Jones, Kenny
  See The Who
Jones, Michael
  See Kronos Quartet
Jones, Mick
  See The Clash
Jones, Quincy **2**
Jones, Rickie Lee **4**
Jones, Spike **5**
Jones, Steve
  See the Sex Pistols
Jones, Will "Dub"
  See the Coasters
Joplin, Janis **3**
Jordan, Stanley **1**
Jorgensor, John
  See the Desert Rose Band
Joyce, Mike
  See the Smiths
Judds **2**
Jurado, Jeanette
  See Exposé
Kahlil, Aisha
  See Sweet Honey in the Rock
Kakoulli, Harry
  See Squeeze
Kalligan, Dick
  See Blood, Sweat and Tears
Kaminski, Mik
  See Electric Light Orchestra
Kanawa, Kiri Te
  See Te Kanawa, Kiri
Kane, Big Daddy **7**

Mazibuko, Albert
    See Ladysmith Black Mambazo
MCA
    See Yaunch, Adam
McCarrick, Martin
    See Siouxsie and the Banshees
McCartney, Paul **4**
    Also see the Beatles
McCracken, Chet
    See the Doobie Brothers
McDaniels, Darryl "D"
    See Run-D.M.C.
McDonald, Barbara Kooyman
    See Timbuk 3
McDonald, Michael
    See the Doobie Brothers
McDonald, Pat
    See Timbuk 3
McDorman, Joe
    See the Statler Brothers
McDowell, Hugh
    See Electric Light Orchestra
MC Eric
    See Technotronic
McEuen, John
    See the Nitty Gritty Dirt Band
McFee, John
    See the Doobie Brothers
McFerrin, Bobby **3**
McGeoch, John
    See Siouxsie and the Banshees
McGuinn, Jim
    See McGuinn, Roger
McGuinn, Roger
    See the Byrds
McIntosh, Robbie
    See the Pretenders
McIntyre, Joe
    See New Kids on the Block
McKagan, Duff
    See Guns n' Roses
McKay, John
    See Siouxsie and the Banshees
McKean, Michael
    See St. Hubbins, David
McKernarn, Ron "Pigpen"
    See the Grateful Dead
McKnight, Claude V. III
    See Take 6
McLean, Don **7**
McLeod, Rory
    See Roomful of Blues
MC Lyte **8**
McMeel, Mickey
    See Three Dog Night
McShane, Ronnie
    See the Chieftains
McVie, Christine
    See Fleetwood Mac
McVie, John
    See Fleetwood Mac
Mdletshe, Geophrey
    See Ladysmith Black Mambazo
Medley, Bill **3**
Meisner, Randy
    See the Eagles
Mellencamp, John "Cougar" **2**
Merchant, Natalie
    See 10,000 Maniacs
Mercier, Peadar
    See the Chieftains
Mercury, Freddie
    See Queen
Metallica **7**
Methembu, Russel
    See Ladysmith Black Mambazo
Metheny, Pat **2**
Meyers, Augie
    See the Texas Tornados

Midler, Bette **8**
Midori **7**
Mike D
    See Diamond, Mike
Miller, Glenn **6**
Miller, Roger **4**
Miller, Steve **2**
Milli Vanilli **4**
Mills, Fred
    See the Canadian Brass
Milsap, Ronnie **2**
Mitchell, John
    See Asleep at the Wheel
Mitchell, Joni **2**
Mizell, Jay
    See Run-D.M.C.
Molloy, Matt
    See the Chieftains
Moloney, Paddy
    See the Chieftains
Monk, Meredith **1**
Monk, Thelonious **6**
The Monkees **7**
Monroe, Bill **1**
Montgomery, Wes **3**
Moon, Keith
    See The Who
Moore, Angelo
    See Fishbone
Moore, Melba **7**
Moore, Sam
    See Sam and Dave
Moraz, Patrick
    See Yes
Morris, Kenny
    See Siouxsie and the Banshees
Morrison, Bram
    See Sharon, Lois & Bram
Morrison, Jim **3**
    Also see the Doors
Morrison, Sterling
    See the Velvet Underground
Morrison, Van **3**
Morrissey, Patrick
    See the Smiths
Morton, Jelly Roll **7**
Morvan, Fab
    See Milli Vanilli
Mosely, Chuck
    See Faith No More
Moser, Scott "Cactus"
    See Highway 101
Mötley Crüe **1**
Motta, Danny
    See Roomful of Blues
Mullen, Larry
    See U2
Murray, Anne **4**
Mustaine, Dave
    See Metallica
Mwelase, Jabulane
    See Ladysmith Black Mambazo
Mydland, Brent
    See the Grateful Dead
Myles, Alannah **4**
Nagler, Eric **8**
Nascimento, Milton **6**
Navarro, David
    See Jane's Addiction
N'Dour, Youssou **6**
Near, Holly **1**
Neel, Johnny
    See the Allman Brothers
Negron, Chuck
    See Three Dog Night
Neil, Vince
    See Mötley Crüe
Nelson, Rick **2**
Nelson, Willie **1**

Nesmith, Mike
    See the Monkees
Neville, Aaron **5**
    Also see the Neville Brothers
Neville, Art
    See the Neville Brothers
The Neville Brothers **4**
Neville, Charles
    See the Neville Brothers
Neville, Cyril
    See the Neville Brothers
The New Grass Revival **4**
New Kids on the Block **3**
Newman, Randy **4**
Newmann, Kurt
    See the BoDeans
Newton, Wayne **2**
Newton-John, Olivia **8**
Nicks, Stevie **2**
    Also see Fleetwood Mac
Nico
    See the Velvet Underground
Nirvana **8**
The Nitty Gritty Dirt Band **6**
Noone, Peter
    See Herman's Hermits
Norica, Sugar Ray
    See Roomful of Blues
Norman, Jessye **7**
Norman, Jimmy
    See the Coasters
Novoselic, Chris
    See Nirvana
Nugent, Ted **2**
Nunn, Bobby
    See the Coasters
N.W.A. **6**
The Oak Ridge Boys **7**
Oakley, Berry
    See the Allman Brothers
Oates, John
    See Hall & Oates
Ocasek, Ric **5**
Ocean, Billy **4**
Oceans, Lucky
    See Asleep at the Wheel
Ochs, Phil **7**
O'Connell, Chris
    See Asleep at the Wheel
O'Connor, Mark **1**
O'Connor, Sinead **3**
Odetta **7**
O'Donnell, Roger
    See The Cure
Ohanian, David
    See the Canadian Brass
Olson, Jeff
    See the Village People
Orbison, Roy **2**
O'Riordan, Cait
    See the Pogues
Orzabal, Roland
    See Tears for Fears
Osborne, Bob
    See the Osborne Brothers
The Osborne Brothers **8**
Osborne, Sonny
    See the Osborne Brothers
Osbourne, Ozzy **3**
Oslin, K. T. **3**
Osmond, Donny **3**
Ott, David **2**
Owen, Randy
    See Alabama
Owens, Buck **2**
Owens, Ricky
    See the Temptations
Page, Jimmy **4**
    Also see Led Zeppelin

Winfield, Chuck
　　See Blood, Sweat and Tears
Winter, Johnny **5**
Winwood, Steve **2**
Womack, Bobby **5**
Wonder, Stevie **2**
Wood, Danny
　　See New Kids on the Block
Wood, Ron
　　See the Rolling Stones
Wood, Roy
　　See Electric Light Orchestra
Woods, Terry
　　See the Pogues
Woodson, Ollie
　　See the Temptations
Woody, Allen
　　See the Allman Brothers
Wright, Norman
　　See the Country Gentlemen

Wright, Rick
　　See Pink Floyd
Wright, Simon
　　See AC/DC
Wyman, Bill
　　See the Rolling Stones
Wynette, Tammy **2**
Ya Kid K
　　See Technotronic
Yamamoto, Hiro
　　See Soundgarden
Yamashita, Kazuhito **4**
Yankovic, "Weird Al" **7**
Yarrow, Peter
　　See Peter, Paul & Mary
Yates, Bill
　　See the Country Gentlemen
Yaunch, Adam
　　See the Beastie Boys
Yella
　　See N.W.A.

Yes **8**
Yoakam, Dwight **1**
York, John
　　See the Byrds
Young, Angus
　　See AC/DC
Young, Faron **7**
Young, Fred
　　See the Kentucky Headhunters
Young, Malcolm
　　See AC/DC
Young M.C. **4**
Young, Neil **2**
Young, Richard
　　See the Kentucky Headhunters
Yule, Doug
　　See the Velvet Underground
Zappa, Frank **1**
Zimmerman, Udo **5**
Zukerman, Pinchas **4**
ZZ Top **2**